CONDUCTING THE BRAHMS SYMPHONIES

JOHANNES BRAHMS

CONDUCTING
THE BRAHMS SYMPHONIES

FROM BRAHMS TO BOULT

Christopher Dyment

THE BOYDELL PRESS

The right of Christopher Dyment to be identified as
the author of this work has been asserted in accordance with
sections 77 and 78 of the Copyright, Designs and Patents Act 1988

First published 2016
The Boydell Press, Woodbridge

ISBN 978 1 78327 100 9

The Boydell Press is an imprint of Boydell & Brewer Ltd
PO Box 9, Woodbridge, Suffolk IP12 3DF, UK
and of Boydell & Brewer Inc.
668 Mount Hope Ave, Rochester, NY 14620–2731, USA
website: www.boydellandbrewer.com

A catalogue record for this book is available
from the British Library

The publisher has no responsibility for the continued existence or accuracy of URLs for
external or third-party internet websites referred to in this book, and does not guarantee that
any content on such websites is, or will remain, accurate or appropriate

CONTENTS

ILLUSTRATIONS

The author and publishers are grateful to all the institutions and individuals listed for permission to reproduce the materials in which they hold copyright. Every effort has been made to trace the copyright holders; apologies are offered for any omission, and the publishers will be pleased to add any necessary acknowledgement in subsequent editions.

PREFACE

The reader must forgive some initial reference to autobiographical matters. My early publications included a discography of Albert Coates (1975) and my first book, on Felix Weingartner (1976).[1] When researching material during the 1960s for these and other publications I had the distinct feeling of being little more than a fossil hunter. Interest in recordings by conductors so much of the past was minimal, even considered by the then critical mainstream as rather eccentric. And I well recall the merriment with which my extramural interest in 'discographies' was met by professional colleagues. Who had ever heard of such a ridiculous made-up word, so they thought; and that despite the fact that *Gramophone* had been publishing lists of 78rpm discs so labelled since at least 1928. Vocal recordings were in a different category: the scholarship was already considerable, the limitations of pre- and early electric recordings more easily overlooked.

It was easy enough, then, for some very odd views about what conductors got up to in former times to obtain currency. During my collecting days, again in the 1960s, I got hold of wonderful, mint 78rpm copies of one Max Fiedler conducting the Second and Fourth Symphonies of Brahms and was puzzled by what I heard. All those little – occasionally monstrous – stops and starts, the *Luftpausen*; and what about those first few bars of the Fourth, where the conductor increased the tempo at bar 8 by one-half and resumed his opening tempo at bar 12 as if nothing untoward had occurred? Surely something remarkably eccentric was going on here? Not at all, said a well-informed friend: 'They all did that sort of thing in those days.' But that was clearly at best only partly correct, as my knowledge of recordings by Weingartner and Karl Muck made obvious.

Eventually I determined to consult the most eminent British authority with the longest and clearest memories of the conductors of his youth, Sir Adrian Boult, who kindly received me in his Wigmore Street office in September 1972. Before switching on my recorder, I made some preliminary remarks about the purpose of my visit and in that context described Fiedler's opening of the Brahms Fourth Symphony – 'Extraordinary', said Sir Adrian; 'why did he do that?' I then quoted my well-informed friend to the effect that 'they all did that sort of thing'; this was met with Boult's immediate

---

[1] The Coates discography is in 'Recorded Sound', Nos. 57–8, January–April 1975, pp. 382–405 and p. 464 (errata); for the Weingartner book, see the Bibliography.

and sharp retort, 'a lot of *rot!*' So then the interview proceeded, with results that the patient reader will observe scattered throughout this book.

Over the years, when the increasingly vocal advocates of recordings by such variously arch-Romantic figures as Mengelberg, Furtwängler and Stokowski made known their views (*molto crescendo* in the doing), I felt just a little lonely in adhering to a lifelong subscription to Classical rectitude, whether at the hands of Toscanini, Weingartner, Fritz Busch, Erich Kleiber or other eminences. Over the years I searched for the opportunity to consider at length the correctness or otherwise of the precious information given so many years before by the now long-deceased Boult, as well as much further information published over several decades by noted professional musicologists in an area which had been for so long dormant. My opportunity came about with the publication of my book *Toscanini in Britain* (Boydell 2012), in which, in an Annex to that book, I tested my views in the context of a study of the historic styles of performance shown to have been approved by Brahms, specifically in relation to his symphonies. Its title, 'Brahms and Toscanini: An Historical Excursus', indicated how Toscanini-centric that study proved to be – intentionally so, given its place in that book.

I thought at the time of that publication that my study covered the ground in sufficient detail but in 2014 I changed my view and undertook the further research resulting in the present, much-expanded work. It is no longer Toscanini-centric, although, given the weight of documentation both on paper and in sound, that conductor continues to figure with due prominence. But the motivation remains, at least in part, the same: to test the evidence, here exhaustively, about historical conducting styles, specifically, first, in the context of Brahms's own performances and his known wishes about the performance of his symphonies and, secondly, in the context of recordings (if any) which have preserved aural evidence of those wishes through the medium of those conductors whom he favoured, together with their disciples and admirers.

All, doubtless, intriguing, but the disinterested observer might regard the results as something short of earth-shaking significance: a subject for the proverbial rucksack of the tedious enthusiast, but for the general listener a matter more likely to induce a reaction of only mild interest. However, the game of interpretative quirks and their place in the history of orchestral performance is but a limited aspect of this study's wider compass. Knowledge of what Brahms aimed for in his own performances and what he expected of his interpreters is essential for a deeper understanding of how he expected his unique fusion of high Romantic emotion and Classical form to be projected for its maximum advantage. Did anything go in the late nineteenth-century era of the hyper-Romantics?[2] Were, say, Fiedler's (from our current viewpoint) eccentricities part and parcel of what the composer expected within the then range of interpretative options? Or would he have regarded such extremes, as some of us

---

[2] For usage in this context of the terms 'Classical' and 'Romantic', see further pp. 4 and 26.

may do today, as disruptive of his intensively interlocked structures and so outside the realms of what would have been acceptable to him? Only by careful tracing of the interpretative styles current in the latter years of the composer's life and his reactions to them can these questions receive a convincing answer. So our contemporary habit of comparing the interpretative little more or little less, so beloved of all who indulge extensively in recorded music of that era, becomes in the present context an essential element in our understanding of the composer's mind – the interpretative approaches he himself worked towards or favoured in others to express fully both the emotional and the intellectual force of his symphonic masterworks.

Further, in an age in which the search for interpretative validation seems increasingly to delve into, if not to rely on, performance practices of the past – including Brahms's music, as is evidenced by the utterances of several distinguished contemporary names[3] – it becomes of increasing importance to nail the truth: that is, to establish Brahms's own range of tolerance for interpretative approaches in his largest orchestral works. A conductor's excessive adherence to the straight and narrow or reliance on the opposite pole of constant and extreme exaggeration may in either case carry real dangers of misleading today's audiences about the essential Brahmsian message; only a solidly based knowledge of the composer's range of interpretative approbation provides a secure foundation for avoiding such dangers.

If, then, the methods adopted in this attempt to recapture the authentic voice of Brahms the symphonist – a thorough examination of the styles of his own performances, of his favoured conductors and of recorded evidence by them and their disciples – have resulted in, at any rate, some important leads, the inevitable query arises: can such methods throw similar light on the favoured approach of other symphonists of the nineteenth or early twentieth centuries? In attempting to provide a coherent answer, it has to be borne in mind that Brahms lived and created his symphonic masterworks in a tantalising period, the era in which the virtuoso conductor was spreading his wings to an unprecedented degree but, with a few conspicuous exceptions, lived and died before he could tell us his tale through the medium of recorded sound. Thus to a substantial degree we are necessarily reliant on the printed word to bring us near to the spirit of conductors contemporary with the composer, following through as best we may with at least a sufficiency of recordings by their disciples. A brief survey of pre- and post-Brahms symphonists suggests that the methodology that provides us with substantial information about Brahms's preferences in performance depends on the presence of factors perhaps unique to that 'tantalising' period of creativity. Before or after that period it becomes difficult, if not impossible, to replicate the methods used in this study in order to provide similarly useful results.

---

[3] See pp. 4, 230 and 235.

Consider, as a first example, a step back of less than a full generation to Brahms's revered senior, Robert Schumann. The connecting threads, in terms of a tradition or traditions in the performance of his symphonies created in an era predating the arrival of the virtuoso conductor, are frayed indeed. There seems to be only one such distinguished thread of continuity in the shape of the thirty-one-year-old Adrian Boult playing through the symphonies on the piano in 1920 (taking the bass part) with the fifty-nine-year-old Fanny Davies, Clara Schumann's last surviving eminent pupil with an international reputation.[4] Boult came away from this experience with enlivened ideas about, in particular, rhythmic acuity in the finale of the Second Symphony and, more generally, some radical views about tempos throughout the four symphonies – as the opening movements of the Second and Third Symphonies attest in his recording of the cycle.[5] But how likely is it that this one thread could lead us accurately or reliably to Schumann's own desired approach? Davies gathered her ideas at second-hand from Clara's distinctive 'take' on the interpretation of her husband's works, honed over several decades before Davies became her pupil. It is true that perhaps no other pair had such a 'symbiotic relationship' (as one commentator has termed it) as Schumann and Clara as his anointed interpreter and that Clara's many distinguished pupils, Davies among them, exhibited a degree of family resemblance.

But the continuity of any tradition linking the preferred interpretative approach of the symphonist in the 1840s and the pianist disciple in the 1920s is too open to question to require further comment or investigation. Moreover any pianist, however distinguished, can too easily rush orchestral fences as, for example, did Shostakovich in claiming that his First Symphony should last just twenty-five minutes and rattling through it on the piano to prove his point.[6] In any event, no-one has followed Boult's lead and, leaving Boult aside, the generational removes from the composer as conductor must be accounted too many and any threads of authority too attenuated to be credible as genuine links with Schumann's way of conducting his symphonies – even

---

[4] Fanny Davies (1861–1934), English pianist who studied with Clara Schumann in 1883–5. See further Jerrold Northrop Moore's notes to the CD issue of all Davies's recordings on Pearl GEMM CD 9291.
[5] Recorded with the London Philharmonic Orchestra for Nixa in August 1956, CD transfer NixCD 1005. Boult left two accounts of his experience with Fanny Davies, in his autobiography, *My Own Trumpet*, London: Hamish Hamilton, 1973, p. 50, where he says their four-handed play through covered all four symphonies, and in Michael Kennedy, *Adrian Boult*, London: Hamish Hamilton, 1987 (Kennedy), p. 78, where he says it covered only the first two; but the distinctiveness of Boult's account of the Third Symphony suggests that his autobiography is the more accurate. Boult's tempos in this symphony were no passing fancy: I have vivid memories of the work taking off like a rocket at Boult's eighty-fifth birthday concert with the LPO in London's Royal Festival Hall on 4 April 1974.
[6] See Elizabeth Wilson, *Shostakovich: A Life Remembered*, London: Faber and Faber, 2006 (2nd ed.), p. 54.

discounting his notorious shortcomings as a conductor of his own or, indeed, any other works. There is unfortunately a dearth of authority by comparison with the links explored in the present study of the Brahms symphonies.

Moving even further back to Beethoven's era, the threads have been broken as surely beyond repair as the Norns' golden rope of world knowledge. A performing tradition in Beethoven's orchestral works, in the particular sense adopted in the current investigation,[7] has been preserved only in the rather pathetic attempt – as we now see – by Willem Mengelberg to justify his idiosyncratic approach by reference to a multi-generational but highly questionable pupil–teacher relationship extending back to the composer.[8] This highly dubious specimen apart, the threads of authority, in terms of a direct line of descent through the stylistic approach adopted by successive eminent conductors, are non-existent. In short, moving back in time from Brahms's era meets with almost insuperable difficulties in adopting the particular methodology of the present study.

Moving forward in time from the Brahms era meets with different, if equally weighty, problems. To take an obvious example, only fourteen years separate the deaths of Brahms and Mahler; but with the latter hovering yet more closely on the edge of the age of recording, one is met with a mountain of performance information of differing degrees of reliability: the composer's suggestive piano rolls of movements from the Fourth and Fifth Symphonies; the countless vivid and seemingly exact but far from consistent descriptions collected in Henri Louis de la Grange's monumental biography; and the many recorded performances of Mahler's symphonies by his devoted disciples, Mengelberg, Oskar Fried, Bruno Walter and Otto Klemperer, each with his highly distinctive approach.[9] Those wishing to construct a portrait of Mahler conducting his works meet with a too ample array of evidence, written and recorded: lines of authority are many and almost irremediably conflicting, so much so that those arguing for one or another view of Mahler's own approach – ranging from stern rectitude to the extravagantly mannered – will find all they need in support of whichever view they espouse. A true portrait can emerge, therefore, only by the use of techniques of analysis rather different and perhaps yet more sophisticated in terms of selectivity than those employed in the present study.

---

[7]   There are, of course, alternative routes, such as the performance practice of Weber leading to the wider reforms in performance propounded by Wagner; but the latter's two essays 'On Conducting' (written in 1869) and 'On Performing Beethoven's Ninth Symphony' (1873) interweave inextricably the 'as it (allegedly) was' and 'as it ought to be' – convincing for many at the time but quite distinct from our current pursuit of the actual voices of the various composers touched on in the course of Wagner's essays and, further, in sharp contrast to the detailed descriptions of the route to be taken in pursuit of the authentic voice of Brahms, both in the present study and in other sources brought forward as evidence within it.
[8]   See further p. 115.
[9]   See further, pp. 115, 120 and 122.

This necessarily summary survey indicates beyond any real doubt that, as propounded at the outset, it is Brahms's unique position in time which permits, indeed requires, the particular combination of detective work in the examination both of the documentary and the recorded evidence characterising the methods in the present study, enabling us to discern genuine lines of authority and how they were, at least in part, preserved for future generations.

If the resultant text appears on occasion to indulge in over-insistent tilting at windmills, this is no mere Quixoticism: this study deals for the first time with, if not an army, at any rate an important body of major musicians (including the composer himself), some of whom have, until now, been without a voice in this field of research. The book's conclusions, which I will not anticipate here, may indeed be accounted heterodox according to current wisdom; but that is simply where the evidence led – and that evidence, as the preceding pages have suggested, stands perhaps uniquely in time, from which it is our good fortune to draw conclusions probably impossible to replicate in any study of an earlier era.

Whether or not this study's conclusions are challenged, I trust that it adds to the current state of knowledge concerning historical practice in the performance of one of the supreme canonical sets of work in the pantheon of Western music, the four symphonies of Johannes Brahms – and thereby leads to a more complete understanding of the composer's mind and intentions.

Christopher Dyment
September 2015

ACKNOWLEDGEMENTS

I must give thanks with due prominence to Michael H. Gray, discographer extraordinaire and great friend over four decades. Not only did he quickly rectify discographical errors in my text and update existing tabular work with scarcely a murmur – these were but minor aspects of his assistance – but, guided only by my dating of a large number of London and New York concerts by various conducting luminaries, he exhumed for my benefit a veritable cache of treasure trove from contemporary journals and newspapers that figures extensively throughout the second chapter of this book. I must also thank for his patience with my queries the biographer of Toscanini, Harvey Sachs, whose new magnum opus on that conductor cannot be published too soon. Allan Steckler, guardian and legal representative of Toscanini's estate, helped me in ways that no-one else could and I am grateful.

Other individuals and organisations must be thanked for their assistance, among whom I mention first Dr. Maren Goltz, curator of the Meiningen Museum's musical archives. Her own publications, whether online or within hard covers, are extensive and essential to anyone interested in the history of the Meiningen orchestra and its conductors; in addition, Dr. Goltz kindly provided me with supplementary information of considerable value. Other archivists who have provided essential assistance are Irena Lucke-Kaminiarz, Weimar archivist and biographer of Hermann Abendroth, and Jürgen Schaarwächter, of the Max Reger Institute Karlsruhe, and the Busch Brothers Foundation. I am grateful to the last-named for permitting reproduction of one of Fritz Steinbach's letters to Fritz Busch (p. 174).

I thank Nicholas Chadwick for translating some texts, including Brahms's knottiest German and the Steinbach letter referred to above, and Pieter van der Grinten for translations from the Dutch. My thanks to Edward Johnson, not only for discographical details about Stokowski's recordings of the Brahms symphonies (and copies of many of those recordings), but for the image of that never camera-shy maestro used at p. 68. Others to whom I am indebted include Peter Aistleitner, Kevin Mostyn and sound-recording engineer Aaron Snyder. Simon Marcus in Berkeley suggested many titles for this study, all superior to those of my devising, for which I am grateful – but the ultimate choice was, of course, mine.

I am indebted to John Casey for much advice and help on technical matters. Without his ministrations the – frequently ancient and compromised – photographic work would have remained unacceptable; its appearance here speaks for itself and for the level of John's accomplishments. I am also indebted once again to Michael Middeke of Boydell and Brewer, in particular for his sympathetic response to personal problems, and to his efficient and friendly colleagues, including copy-editor Hester Higton.

Finally, my thanks to Michael Halpern, but for whose friendly encouragement I would in all probability not have embarked on this major expansion of a relatively minor aspect of my *Toscanini in Britain*. Some critics thought the essay about Toscanini and Steinbach in that work had no essential connection with the rest of it; Mike was the only reader who urged further elucidation and, with his librarian friend Chris Lubicz-Nawrocki, made suggestions that helped clear my deck for action. But all blame for that action and for any inaccuracies and shortcomings in the resultant work rest with the author.

Christopher Dyment
September 2015

Note

Shortly after this book went to press, in September 2015 Classical Recordings Quarterly Editions reissued Sir Adrian Boult's long unavailable cycle of the Brahms symphonies recorded in 1954 (CRQ CD202-204), to which detailed reference is made throughout Chapters 3 and 4.

CHAPTER 1

BRAHMS CONDUCTS: THE COMPOSER AND HIS CONTEMPORARIES

Problems and conundrums

> Brahms played his Pianoforte Concerto in D minor superbly. I especially noted his emphasizing each of those tremendous shakes in the first movement by placing a short rest between the last note of one and the first small note before the next. During those short stops he would lift his hands up high and let them come down on the keys with a force like that of a lion's paw.[1]

George Henschel's vivid description of Brahms at the piano, dating from 5 February 1876, encapsulates the composer's stylistic approach: commanding yet free, almost improvisatory and intensely personal. Half a hundred other such descriptions attest its accuracy, at least during his prime as a pianist in the 1850s–70s, and throughout the essential elements remain constant.

Was there an analogous style (or styles) in the conducting of Brahms's symphonies, in the sense that some performances, but not others, approximated to what the composer aimed for in his own interpretations? That question is, in a nutshell, the principal concern of this study; it is not concerned with the wider question of what may be or may not be a valid interpretative approach to these works, consideration of which would occupy a work far larger, and with wider ramifications, than the present volume. To attempt a coherent answer to the initial question, the study pursues two underlying issues. The first is whether Henschel's description of Brahms's powerful but highly idiosyncratic style when performing his piano music had its counterpart in his style on the rostrum when conducting his own major works – assuming, that is, that

---

[1]   George Henschel, *Personal Recollections of Johannes Brahms*, Boston: Gorham Press, 1907, p. 18.

he achieved his intentions with his orchestras as fully as, in his early years, he was able to do at the piano. The second issue is whether recorded sound preserves traces of that style or of other stylistic approaches to conducting his symphonies that received his approbation. Taken together, the answers to these issues may lead to a deeper appreciation of the composer's mind and intentions – for establishing the parameters of performance may indicate how best the composer expected his unique fusion of Classical form and high Romantic emotional thrust to be projected and balanced.

The groundplan of the study is best indicated by a series of questions. Contemporary research has provided trustworthy answers to some of these but to others has given answers which have not, in the author's view, been supported with sufficient evidence.

- To begin with the composer himself: when Brahms conducted his own works, in particular the four symphonies, what were the performance characteristics?
- Did Brahms's interpretations differ from those of other conductors entrusted by him with their performance?
- What conclusions may be drawn about the composer's interpretative approach?
- What were Brahms's expectations when other conductors put their interpretative glosses on these works?
- Did Brahms favour one approach more than another? If he did, what were the elements of the various performing styles among his contemporaries and juniors that led him to opt for that preferred approach – and why?
- Were there other and perhaps incompatible stylistic approaches which were also acceptable to Brahms?
- Is there sufficient information, whether by way of written documentation or of recordings, to provide evidence of continuing traditions of performance that can be linked with certainty to the interpretative approaches of those conductors favoured by Brahms?
- What of other twentieth-century conductors who had no apparent link with Brahms but whom posterity, nonetheless, credits with a special authority in their performances of his symphonies?[2] Is posterity's acclaim in these cases founded on nothing more than the intrinsic merits of the performances or were there other links with the stylistic approaches known to have been favoured by the composer?

Although recent research has explored some of the issues raised by these questions, sometimes in considerable depth, the greater part of that research has been directed to identifying particular stylistic elements known to be favoured by the composer in the

---

[2]   See in particular n. 3 below.

performance of his orchestral music, elements that differ from later twentieth-century performance practices. Less has been done to identify traditions of performing styles referable to individual conductors having a connection with the composer and, in turn, such recorded performances as may perpetuate traces of those styles.

There is, however, one exception to the relative neglect in current research about historic performing styles, an exception of unique importance: considerable attention has been given to the work of the conductor who, by the opening years of the twentieth century, occupied the premier position throughout Europe as an exponent of Brahms's orchestral works, the Meiningen conductor Fritz Steinbach.[3] The concentration of research on Steinbach's style stems both from the special esteem that Brahms himself is known to have bestowed on him on frequent occasions during the 1880s and 1890s and from the substantial body of information that, at first sight, provides evidence of Steinbach's stylistic approach. Conclusions about the character of that approach, together with descriptions of the recorded evidence of particular conductors whose work is believed to suggest a strong Steinbachian element, have been set out elsewhere in some detail.

As yet, however, relatively little research has been directed towards exploring in depth the legacy of conductors other than Steinbach (recorded or not) who, alongside him, might have legitimate claims to be standard bearers of distinct stylistic approaches having Brahms's approval. Nor has there been any research directed towards the achievements of those recording conductors who, beyond dispute, heard Steinbach perform Brahms and expressed admiration for his work – and, crucially, were explicit about Steinbach's influence upon them. Those conductors include the great Italian Arturo Toscanini, who throughout his career acknowledged Steinbach's supremacy in the performance of the Brahms symphonies. So, too, did other conductors who knew Steinbach's performances; the most noteworthy of them were Adrian Boult and Steinbach's foremost conducting pupil, Fritz Busch. Such a degree of unanimous admiration among these noted Brahms interpreters might have been expected to provide a window of opportunity for those wishing to probe for clues about Steinbach's style, yet no effort has hitherto been made to assess whether any Steinbach imprint may be traced in their recorded performances.

---

[3] See Michael Musgrave and Bernard D. Sherman (eds), *Performing Brahms: Early Evidence of Performance Style*, Cambridge and New York: Cambridge University Press, 2003 (Musgrave and Sherman), in particular Robert Pascall and Philip Weller's Ch. 8, 'Flexible Tempo and Nuancing in Orchestral Music: Understanding Brahms's View of Interpretation in his Second Piano Concerto and Fourth Symphony' (pp. 220–43). This authoritative essay is the most detailed survey of the subject, marred only by an unsupported suggestion that Mengelberg, Abendroth and Furtwängler, who, as the present study demonstrates, had no known connection with Brahms's or Steinbach's interpretative approaches, nonetheless '*may well have retained vestiges of the Brahmsian ideal, and passed these on to us through their important legacy of orchestral recordings*' (p. 237, emphasis added). On these conductors, see pp. 125, 136 and 166.

Current scholarship has instead concentrated on two other threads of evidence.[4] First, attention has centred on annotations of the scores of the Brahms symphonies in accordance with Steinbach's style, as compiled after his death by the otherwise little-known conductor Walter Blume – a work that was, remarkably, dedicated to Fritz Busch. The increasing importance now attached to Steinbach's significance in the history of Brahms interpretation is reflected in the 2013 republication in facsimile of Blume's work in its original typed text, as it was first issued in 1933.[5] Attempts to observe the substance of Blume's annotations have been made in certain recorded performances, notably in the Brahms cycle dating from 1997 conducted by Sir Charles Mackerras – although in the recorded interview with him accompanying this cycle the conductor's understanding of Steinbach's style seems, as will appear, to be misjudged in various respects.[6] The second thread has explored the recorded Brahms interpretations of Steinbach's successor in Cologne, Hermann Abendroth, which, it is contended, provide a significant indication of Steinbach's approach, because – in the view of certain scholars – they pay close regard to Blume's annotations. Abendroth's emphatic and sometimes (to ears attuned to contemporary performances of Brahms) exaggerated tempo shifts are therefore proposed as suggestive evidence in the search for Steinbach's performance practice. Again, at least one contemporary conductor, Sir John Eliot Gardiner, has taken due notice of Abendroth's recordings in his own performances of the Brahms symphonies.[7]

There are obvious difficulties about the evidential approach taken to establish the Steinbach style described above. Quite how Blume came to set down his observations and the degree to which they reflect Steinbach's practice is unclear. Why did Blume dedicate his work to Fritz Busch? And what was the link, if any, between Abendroth and Steinbach? Crucially for the present study, Toscanini, Boult and Fritz Busch each in their distinct ways practised what may conveniently be termed a Classical restraint in their interpretative approach, both generally and specifically in their Brahms performances: that is, their fluctuations of tempo from the basic pulse were

---

[4] See Musgrave and Sherman, Ch. 9, Walter Frisch, 'Brahms in the Meiningen Tradition: His Symphonies and *Haydn* Variations in the Markings of Fritz Steinbach, Edited by Walter Blume – Excerpt: The First Symphony, Introduced and Translated by Walter Frisch', and Ch. 10, Walter Frisch, 'In Search of Brahms's First Symphony: Steinbach, the Meiningen Tradition, and the Recordings of Hermann Abendroth'. See also Walter Frisch, 'A Brahms Tradition Lives in Remnants', *New York Times*, 5 October 1997.

[5] Walter Blume, *Brahms in der Meininger Tradition. Seine Sinfonien und Haydn-Variationen in der Bezeichnung von Fritz Steinbach*. Stuttgart: Ernst Surkamp, 1933; reprinted in facsimile with introduction by Michael Schwalb, Hildesheim: Georg Olms Verlag, 2013 (Schwalb/Blume); see further pp. 5, n. 9 and 150.

[6] See further p. 235.

[7] See further p. 236, n. 54.

held in check, abjuring sudden or extreme deviations.[8] Would these conductors have accorded Steinbach such veneration if they had witnessed Abendroth-style extremes in the matter of tempo manipulations? If a negative answer is the more likely, how reliable are Abendroth's Brahms recordings as evidence of the Steinbach way and hence of Brahms's preferred interpretative approach? To what extent, if at all, do the Brahms recordings of the known Steinbach admirers suggest his influence at work? And what of other conductors – was Steinbach the only one to be favoured by Brahms so closely and unequivocally? If not, what lines of investigation should be pursued to uncover audible traces of any alternative styles favoured by the composer?

Given Steinbach's acknowledged links with Brahms, and given also the various conundrums and contradictory pointers outlined above, some of the major issues demanding consideration are, first, how exactly did Steinbach perform Brahms's major orchestral works and with what degree of freedom? Secondly, how closely did his successors and admirers cleave to his performance practice? These issues require that the available evidence, both documentary and recorded, be sifted with maximum care. Such an examination, extending also to evidence of other seemingly legitimate performing styles with no apparent connection to Steinbach's, provides the bulk of the following chapters. First, however, in order to establish the nature of the Brahms–Steinbach nexus, and also to raise the question whether Brahms's links with other conductors justifies the unique treatment accorded that nexus, an overview is needed of the composer's own style of conducting, what he demanded of his contemporaries when undertaking early performances of his new orchestral works, and, not least, why these demands: in other words, what drove the composer to favour certain interpretative approaches and not others?

Recent research has brought together and analysed many sources of information about some of these matters.[9] Problems stem from the interpretation of this ample

---

[8] The term 'Classical' is used throughout this study in this sense, although in the nineteenth century it usually referred to interpretative values having a particular degree of authenticity as a result of their long usage.

[9] In addition to Musgrave and Sherman, *Performing Brahms*, Chs 8, 9 and 10, cited in notes 3 and 4 above, see also Ch. 4, Bernard D. Sherman, 'Metronome Marks, Timings, and Other Period Evidence Regarding Tempo in Brahms', and Ch. 13, Robert Philip, 'Brahms's Musical World: Balancing the Evidence'. See also Walter Frisch, *Brahms: The Four Symphonies*, New York: Schirmer, 1996 (Frisch), Ch. 8, 'Traditions of Performance' (but note my review of this chapter: 'Gunther Schuller: The Compleat Conductor and Walter Frisch: Brahms – The Four Symphonies', *ARSC Journal*, 1998, vol. 29, no. 1, pp. 112–16). I have also referred to two major dissertations on the subject: James K. Bass, 'Johannes Brahms the Conductor: Historical Context, Chronology, and Critical Reception', DMA dissertation, University of Miami, 2005 (Bass); and Jonathan R. Pasternack's translation of Walter Blume's text (n. 5), 'Brahms in the Meiningen Tradition – His Symphonies and *Haydn* Variations According to the Markings of Fritz Steinbach, Edited by Walter Blume: A Complete Translation with Background and Commentary', DMA dissertation, University of Washington, 2004 (Pasternack/Blume). These works

material: any summary is liable to reflect the predilections and ultimate intent of the writer rather than the often contradictory indications to be found in the sources. The following exposition, including quotations by Brahms himself, concentrates on Brahms's stylistic approach and those of his favoured contemporaries (by which is meant the conductors born in the 1830s and early 1840s), with a commentary sufficient to place this evidence in context. Within the scope of what is intended to be a prefatory chapter, the survey cannot avoid being somewhat selective in the choice of evidence, but the conclusions reached may well seem self-evident.

Brahms conducts his symphonies

As each symphony appeared, Brahms conducted a series of performances of the new work throughout Austro-Germany and beyond. Save for the Fourth Symphony, he himself did not undertake the first performance: that was entrusted to chosen contemporaries, of whom more below. Thus after the first performance of his First Symphony, conducted by Otto Dessoff at Karlsruhe on 4 November 1876, the composer conducted a further five performances, introducing it to Munich, Vienna and Leipzig in the course of a little over two months. Later performances under his baton took place at Hamburg, Bremen and Utrecht, with a total number of fifteen performances of the work. This total compares with the nineteen composer-conducted performances of the Second Symphony, of which five were given within the five weeks following its premiere under Hans Richter in Vienna on 27 December 1877.

Brahms took up the task of introducing his Third Symphony more intensively: following Richter's premiere in Vienna on 2 December 1883, the composer led a series of ten performances between January and early June 1884; he conducted the work eighteen times in all. But Brahms outstripped all these efforts with the Fourth Symphony: he conducted the premiere at Meiningen on 25 October 1885 and went on tour with the Meiningen Court Orchestra (Hofkapelle) until 15 April 1886 with a further nine performances in Germany and Holland; he conducted the Fourth Symphony on no less than twenty-three occasions.[10] A similar series of performances marked Brahms's last orchestral work, the Double Concerto, with five performances in October 1887–January 1888 and two more in the following twelve months. Thereafter he conducted

---

are available online. I footnote them hereafter in all cases where information or conclusions are referable to any material in these theses. Bass covers part of the same ground as Renate and Kurt Hofmann, *Johannes Brahms Als Pianist und Dirigent. Chronologie Seines Wirkens Als Interpret*, Tutzing: Hans Schneider, 2006 (Hofmann), but also contains valuable material on the press reception of Brahms's conducting, as well as an extended prefatory essay.

[10]   These figures are collated from the chronology of all Brahms's appearances as conductor in Bass, Ch. 3. See also Frisch, Appendix I, 'A Chronology of the Brahms Symphonies'.

with decreasing frequency, last appearing in a substantial concert in Berlin on 10 January 1896. In the great majority of Brahms's symphonic concerts in these years, he conducted only his own works: in particular, during the Meiningen Hofkapelle's tour with the Fourth Symphony the other works were in every concert conducted by Hans von Bülow.

Brahms had built his experience as a conductor in a succession of posts, many of them ultimately unhappy or unsatisfactory experiences for him. During several months of the three years commencing in October 1857, he conducted the small orchestra and amateur chorus at the tiny court of Detmold. By 1860 he found himself constricted by the means available and concentrated more on work in Hamburg, first with its Frauenchor from 1859 and then from 1860 with the Hamburg Philharmonic's concerts. While his talents were greatly appreciated by the former, he was passed over for a permanent position with the latter in favour of the noted singer Julius Stockhausen. In the face of this snub, it was many years before Brahms returned to his native city and for the rest of his life he resided in Vienna. There, for the seasons 1863–5, he was conductor of the Singakademie, an organisation far less renowned than Vienna's Gesellschaft der Musikfreunde. After his first concert with them one writer appraised Brahms's appointment as 'by far the most noteworthy achievement in the record of the Singakademie, and gave us the opportunity to see Brahms' rare talent as a conductor'.[11] The second concert, however, was disastrous and this rocky path typified Brahms's relations with the musical forces and critics in the majority of his posts. His last permanent post was with the Gesellschaft der Musikfreunde in the three seasons from October 1872 until his final concert in April 1875, after which he sought no permanent post. Again, he started well, but, to take but one example, a prominent journal pronounced that 'Johannes Brahms ... was not equal to the task' of conducting Bach's *St Matthew Passion*, a concert on 23 March 1875 during his final season.[12]

During his years as a professional conductor, which it will be noted preceded the premiere of his First Symphony, estimates of Brahms's podium abilities varied widely and wildly: in his own works he was invariably very successful, but other composers under his baton often fared less well. It is therefore hardly surprising that this gamut of critical appreciation was absent in the years he spent introducing his four symphonies, usually the premieres in the cities he visited for that purpose. Of course, contemporary critics were more concerned with examining this new music than with the qualities of the performances; but nowhere do we find in the many reviews of Brahms's concerts, commencing in November 1876, any complaint about his competence as a conductor of his symphonic works. By the same token, only rarely did the

---

[11] Florence May, *The Life of Brahms*, London: William Reeves 1948 (2nd ed.), vol. 1, p. 346, cited by Bass, p. 64.
[12] *Deutsche Kunst Musik-Zeitung*, 6 April 1875, p. 8 cited by Bass, p. 157.

reviews describe his performances in sufficient detail to permit comparison between Brahms's conducting and that of others, which might have revealed elements of the composer's stylistic approach to interpreting his own symphonies. Just two comments stand out: in Berlin in 1884 it was noted that he conducted the *poco allegretto* movement of the Second Symphony 'a shade faster ... than it had been by Joachim', while in an 1889 performance of the Fourth Symphony in Hamburg a commentator noticed that he conducted the third movement of the Fourth Symphony in 'slow (strict minuet) tempo', which surprised those expecting something more brisk.[13]

For the rest, assessment of how Brahms himself conducted his symphonies can be effected only by reference to his relatively few instructions to contemporary conductors[14] and by drawing on eye-witness reports by musicians comparing his approach with that of his major contemporaries.[15] Even so, these mostly broad-brush observations tell us relatively little about interpretative details; for anything more enlightening one must turn to his observations on and stated preferences about the work of other conductors, a survey of which follows. From their performance practice and also from comments made by them, it is possible to draw some broad conclusions about Brahms's conducting style and what he wanted to achieve.

Metronomic and sloppy? Hans Richter in Vienna and London

From the mass of sometimes conflicting data about Brahms's preferences in the performance of his orchestral music by professional conductors, one factor is constant, namely, his abhorrence of unfelt, under-rehearsed run-throughs. Hans Richter (1843–1916) with the Vienna Philharmonic Orchestra were here too often the guilty parties: the composer was on occasion known to have deliberately avoided Richter conducting the First Symphony and to have walked out of one of his metronomically inclined performances of that work.[16] It was not merely the lack of understanding seemingly betrayed on these occasions: Brahms was, if anything, more angry at evidence of

---

[13] The comments are noted by Bass, p. 140 (Fourth Symphony), citing Walter Hübbe, *Brahms in Hamburg*, Hamburg: Lütcke und Wolff, 1902, p. 55; and p. 160 (Second Symphony) citing the *Musikalisches Wochenblatt*, January 1884, p. 15. For more about the Hamburg concert, see p. 24.

[14] See p. 215.

[15] See p. 23.

[16] Musgrave and Sherman, Ch. 8, pp. 232–4, citing at p. 233 Charles Villiers Stanford, *Pages from an Unwritten Diary*, London: Edward Arnold, 1914, pp. 201–2, and *Interludes: Records and Reflections*, London: John Murray, 1922. See also Christopher Fifield, *True Artist and True Friend: A Biography of Hans Richter*, Oxford: Oxford University Press, 1993 (Fifield), pp. 468–9, where the second extract from Stanford is set out in full, and Richard Heuberger (ed. Kurt Hofmann), *Erinnerungen an Johannes Brahms*, Tutzing: H. Schneider, 1976, pp. 58, 88 and 147, also cited in Musgrave and Sherman, Ch. 8 pp. 233–4.

1. HANS RICHTER, LONDON, 1898

Richter's lack of preparation and the sloppy orchestral response resulting from this negligence. Yet Richter, although customarily sparing of rehearsals, could also rise to the occasion with a properly prepared presentation, as he did at the premiere of the Second Symphony and, later, the Third Symphony.[17] On such occasions, as Adrian Boult observed to me, Richter's straightforward grasp of the large design had the composer's confidence.[18] Indeed, it was at the composer's request that Richter gave the

---

[17] Fifield, p. 138, citing and translating Hanslick's review in the *Neue freie Presse*, 3 January 1878. Brahms was also enthusiastic about Richter's handling of Bach's St Matthew Passion: Styra Avins (ed.), *Johannes Brahms: Life and Letters*, Oxford: Oxford University Press, 1997 (Avins), p. 620.

[18] Christopher Dyment 'Adrian Boult: The Formative Years' (edited transcript of interview in 1972), *CRC*, Spring 2003 (Dyment interview), p. 40.

premiere of the Second Symphony, and Hanslick reported that Richter 'had studied the work with loving care and performed it to perfection'.[19]

The characteristics of Richter's Brahms at its best were captured by some contemporary reviews in the London press. Thus, for example, *The Times* on 18 May 1886 remarked of the preceding day's London premiere of the Fourth Symphony that 'Such accuracy and refinement of phrasing, such fire, such genuine inspiration, such richness of tone in the strings, such perfect balance of the various components of brass and woodwind, have seldom been equalled, never surpassed, within our experience.'

Again, after a London performance of the First Symphony on 30 October 1899, the *Musical Times* thought that

> there was a dignity about his reading that caused the music to stand more than ever aloof … No nervous excitement was there, no frantic hurrying up to sensational climax, no explosion of musical powder magazines … but order and strength, beauty and nobility.[20]

Of that same performance, *The Times* on 31 October took a different line, if with an equal measure of praise:

> all that once seemed remarkable rather for intricacy than actual beauty was transformed into an inspired poem, the logical sequence of which, though absolutely clear, was yet subordinate to its emotional power … the execution of the whole was of rare and faultless excellence.

Evidently, at that time Richter took his duties in London more seriously than he sometimes did in Vienna; indeed, his combination of dignity and inspiration was a constant for London critics over three decades until his final departure from Britain in 1911. But here it must be noted that dignity was not always synonymous with broad tempos: some of Richter's tempos for his premiere of the Second Symphony were, especially in the outer movements, faster than those which later became customary.[21]

It may also be objected that, in relation to the reviews quoted above, critical terminology has to some extent changed its meaning over the years and that descriptions of Richter's performances do not convey to us today the meaning they would have had for Richter's contemporaries, however unequivocal the value judgements appear to be.

---

[19] See Musgrave and Sherman, Ch. 13, p. 359.

[20] *Musical Times*, vol. 40 (1 December 1899), p. 819.

[21] See Musgrave and Sherman, Ch. 4, tables at pp. 115–17 and notes thereto; the movement timings were, allowing for no repeats: I 14:00, II 11:00, III 5:00, IV 8:00. For a comparison with later conductors, see Table 1, p. 169, from which it appears that only the second movement under Richter was exceptionally broad in tempo.

How else, it may be argued, can such radically different views of the same performance of Brahms's First Symphony be explained save by reference to Richter's use of a range of tempo variation taken for granted by his contemporaries, but unusual, if not eccentric, in today's terms? That possibility requires further and separate consideration.[22] For immediate purposes it suffices to seek support from the response of Adrian Boult to my question put to him on this very issue: if Richter's performances were given today, would they appear to be eccentric, as some of Nikisch's might? The answer: 'Some of Nikisch's certainly would. I should think that Richter's would certainly not [although] he might occasionally be thought by some of his audience to be dull.'[23] The great bassoon player Archie Camden, who between 1906 and 1910 played many times in the Hallé Orchestra under Richter, remarked to me that Richter was like the latter-day Klemperer, 'but much greater!'[24] This impression of granitic strength is further reinforced by the twenty-year-old Boult's remarks on the three types of conductor he observed at the time:

> … there are the men who beat time, like Dr. Richter; who guide the orchestra, like Mr Safonoff; and who hypnotize the orchestra, like Mr Nikisch … No one who has ever heard [Richter] can forget the magnificent breadth, dignity and power of his performances … and his steady beat which produces *an absolutely even tempo, unbroken sometimes from beginning to end of the longest symphonic movement.* But this is all he does at performance. All the expression he wishes for – usually exactly what is indicated and nothing more – is arranged at rehearsal.[25]

From the totality of these authentic eye-witness sketches, it must be clear beyond doubt that the critical descriptions we have of Richter's performances in London, including those of his Brahms symphonies, convey a reasonably reliable impression of the actuality, despite the passage of time.[26]

---

[22] See further p. 155.

[23] See Dyment interview, pp. 39–40.

[24] Unpublished interview with the author, 1972.

[25] Jerrold Northrop Moore (ed.), *Music and Friends: Letters to Adrian Boult*, London: Hamish Hamilton, 1979, the 'Prologue' of which includes Boult's paper 'Some Notes on Performance', given at a meeting of the Oriana Society, Oxford, in November 1909 (this quotation at p. 12, emphasis added).

[26] Here it should be noted that Wagner's advice on conducting and the (in practice often more extreme) example of Wagner's own performance style form an unavoidable background to any discussion of late nineteenth-century conducting styles; this background is referred to at the appropriate places in this and the following chapter. However, the descriptions of various conductors' styles in these chapters relate – so far as it is possible to separate stylistic approaches to the performance of the two composers – only to their approach to the music of Brahms. For a thorough and detailed assessment of these conductors' physical deportment and their stylistic approach to the music of Wagner, reference should be made to the following chapters

The early champions: Levi, Wüllner and Dessoff

If the burden of Brahms's complaint about Richter was his sometimes neglectful and sloppy preparation, did he welcome any thoroughly prepared, sincerely felt performance with impartial approbation? Certainly, as will be seen, he approved a wide range of interpretative styles. But precisely what range of styles was adopted by the composer's earliest champions in the 1860s and 1870s remains somewhat unclear since at that stage comment was reserved for the works rather than their interpretation.[27] Moreover the conductors concerned left relatively few musical footprints and clues tend to be contradictory. Among them, three stand out: one, Hermann Levi (1839–1900) was undoubtedly great; two others, Franz Wüllner (1832–1902) and (Felix) Otto Dessoff (1835–92) were no more, and no less, than distinguished Kapellmeisters.

Levi was the earliest among the great conductors to champion Brahms's orchestral music. Of that greatness there can be no dispute: in his one London concert given on 25 April 1895, only a few months before his retirement, he was hailed by critics as combining the virtues of Richter and Mottl, with a divinatory quality and 'electric' control of his forces peculiarly his own.[28] Brahms and Levi had a remarkably close relationship for a time, yet the composer never clearly stated what he thought of his friend, save that late in 1869 he declared him superior to Dessoff and others then in Vienna.[29] Unfortunately, for a variety of reasons, including Levi's increasing involvement with Wagner as a major element, his friendship with Brahms terminated in 1875 and after 1877 their correspondence ceased. This breach was 'the most painful experience of my entire life', wrote Levi to a mutual friend, 'a friend to whom I owe everything I am and have, deserted me because he would have nothing to do with a Wagnerian'.[30] His eventual first performance of Brahms's First Symphony in Munich on 27 March 1878 was the worst failure of his life, which he himself accounted his

---

of Jonathan Brown's monumental *Great Wagner Conductors: A Listener's Companion*, Canberra: Parrot Press, 2012 (Brown): Ch. 2, Hans von Bülow; Ch. 3, Hans Richter; Ch. 4, Anton Seidl; Ch. 5, Hermann Levi; Ch. 6, Felix Mottl; Ch. 7, Karl Muck; Ch. 8, Arthur Nikisch; Ch. 11, Felix Weingartner; Ch. 12, Bruno Walter; Ch. 13, Arturo Toscanini; Ch. 15, Wilhelm Furtwängler; Ch. 16, Fritz Busch; Ch. 17, Erich Kleiber; Ch. 18, Hans Knappertsbusch.

[27] See also p. 155 about possible change in critical vocabulary and meaning.

[28] The programme contained Wagner excerpts, including the Prelude to Act 1 of *Parsifal*, and Beethoven's Seventh Symphony. See *The Times*, 26 July 1895; *Musical Times*, vol. 36 (1 June 1895), p. 381; *Musical Standard*, 4 May 1895, pp. 349–50; also Brown, pp. 146–8.

[29] See Frithjof Haas, *Zwischen Brahms und Wagner. Der Dirigent Hermann Levi*, Zürich: Atlantis Musikbuch-Verlag, 1995 (Haas), p. 138; transl. Cynthia Klohr as *Hermann Levi: From Brahms to Wagner*, Washington, DC: Scarecrow Press, 2012 (Haas/Klohr), p. 92. Levi was at that time pondering an invitation to the Vienna Court Opera, which he turned down because it would have required him to share authority with the conductors already in place there.

[30] Haas, p. 199; Haas/Klohr, p. 138.

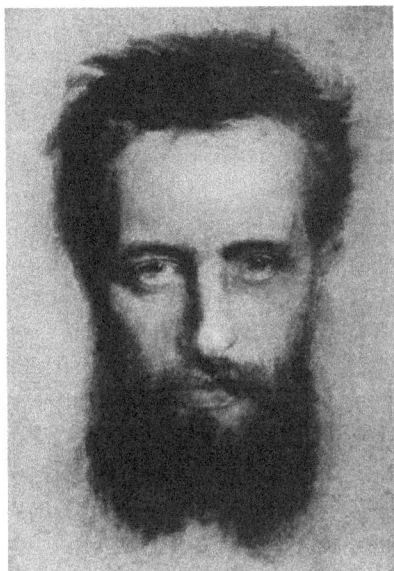

2. HERMANN LEVI,
LENBACH'S EARLY PORTRAIT

most embarrassing experience. Thereafter his performances of Brahms, although not infrequent, lacked conviction, especially after he conducted the premiere of *Parsifal*, because 'he no longer believed in them'.[31] Not without justification, after a Brahms concert on 17 November 1884 with the Meiningen Hofkapelle under Hans von Bülow in Munich, where Levi had been Kapellmeister since 1872, Bülow remarked to his wife that 'one day of mine accomplished *more* than a Levitical decade'.[32]

Of Levi's stylistic approach to Brahms – as distinct from his Wagner, especially *Parsifal* – we have only some broad clues. For example, after a Karlsruhe performance on 12 May 1869 of the *German Requiem*, prepared by Levi but conducted by Brahms, Levi found the performance more free and nuanced than under his own direction.[33] In his farewell concert at Karlsruhe in June 1872 before his move to Munich Levi gave the

---

[31] Haas, pp. 165 and 210–11; Haas/Klohr, pp. 115 and 145. Haas lists Levi's Munich performances of the First Symphony (1893), the Second (1879, 1888), the Third (1884) and the Fourth (1886), together with six further performances of other orchestral/concerted works: Haas, pp. 211–12; Haas/Klohr, pp. 145–6. Styra Avins suggests that factors other than Levi's involvement with Wagner caused this breach: 'Brahms the Godfather', in Walter Frisch and Kevin Karnes (eds), *Brahms and His World*, Princeton: Princeton University Press, 2009 (2nd ed.), pp. 41–56 at p. 52; see also Avins, pp. 473–5.

[32] Marie von Bülow (ed.), *Hans von Bülow. Briefe und Schriften*, Leipzig: Breitkopf und Härtel, 1895–1908 (Bülow Briefe), vol. 7, p. 318, quoted in Hans-Joachim Hinrichsen (ed.) (transl. Cynthia Klohr), *Hans von Bülow's Letters to Johannes Brahms*, Washington, DC: Scarecrow Press, 2012 (Hinrichsen/Klohr), p. 79.

[33] Haas, p. 131; Haas/Klohr, p. 87.

premiere of the complete *Triumphlied*, but later, in Munich, reported to Brahms about a terribly metronomic allegro-tempo performance of the work by his co-conductor Wüllner, sheer 'torture' for Levi, who regarded Wüllner as incapable of performing Brahms adequately.[34] From these clues one may deduce that Levi adopted a flexible approach in his performances of Brahms, if perhaps not as free or nuanced as that of the composer himself.

Wagner's extremely low opinion of Wüllner – the most incapable of all conductors and a 'bungler'[35] – doubtless stemmed from his furious opposition to the Munich premieres under that conductor of *Das Rheingold* (1869) and *Die Walküre* (1870), following Bülow's abrupt exit from his post there in 1869. However, Bülow's own view coincided with Wagner's: for him both Wüllner and the great violinist Joseph Joachim were bad (*schlechtes*) conductors.[36] Nevertheless, Brahms entrusted Wüllner with early performances of the *Haydn* Variations and First Symphony and in 1884 recommended him as successor to Ferdinand Hiller as Director of the Cologne Conservatoire and conductor of the Gürzenich orchestra; these posts he held with some distinction until his death in 1902. Evidently Brahms trusted his musicianship in dealing with his early symphonic works, whatever his shortcomings in technique and temperament. Whether there remains any subsequent trace of his stylistic approach to the Brahms canon is considered later in connection with the recordings of one his most famous pupils, Willem Mengelberg.

The last of this trio of now remote early champions of Brahms, Otto Dessoff, was in 1876 entrusted by Brahms with the premiere of the original version of his First Symphony at Karlsruhe, where Dessoff was director of music in succession to Levi. Dessoff had been appointed conductor of the Vienna Philharmonic at the age of twenty-five in 1860 but, after typical Viennese intrigues against him, left for Karlsruhe in 1875. One of his Viennese players, Josef Sulzer, left a description of his rather strange style, including excessive attenuation of notes bearing pause marks and extreme exaggeration of dynamics at both ends of the aural scale.[37]

Brahms was ambivalent about the conductorial powers of his old friend: in April 1869 he thought him 'not the right man' for the Viennese position, with the orchestra having 'gone to pot' under him[38] – an opinion not shared by Hanslick in his eulogy

---

[34] Levi's letter to Brahms on 3 December 1873, in *Johannes Brahms Briefwechsel*, Berlin: Deutsche Brahms-Gesellschaft 1912–22 (repr. Tutzing: Hans Schneider, 1974), vol. 7, quoted in Haas, pp. 181–2; Haas/Klohr, p. 126. See also Carl Krebs, *Meister des Taktstocks*, Berlin: Schuster & Loeffler, 1919, p. 206, quoted in Frits Zwart, *Willem Mengelberg (1871–1951). Een Biografie 1871–1920*, Amsterdam: Prometheus, 1999 (Zwart), p. 31.

[35] See Martin Gregor-Dellin and Deitrich Mack (eds) (transl. Geoffrey Skelton), *Cosima Wagner's Diaries*, New York: Harcourt Brace Jovanovich, 1978–80, vol. 1 (1869–1877), pp. 146, 194.

[36] Zwart, p. 32.

[37] Erwin Mittag, *The Vienna Philharmonic*, Vienna: Gerlach & Wiedling, 1950 (Mittag), p. 26.

[38] Letter to Hermann Levi, April 1869, in Avins, p. 393.

3. FRANZ WÜLLNER

4. OTTO DESSOFF

when Dessoff left that post.[39] On the other hand, Brahms readily accepted advice on practical points from Dessoff, recognising his careful preparation of and empathy for his works. When intent on entrusting him with the premiere of the First Symphony – at a time when friendship with his erstwhile champion Hermann Levi was on course to terminate – Brahms wrote to him of his wish to 'hear the thing for the first time in the small town which has a good friend, good conductor, and good orchestra' – that is, Dessoff himself – views which he repeated after the conductor's relatively early death.[40] It may well have been Dessoff's comments about the second movement that stimulated Brahms to rewrite it. However, a neutral observer of Levi and Dessoff, Heinrich Ordenstein, pianist and director of the conservatory in Karlsruhe, wrote that the latter 'had much less fiery temperament and inspirational might. But he was unsurpassed at carefully working out every detail to the highest standards of artistic intellect.'[41] As with Richter in the Second Symphony, timings of Dessoff's premiere of the First Symphony suggest a rapidity not often encountered in the later twentieth century.[42] He numbered both Nikisch and Mottl among his pupils in Vienna and his general approach is further considered in the context of the latter's reactions to his teaching.[43]

[39] Mittag, p. 27.
[40] Letter to Dessoff, October 1876, in Avins, pp. 495–6.
[41] Heinrich Ordenstein, *Musikgeschichte der Haupt- und Residenzstadt Karlsruhe bis zum Jahre 1914*, Karlsruhe: Müller, 1915, p. 28, quoted in Haas/Klohr, p. 111.
[42] Musgrave and Sherman, Ch. 4, p. 113 and Table at p. 115 with the notes thereto; the movement timings are: I 14:00, II 9:00, III 4:00, IV 16:00. Compare these figures with Table 1, p. 169.
[43] See p. 49 below.

Joseph Joachim: 'Just watch me'

The unchallengeable stature of Joseph Joachim (1831–1907) as the premier Austro-German violinist of the nineteenth century and dedicatee of both Brahms's Violin Concerto and (jointly) his Double Concerto overshadows his efforts as a conductor, in particular of Brahms's works. Rightly overshadowed, his contemporaries would probably have responded; Bülow's comment has been noted and he was not alone. The choral conductor Siegfried Ochs thought him an 'insecure and inadequate' conductor: his 'great weakness was his almost childish penchant for conducting ... In his enthusiasm he fooled around in an imprecise and indecisive manner; he was incapable of any interpretational refinement whatsoever.'[44] But he was sublimely unaware of his own limitations with the baton, so much so that, when rehearsing an orchestra for Brahms early in the composer's career, he remarked, 'Your best opportunity of learning how to conduct is surely to see me do it. Just watch carefully what I do, and you will do well enough later on.'[45]

Whatever his shortcomings as a conductor, Joachim was a tireless advocate of Brahms's works and in 1877 gave the first performance in England of the First Symphony. Among the composer's early interpreters, Joachim is significant in the present context as the recipient of the most detailed statement of Brahms's preferences in the performance of his symphonic music. The letter was occasioned by Joachim's request for metronome markings for the Fourth Symphony prior to his performance of the work in Berlin on 1 February 1886. Refusing the request, Brahms instead accompanied the parcel containing score and parts with a letter,[46] the subject of which was certain unmarked instructions pertaining to expression and related matters that he had pencilled into the score sent to Joachim. These instructions were, Brahms said, 'tempo modifications [that are] useful, even necessary, for a first performance', but unnecessary and undesirable to print, because:

> Such exaggerations are only really necessary as long as a work is unknown to the orchestra ... In that case I often cannot do enough pushing forward and holding back, so that passionate and calm expression is produced more or less as I want it.

[44] Siegfried Ochs, *Geschehenes, Gesehenes*, Leipzig: Grethlein, 1922, p. 90, cited in Kenneth Birkin, *Hans von Bülow: A Life for Music*, Cambridge: Cambridge University Press, 2011 (Birkin), p. 331.
[45] Konrad Huschke, *Johannes Brahms als Pianist, Dirigent und Lehrer*, Karlsruhe: Friedrich Gutsch, 1935, p. 51: '*Sehen Sie also nur ordentlich zu, wie ich es mache, dann wird es später schon gehen.*'
[46] Dated c. 20 January 1886, in Andreas Moser (ed.), *Johannes Brahms Briefwechsel V und VI. Johannes Brahms im Briefwechsel mit Joseph Joachim*, Berlin: Deutsche Brahms-Gesellschaft, 1912 (repr. Tutzing: Hans Schneider, 1974), p. 220.

5. JOSEPH JOACHIM WITH DONALD FRANCIS TOVEY, BERLIN, FEBRUARY 1902[47]

Once a work has got into the bloodstream, there should be no more talk of such things ... and the more one departs from this, the more inartistic I find the performing style ... But how people like to impress these days with this so called 'free

---

[47] Tovey was in Berlin for concerts of his own music with the Joachim Quartet. Joachim later wrote to Tovey's piano teacher, Sophie Weisse, that the photograph was taken by 'Fräulein Essler' and that Tovey told him constantly to stop smiling. To compose himself, Joachim had to adopt a 'ferocious glare', while Tovey complained that he himself looked like the 'Ameer of Afghanistan'. See further Donald Francis Tovey (ed. Michael Tilmouth and others), *The Classics of Music: Talks, Essays and Other Writings Previously Uncollected, Part 2, Journalist, Reviewer and Obituarist (1902–1934)*, Oxford: Oxford University Press, 2001, p. 257. This copy in my collection formerly belonged to Frances Dakyns (1877–1960), who knew both musicians well. Joachim presumably gave the copy to her on the date of his signature. Later Dakyns was a close friend of Adolf Busch and helped John Christie in founding the Glyndebourne Festival. See further p. 37 and Dyment 2012, p. 49.

artistic' performing style – and how easy that is even with the worst orchestra … An orchestra like the Meiningen should take pride in showing the opposite!

The letter has been subject to extensive exegesis,[48] but the principal message seems clear on its face: a conductor must always require some flexibility in order to render explicit the 'passionate or calm' expression implicit in the music, even if that 'pushing forward and holding back' is not marked in the score; but expressive licence must be avoided as 'inartistic'. It is clear, therefore, that Brahms preferred 'pushing forward and holding back' to its absence, as sometimes occurred with Richter, at least in Vienna. His last sentence, however, is a not-so-veiled criticism of the way in which his works had been conducted by Bülow at Meiningen, to which we now turn.

Hans von Bülow: 'If I'd wanted that, I would have written it in'

With the advent of Hans von Bülow (1830–94) there at last emerged a distinct and characterful interpretative approach to the developing Brahms canon that had a marked influence on some of his successors. During the late 1870s Bülow became as ardent a champion of Brahms as before that time he had been of Wagner and Liszt. His enthusiasm for Brahms was, contrary to popular perception, probably not a reaction against Wagner's works on account of that composer's treatment of him in their personal lives. Rather, it stemmed from his growing distaste for the music of his former father-in-law, Franz Liszt, and his renewed appreciation of Schumann, Mendelssohn and, above all, Beethoven, whose successor Bülow believed he could espy in Brahms.[49]

Bülow's early interest in Brahms commenced in 1872 with the addition of some of the composer's major piano works to his repertoire and, in 1875, the London premiere of the Piano Quintet.[50] This increasing appreciation culminated in his Hanover premiere of the revised score of the First Symphony in October 1877 and came to full fruition during his years with the Meiningen Hofkapelle from 1880 to 1885. There, starting with the Second Piano Concerto in October 1881, Brahms had the chance to rehearse new works in congenial surroundings with the forty-eight members of the orchestra, which Bülow drilled incessantly until it became the almost ideal vehicle for Brahms's purpose (even if sometimes he wished for more players).[51]

---

[48] See, in particular, Musgrave and Sherman, Ch. 8 pp. 224–30, from which I have drawn this translation. See further p. 219.
[49] See Hinrichsen/Klohr, p. xv.
[50] See Birkin, pp. 209, 228.
[51] Bülow's 'brilliant string quartet', as Brahms termed it in a letter to Wüllner in October 1885 (Avins, p. 629). This description, here used derisively by Brahms, was actually Bülow's own

6. HANS VON BÜLOW

The Meiningen Brahms cult during Bülow's time is sometimes exaggerated; in fact, including the orchestra's frequent tours, he conducted Brahms's symphonies on only 31 occasions during his Meiningen tenure – a small number indeed compared with his 198 performances of Beethoven's symphonies, including his famous 'double performances' of the Ninth Symphony.[52] Moreover, it is not an easy task to re-imagine in contemporary terms just how Bülow treated the scores for which he had the greatest reverence – Beethoven, Schumann and, as they appeared sequentially from the composer's pen, Brahms.[53] One of the clearest expositions of the elements of his style came from a Berlin critic when the Meiningen Hofkapelle played at a concert in the capital in February 1884:

---

deprecatory label for his Meiningen strings: see his letters of 15 August and 13 September 1881 to Brahms in Hinrichsen/Klohr, pp. 3–4.

[52] Numbers derived from Birkin, Appendix, 'Bülow Performance Chronology', pp. 583–641. The figures include performances on Bülow's nine tours with the Meiningen Hofkapelle and break down as follows: during the Bülow years, Brahms himself conducted the Hofkapelle in fifteen performances of his symphonies, No. 1 (one performance), No. 3 (four, including a double performance at the Meiningen concert on 3 February 1884), No. 4 (ten, including the work's first performance on 25 October 1884 and then on tour). Bülow conducted No. 1 (eight performances), No. 2 (seven), No. 3 (fourteen) and No. 4 (two). As to Beethoven's symphonies, Bülow conducted No. 1 (thirty-three performances), No. 2 (one), No. 3 (twenty-three), No. 4 (twenty-two), No. 5 (forty-one), No. 6 (fourteen), No. 7 (twenty-five), No. 8 (thirty-three) and No. 9 (six, being performed twice on three occasions).

[53] But see p. 82 for Weingartner's description of what he thought were Bülowian excesses in specified works.

Every note, every pause, each inflection is significant, hence the tremendous clarity which distinguishes performances which can only be described as creative acts in their own right. We seem to have the score laid out before us; we see the compositional process at work, built up *Motiv* by *Motiv* before our very eyes – but the music does not disintegrate in Bülow's hands, no – and this is the remarkable thing – he fuses the whole thing together in a veritable act of genius. Each element succeeds the other with such inevitability that it leaves the impression of spontaneous improvisation.[54]

Pauses, inflections, an emphasis thereby on every significant item of the subject matter – thus a seeming improvisation held together by the conductor's masterful vision. To much the same effect was Hanslick's slightly indulgent description of Bülow and the Meiningen Hofkapelle in Vienna in 1884, when he declared that Bülow's training:

has transformed it into an instrument upon which he plays with utter freedom and from which he produces nuances possible only with a discipline to which larger orchestras would not normally submit. Since he can achieve these nuances securely, it is understandable that he applies them at those places where they would seem appropriate to him if he were playing the same piece on the piano. It would be unjust to call these tempo changes 'liberties', since conscientious adherence to the score is a primary and inviolable rule with Bülow ... A few things struck me as unmotivated and affected, among them the almost mannered phrasing of the scale fragment which introduces the finale of Beethoven's Symphony No. 1. And I had certain reservations about certain rubati in the Overture to *Der Freischütz*. These are interpretative peculiarities common to Bülow's predilection for individual touches.[55]

'In its day' has to be borne in mind when discussing Bülow's achievements in Meiningen, for a unanimous response to such subtle (or rather less subtle as it sometimes

---

[54] *Musikalisches Wochenblatt*, vol. 25, no. 9, 21 February 1884, p. 112, quoted and translated by Birkin, p. 308.

[55] Henry Pleasants (ed. and transl.), Eduard Hanslick: *Music Criticisms 1846–99* (first published in the USA, 1950), revised ed., Harmondsworth: Penguin, 1963, pp. 234–5. Hanslick wrote his critical review after hearing the three concerts in 1884 by the Meiningen Hofkapelle under Bülow in the Musikvereinssaal: on 20 November an all-Beethoven programme, the principal works being Symphonies Nos. 1 and 5 and the *Grosse Fuge*; on 25 November, the principal works including Brahms's 1st Piano Concerto (soloist Bülow without conductor) and 3rd Symphony, Weber's Overture *Der Freischütz* and Beethoven's Overtures *Leonoras Nos. 1* and 3; and on 2 December, the principal works including Brahms's 2nd Piano Concerto (soloist Bülow, Brahms conducting), *Haydn* Variations and Beethoven's 8th Symphony. Additionally, on 1 December the orchestra assisted Bülow's concert, playing two overtures under him and also Beethoven's 4th Piano Concerto and the Schubert/Liszt *Wanderer* Fantasia, both with Bülow as soloist.

seemed) nuancing would now be taken in the stride of many modern orchestras. So, too, would the 'astounding feat', as Hanslick termed it, of the whole strings playing 'flawlessly' the *Grosse Fuge*. Bülow's orchestral training nonetheless set standards to be emulated by all who followed and some elements of his style left a permanent imprint on his juniors. The totality of his approach in the Brahms symphonies, however, was captured by few, if any, of his successors. Max Fiedler may have come closest, but his manipulations of tempo, as recorded, are sometimes so crude and obvious that it may be doubted whether, for all his worship of Bülow, he was capable of reflecting the latter's sometimes subtle fluxing and treatment of detail.[56] Aside from Brahms, perhaps Richard Strauss, Bülow's caretaker successor in Meiningen, approached aspects of the style most successfully, in both his Wagner recordings and his brilliant and flexible account of Beethoven's Fifth Symphony.[57]

But what of the composer's reactions? To some extent Brahms appreciated Bülow's didactically shaped, fully nuanced, precisely drilled performances of his symphonies with the Meiningen Hofkapelle; the ample rehearsal time taken in order to produce such results came as manna after some of his experiences in Vienna.[58] And here, it may be noted once more, Bülow's timings for his own performances of the first three symphonies were more brisk than was the custom in the latter part of the twentieth century: he wrote, '[No.] I lasts 37 minutes, II lasts 38, III takes 34 minutes. (However, in I and II we skip the repeat of the first movement, which the Master has authorised me to do!).'[59]

It is nonetheless clear that Brahms resisted elements of Bülow's elaborately planned approach, objecting to his constant, premeditated manipulation of tempos, which for him, evidently, were not always 'fused together in a veritable act of genius': his conducting, complained Brahms, was 'always calculated for effect. At the moment when a new phrase begins, he gets [the players] to leave a tiny gap, and he also likes to change the tempo ever so slightly … if I had wanted [this], I would have written it in'.[60] Brahms's formulation of his objections was anticipated by his friend Elisabeth

---

[56] See further p. 72 (Max Fiedler) and also p. 80 (Walter Damrosch).
[57] Richard Strauss's recordings of Wagner – his *Flying Dutchman* Overture, Polydor 66830, and Prelude to Act 1 of *Tristan*, Polydor 66832 – were made with the Berlin Philharmonic in December 1928, Beethoven's Fifth Symphony with the Berlin State Opera Orchestra, Polydor 66814–7, in early October 1928; CD transfers in DGG 00289 479 2703. See further Carsten Schmidt, 'Richard Strauss and the Recording Media', *Classical Recordings Quarterly*, Winter 2014, p. 13.
[58] See e.g. Avins, pp. 581–2 (Brahms's letter to Ferdinand Hiller, October 1881).
[59] Bülow's letter to the Vienna publisher Albert Gutmann about a proposed concert (the programme ultimately dropped two of the symphonies), 9 October 1884, in Bülow *Briefe*, vol. 7, p. 303, quoted in Hinrichsen/Klohr, p. 78.
[60] Musgrave and Sherman, Ch. 8, p. 230, citing Max Kalbeck, *Johannes Brahms*, 4 vols, Berlin: Deutsche Brahms-Gesellschaft, 1904–14, vol. 3, p. 495. Alan Walker, *Hans von Bülow: A Life*

von Herzogenberg, who in the course of a letter to the composer about Bülow's style at the piano, dated 27 March 1881 from Meiningen, remarked that 'Bülow's affected little pauses before every new phrase, every notable change of harmony, are quite unpardonable.'[61] True, due to a mutual misunderstanding about each other's appearances with the Meiningen Hofkapelle on tour, Brahms was at loggerheads with Bülow at the time he made his remarks but the witness of his friend and also of the young Felix Weingartner (noted hereafter) attest to the accuracy of the performance characteristics occasioning his reservations.

Notwithstanding these major quibbles, taken as a whole there can be no doubt about Bülow's supreme stature as the virtuoso conductor – indeed the first such virtuoso – of his era. Of the many tributes to his power and perception, that of Liszt's pupil Frederic Lamond may serve for all:

> He was the greatest conductor who ever lived – not even Toscanini approaching him. I have seen and heard them all. No one, Nikisch, Richter, Mahler, Weingartner, could compare with him in true warmth and expression ... [Brahms] was a good conductor, but did not compare with Bülow, who could galvanise the most villainous, straggling band of musicians into an array of heaven-sent archangels. Brahms, in the rehearsals [for the premiere of the Fourth Symphony at Meiningen in October 1885], repeatedly said to the orchestra: 'Wait, gentlemen, until you hear this work conducted by Bülow.'[62]

Post-Bülow conductors: encouraging words for juniors

Felix Weingartner's early devotion to Liszt and Wagner was well known to Brahms and it was therefore with some suspicion that the composer first greeted him when the Berlin Philharmonic visited Vienna for three concerts in 1895. Brahms attended all three – the two others were conducted by Felix Mottl and Richard Strauss – but, in the end, it was the one conducted by Weingartner that he found by far the most interesting. After the performance of his Second Symphony in this concert, Brahms showed his especial respect for Weingartner by rising from his customary chair in the Roter

---

and Times, Oxford: Oxford University Press, 2010 (Walker), p. 308, throws doubt on Kalbeck's reliability in general, but the cited quotation has not been called into question; see also n. 73. For a balanced assessment of Kalbeck's reliability, see Avins, p. 3.

[61] Max Kalbeck (ed.), *Johannes Brahms Briefwechsel I. Johannes Brahms im Briefwechsel mit Heinrich und Elisabet von Herzogenberg, vol. 1*, Berlin: Deutsche Brahms-Gesellschaft, 1907, pp. 145–6, transl. Hannah Bryant as *Johannes Brahms: The Herzogenberg Correspondence*, London: John Murray, 1909 (repr. with introduction by Walter Frisch, New York, 1987), pp. 124–8.
[62] Frederic Lamond, *The Memoirs of Frederic Lamond*, Glasgow: William McLennan, 1949, pp. 40 and 49.

Igel, greeting him with the words: 'I am delighted with the way my piece was reflected in your head' ('*Ich freue mich wie sich mein Stücke in Ihrem Kopfe gespiegelt hat*').[63] Later he told his publisher, Fritz Simrock, that the performance was 'quite wonderful', while Weingartner's 'healthy and fresh personality was uncommonly appealing'. The uncluttered but spontaneous freshness of approach characterising performances under the young Weingartner showed Brahms one secure way forward for his music in the future.[64] Weingartner's Brahms legacy is considered below.[65]

Only three months later Brahms expressed equal delight at the performance of the Fourth Symphony given in Leipzig by Arthur Nikisch: 'Nikisch is an extraordinarily gifted conductor. When he is dealing with things about which he is enthusiastic (and my symphonies are among these) he does his work perfectly … It is impossible to hear it [the Fourth] better done.'[66] Nikisch's few recordings include nothing of Brahms, but from all contemporary accounts it is clear that his poetic abandon was at the opposite pole from Weingartner's straightforward approach. The styles of these two, in their time regarded by some in Germany and elsewhere as the greatest concert conductors of their generation,[67] probably mark the extremes of what was interpretatively acceptable to the composer, avoiding both unfelt metronomics and the reservations he found it necessary to make in the case of Bülow. Their performances of Brahms are further documented hereafter.[68]

Brahms's contemporaries on his conducting of the symphonies

The conductors surveyed in this chapter left their own appraisals of Brahms as interpreter of his works. The earliest, at least among those who supported Brahms and

---

[63] See Felix Weingartner (transl. Marguerite Wolff), *Buffets and Rewards*, London: Hutchinson, 1937, pp. 221–2 (this translation of the two volumes of Weingartner's *Lebenserinnerungen*, Zürich: Orell Füssli, 1928–29, is severely cut; both are therefore cited in this study), and *Lebenserinnerungen*, vol. 2, pp. 62–3. See also Christopher Dyment, *Felix Weingartner: Recollections and Recordings*, Rickmansworth: Triad Press, 1976 (Dyment 1976), p. 27, for Weingartner's pupil Stewart Deas's literal translation quoted here of Brahms's words.

[64] Brahms to Simrock, in Max Kalbeck, *Brahms Briefwechsel*, vol. 12, Berlin, 1919, transl. in Avins, p. 726; quoted more extensively at p. 84.

[65] See p. 84 for the full text of this extract and the recorded legacy.

[66] Berthold Litzmann, *Letters of Clara Schumann and Johannes Brahms 1853–1896*, New York: Longmans, 1927 (Brahms–Schumann), vol. 1, p. 295, letter from Brahms dated 4 February 1896. See also Brahms's letter to Simrock in similar terms in Avins, p. 730.

[67] Reporting from Berlin in 1905, the *Musical Courier*'s correspondent remarked that 'we are constantly hearing the world's two greatest conductors, Nikisch and Weingartner. Weingartner conducts with wonderful élan, and with remarkable perfection of detail … Nikisch is more poetic, more impulsive' (8 February 1905).

[68] See pp. 60 and 92.

conducted his early works, was Hermann Levi, who remarked to Brahms, 'you have a gift for conducting beyond any others', but the compliment came within a lengthy letter sent in response to Brahms's request to him for advice on whether to accept a conducting position in Vienna. In fact, the letter's compliment seems to have been wrapped up in a negative message, the thrust of which was that Brahms's gifts were not best put to use in the position offered – a message that the composer may well have resented.[69] In any event it tells us little and came at a time before the composition of the First Symphony. More to the point, Bülow clearly felt that Brahms's conducting at the Meiningen premiere of the Fourth Symphony should have been left to him, since the work would have been clearer, livelier and more impressive in his hands.[70] On the other hand, Bülow also remarked on one occasion that, next to Wagner, he knew of no other conductor who understood how to transport one by his conducting.[71]

These assessments are no more than conflicting generalities that take us little further in the task of understanding Brahms's own style. Weingartner's general comments about Bülow and his comparison with Brahms take us a step further. His testimony about Bülow's eccentricities, particularly in Beethoven's overtures and symphonies, was extensive in both his memoirs and his expository works. In the present context, his recollections are of particular value for his witness of a concert in Hamburg, when he saw Brahms conduct his Fourth Symphony in the first half of the concert and Bülow conduct Beethoven's Eighth Symphony in the second.[72] He commented on the composer's 'restrained movements and broad conceptions (*ruhigen grosslinigen Bewegungen*)' as against the 'mercurial unrest (*quecksilberartigen Unruhe*)' of Bülow, even though at the time he failed to understand Brahms's Fourth Symphony.[73] By

[69]　Huschke, p. 62. Levi's words were: '*Dass Du die Fähigkeit zum Dirigieren besitzest, wie mein Zweiter, habe ich ... gesehen*'.

[70]　Richard Specht (transl. Eric Blom), *Johannes Brahms*, London: J. M. Dent, 1930, p. 252.

[71]　Huschke, p. 43.

[72]　Weingartner is hazy about dates, but he was without doubt referring to the Philharmonic concert in Hamburg on 9 March 1889, in which, in the first half, Bülow conducted Reinecke's *Trauermarsch* Op. 200 in memory of Kaiser Wilhelm I and Beethoven's *Coriolan* Overture, followed by Brahms conducting his Fourth Symphony; in the second half Bülow conducted Beethoven's Eighth Symphony, followed by Brahms conducting his *Academic Festival Overture*: Birkin, p. 671; Hofmann, pp. 278–9. This concert was Brahms's last appearance as a conductor in Hamburg.

[73]　Weingartner 1937, p. 165; *Lebenserinnerungen*, vol. 1, p. 311. Typically, the translated paragraph is half the length of Weingartner's original, omitting all mention of his failure to appreciate the Brahms symphony at the time. Walker, pp. 364–6, in a sustained attack on Weingartner's credibility and stature, maintains that he was motivated purely by revenge in his remarks about Bülow after 1887, following their acute differences in that year over the interpretation of Bizet's *Carmen* in Hamburg (see further p. 82 below). However, his book does not examine Bülow's style in any detail or refute the examples which Weingartner gave of what, in his opinion, were Bülow's distortions (e.g. in the *Egmont* and *Coriolan* overtures and the Eighth

'broad conceptions', we may perhaps understand that Brahms manipulated his tempos to some extent for expressive purposes without going to the extremes of frequency, detail and degree that characterised Bülow's practice.

Weingartner's comparison was to some extent corroborated by Richard Strauss and Charles Villiers Stanford. Strauss, assistant Kapellmeister to Bülow at Meiningen before and immediately after the latter's sudden and headstrong resignation in November 1885, described Bülow's handling of Brahms's music as 'hyper-refined, inventive and resourceful', whereas Brahms himself had a 'simpler and more sober way of conducting these pieces' in which 'one heard the work itself'.[74] Stanford, commenting on Brahms's dislike of Richter's sometimes pedestrian and metronomic performances already cited, described the composer's own approach as 'very elastic, as much so in places as von Bülow's, though more restrained'.[75]

Perhaps most revealing of all is Brahms's own description of his difficulties described in his letter to Joachim, quoted above.[76] The letter makes clear that when conducting a piece new to orchestras Brahms sometimes encountered resistance to 'pushing forward and holding back, so that passionate or calm expression is produced more or less as I want it'. But, carried to excess, expressive liberties resulted in a performance style – implicitly a style akin to Bülow's excesses – for which he expressed his distaste. As the letter indicates, Joachim's request for further elucidation led the composer to insert extra, pencilled markings into his autograph score of the Fourth Symphony, but these were deleted before publication.[77] Such instructions were, he thought, necessary only at the stage when conductors were learning to 'feel' the expressive requirements of this new language cast in Classical form. The correct route should reject a 'free artistic' performance style. 'The so-called elastic tempo is not a new discovery', wrote Brahms in 1880 to his young friend George Henschel, 'and to it, as to many another, one should attach a *con discrezione*.'[78]

A reasonably clear, if not always consistent, picture emerges. As a conductor, Brahms himself attempted, with intermittent success, to inject a 'pushing forward and holding back' into the basic pulse which would provide in sufficient measure 'passionate or calm expression' explicit or implicit in his symphonic music. In performances of

---

and Ninth Symphonies in his *On Conducting*, 3rd ed., 1905, trans. Ernest Newman, New York: Dover reprint, 1969, pp. 12–18). The witness of Brahms himself, among innumerable contemporaries, is sufficient confirmation of Weingartner's stature. Walker's view that Weingartner's style was characterised by 'self-effacement to the point of redundancy' and that his Beethoven recordings give 'the whole text and not much more than the text' (*ibid.*) suggests a rather limited acquaintance with his recorded legacy. See further p. 89.

[74] Huschke, p. 49: '*Aber man hat das Werk gehört!*'
[75] See n. 16 above.
[76] See p. 16.
[77] See Musgrave and Sherman, Ch. 8, p. 224, and p. 219 below.
[78] Henschel, pp. 78–9; see Avins, p. 559, from which this translation is drawn.

his symphonies by others, he approved of a wide range of approaches: those of his early Kapellmeister champions (insufficiently documented to dogmatise about details of their styles); later the clean, unmannered Weingartner and the uninhibitedly Romantic Nikisch.[79] But he vehemently rejected pedestrian and under-rehearsed routine and accepted only with considerable reservations Bülow's constant, consciously mannered and manipulative exegeses. His undoubted admiration for Bülow was directed more towards the conductor's achievement in drilling his modestly sized orchestra – far smaller than those in the principal cities of the German-speaking world – to a perfection unique in its time.[80]

Facing the issues: an assembly of witnesses

In the context of the seemingly irreconcilable stylistic divergences described in preceding pages, Fritz Steinbach's performances achieved a special distinction in the eye (or ear) of the composer: they avoided what some saw as Bülow's exaggerations but delivered the world of flexibility and nuance envisaged by Brahms if his orchestral music's expressive intentions were to be most fully realised. 'Pushing forward and holding back', and knowing when to do so, was a fundamental element in Brahms's interpretative intentions, expressing in equal measure the music's structural integrity and emotional thrust. That was Steinbach's seemingly unique achievement, but just how much flexibility and nuance he infused in his Brahms performances has been the subject of significant debate. Clarifying that crucial issue requires a renewed assessment, not only of contemporary evidence about Steinbach but also of the career and stylistic affinities of those conductors who witnessed Steinbach's approach.

Of significant (but perhaps not equal) importance, similar questions must be addressed about other conductors, outside the circle of orthodox Brahmsians, who may be credited with establishing valid interpretative norms in the performance of Brahms's symphonic works. Some of the conductors falling in the latter category, such as Nikisch and Weingartner, won the composer's approval and may therefore plausibly be credited with carrying forward valid traditions in the performance of Brahms's symphonies almost certainly unconnected with the Steinbach line of authority. Others, such as Mengelberg and Wilhelm Furtwängler, are, with their characteristic interpretative licence, sometimes credited with providing an indication of Steinbach's

---

[79] This study uses the term 'Romantic' to indicate, in broad terms, those conductors who espoused a 'free artistic' performance style (to use Brahms's own ironic term) as distinct from the Classical line mentioned at the outset (see p. 4 above).

[80] For the significance of the qualification 'in its time', see p. 20 and Musgrave and Sherman, Ch. 13, pp. 358–9; see also below, p. 195.

approach and, hence, of possessing a special authority in their performances of Brahms's symphonies:[81] such claims need to be tested.

In addition to the elucidation of stylistic affinities mentioned above, a further objective in the next chapter is to assess the remains in the twentieth century, if any there be, of the traditions or, more properly, lines of authority established by the conductors of whom Brahms approved without significant reservation, whether or not these conductors concerned left recorded evidence of their interpretative approaches. Where no evidence exists in recorded sound, it is necessary to establish, with as much precision as the evidence permits, just how those conductors who are documented only in the words of their contemporaries approached their task. That in turn requires an assessment of whether that documentary evidence is couched in terms which convey the same meaning today that they conveyed to their contemporaries – a possible difficulty already adumbrated in the instances of Bülow and Richter. Where necessary, a provisional assessment of this difficulty is made in each case, but general comments on the problem are considered after the totality of the evidence has been set out.[82]

Of course, recorded sound, if it can help establish the character of the lines of authority, must be explored with as much vigour as the documentary evidence, with the aim of discerning any hints that may exist of the nature and character of the lines of authority linking us with the performances most cherished by the composer – inevitably, in most cases, at second hand through the medium of proven disciples of the conductors who secured Brahms's approval.

The scheme of the next two chapters is therefore an examination of all relevant documentary evidence in Chapter 2 and a similar examination of recorded evidence in Chapter 3. As will become evident, the combined chapters provide a roll call of some of the most distinguished musicians – the majority of them conductors – of the past century and a half. These witnesses await cross-examination about their careers, influences (upon them and emanating from them), stylistic characters and, not least, the nature of their connections, if any, with the composer himself.[83]

---

[81] See e.g. note 3 above. See also comments to like effect by Sir Charles Mackerras, p. 235.

[82] See p. 155.

[83] The scope of this study has intentional limitations. It deals with those conductors linked to Brahms because he welcomed their interpretations of his works, together with their podium descendants. It does not deal with other musicians linked to Brahms by friendship and approval who numbered among their pupils those who went on to become distinguished conductors. Thus Joseph Krips, as a pupil of Weingartner, falls within the scope, but Karl Böhm (1894–1981), as a pupil of Brahms's amanuensis Eusebius Mandyczewski, falls outside, even though the latter's performances of the Brahms symphonies would be accounted by many as superior to the former's. See further pp. 59 and 95.

CHAPTER 2

THE DOCUMENTARY EVIDENCE: LINES OF AUTHORITY

The last chapter's conclusions outlined the lines of enquiry required in the present chapter by the sometimes problematic 'assembly of witnesses' brought to the fore in the search for Brahms's authentic voice. In the following pages the musicians – most but not all of them conductors – who in a variety of ways provided (or are alleged to have provided) lines of authority traceable to the composer are presented in more or less chronological order with the exceptions of the first, Alexander Berrsche, and the last, Walter Blume, whose importance lies now in the documentary evidence they left to posterity. It should be noted that, where the careers of recording conductors are too well known to merit a full biographical account, they are outlined here only in so far as the context requires.

Alexander Berrsche: Munich's recording angel (or Beckmesser?)

The first witness in the search for any authentic 'tradition' or line of authority traceable to the composer is the outstanding critic Alexander Berrsche (1883–1940). Berrsche was a pupil of Max Reger and wrote for the *Augsburger Postzeitung* (1907–12) and the *Münchener Zeitung* (1912–40). Along with other essays, his critical reviews were collected posthumously in *Trösterin Musika*, an 800-page volume published in two editions, the first in 1942 (Munich: Callweg), the second in 1949 (Munich: Hermann Rinn). The latter added items on musicians *verboten* in 1942, including the Jewish Gustav Mahler and Bruno Walter and the self-exiled Busch brothers; the footnoted references hereafter are to the page numbers of this edition. Berrsche's vantage point in Munich means that some desirable names are missing – Abendroth, Toscanini and the Brahms performances of Weingartner and Fritz Busch (he commented on the Beethoven performances of both, with some reservations on account of their, as he thought, quick tempos). In his concert reviews there is an excusable focus on those with posts in Munich during his time, such as Franz Fischer, Hans Pfitzner and Hans

Knappertsbusch.[1] Nevertheless, Berrsche's detailed comments on the Brahms style of those conductors he did hear are invaluable. For him, none measured up to Steinbach and it is with this conductor, so central to the understanding of what Brahms required in the performance of his orchestral music, that we commence the roll call of witnesses in the search for authenticity of style.

Fritz Steinbach: 'all is perfection'

Steinbach's early career: the Mühlfeld effect

Steinbach is perforce a principal witness in this chapter by virtue of his close connection with Brahms and the unstinting approval the composer bestowed on his performances of works across the repertoire, including his own. A pupil of the Leipzig Conservatory and of Gustav Nottebohm in Vienna, to whom Brahms recommended him after he first met the young student in 1875, Fritz (born Friedrich Adolf) Steinbach (1855–1916), went on to study in Karlsruhe with Otto Dessoff.[2] On Bülow's recommendation, he became assistant Kapellmeister in Mainz, where his elder brother Emil was Kapellmeister.[3] This 'sensitive, yet strapping young conductor', reported Bülow to Brahms in October 1884, was, together with Mottl, 'the best' orchestral conductor of the younger generation.[4] Steinbach succeeded that master (and his interim successor, Richard Strauss) as Kapellmeister of the Meiningen Hofkapelle in 1886; he owed the post to Brahms's recommendation to the theatre- and music-loving Herzog (Duke) Georg II at Meiningen, whose personal interest was responsible for the continued funding of the small orchestra.[5]

---

[1] Franz Fischer, conductor at the Munich opera from 1879, Generalmusikdirektor of Bavaria after the death of Mottl but relinquishing the post when Walter was appointed in January 1913: see Erik Ryding and Rebecca Pechevsky, *Bruno Walter: A World Elsewhere*, New Haven: Yale University Press, 2001, p. 103. Hans Pfitzner was appointed Senator of the German Academy, Munich, in 1925 and was a life member of the Munich Academy of Music, 1927–34. Hans Knappertsbusch (see further p. 148) was, in succession to Walter, music director of the Bavarian State Opera in Munich, 1922–36.

[2] See Maren Goltz, *Musiker-Lexicon des Herzogtums Sachsen-Meiningen (1680–1918)*, Meiningen, 2012 (Goltz 2012), p. 373; Herta Müller's entry in the *New Grove Dictionary of Music and Musicians*, 2nd ed., vol. 24, pp. 334–5, and her more detailed treatment in 'Fritz Steinbachs Wirken in Meiningen und für Johannes Brahms von 1886–1903', *Südthüringer Forschungen* 30 (1999), pp. 87–120 (Müller); see also Tully Potter, *Adolph Busch: The Life of an Honest Musician*, London: Toccata Press, 2010 (Potter), pp. 1118–19.

[3] Emil Steinbach (1849–1919), a competent but unremarkable conductor who was in charge of Covent Garden's Wagner in 1893.

[4] Bülow's letter to Brahms, 18 October 1884, in Hinrichsen/Klohr, p. 22.

[5] Herzog Georg II of Sachsen-Meiningen (1826–1914) refers to Brahms's recommendation in his letter to Brahms of 28 April 1887, in Herta Müller and Renate Hofmann (eds), *Brahms*

Steinbach maintained a very close relationship with Brahms until shortly before the composer's death. He took every opportunity to observe him at work and it is probable that his own Brahms performances were influenced by this thorough study.[6] Brahms continued the regular visits to Meiningen begun during Bülow's tenure, which gave him the opportunity to hear the repertoire, including his own works, rehearsed and conducted by 'the dear Conductor' – Steinbach – to his profound satisfaction.[7] On one occasion, in December 1891, his First Symphony conducted by Steinbach pleased the composer so much that he asked for it to be repeated: Brahms was 'taken by surprise and overwhelmed' by its 'elemental effect'.[8] On another visit, for a festival organised by Steinbach at the end of February 1895, Brahms was overheard to say: 'The chorus, the orchestra and that incomparable Steinbach; everything is perfection.'[9]

Brahms's attendance at this festival was exceptional. In the ordinary course he made only private visits to hear his works, staying as guest of Herzog Georg and Freifrau Helen in the Schloss Elisabethenburg; but on this occasion Brahms was attracted by Steinbach's inclusion of works by other composers, including *Fidelio* performed in the ducal theatre.[10] After yet another festival organised and conducted by Steinbach on 27–29 September of that year, in a letter to the conductor dated 30 September the normally gruff composer found it hard to express adequately his grateful thanks: the letter, one of his last to Steinbach, measures the depth of his gratitude to him. The

---

Briefwechsel Vol. XVII: Johannes Brahms in Briefwechsel mit Herzog Georg II von Sachsen Meiningen und Helene Freifrau von Heldburg, rev. Otto Biba and Kurt and Renate Hoffman, Tutzing: Hans Schneider, 1991 (*Herzog-Briefe*), p. 71. Freifrau Helen, originally Ellen Franz (1839–1923), a piano pupil of Bülow in Berlin, later chose acting as a profession and was a member of the Meininger Hofschauspieler when she married Herzog Georg, with the morganatic title of Freifrau von Heldburg.

[6]   See Musgrave and Sherman), Ch. 8 (Pascall and Weller), p. 242, citing Max Kalbeck, *Johannes Brahms*, 2nd ed., vol. 4, Berlin: Deutsche Brahms-Gesellschaft, 1915, p. 81. Steinbach was promoted to Generalmusikdirektor in 1893 and Intendant in 1896.

[7]   Brahms–Schumann, vol. 2, p. 267, Brahms's letter of 17 November 1894. Brahms made fourteen visits to Meiningen from 1880 onwards, staying there for a total of around 100 days: Goltz 2012, p. 52.

[8]   Translation in Pasternack/Blume, p. xi of Pasternack's Preface, of Kalbeck, *Johannes Brahms*, vol. 4, pt 1, p. 224, quoted in Robert Pascall (ed.), *Symphonie Nr. 1 c-moll op. 68*, Series I/1 of *Johannes Brahms Gesamtausgabe*, Munich: G. Henle, 1996, p. x.

[9]   Edward Speyer, *My Life and Friends*, London: Cobden-Sanderson, 1937, p. 101, quoted by Potter, p. 1118. On this visit Brahms also participated as pianist in a chamber music concert on 25 February, playing both the Sonatas Op. 120 with Mühlfeld and the Piano Quartet Op. 25 with Bram Eldering, Alfonss Abass and Carl Peining, principals in the Meiningen Hofkapelle: Hofmann, pp. 303–4.

[10]   Heinrich Reimann, *Johannes Brahms*, Berlin: Harmonie, 1903, p. 113. Brahms attended all three performances of *Fidelio*, declaring that 'the performance was in every respect excellent': Brahms–Schumann, vol. 2, p. 274, Brahms's letter of 10 March 1895. Brahms also participated as pianist in a concert conducted by Steinbach on 28 September, accompanying four solo voices in songs from Op. 31, 64 and 112: Hofmann, p. 305.

7. THE MEININGEN HOFKAPELLE WITH FRITZ STEINBACH

following, addressed to his 'dear friend' in somewhat knotty and slapdash German, is the complete text:

> Much though I should like to, I must not interrupt your well-deserved repose; however, on your happy awakening you shall find my heartfelt greeting waiting for you—no need for me to tell you at length *how heartfelt*, and how *sincerely full of gratitude* it is. Each day you must have felt what a tremendous pleasure you were giving me and all who were taking part in your splendid festival. You probably have to be satisfied with this quite certain feeling, however, as neither in writing nor face to face can one completely express how exceptional your festival was in every respect. Were I at all able to achieve this, I would stay here for the whole day in order to make the attempt. With heartfelt greetings to you all, Yours, J. Brahms.[11]

Steinbach inherited from Bülow not only a crack orchestra (in late nineteenth-century terms) but the services of the inestimable Richard Mühlfeld (1856–1907), the orchestra's principal clarinettist. He had occupied that position since 1879 and his great worth was immediately apparent to Bülow and also to Herzog Georg, who saw to it that Mühlfeld's unique qualities were properly rewarded and his sometimes precarious health carefully tended. So it was that, despite many offers from elsewhere, Mühlfeld's strong sense of obligation kept him at Meiningen throughout his career. He was, however, permitted to accept some solo engagements and from 1884 to 1896 played in the summer months with the Bayreuth Festival orchestra, whose woodwind

---

[11] Reimann, p. 113, emphasis in original. Comment on the composer's language by the translator, Nicholas Chadwick.

8. STEINBACH WITH
RICHARD MÜHLFELD

ranks he outshone; all the conductors – Richter, Levi, Mottl – again recognised his remarkable qualities.

Mühlfeld forged a particularly close relationship with Steinbach, who was well aware of the player's position of trust and artistic influence in the Hofkapelle; the conductor frequently took the player's advice on artistic matters and allowed him more frequent solo engagements throughout Germany. It was probably as a result of Brahms's request to hear Mühlfeld as soloist that, with a quartet drawn from the orchestra, he performed Mozart's Clarinet Quintet especially for the composer on a visit to Meiningen in March 1891, with results that brought forth Brahms's late masterpieces. 'It is impossible to play the clarinet better than Herr Mühlfeld does here', wrote Brahms to Clara Schumann in March 1891, a view he repeated after his completion of the Clarinet Trio and Quintet three months later, adding 'he is absolutely the best I know'.[12] Mühlfeld performed the Quintet and the other late clarinet works throughout Germany, often with the composer or Joachim (in Op. 114 and 120), and even travelled to London for the Quintet's premiere there in March 1892.[13] His unique artistry contributed to the style of Brahms performances by the Meiningen Hofkapelle, accounting for both

---

[12] Brahms–Schumann, vol. 1, pp. 190 and 196, letters of 17 March 1891 and (?)July 1891. Brahms played in four performances at Meiningen of the Clarinet Trio Op. 114 in November 1891 and again on 30 January 1893, when the Clarinet Quintet Op. 115 was also played, Mühlfeld participating: Hofmann, pp. 284–5, 292.

[13] At St James's Hall on 28 March, with Joachim leading a quartet (Ries, Straus and Piatti).

the special cohesion of the woodwind forces and their prominence in the orchestral balance on which the critics so frequently remarked.[14]

The tours and later career

Continuing the tradition established by Bülow, from the start of his Meiningen tenure Steinbach toured with the Hofkapelle, tirelessly promoting Brahms, at first only to neighbouring towns, but from 1897 across Germany.[15] Three years later in the course of a thirty-concert tour they ventured to Holland for six concerts, including three in Amsterdam's Concertgebouw, and in March 1902 travelled to Paris for one concert.[16] In November of that year, under the auspices of Edward Speyer, they gave five concerts in London's St James's Hall, including the four symphonies and the Violin Concerto. There were some superlative critiques, for here were the symphonies 'rendered with such life and impulse, with such a spirit of romance, that one felt their power in a quite unaccustomed degree; the conductor seemed to be recreating rather than giving a rendering of the music'.[17]

[14] See p. 43 below. This paragraph draws on Maren Goltz and Herta Müller, *Der Brahms Klarinettist Richard Mühlfeld*, Balve: Artivo, 2007, pp. 21–37, 95–7.

[15] See Maren Goltz, *Die Brahms-Programme auf den Konzertreisen der Meininger Hofkapelle (1882–1914)*, Meiningen, 2009 (Goltz 2009). This website tabulation shows that, during Bülow's tenure, the orchestra gave 68 concerts on tour, including 9 conducted by Brahms. During Steinbach's tenure the orchestra gave 184 concerts on tour, all conducted by him, including his single concert in Paris with this orchestra, on 28 March 1902, reported in *The Times* the following day, in which Brahms's Second Symphony was performed (this concert is not included in the quoted tabulation).

[16] See preceding note. The programmes for the six concerts in Holland contained the 2nd Symphony in the first three concerts and the *Haydn* Variations in those following: Goltz 2009. Steinbach had already appeared in Paris and was to do so again; he conducted one concert on 28 March 1901 (Grand concerts symphoniques du Vaudeville), two concerts with the Lamoureux orchestra in January 1908 and, just before his fall from grace, one concert with the Colonne orchestra on 29 March 1914: Joëlle Caullier, 'Les chefs d'orchestre allemands à Paris entre 1894 et 1914', *Revue de Musicologie*, vol. 67, no. 2, (1981) pp. 193–5 and 202.

[17] *Musical Times*, vol. 43 (December 1902), p. 819 (concerts 17–21 November 1902); but see Mary Grierson, *Donald Francis Tovey: A Biography Based on Letters*, Oxford: Oxford University Press, 1952 (repr. Westport, CT: Greenwood Press, 1970) (Grierson), pp. 104–5, for the discord among London critics of which the visiting Meiningen orchestra was an unwitting victim. Walker, p. 332, takes the view, shared by no other writer, that under Steinbach Bülow's 'marvellous machine … began slowly to unwind'. The cited *Musical Times* review stated that Bülow established the orchestra's fame and under Steinbach 'that fame has not in any way diminished'. The orchestra was disbanded in 1914, soon after the resignation on health grounds of one of Steinbach's successors, Max Reger, its conductor from 1911 to 1914, under whom in 1913 the orchestra was still 'remarkable for precision and clarity': W. J. Turner, Music and Life, London: Methuen, 1921, 'Max Reger', p. 82, quoted in Potter, p. 172.

9. STEINBACH IN THE COLOGNE YEARS, C. 1905

Steinbach's tours with the Meiningen Hofkapelle ended in February 1903 and later that year he took over the Cologne Conservatoire and Gürzenich Orchestra in succession to Brahms's friend Franz Wüllner.[18] By then this dominating musician, outwardly prickly but inwardly warm-hearted, was recognised throughout Europe as the foremost exponent of Brahms's orchestral music. Steinbach was not, however, a mere Brahms specialist. Under his baton Bach Passions flourished, his Beethoven Ninth Symphony was a speciality lauded by Boult and Fritz Busch, and his friend Max Reger featured prominently (in world and Cologne premieres), as latterly did Mahler, Korngold and Braunfels.[19]

Steinbach's tenure in Cologne consolidated his position and launched him in conquest of fresh territories as guest conductor – with the London Symphony Orchestra as a regular guest until 1914;[20] in Italy, Russia, France and Spain; throughout German-speaking Europe and in New York.

In only two centres throughout his career did his success seem less than total, for which in each case there were readily explicable reasons. In the Meiningen Hofkapelle's Concertgebouw concerts on 4, 5 and 7 November 1900, when they played the *Haydn Variations* and *Second Symphony*, the small orchestra remained in the shadow of Mengelberg's Concertgebouw players, already trained by him to a degree that matched Steinbach's Meiningen band – and with a far greater orchestral complement. The public was largely indifferent and the critic Hugo Nolthenius[21] remarked that it was nonsensical to make a fair comparison between the two orchestras: 'no-one

---

[18] For the later history of the Meiningen Hofkapelle, see p. 65 below.

[19] For Steinbach's Cologne programmes, see Irmgard Scharberth, *Gürzenich Orchestra Köln 1888–1988*, Cologne: Vienand Verlag, 1988 (Scharberth), pp. 214–227.

[20] For Steinbach's first concert with the LSO on 15 December 1904 (Beethoven's Overture *Leonore No. 2*, Bach's Brandenburg Concerto No. 3, Beethoven's Violin Concerto (Zimmerman) and Brahms's Fourth Symphony) see Percy A. Scholes, *The Mirror of Music 1844–1944*, London: Novello/Oxford University Press, 1947, p. 393, and Kennedy, p. 226. For some of his later concerts, see the following issues of the *Musical Times*: vol. 53 (April 1912), p. 258 (concert of 18 March 1912 including Beethoven's *Overture Leonore No. 3*, Brahms's Fourth Symphony and Adolf Busch's London concerto debut in the Brahms Violin Concerto – see also pp. 44 and 48 below); vol. 53 (December 1912), p. 805 (two concerts, the first on 28 October 1912 including Schubert's Symphony No. 8, Adolf Busch in the Beethoven Violin Concerto – this notice referred in error to the Brahms concerto – and Brahms's First Symphony, as to which see further p. 48; the second concert on 11 November 1912 including Mozart's Symphony No. 40); vol. 55 (January 1914), p. 45 (23 November 1913 including Brahms's Fourth Symphony and Mozart's Symphony No. 39; and 24 November 1913 including the *Eroica* Symphony and other works); vol. 55 (March 1914), p. 188 (9 February 1914 including Beethoven's Symphonies Nos. 2 and 6 and the Brahms Violin Concerto with Bronisław Huberman). Extracts from the *Times* reviews of some, but not all, of these concerts are set out at pp. 43–7. For further reference to the impact of Steinbach's Brahms on London audiences, see Maurice Pearton, *The LSO at Seventy*, London: Gollancz, 1974 (Pearton) p. 32.

[21] (1848–1929), a noted Wagnerian.

could have possibly done such a thing'.[22] Again, in New York for two concerts with the Philharmonic on 23 and 24 March 1906, *Musical America* opined that Steinbach was 'not of the stature of Weingartner or Safonov' and his Brahms Second Symphony, aside from the finale, 'too slow'. Slower, that is, than, among others, Weingartner's two performances with the New York Symphony Orchestra earlier in the season – but the latter's unusually swift rendition (at least on some occasions[23]) was later to be criticised on that account by the Steinbach devotee Adrian Boult.[24] Walter Damrosch's traversal in the 1902–3 Symphony season may also have been in mind.[25] In any event, as noted below, *Musical America*'s view of Steinbach's work was vigorously refuted elsewhere.[26]

The German Brahms Festival organised by Steinbach at the Königliche Odeon, Munich, during 10–14 September 1909 was one of the peaks of his career.[27] For the festival he brought together the wind and brass of his former orchestra, the Meiningen Hofkapelle, at that time headed by composer-conductor Wilhelm Berger, with the Munich Tonkünstlerorchester (formerly the Kaim orchestra). One of Steinbach's favourite composition pupils in Cologne, Adolf Busch, played in the first violins[28] and he also imported his 260-strong Gürzenich chorus for the choral works. There were some distinguished soloists for lied recitals and a selection, too, of Brahms's chamber works. The anticipation was immense and to the overflowing audiences were added an assortment of princes, grand and other dukes, critics from all over Austro-Germany and many famous musical guests, among them Vassily Safonov, Reynaldo Hahn and another maestro of already burgeoning fame, Arturo Toscanini, who was accompanied by his friend the composer Leone Sinigaglia.

Of the three gigantic concerts that Steinbach conducted, the first began with the *German Requiem*, followed by the First Symphony, both acclaimed ecstatically by the audiences, particularly after the First Symphony's finale, 'played with unusual fire and spirit'. The second included the *Haydn* Variations, *Schicksalslied*, the Third Symphony and the Alto Rhapsody, concluding with the Second Symphony. The *vivace* fifth *Haydn* Variation was taken so swiftly and with such virtuoso address that, as

---

[22] Zwart, p. 94; translations from the Dutch here and on p. 116 courtesy of Pieter van der Grinten.

[23] But see p. 86.

[24] Kennedy, p. 87; see p. 93 below.

[25] See James Gibbon Huneker, *The Philharmonic Society of New York and its Seventy-fifth Anniversary: A Retrospect* New York, 1917; repr. Boston: Da Capo, 1979, pp. 63–4. See further p. 81.

[26] See p. 42.

[27] See Scharberth, p. 54. According to Müller, p. 115, about half of Steinbach's former Meiningen orchestra served in the festival orchestra, amounting therefore to some twenty to twenty-five players out of the Meiningen complement of forty-eight.

[28] Potter, p. 105. Another distinguished composition pupil was Erwin Schulhoff (1894–1942).

Toscanini recollected late in life, it evoked calls for a *bis*, granted forthwith.[29] The festival ended with Steinbach's third concert, opening with the *Triumphlied*, continuing with the *Gesang der Parzen* and the Violin Concerto (with Adolf Busch's teacher, Bram Eldering, as soloist[30]) and concluding with the Fourth Symphony, after which there was 'frantic enthusiasm' – flowers, wreaths and even laurel trees.[31] Summing up for the benefit of French readers shortly after the festival concluded, *Le Mercure Musical*'s correspondent William Ritter[32] maintained that

> anyone who has not encountered [Steinbach]'s rendition of the four symphonies – coming at one like a blow straight to the chest (*en pleine poitrine*) – does not know them. We have been satiated with the Brahms symphonies in Vienna, Paris, Prague, in Munich with Richter, and with Weingartner, Lœwe, Lamoureux, Chevillard, Hausegger, Schnéevoigt, Nedbal and Zemánek, but we had never thought to hear a transfiguration comparable to the First and Fourth under Steinbach's direction [which] became hymns of energy and power …

On these travels from his Cologne base Steinbach never carried his Gürzenich orchestra's parts for the Brahms symphonies since, as he later remarked to Adolf Busch, 'we [*sic* – presumably his librarian and himself] have not written anything special in them'.[33] Such insouciance was a measure of his technique, which astonished Tovey at Meiningen in October 1900: 'the most amazing conductor I ever dreamt of. Flies into three pieces with a strong electric spark at the *fortissimos*, but never loses clearness or lets the orchestra mistake his meaning.'[34]

Steinbach's last years must be detailed for reasons which will be apparent from the claims made about him by certain followers.[35] His position in Cologne was unchallenged until in mid-1914 scandal enveloped him. A female Conservatory pupil

---

[29] See p. 98.

[30] Bram Eldering (1865–1943), student of Jenő Hubay in Brussels and Joachim in Berlin, was Konzertmeister of the Berlin Philharmonic before he was engaged by Steinbach in 1894 as Konzertmeister for the Meiningen Hofkapelle, a position he left in 1899 to teach in Amsterdam. However, in 1903 he followed Steinbach to Cologne, where he taught violin at the Conservatoire.

[31] Details and quotes from the special report by Paula Gericke for the *New York Tribune*, dated 3 October 1909; see further p. 45 below.

[32] (1867–1955), French writer, painter, art and music critic, and a friend of Mahler. He was at the time based in Munich but, after a peripatetic life, eventually settled in Switzerland.

[33] Irene Busch-Serkin (compiled and transl. Russell Stockman), *Adolph Busch: Letters–Pictures–Memories*, 2 vols, Walpole, NH: Arts and Letters, 1991 (Busch-Serkin), vol. 1, p. 86.

[34] Grierson, p. 84. Donald Francis Tovey (1875–1940), the foremost British musical analyst of his day, also composer, conductor and pianist, was on this occasion at a festival for the unveiling of a Brahms memorial, a photograph and further details of which are in Müller, p. 107. Tovey later became a close friend of the Busch family, especially Adolf; see also Fig. 5 and n. 47.

[35] See p. 151.

accused him of improper behaviour; the whole incident, if it ever happened, was, for Steinbach, a misunderstanding. Nevertheless, he felt obliged to resign all his Cologne posts and fled initially to Vienna, where for a time he and his wife occupied Adolf Busch's then vacant apartment.[36] With the onset of war, he moved over the border to Munich but recurrence of a serious heart ailment prevented him from re-establishing himself. According to his copious correspondence with Adolf, he had a mere couple of unpaid charity events in Munich, including Brahms's First Symphony in October 1914 and another in November; but he complained of poor orchestral standards and soon gave up conducting there. A few engagements followed in other centres, including Frankfurt and Karlsruhe, with the odd triumph in Berlin. Pathetically, he complained to Adolf of penury and poor health; from early December 1915 until his death in August the following year he was too ill for any musical activity. As Adolf summed up these years in a letter to his brother Fritz, Steinbach was, 'thanks to the Cologne business, *condemned* to inactivity. One can think of his death as a salvation for him, but his fate was not a nice one'; 'I had to be consoling and to pretend that a better time would come', but, after Cologne, Steinbach's career was finished.[37]

Steinbach's stylistic approach – to Brahms and others

Contemporary eyewitness comment by fellow musicians makes clear beyond doubt that, in his approach to the pre-Brahms repertoire, Steinbach adhered to Classical ideals in the line of Hans Richter, if with greater animation and imagination. There was none of the far-flung abandon of a Nikisch and, indeed, the Viennese-born composer Hans Gál remarked that, while Steinbach 'was an excellent conductor in the Classical line', he was 'a little stiff compared with Nikisch, who was a little too loose and relaxed. They were absolute opposites.' Gal's impression is corroborated by virtually all musicians. So, for example, the American-born violinist and composer and sometime partner of Elly Ney, Florizel von Reuter, considered that even Steinbach's Brahms conceptions 'stressed the rugged side of the … symphonies', although 'he never disregarded the lyrical element completely'.[38] Again, although strongly distancing himself from negative comments about Steinbach, his most distinguished conducting pupil, Fritz Busch, quoted others who condemned his performances as militaristic and

---

[36] Busch-Serkin, vol. 1, p. 97. As to Steinbach's fall, see also Potter, p. 181.

[37] For references to Steinbach's post-Cologne concerts, his illness and death, see Busch-Serkin, vol. 1, pp. 107, 115, 128, 139, 142, 145, 150, 156 and 171.

[38] For the Gál quotation, see Potter, p. 67 (his interview with the composer in 1979). For the Reuter quotation, see Florizel von Reuter, *Great People I Have Known*, Waukesha, WI: Freeman, 1961, pp. 79–80, quoted in Potter, p. 1118.

10. STEINBACH CONDUCTS

unvaried – once more, even if decried, an emphasis on a non-Romantic approach.[39]
Fritz also admired Steinbach as 'an outstanding conductor of Beethoven, and I have
never heard, for example, the *Adagio* of the Ninth Symphony played with such obviously right tempo, so warmly and tunefully, with such correct phrasing – in a word, in
such a convincing matter – as by him'. One may infer from this assessment that Busch
was influenced by Steinbach in his own performances of the Ninth's *Adagio*, its warm,
mobile and unmannered character fortunately preserved on record.[40]

Finally, among the continental commentators, the great violin teacher Carl Flesch
painted, as was usual for him concerning conductors, an unsympathetic portrait in his
1936 Memoirs:

> At the beginning of the [twentieth] century, Fritz Steinbach was thought to be the
> only great German conductor; for Nikisch, Mottl, Weingartner, Muck, Richter and
> Mahler all hailed from various parts of the Austro-Hungarian empire. As a conduc-
> tor, Steinbach was a contradictory personality. Heavy-handed in his beat, one-sided
> in the choice of his repertoire, he yet was an important figure because, through his
> enthusiasm, he succeeded in bringing the works of Brahms to the masses; in the
> best sense of the word, he popularized what had at first seemed such dry, intractable
> music. He was also the first who, by way of refined dynamics and agogics, achieved
> 'effective' interpretations of the works of Bach and Handel. Irascible and rude, he
> could be called a German edition of Lamoureux whom, however, he far surpassed as
> a musician and conductor.[41]

Boult would probably have rejected some – perhaps all – of the assertions in Flesch's
portrait, relating, for example, to an alleged heavy-handedness; and, as already noted,
Steinbach's repertoire was in fact broad and varied. Moreover, Flesch's description
of alleged shortcomings in Steinbach's technique hardly tallies with Tovey's amaze-
ment at his prowess with the stick. As Boult described Steinbach to me, although his
conducting method was rather more demonstrative than the relative minimalism of
Richter and Weingartner, his interpretative approach was in the tradition of the former: 'I heard performances of the Brandenburg Concertos and the Ninth Symphony

---

[39] The words that Fritz used were '*militärisch*' and '*undifferenziert*'; see Fritz Busch *Aus dem
Leben eines Musikers*, Zürich: Rascher & Cie, 1949, translated by Marjorie Strachey as *Pages
from a Musician's Life*, London: Hogarth 1953 (Fritz Busch), p. 48 (English translation not followed here). His reference to Steinbach's Beethoven's Ninth is on p. 57.
[40] Guild GHCD 2343, a 1950 concert performance.
[41] Hans Keller (ed. and transl., in collaboration with C. F. Flesch), *The Memoirs of Carl Flesch*,
London: Rockliff, 1957; centenary ed. Harlow: Bois de Boulogne, 1973 (Flesch), p. 209. Flesch
describes Charles Lamoureux (1834–99) as an energetic, hot-tempered time-beater, albeit a fine
orchestral trainer: *ibid.* pp. 72–4.

of Beethoven which were absolute models for me.'[42] Only in Brahms did he 'let himself go a little more'; so Boult's own score of the Fourth's passacaglia, annotated on a hearing of Steinbach, contained 'up to ten different tempo markings' in the course of it. Steinbach 'wasn't always doing that, but he certainly did in that movement express himself very freely'.[43] Nevertheless, Boult was adamant that Steinbach's style differed sharply from those of Nikisch and Furtwängler, whom he bracketed together as forming a distinct contrast with Steinbach. This view, expressed in his old age, was consistent with his remarks made, first, in his diary entry on 9 May 1908 about the remarkable performance he had just heard of Brahms's First Symphony under Nikisch, the extravagance of which nonetheless made him wish for 'a dose of Steinbach to make me see straight';[44] and, secondly, his assessment in 1922 of Furtwängler's Beethoven Ninth Symphony in Leipzig, when 'sometimes one felt it was in danger of falling to pieces, but one must not compare it with the monumental performances of Richter and Steinbach'.[45]

It is hardly necessary to stress once more that, as in the case of Hans Richter,[46] Boult and the preceding witnesses speak and describe in terms understandable to the contemporary reader, with a vocabulary that means what it says. No allowance need be made, as may sometimes be required, for changes in critical language or musical terminology since the late nineteenth/early twentieth century.[47] That conclusion is also crucial in assessing the real meaning of the descriptions by professional critics which follow: to all intents and purposes they can still be relied on to convey to us today the meaning intended for their contemporaries.

Turning to these critical assessments of Steinbach's approach to Brahms, the most detailed and vivid characterisation in general terms is to be found in Berrsche's review of the 1909 Brahms Festival in Munich:

> There is a shaping of the large line without any neglect of the smallest detail, there is a loving cultivation of details, without for a moment losing sight of the relationship with the whole. Thus we can once again see what phrasing means, where and how slurs and caesuras are placed, how the differing groups of instruments play out and balance against each other, how great climaxes are planned and how, through dynamic and agogic refinements, a melody attains declamatory power. Through

---

[42] According to a note in the *Musical Times* for 1 July 1904, p. 462, Steinbach's Cologne strings for the Third Brandenburg Concerto totalled ninety players: thirty-six violins, twenty-four violas, eighteen cellos and twelve basses.

[43] Dyment interview, pp. 40–1.

[44] Kennedy, p. 34; Boult had also heard Nikisch's LSO performance in 1906, 'which I disliked'; see further p. 60.

[45] Kennedy, p. 86.

[46] See p. 10.

[47] See further, p. 155.

the whole execution flows the pulse of a strict, intensely musical rhythm, which is the unmistakeable distinguishing mark of a true and complete master musician ... Steinbach ... achieved directly through his iron rhythm a thrilling and irresistibly overwhelming effect.[48]

Again, in his obituary of Steinbach, Berrsche wrote of the 'great expressive power of the cantilena, the dynamic shading, the absolutely plastic phrasing and the rarely used but so natural rubato'.[49] For Berrsche, when Steinbach died, Brahms 'died a second time. A true and correct tradition has perished, even before it could put down roots, along with its culture of music-making with the orchestra without which the meaning of this tradition cannot be expressed.'[50] He was *the* Brahms conductor with whom all successors stood to be compared and were almost always found – by Berrsche – to be wanting.

Many of the qualities noted by Berrsche were recognised, too, in reviews of individual concerts, both in New York and London. The foremost New York critic, Richard Aldrich,[51] left a detailed and magisterial description of Steinbach's March 1906 concerts with the Philharmonic so indifferently reviewed by *Musical America*, which must be quoted at length:

Mr Steinbach is a conductor of authority and of much force and energy. His motions and signs are extremely abundant, to the point of restlessness; but it is clear that they are for the orchestra, not the audience ... He obtained from the Philharmonic players a higher degree of finish than they have sometimes put into their work, and there was a certainty and precision in the way he produced his effects that disclosed in him, not only a master of detail, but a man who can impress upon those under him the logic and the feeling of the larger proportions of a work of art. His performance of Brahms's symphony [No. 2] was in many respects a singularly fine one. It was the product of a perfectly clear and well-ordered conception, in which every detail was adjusted with a view to its place in the whole. It was a reading that emphasized the lyric quality, especially of the first movement. Mr Steinbach took this at a tempo slower than that to which we are accustomed.[52] The allegretto grazioso was also taken at a measured tempo. He conceives the work with warmth and poetical feel-

---

[48] Alexander Berrsche, *Trösterin Musika*, 2nd ed. Munich: Hermann Rinn, 1949 (Berrsche), pp. 276–7.
[49] *Ibid.* pp. 590–1; see further p. 157.
[50] Berrsche, pp. 590–1.
[51] Aldrich (1863–1937) was, music critic of the *New York Times* 1902–23.
[52] Aldrich prefaced his review by pointing out that the Second Symphony had already been heard 'four or five' times in New York that season, including the two by Weingartner noted above: see p. 36.

ing, undoubtedly. He brought out the melodic line with a true appreciation of where and what it was, and what it meant. His modelling of the phrase was plastic, and he did not hesitate to accentuate it with incessant modifications of tempo and skilful nuance of all sorts. Withal there was life and spirit in it.[53]

The two reviews here quoted, Berrsche and Aldrich, coincide to a remarkable degree in pinpointing the distinctive elements of Steinbach's style: the clarification of the melodic line, with constant nuances and other expressive devices illuminating that line without harm to the clearly grasped larger design. To a substantial degree it is possible to gauge what Aldrich had in mind when he specifies, with approbation, 'incessant modifications of tempo and skilful nuance of all sorts' as elements of Steinbach's style. As will be seen, the same critic judged harshly Max Fiedler's major deviations of tempo in Brahms which had disruptive results – and, fortunately, Fiedler left recordings of the Second and Fourth Symphonies which allow us, in turn, to assess Aldrich's meaning as to what he found acceptable and what he thought unduly disruptive to the structure of Brahms's symphonies.[54]

The London reviews corroborate Berrsche and Aldrich; thereby, they assist in building a clear portrait of the conductor, commencing with his presentation of all four Brahms symphonies with the Meiningen Hofkapelle in October 1902, which remained in the memory of London audiences for many years. The day after their first concert on 17 November the *Times* remarked of the First Symphony that:

Even those who knew it best must have been unprepared for all the surprises that awaited them, many of which were the result of a slightly different balance between wind and strings from that to which we are accustomed [that is, from Richter]. The delicate gradations of pace and the play of light and shade lent to every movement a new beauty and meaning … the style of Herr Mühlfeld was unmistakably felt. The band has been called 'an orchestra of Mühlfelds', and there is a good deal of truth in the criticism that points to him as a leading influence in the whole.

Again, the day after Steinbach's first concert with the newly formed London Symphony Orchestra on 16 December 1904, the *Times* reported that he conducted the Fourth Symphony 'with an infinite variety of slight changes of tempo', as well as 'a curious and unexpected balance of the parts in the finale'. Boult, too, was present and wrote in his diary, 'The performance of the Brahms was magnificent. One always heard the woodwind'[55] – an indication that Steinbach had already imprinted the 'Mühlfeld effect' on the LSO's Brahms. Of Steinbach's next concert with the LSO, on 14 December 1905,

[53] *New York Times*, 24 March 1906.
[54] See p. 75.
[55] Kennedy, p. 25.

the *Times* reported on the following day that Brahms's Second Symphony 'was played in a manner which has scarcely been equalled since the famous visit of the Meiningen players some years ago. Every point was brought out, yet each movement took its place in the general design, while that was seen to be a creation of exquisite beauty.'

When Steinbach returned after some years' absence for an LSO concert on 28 January 1913, the following day's *Times* emphasised another aspect of his style in a programme containing Bach's Third Brandenburg Concerto, Beethoven's Eighth and Brahms's Second Symphonies, rounded off by the latter's *Haydn* Variations. Remarking that the Brandenburg's strings were rather unsteady at times, the critic continued:

> Any unsteadiness of this sort is particularly noticeable with Herr Steinbach's insistence on a pulsating fundamental rhythm. This rigidity of his beat was rather merciless in the Scherzo and Trio of the Beethoven symphony and in the first of the two movements of the concerto by Bach, but it enabled the conductor to obtain some wonderful effects in the long crescendos leading up to climaxes that occur in the symphonies, and the last of the variations by Brahms was very impressive with its fullness and sense of reserved force, while every detail both here and in places like the Allegrettos of the two symphonies was beautifully clear and articulated.

The qualities of iron rhythm and building of climaxes here noted had their counterpart in Berrsche's summing up. Two months later, on 18 March 1912, a concert which also marked Steinbach's composition pupil Adolf Busch's concerto debut in London, *Musical Opinion* was eloquent on the stature that the conductor had attained in the musical life of the capital: of the Brahms Fourth Symphony, it was

> safe to say that no finer interpretation of this ... work has been given in London ... the playing was not merely highly finished but ... charged with meaning. Even the last movement claimed authenticity by the virtuosity of the performance. Steinbach has now unquestionably established a high reputation in this country.[56]

Taken together, all the evidence strongly suggests that Steinbach's general approach to Brahms with the Meiningen players and in his early concerts with the LSO might be characterised as a species of animated Classicism. The long line was always preserved but within its span Steinbach accommodated a wide variety of small and frequent deviations of tempo and nuance. There is nothing in any Anglophone critical review at that time – that is, for a decade commencing in 1902 – to suggest either major or abrupt changes of tempo, or emphases that broke the line, whether by *Luftpausen* or over-emphatic, over-distended, phrasing. Indeed, it is evident from the above-quoted

---

[56] *Musical Opinion*, April 1912, p. 258.

reactions of his fellow musicians and of some critics, too, that some at least of Steinbach's finer points of phrasing and nuance were so slight as not to register at all as positive deviations from the straight and narrow. As late as 1913 the *Manchester Guardian's* London critic, Ferruccio Bonavia, in commenting on the Fourth Symphony given by the LSO under Steinbach on 24 November, remarked that, unlike other conductors, Steinbach did not hurry the music's inherent 'little refinements [and] clever devices' and thereby he alone showed both 'the loveliness as well as the majesty of the design'.[57] In other words, Steinbach's chosen tempos allowed him to expose and characterise everything in the music without resort to obvious manipulations. His approach in that first decade of the twentieth century, as described with such clarity on both sides of the Atlantic, was without doubt what Brahms himself heard at Meiningen and whole-heartedly approved: unlike Bülow's self-conscious manipulations, the constant 'slight changes of tempo' (to use the *Times* description) fulfilled Brahms's desired 'pushing forward and holding back' without drawing attention to themselves. If Steinbach could be characterised as 'Bülow-lite', it is clear that, drawing his inspiration from watching Brahms himself and possessing a technique far more accomplished than the composer, he was also supremely 'Brahms-heavy'.

A changing style?

There is some evidence that during the last few years of Steinbach's career his treatment of Brahms to a certain degree became less subtle. Paula Gericke's description of the overwhelming reception accorded Steinbach at the Munich Brahms Festival has already been quoted.[58] Her own assessment of Steinbach's approach was more critical. Of the Second Symphony, she maintained that 'more grace would have been acceptable [in the first movement] and a lesser orgy of power in the finale'. And of the whole series, she observed that the conductor

> threw himself body and soul into his task, sometimes with happiest results, at others showing a tendency to exaggeration … In his eagerness to bring out every detail and every beauty, he not only … let Brahms speak, he also let him scream. He loves to emphasise every accent, to put it on always still more strongly, if possible … Still, there was a great deal to be honestly admired, and not the least his untiring energy and his unflagging zeal to the very end of these enormous programmes.[59]

But she also found the hall too small for orchestra, chorus and 'such a high spirited conductor': sometimes, during the *Triumphlied* and parts of the Fourth Symphony,

[57] *Manchester Guardian*, 25 November 1913.
[58] See p. 36 above.
[59] Special report by Paula Gericke for the *New York Tribune*, 3 October 1909.

'the very walls seemed to shake with the masses of sound'. None of these entertaining observations, however, can be taken at their full face value, for the writer was the wife of Wilhelm Gericke, erstwhile conductor of the Boston Symphony Orchestra, famous, or rather notorious, for his polished, prim and wholly undernourished performances of the repertoire, including Brahms;[60] one hears too obviously the dissentient voice of her pianissimist husband whispering in her ear. Her observations do, however, serve to bring alive Steinbach at his peak, when, for the vast majority of those who witnessed him – including, it may be noted, Adolf Busch and Toscanini – the expressive range he brought to bear on Brahms never harmed the larger design.[61]

More reliably, the *Times* reviews of Steinbach's Brahms performances in the years 1913–14 began to sound some doubts; these were among those occasions on which Steinbach returned as guest conductor of the LSO after some years of absence. On 25 November 1913 the critic observed of the previous evening's Fourth Symphony with the LSO,

> It may be felt now that the music is so familiar that some of the points in the first move-
> ment do not require quite the emphasis which Herr Steinbach lays upon them, but
> nevertheless such complete clearness of effect as he produces is something for which
> we must always be grateful, and the slow movement in his hands is unsurpassable.

If that suggested only that the very familiarity of the music made for a different critical reception, the *Times* report on Steinbach's previous concert on 27 October 1913, when he conducted the Third Symphony, is more explicit:

> Herr Steinbach conducted with that wonderful grip and energy which has made his
> performances famous and especially has made people realise the melodic and rhyth-
> mic power of Brahms. The first movement … was played with an exuberance which

---

[60] Wilhelm Gericke (1845–1925), Hans Richter's assistant in Vienna and conductor of the Boston Symphony Orchestra, 1884–88 and 1898–1905. Although Aldrich spoke highly of his Brahms Third Symphony in a Boston SO concert in New York on 8 December 1904 (see Richard Aldrich, *Concert Life in New York 1902–1923*, New York: Putnam, 1941 (Aldrich), pp. 84–5), the *Musical Courier* was full of complaints. Of one Boston SO concert in New York, on 26 February 1902, their reviewer wrote 'we know in advance just how piano will sound the fortissimos and how pianissimo the pianos … we had a very careful reading of [Tchaikovsky's Sixth Symphony] in which the strings sang beautifully. For the rest it might have been composed by Mendelssohn.' Of Gericke's account of Brahms's Fourth Symphony in New York, 26 March 1902, the comment was: 'though he played every blessed little note of the work, not at any time did he succeed in making the work cohere intelligibly. The phrases were neatly trimmed as though with manicure scissors and it was polished until it glistened … but in the process the spirit of Brahms evapo-rated.' For more about Gericke and his wife, see Bruno Walter, *Theme and Variations*, London: Hamish Hamilton, 1947 (Walter memoirs), p. 263.

[61] See p. 132.

was calculated to show the futility of [the] complaint that Brahms could not exult. The two middle movements were a little less satisfying. Herr Steinbach's treatment seems to have grown a little heavy-handed … It appeared in a tendency to lay on the sentiment thickly and to emphasise points which one would rather have suggested. But the finale of [the] symphony, especially the wonderful coda, was a splendid piece of rhythmic control and balance of tone: especially the resonance without hardness of the wind parts made the whole scene glow with living colour.

Much remained as it ever was with this supreme Brahms interpreter – but not quite all. Perhaps critical taste was undergoing a change after so many performances of these works, but so, in certain respects, was Steinbach's style. That, at least, remained the opinion of the *Times* critic some fifteen years later on 16 February 1929, looking back at evolving interpretations of the canon after experiencing a performance of the First Symphony with the LSO under Hermann Abendroth on 11 February that year. When the Meiningen players in 1902, 'trained to phrase like an enlarged combination of chamber music players', showed how clearly Brahms's orchestration could sound, 'Herr Steinbach was hailed as the great exponent of Brahms, which he undoubtedly was at that time about twenty-five years ago'. But later, when he returned as guest conductor of the LSO, he

> began the process of insisting on this, that and the other, some of which seemed demanded by circumstances and the rest by the desire to intensify a reputation already complete. Those who say, and some do, that Herr Abendroth follows the example of Herr Steinbach, speak truly, but it is the example of the later Steinbach, not that of the Meiningen model.

This less subtle approach was explicable, remarked this critic, because a conductor leading a large, Strauss-sized orchestra without doubled wind could achieve his expressive purposes only by 'broadening every tune and bloating every climax'. The column ended with a detailed dissection of one example of Abendroth's striving for alien effects in his treatment of the pizzicato passages in the introduction to the finale of the First Symphony; this feature is examined in context below.[62]

Whether there were, indeed, any resemblances between the Brahms performances of Steinbach and Abendroth is a subject considered hereafter.[63] In the present context it is necessary only to stress that the *Times* critic was making no such direct comparison: his concern was the coarsening effect on both conductors arising from the system of guest conducting and, with London rehearsal times in short supply, the consequent need for quickly impressing individual interpretations on large, perhaps unreceptive, orchestras.

---

[62] See pp. 132 and 191.
[63] *Ibid.*

In the case of Steinbach, earlier *Times* reviews suggest that this coarsening effect touched only the inner two movements of the Third Symphony and the opening movement of the Fourth. In the case of Abendroth, the *Times* critic in 1929 thought that the coarsening resulted in a blatant misreading of the score, a charge rarely laid against Steinbach.[64]

Irrespective of possible changes in Steinbach's interpretative approach, it was, of course, the more subtle Steinbach of the Meiningen years who had Brahms's absolute confidence, while it was the later Steinbach, changed stylistically or no, who inspired the recording conductors identified at the outset of this study: Toscanini, Fritz Busch and Adrian Boult. It is also clear that, more flexible though Steinbach's approach was in Brahms compared with the rest of his repertoire, even that flexibility operated within circumscribed limits. Precisely what those limits were, or may have been, is examined in the course of this study. But whatever answer may be given to that issue, it is again beyond doubt that, according to the unanimous view of his eye- (and ear)witnesses at the time, Steinbach's approach to Brahms differed fundamentally from that of Nikisch and fellow Romantics of his generation. As the *Times* summed him up the day after a 'magnificent' performance of the Fourth Symphony with the LSO in 1912 (the one also reviewed by *Musical Opinion*), 'it is this long-sightedness which make Herr Steinbach's playing of Beethoven and of Brahms a unique thing'.[65] Steinbach's performing style, consistent with his standing in the Brahms circle, eschewed the extravagances of those who followed in the footsteps of Wagner's conducting practice: until the twentieth century – and notwithstanding the dutiful Wagner performances of Dessoff and Wüllner – adherents of Wagner and Brahms too often occupied separate camps, whether as performers, composers or critics. How the twentieth century dealt with this disjuncture will become evident in the course of this chapter, as will the legacy of Steinbach's Brahms performances.

Felix Mottl: Wagnerian immersion and disastrous Brahms

Mottl's career

The profound disjuncture between the Brahms and Wagner traditions of performance is nowhere better exemplified than in the career and musical affinities of Felix Mottl (1856–1911), but for that very reason the testimony of this complete Wagnerite is of great value for the light it throws on the later history of Brahms performing style.[66]

---

[64] But see p. 201 for a posthumous criticism of Steinbach's performance of the finale of the First Symphony.

[65] See further Potter, p. 140.

[66] See also, as to Hermann Levi, p. 12. Another case in point is that of Anton Seidl (1850–98), for whom see p. 53.

11. FELIX MOTTL IN 1895

From his earliest musical days immersed in Wagner, Mottl felt little in common with his conducting and orchestration teacher at the Vienna Conservatoire, Otto Dessoff. In his diary for February 1873 Mottl remarked that Dessoff 'was a strong supporter of Brahms but did not get on particularly well with Wagner and Liszt'.[67] Although Dessoff did indeed do his best for those composers in his programmes as conductor of the Vienna Philharmonic, his reputation as a devoted Brahmsian evoked no sympathy from Mottl, who had no understanding of Brahms, then or later.[68] Nor could he warm to Dessoff's mere formal proficiency, which lacked a 'spirit of love'. When Mottl was summoned by Wagner to Bayreuth, where as a member of the 'Nibelungen-Kanzlei' he acted as stage conductor for the first *Ring* cycles in 1876, his Wagnerian immersion and hero worship were total; so much so that, after his appointment as Hofkapellmeister in Karlsruhe in 1881, some regarded the centre of Wagner performances par excellence as shifting with him, after Wagner's death, to this '*kleine* Bayreuth'.[69] Appointed in 1903

[67] Willy Krienitz, 'Felix Mottls Tagebuchaufzeichnungen aus den Jahren 1873–1876', *Neue Wagner-Forschungen*, Karlsruhe: G. Braun, 1943, p. 175.
[68] See Frithjof Haas, *Der Magier am Dirigentenpult. Felix Mottl*, Karlsruhe: Hoepfner-Bibliotek, 2006 (Haas/Mottl), pp. 14–15; and Mittag, pp. 23–7. The *New Grove Dictionary of Music and Musicians*, 2nd ed., vol. 17, pp. 232–3, gives Joseph Hellmesberger (Sr) as Mottl's conducting teacher. Haas gives Dessoff as his conducting teacher, but Mottl, played as timpanist in the Vienna Conservatoire orchestra, whose conductor was Hellmesberger; Mottl disliked him just as much as he did Dessoff: see Haas/Mottl, p. 15.
[69] Haas/Mottl, p. 41.

as Hofkapellmeister in Munich and from 1904 Director of its Akademie der Tonkunst, Mottl later assumed the directorship of music for the whole of Bavaria. Only his failure in 1907 to secure release prevented his succeeding Mahler in Vienna. He continued in Munich until he collapsed while conducting *Tristan und Isolde* in 1911, dying a few weeks later.

Repertoire and style

Mottl's tastes were wide: his Mozart operas were thought outstanding (Berrsche considered Beecham perhaps his nearest stylistic analogue[70]) and he championed French music, particularly Berlioz, copiously. But Wagner occupied centre stage throughout Mottl's career and in his stylistic approach to the orchestral repertoire he adopted fully all that he had learned from the master – who by some accounts was in practice even more extravagant in his freedom of tempo than his revolutionary advice to conductors suggested.[71] Mottl's practice in this respect was reinforced by his Bayreuth experiences when, from 1886 onwards, he submitted to Cosima Wagner's demands for changing and expanding hitherto hallowed tempos – with results in the 1888 presentation of *Parsifal* that caused Weingartner (who elsewhere claimed friendship with Mottl) to impale it in 1897 as

> one of the greatest artistic crimes, the greatest of all perhaps, that Bayreuth has ever perpetrated ... The new gospel of the slow time was also preached in the concert hall and soon every fresh and energetic tempo seemed to have disappeared ... [and] as one witty Berlin musician is said to have expressed it, 'he Mottlizes' (*er vermottelt*) (since it was Mottl by his conducting who had 'saved' Parsifal, which made him the darling of the house of Wahnfried and beyond criticism). Furthermore, Bülow, now no longer young, had already begun to incite others to exaggerations by arbitrariness in his conception and rendering of individual pieces of music. Soon this dragging of the tempo à la Bayreuth and these distortions à la Bülow, knowing the affinity of their natures, entered into the bonds of matrimony, and brought forth a strange child that was nothing else than the tempo rubato conducting which I have once before attacked.[72]

---

[70] Berrsche, p. 626.
[71] See Clive Brown 'Performing Practice', in Barry Millington and Stewart Spencer (eds), *Wagner in Performance*, London: Yale University Press, 1992, pp. 117–18; however, the citations date from Wagner's London visit in 1855 when the critics were, notoriously, either ignorant of Wagner's works or unsympathetic to his aims in performance.
[72] Felix Weingartner, *Bayreuth (1876–1896)*, Berlin: Fischer Verlag, 1897, pp. 19–20, transl. Lily Antrobus, London: Weekes, 1898, p. 13, reprinted in Dyment 1976, pp. 97–110, this passage at p. 101. The lines in parentheses were added by Weingartner for the second, German edition (Leipzig: Breitkopf & Hartel, 1904), p. 31. On Mottl's death, Weingartner wrote a full and

Weingartner was not alone. On the occasion of Mottl's London concert debut in April 1894, the critics (Bernard Shaw especially) welcomed his freedom of tempo in some powerful and convincing Wagner, but soon they were at play in objecting to his extravagant point-making and tempo distensions in a stream of masterpieces. So, opined the *Musical Times* as early as May 1894, in the first movement of Beethoven's Fifth 'the conductor's desire to "make points" rather detracted from the impulse'; in the *Pastoral*, every detail was brought out but the spirit missed; in Tchaikovsky's *Pathétique*, his 'inclination to exaggerate accentuation led people to expect something new ... he certainly satisfied [this] anticipation ... but it is doubtful if the unusual interpretation gave satisfaction'; Schubert's *Unfinished* symphony suffered from 'too much zeal' – it was 'articulated and polished to such a degree that its atmosphere of mystery, tragedy and romance evaporated'. All these symphonies, it seems, were subjected to this unwonted strain of novelty. Although Mottl's *Eroica* 'brought out with a sureness of touch, an alertness, an infinitude of resource' its 'constantly changing emotional phases', the *Musical Times* complained of Beethoven's Ninth Symphony in 1897 that 'such a slow, lumbering *Adagio* we have never heard. The heavenly melodies appeared dragged out of all proportion.' In the following year even Wagner's then popular *Kaisermarsch* suffered 'once more' from his 'tempo rubato reading' – yet another *Musical Times* complaint, which in the very same notice turned with relief to the London debut of Felix Weingartner, who, by contrast, was 'no tempo rubato faddist' but sane and direct, as well as undoubtedly great.

Mottl's final London notices were for his Covent Garden Wagner in 1900. They showed no improvement on what had gone before: now, even his great speciality met with disapproval. Of a *Ring* performance, of which *Götterdämmerung* was witnessed by Toscanini on his first visit to London,[73] the *Times* remarked that, famed as he was in Germany for his funereal pace, Mottl 'keeps his slowest rate of progress' for the well-known concert extracts, 'allowing the band to get on at quite the ordinary measure in the intervals', thereby robbing even the *Trauermusik* 'of all impressiveness'.

---

friendly obituary for the Paris journal *Monde musicale*, Summer 1911, in which he recalled their first meeting in Liszt's circle in 1882 and passed over their musical differences in a single short sentence; the obituary was included in Weingartner's collection of essays, *Akkorde*, Leipzig: Breitkopf & Hartel, 1912, repr. Walluf-Nendein: Sandig, 1977, pp. 119–22. In a letter to EMI's recording impresario Fred Gaisberg dated 17 August 1938, Weingartner excused himself from the proposal that he record what he termed the Gluck–Mottl Ballet Suite (Mottl's 1896 suite of dances by Lully, Rameau, Grétry and Gluck) because 'Mottl was indeed a good friend of mine' but he had no sympathy for this suite (EMI archive).

[73] See Christopher Dyment, *Toscanini in Britain*, Woodbridge: The Boydell Press, 2012 (Dyment 2012), pp. 3–6, which also sets out at greater length the extracts here given from the *Times* of 11 June 1900.

By these persistent criticisms London writers pinpointed inescapable aspects of Mottl's style; [74] furthermore, their notices contrasted considerably with the welcome for Steinbach's debut with the Meiningen Hofkapelle just two years after Mottl's last appearance, which, as extensively illustrated above, expanded in a crescendo of approbation that established Steinbach in London eyes as one of the greatest conductors of his time – strong evidence of a telling difference of interpretative approach.

Weingartner's attacks and Mottl's reputation as a 'slow tempo' conductor barely touched his stature within the Austro-German world. Indeed, Berrsche's analyses of his way in, say, an expansive and songful Schubert Ninth and the *Eroica*'s *Marcia funebre* were detailed and appreciative – he much preferred Mottl's Beethoven to Weingartner's 'hurried' and 'cool' approach.[75] Further, Mottl's temperament, with his search for peace and harmony in music as in life, made him the ideal Viennese conductor, in contrast to the uncompromising and fanatical Mahler.[76]

On the other hand, there seems to have been a critical consensus about Mottl's failure in the music of Brahms. His diaries record how, in his early years and particularly after he was enveloped by the atmosphere of Bayreuth, he found much that was boring and meaningless in the first two symphonies.[77] As Hofkapellmeister in Karlsruhe he conducted the Fourth Symphony in 1886, but that was an isolated effort and until the end of the century he ventured little into Brahmsian territory.[78] When in 1906 he essayed the Third Symphony in Vienna he was roundly condemned for his pains:

> In the first movement the correct shaping was missing, the woodwind phrases suffering from excessive haste. The graciousness of the *Allegretto* grew torpid with muddy heaviness and in the finale the conductor's temperament ... did not find the right transition to the radiant close.

The effort damaged his reputation.[79] Again, during his Munich years he felt obliged to conduct works by a composer whose stature was by then unchallengeable, but, as

---

[74] For Shaw's comments, see Bernard Shaw, *Music in London*, London: Constable, 1932, vol. 3, pp. 195–8. For the *Musical Times* notices, see vol. 35 (June 1894), p. 391 (Beethoven's Fifth Symphony); vol. 36 (December 1895), p. 814 (Schubert's *Unfinished* Symphony); vol. 37 (January 1896), p. 22 (*Eroica* Symphony); vol. 37 (June 1896), p. 384 (*Pastoral* Symphony); vol. 38 (May 1897), p. 313 (Beethoven's Ninth Symphony); vol. 38 (December 1897), p. 817 (Tchaikovsky's Sixth Symphony); vol. 39 (June 1898), p. 389 (Wagner's *Kaisermarsch* and Weingartner's London debut concert); vol. 41 (July 1900), p. 477 (*Ring* cycle and *Tannhäuser*), vol. 41 (August 1900), p. 537 (Mottl's *Meistersinger*, his final appearance in London, and Emil Paur's *Tannhäuser*, where items were 'for the first time this year ... [by contrast with Mottl] taken at the proper pace').
[75] Berrsche, pp. 174 and 594.
[76] See Haas/Mottl, pp. 350 and 352; Mittag, p. 39.
[77] Haas/Mottl, pp. 27–8.
[78] *Ibid.* p. 172.
[79] *Ibid.* pp. 292–3.

many entries in his diaries indicated, Mottl could not refrain from giving voice to a constant antipathy towards him. That lack of belief in the works themselves accounted for his own relative lack of success in his not infrequent performance of the symphonies in both Munich and Vienna.[80] A later critic summed up Mottl's failings: 'The pupil of Wagner and interpreter of the pathetic and demonic, could make nothing of Brahms's scores; for a conductor who luxuriated in Wagnerian orgies of sound, the grey atmosphere of Brahms's orchestral palette was offensive.'[81]

Mottl's recordings were limited to some Welte-Mignon piano rolls, including the Prelude to Act 1 of *Tristan und Isolde* made in February 1907, and fragments in certain cylinders.[82] In the absence of more reliable recorded mementoes of his art, Mottl's star, like Steinbach's, has sunk below the horizon. Today he is remembered for his orchestrations, particularly of Wagner's *Wesendonck Lieder*, and as the influential Munich exemplar of Abendroth and also of Furtwängler, whose *Tristan*, according to Mottl's biographer, closely resembled his mentor's;[83] both of them are considered later in this chapter.

Aside: Anton Seidl and another Wagnerian immersion

Too long to footnote but rather on the periphery of this study, mention must be made of the great but short-lived Anton Seidl (1850–98), who once more illustrates the almost unbridgeable divide between the Wagnerians and the Brahmsians during the second half of the nineteenth century. He was beyond doubt a supreme conductor of Wagner's music dramas, perhaps the greatest of all. He assisted Wagner from 1872, worked alongside Mottl at Bayreuth in 1876 and was responsible for the German opera (primarily Wagner) craze in New York from 1885. He was also the New York Philharmonic's conductor from 1891 until his death. Although critics have left us a substantial range of comment about his Wagner performances – their acute reaction to every passing emotion evoked in the music dramas, painted with constant changes of tempo, some slight, some emphatic, and with many a *Luftpause*[84] – there is less

---

[80] *Ibid.* p. 356.
[81] Gaston Dejmek, *Max Fiedler*, Essen: Vulcan, 1940 (Dejmek), pp. 152–3; translations from Dejmek courtesy Nicholas Chadwick.
[82] Haas/Mottl, pp. 354 and 425; Brown, p. 722. A Mapleson cylinder recording dated 17 January 1904, identified as Mottl conducting Wagner's Kaisermarsch in New York's Metropolitan Opera, is in *100 Jahre Bayreuth auf Schallplatte. Die Frühen Festspielsänger 1876–1906*, Gebhart (2004) JGCD 0062-12, CD 10, Track 7. However, William H. Seltsam's *Metropolitan Opera Annals: A Chronicle of Artists and Performances*, New York, H. W. Wilson, 1947, p. 140, does not list this work in the concert programme Mottl conducted on that day. For the possibility that some of Mottl's characteristics may be present in the recordings of Hans Pfitzner, see p. 135.
[83] Haas/Mottl, p. 355.
[84] See Brown, pp. 122–32, for an exhaustive and illuminating range of critical comment.

12. ANTON SEIDL IN 1885

unanimity about his concert work. According to H. E. Krehbiel, a leading American critic of the period and music editor of the *New York Tribune*, Seidl believed that

> The conductor must penetrate to the heart of the composition and be set aglow by its flames. That done, he must make his proclamation big and vital, full of red blood, sincere and assertive … He had no room in his convictions for mere refinement of nuance or precision of execution. Too much elaboration of detail he thought injurious to the general effect. These beliefs were entirely consistent with his tastes, temperament and training, all of which were … hugely dramatic. His heart went out to music which told a story or painted a picture, and in the presentation of such compositions he became all-compellingly eloquent. Sometimes, too, he found picturesque elements in most unexpected places, as, for instance, in … the last movement of Brahms's symphony in E minor.[85] As a rule, Brahms's music lay beyond the horizon of his sympathies, but this tremendous Passacaglia seemed to warm him, and he read it better than he did anything else of him.[86]

Krehbiel's portrait was by no means fully consistent with other critical views of Seidl's style set out in the volume from which it is extracted, many of which did,

[85] Seidl programmed Brahms's Fourth Symphony with the Philharmonic in its 1894–5 season, the Second Symphony two years earlier.

[86] Henry T. Finck (ed.), *Anton Seidl: A Memorial by His Friends*, New York, Charles Scribner's Sons, 1899; repr. Boston: Da Capo, 1983, p. 135. The book contains appraisals by many contemporaries including the foremost music critics, Finck (1854–1926), James Huneker (1857–1921) and H. E. Krehbiel (1854–1923), as well as numerous tributes from musicians.

indeed, emphasise the delicacy of his responsiveness to the passing mood. In particular, his contemporary Henry T. Finck remarked that 'he had, indeed, a special liking for delicate, dainty music' and thought that, although 'of Brahms he was not a great admirer', he interpreted the Second Symphony 'with the same conscientious care that he bestowed on his favorites'.[87] But the essential point remains: in general, Brahms's music appealed to Seidl little more than it did to Mottl, for the Wagnerian immersion was too overwhelming. That incompatibility among so many of the great Wagnerians was, however, not invariable, as the next witness attests.

Arthur Nikisch: the best of both worlds

Wagnerian baptism and Brahmsian triumphs

A strict chronology would place the next witness, Arthur Nikisch (1855–1922), before Mottl: Steinbach was born on 17 June 1855, Nikisch on 12 October 1855 and Mottl on 24 August 1856. Nikisch is, however, the first true recording conductor in this survey. All subsequent conductors discussed here (other than Walter Blume) also left a recorded legacy, most including works by Brahms; unfortunately, Nikisch's included no Brahms. Still, in general his recordings bear out his reputation for a poetic instinct and wild abandonment, both often to be heard in the same work. However, quite apart from their primitive sound, which creates its own difficulty for even the sympathetic listener in perceiving the greatness of a conductor who was almost universally admired, the Nikisch recordings need to be treated with a modicum of reserve. 'Have you heard that Beethoven Fifth?' Boult demanded of me in 1972, referring to Nikisch's most famous and much analysed recording with the Berlin Philharmonic: 'just ridiculous! He would never have done that [that is, perform it with such liberties of tempo] in London. He was far more frightened of London critics than those in Leipzig [Nikisch's other principal centre of activity]'.[88] In more measured terms in his *Thoughts on Conducting*, Boult remarked that, 'as a musician, he could not command universal approval' and, listening to the Beethoven Fifth recording, he was 'greatly astonished at the little *accelerandos* and *rallentandos* which have been freely brought into the first and last movements. These would have shocked Dr Hans Richter deeply; indeed, they did, as I heard from a friend of his at the time'.[89] It was well known that Nikisch's performances differed one from another, a characteristic evidenced by the

---

[87] *Ibid.* pp. 164 and 172.

[88] See n. 18 above. The quotation here is exact; in my article based on this interview, it is laid out in more formal language.

[89] Adrian Boult, *Thoughts on Conducting*, London: Phoenix House, 1963, p. x.

only duplicate recording of a work in his discography, the Liszt Hungarian Rhapsody No. 14.[90]

While still a student at the Vienna Conservatory, where his composition teacher was Otto Dessoff, Nikisch deputised as second violinist in the Court Opera orchestra and the Philharmonic. This experience afforded him the opportunity to play twice in ten days under Wagner's baton: on 12 May 1872, when in Vienna the programme included the *Eroica* Symphony and Wagner excerpts; and on 22 May, when Nikisch was one of twenty-one Vienna players imported for Wagner's performance of Beethoven's Ninth Symphony at Bayreuth to mark his laying of the foundation stone. The impressions that Nikisch received from the two concerts were the decisive influence on his musical approach. As he put it in the course of a lengthy memoir,

> What I learned in the four rehearsals Wagner held with us had a huge influence on my whole artistic career ... I can say that Wagner's *Eroica* in Vienna and then the Ninth at Bayreuth turned out to be crucial for my conception of Beethoven as a whole, indeed, for my orchestral interpretation in general.[91]

Nikisch was impressed in particular by Wagner's search for the *melos*, seeming to shape the music rather than beat time, and the beautiful singing line that he drew from the strings, an aspect of Nikisch's own conducting that impressed the young Furtwängler.

Nikisch's student days as a deputy in the Vienna Hofoper orchestra were followed by a more formal appointment to membership of that orchestra and on occasion he played under the baton of distinguished composers, including Brahms.[92] After a recommendation by Dessoff, his conducting career began in December 1877 as chorus master in Leipzig. His first Gewandhaus concert took place in 1880, the start of an illustrious partnership – but, first, Nikisch spent the years 1889–93 as conductor of the Boston Symphony Orchestra, with a further two years leading the Royal Opera House in Budapest. At last, in 1895 he was appointed as conductor of the Gewandhaus orchestra, beginning his tenure on 10 October. Later that month he was appointed to succeed Bülow as conductor of the Berlin Philharmonic; he held both positions until his death, conducting about 580 concerts in Leipzig and almost 300 in Berlin. In addition, from 1895 there were some 130 Philharmonic concerts in Hamburg.

---

[90]   The first recording was made with the LSO on 25 June 1913, the second with the Berlin Philharmonic in the period 1920–22. The Beethoven Fifth Symphony was recorded with the Berlin Philharmonic on 20 September 1913. The complete Nikisch recordings have been transferred to CD, Symposium 1087/8.

[91]   In the compilation edited by Heinrich Chevalley, *Arthur Nikisch. Leben und Werken*, Berlin: Bote & Bock, 1922 (Chevalley), pp. 10–14 of Ferdinand Pfohl's biography.

[92]   Nikisch's VPO concerts under Brahms included the *Haydn* Variations (26 November 1876) and First Symphony (17 December 1876): Hofmann, pp. 165–6.

13. ARTHUR NIKISCH IN 1922: THE LAST PORTRAIT

In all these centres Brahms figured prominently in his programmes: in Leipzig, for example, Brahms's symphonies were included (twice as cycles) in 86 of his concerts (in 87, according to another source), along with further concerts containing his other orchestral works;[93] all four symphonies were usually played during each season.[94]

A controversial musical style

Nikisch's combination of consummate technique and the way in which he exercised it to secure performances of the greatest freedom and emotional thrust were extraordinary even in his time, as is clear from the portrait painted by Carl Flesch, which, as was usual with him, analysed Nikisch's attributes in a not altogether positive manner.

> Now [in 1896] for the first time I saw a musician who, impressionistically, described in the air not simply the bare metrical structure, but above all the dynamic and agogical nuances as well as the indefinable mysterious feeling that lies *between* the notes; his beat was utterly personal and original. With Nikisch began a new era in the art of conducting ... [His] technique itself seemed unprecedented and completely individual, in no wise thought out, but experienced, felt – an instinctive expression of his personality ... he combined German musicality with Hungarian fire and Slavonic *morbidezza* [delicacy]. From this rare mixture came an integral whole that left the impression on the hearer of something absolutely unique of its kind, especially when the work in question was in harmony with his individuality. In intellectual respects one would say he was somewhat primitive. He read little or nothing, was fond of cards, women and company ...[95]

With such unique attributes, it is not surprising that Brahms's reaction to Nikisch's performances of his works was sometimes a little uncertain. His response to Nikisch's Leipzig performance of his Fourth Symphony in late January 1896 has been quoted – 'impossible to imagine it better done'[96] – but not all of his comments were so unequivocally approving. Nikisch himself, in the course of giving his views on the function of a modern conductor (as he saw it in the early twentieth century), recounted what happened when he performed one of Brahms's symphonies in the presence of the composer

---

[93] Johannes Fortner (ed.), *Die Gewandhaus-Konzerte zu Leipzig, 1781–1981*, Leipzig: VEB Deutscher Verlag für Musik, 1981 p. 148, quoted in Suzanne Popp, 'Gratwanderung: Regers Brahms-Interpretation', in Suzanne Popp (ed.), *Auf Der Suche nach dem Werk. Max Reger – sein Schaffen – seine Sammlung*, Karlsruhe: Max Reger Institut, 1998, pp. 236–49 (Popp), at p. 239, n. 4. See also Raymond Holden, *The Virtuoso Conductors*, New Haven: Yale University Press, 2005 (Holden), Ch. 2, 'The Magician of the Podium: Arthur Nikisch', pp. 37–60 at p. 49 and n. 57.

[94] See Chevalley, p. 151.

[95] Flesch, p. 148.

[96] See p. 23.

– whether or not it was the same occasion in Leipzig is not clear. Brahms was heard to exclaim in surprise, 'Is it really possible? Did I actually compose that?' – but afterwards he came up to the conductor with a beaming smile and said, 'You have made it all completely different; but you were right – it must be so!'[97] On another occasion, the Berlin concert agent Louise Wolff, sitting with the composer during a performance of the Third Symphony by the Berlin Philharmonic under Nikisch, which she thought the most wonderful and perfectly interpreted ever heard, recounted that afterwards Brahms turned to her with a smile, saying 'I really didn't know that I had written anything so beautiful.'[98]

Such colourful and extremely individual performances of Brahms's symphonies, influenced, like everything Nikisch conducted, by his experience of the extreme deviations from basic tempos practised by Wagner in his conducting, were bound to cause trouble in conservative Vienna. Here was Richter's citadel, where he had long demonstrated to the critics and public how the symphonies (in his view) should go – if sometimes to Brahms's distaste for his sloppy preparation and its metronomic outcome.[99] After a concert of Beethoven, Wagner and Tchaikovsky by the Vienna Philharmonic under Nikisch in May 1901, the Viennese mood was captured for British readers by Brahms's latter-day amanuensis, Eusebius Mandyczewski:

> In all these [works] Herr Nikisch presented to us, not so much the works as they actually are, but as what, in his opinion, they ought to be. It is impossible to entirely acquit this otherwise excellent conductor of the charge of undue and very inartistic exaggeration for the sake of effect. All his performances have been most carefully thought out and prepared, and yet he tears the tempi to pieces and deals with some passages in an outré fashion, which is really incomprehensible. Such deliberate exaggeration cannot be the outcome of spontaneous musical feeling, and is particularly out of place in the works of the classical masters amongst whom, in this connection, Wagner must be classed.[100]

Only after some years, during the succession of guest conductors after Mahler's departure, did the 'far travelled pied piper', as Julius Korngold termed him,[101] win Vienna by

---

[97] See Chevalley, Ferdinand Pfohl's biography, p. 43. Beware slanted translations here, e.g. Curt Riess (transl. Margaret Goldsmith), *Wilhelm Furtwängler*, London: Frederick Muller, 1955 (Riess), p. 46, which has Brahms saying 'Did I really compose this magnificent piece?' Brahms's words, as conveyed by Nikisch himself (Chevalley, p. 43), were '*Habe ich denn wirklich das componiert?*'

[98] '*Ich wusste gar nicht, dass ich so etwas Schönes geschrieben hatte.*' See Chevalley, Louise Wolff, 'Arthur Nikisch und Berlin: aus meinen Erinnerungen', p. 165.

[99] See p. 8 above.

[100] *Musical Times*, vol. 43 (1 June 1901), 'Letter from Vienna'. Eusebius Mandyczewski (1857–1929), eminent musicologist and critic, Romanian-born but resident in Vienna from 1875.

[101] '*vielgereisten Rattenfänger*' – see Ferdinand Pfohl's biography in Chevalley, p. 100. Julius Korngold (1860–1945) was an eminent Viennese critic.

his conducting: '*Er kam, hob den Taktstock und siegte*' ('he came, waved his baton and conquered'), as Pfohl's biography put it, first with Brahms's Third Symphony and then, at the Vienna Festival in 1912, with the Fourth.[102]

Nikisch the Brahms interpreter

How, then, did Nikisch approach the interpretative problems in Brahms's symphonies? The London *Times* was, fortunately, on hand to answer this query with some precision. When Nikisch performed the First Symphony for the first time with the LSO on 9 June 1906, it reported two days later that the conductor:

> gave a highly interesting and effective reading ... Herr Steinbach has on former occasions come in for some blame [not by *The Times*] on account of his anticipation of the composer's indication of alteration of time, more particularly in the first movement; the only printed mark in the score is the 'poco sostenuto' [corrected by Brahms to 'meno allegro'] at the close of that movement, but Herr Steinbach is accustomed to make a rallentando at an important climax (16 bars before letter O [bar 418]); but Herr Nikisch starts his rallentando 48 bars before that point [bar 386]; and in other places there was great freedom of interpretation. For the most part the changes were improvements, for they all went in the direction of increasing the amenity [i.e. the pleasure to be had] of the work, which is, perhaps, a character that has not always been brought out by more orthodox conductors. In the splendid Adagio [*sic*: the Andante sostenuto] there is no apparent reason why the quavers beginning at bar 6 should be taken nearly as slowly as the crotchets in the previous bar; such things as this do not tend to emphasize the unity of the movement. But Herr Nikisch is a person of such commanding will, and such evident musicianship, that he has clearly the right to his own reading ...

The *Times* critique of the first movement *rallentandos* by Steinbach and Nikisch points to the recapitulation; presumably the two conductors made a similar change of pace at bars 145 (Steinbach) and 113 (Nikisch) in the exposition. Steinbach's solution to tempo changes here is one now made, to a greater or lesser extent, by all Brahms conductors and the fact that the *Times* critic underlined it indicates strongly that 'orthodox' conductors – presumably, in this context, Hans Richter – made no noticeable *rallentando*; in modern practice such restraint would be regarded as unusually unbending. On the other hand, Nikisch's *rallentando* at bars 113/386 is not a feature encountered either today or in most pre-Second World War recordings, and points thereby to a freedom of tempo, lauded in its time by the *Times* critic but unlikely to meet with such indulgence today.

[102] Chevalley, p. 100.

Indeed, the evidence here is sufficiently clear to suggest that, over the last century or so, in assessing the value of particular interpretations of the great symphonic literature, it is the critical viewpoint that has changed rather than the language. The approach in the first movement of the symphony adopted by the named conductors, Steinbach and Nikisch, and also by inference Richter, is clear enough from the foregoing description; what has changed is the degree to which playing fast and rather loose with the text has met with critical approbation. Obviously, Nikisch came very near the line set by the *Times* critic from his 1906 vantage point of what was permissible in the treatment of the opening bars of the slow movement, although, taken as a whole, Nikisch's great freedom of interpretation resulted, to the 1906 critic, in a 'highly interesting and effective reading', which made for 'improvements' that enhanced the work's general 'amenity'. A younger generation may well have thought differently; Adrian Boult was present at this performance and disliked it.[103]

As the critics became more used to Nikisch's ways in Brahms, reception of his performances became more accepting of his freedoms. Perhaps, too, Nikisch consciously constrained himself to some extent, aware, as Boult suggested to me, of the London critics' power to make and unmake musical reputations. When Nikisch came to repeat the First Symphony on 9 May 1908, two days later the *Times* remarked that it was one of the works 'in the interpretation of which the conductor most certainly excels' and found fault only with the 'curious freedom of time' at the beginning of the last movement's introduction, which was 'so definite and remarkable an alteration of the text that it must rest on some very good authority' (it did not). For the rest, 'every point of this and the other movements was finely made and in all the effect of the whole was admirably kept in view and not sacrificed to details'. For the *Musical Times*, it was the first movement that contained 'a few individualities in the matter of tempi', but these did not detract from 'the general effect of brilliance and vigour'.[104] Nikisch's performance of the Fourth Symphony with the LSO on 24 May 1910 evoked a similar response. For the *Times* two days later, he brought out 'all the poetic beauty underlying the austere structure', while the *Musical Times* thought that, 'as usual, his individual views threw new light on the familiar' and the work 'assumed an unwonted freshness and spontaneity that added vitality'.[105] Underlying all these assessments lies an obvious critical acceptance of Nikisch's individualities in freedom of tempo that, as Boult told me, might well be regarded today as so extreme as to be an eccentric response to the emotional thrust of the text.

---

[103] See p. 41, where Boult refers to the two performances of the First Symphony under Nikisch that he attended, of which this would have been the first; the second, on 9 May 1908, he found, against his better judgement, more acceptable.

[104] *Musical Times*, vol. 48 (1 June 1908).

[105] *Musical Times*, vol. 50 (1 June 1910), p. 448.

The trans-Atlantic assessment of Nikisch's Brahms was by this time precisely similar, to judge by the ever-perspicacious and descriptively precise estimate of Richard Aldrich. On their North American tour in the Spring of 1912 the LSO, headed by Nikisch, gave the Brahms First Symphony in Carnegie Hall on 8 April 1912. Aldrich duly reported next day that

> There was much to be admired in Mr. Nikisch's beautifully plastic modelling of the phrase; his adjustment of melodic values in the orchestration, so that Brahms's melodic line should never be lost, nor the rounded, rich, and shadowy masses of the instrumental color disturbed; his freedom and flexibility of tempo, that were seldom exaggerated. There was a wealth of significant detail all through it. Nothing was lost, and nothing was unduly obtrusive. The enunciation of the grandiose theme of the last movement was superb, and its entrance artfully prepared to gain the greatest effect. There was a magnificent climax wrought in this movement.[106]

As will be noted hereafter, Max Fiedler did not pass the Aldrich tests of cohesion and continence in the performance of Brahms; on the other hand, Steinbach certainly did, as did Muck and Toscanini.[107] One senses that in Aldrich's view Nikisch only just achieved a similarly praiseworthy coherence – his flexibility of tempo was 'seldom exaggerated'; so, clearly on occasion it was indeed exaggerated, but the conductor's many other virtues outweighed this weakness. That conclusion seems quite closely to reflect the composer's own response.

Given Brahms's (sometimes equivocal) approbation for Nikisch's approach to his symphonies, the obvious question is whether, after the conductor's relatively early death in 1922, there is any evidence that his approach survived elsewhere.

The Nikisch pupils: faint echoes – real or imagined?

As already proposed in this study,[108] Nikisch's handling of Brahms's works probably marked the outward limit of an extreme Romantic style to win, however equivocally, the composer's approbation. Which other conductors, if any, carried forward this line of authority, so heavily influenced by the extravagant spirit of Wagner's practice? For the most part, one cannot look to Nikisch's students in his Berlin or Leipzig classes for anyone perpetuating traces of his stylistic approach. His influence among them lived on to a more solid extent in his stick technique. So, to take the clearest example, in 1912–13 Boult spent six months closely watching the conductor at work in the Leipzig Gewandhaus and noted later that no other conductor was as eloquent with the baton;

---

[106] Aldrich, p. 364.
[107] See pp. 42, 78 and 104.
[108] See p. 23.

14. NIKISCH CONDUCTS:
THE BATON AT SHOULDER HEIGHT;
SILHOUETTE BY OTTO WEIDEMANN

as he remarked in the foreword to his 'little book' (as he described it to me[109]), *The Point of the Stick*, 'nearly all of this book is founded on the practice of Arthur Nikisch, who was the greatest technician in my experience. He spoke little at his rehearsal because the point of his stick described the music with overpowering eloquence.'[110] But Nikisch came first as Boult's favourite interpreter in very few works:

> All the Schumann and Liszt symphonies [viz. the symphonic poems]; the three Weber overtures; a good deal of Wagner – notably *Tristan*; and the Verdi *Requiem*, in which he played under Verdi's direction in Vienna as a boy. But if it was Beethoven, well, Richter, Weingartner and Steinbach all seemed to do greater justice to the music ... Brahms – Steinbach really understood it; and so on. [111]

Traces of Nikisch's stylistic approach in Boult's recorded legacy are certainly hard to find, and, it would seem, wholly absent in his Brahms. Boult's stance towards his teacher is best expressed in this extract from his obituary essay in 1922:

---

[109] See p. 9 above.
[110] *The Point of the Stick: A Handbook on the Technique of Conducting*, London: Paterson, 1968 p. 2; the handbook was written in 1920 for private circulation at the Royal College of Music.
[111] Adrian Boult, *Boult on Music*, London: Toccata Press, p. 94.

15. CARTOON OF MAX REGER
CONDUCTING, 1913,
BY WILHELM THIELMANN

I can remember the most thrilling performance of the Brahms C minor Symphony that I have ever heard – we are not now discussing whether Brahms should be thrilling or not – and, at the end, when the orchestra and audience had been worked up to a white heat and the movement had finished in a blaze of triumph, it occurred to me that Nikisch's hand had never been raised higher than the level of his face throughout the whole movement.[112]

Here, then, was the consummate technician, delivering a slightly dubious musical experience: in this Nikisch was the progenitor of many, influenced by the example, if not by the unique style.

Another witness of Nikisch's style and interpretative approach who, although never one of his students, learned much from him, was, ironically, one of Steinbach's successors at Meiningen. In 1911, after the early death of Steinbach's immediate successor as conductor of the Meiningen Hofkapelle, Wilhelm Berger (1860–1911),[113] Herzog Georg obtained the services of Max Reger (1873–1916), relatively new to the art of conducting but famous already as a composer and pianist. It was, indeed, to Steinbach that Reger in large measure owed the Herzog's decision to engage him.[114] Reger's

---

[112] *Ibid.* p. 101, reprinted from *Musical Opinion*, vol. 3 (April 1922). This performance was probably the one with the LSO in 1908 referred to by Boult at p. 41.
[113] Composer and conductor; Berger continued the tradition of touring with the orchestra with copious Brahms in the programmes.
[114] During 1905–08 Reger sometimes conducted his own works but it was not until 1909 that he conducted a Brahms symphony, achieving a success in Hamburg with the Third that marked his

Leipzig years, 1907–11, gave him ample opportunity to witness Nikisch at work and he owned that Nikisch's approach to Brahms provided an example of the freedom which, as Reger himself stated, distanced his Brahms performances from those of Steinbach: as he put it to Steinbach in 1912, 'in Brahms, you believe in the *letter*, and I in the *spirit*', protesting later to Herzog Georg that he found Steinbach's approach too robust and his phrasing lacking in affection.[115]

Notwithstanding this acutely different approach to the repertoire and Reger's unorthodox baton technique, the Meiningen Hofkapelle, its spirits somewhat flagging under Berger, was revivified under him and kept its standards until ill-health forced his retirement in 1914.[116] Shortly afterwards, with the death of Herzog Georg II, the orchestra was disbanded for the duration of the Great War.[117] Despite their differences, which extended to Reger's heavy retouching of Brahms's symphonies,[118] Steinbach was shattered by his early death, which preceded his own in 1916 by only three months. This sequence of events ensured that Reger's partly Nikisch-influenced approach to Brahms did not outlive him.

Nikisch's star pupils included Albert Coates, whose plentiful discography, rich in Wagner and the Slavs, contains insufficient Brahms to enable us to pass judgement on it.[119] Others included George Georgescu, Karl Krueger and Heinz Tietjen; any search here for a lost Brahmsian tradition would be in vain. For another Hungarian, Fritz Reiner (1888–1963), Nikisch stood midway between teacher and exemplar: during his spell in Dresden early in the Great War, Reiner took every opportunity to witness Nikisch in concert and benefited from his counsel and advice, commenting later that he learned more about conducting from him than from anyone else.[120] Interpre-

---

debut as a conductor in symphonic works other than his own. Reger included this symphony in his first Meiningen programme on 12 December 1911.

[115] '*Sie glauben an den Buchstaben bei Brahms und ich an den Geist*'; entry of 29 August 1912 in Reger's diary, in the Max Reger Institute, Karlsruhe, emphasis in original. Letter to Herzog Georg, 25 September 1912, in *Herzog-Briefe*, p. 322. See generally, Popp pp. 237–43.

[116] See n. 17.

[117] This disbandment caught the eye of Richard Strauss, who, listing for Hofmannstal's benefit the artistic depredations of wartime Germany in a letter dated 8 October 1914, remarked, 'the Duchess of Meiningen turfs her orchestra out into the street': Edward Sackville-West (intro.) (transl. Hanns Hammellmann and Ewald Osers), *A Working Friendship: The Correspondence between Richard Strauss and Hugo von Hofmannstal*, New York: Vienna House, 1961; repr. 1974, p. 211.

[118] See p. 173 below.

[119] With the LSO Coates accompanied Artur Rubinstein's performance of Brahms's Second Piano Concerto, recorded by HMV in the Queen's Hall on 22–23 October 1929, issued on D 1746–50, CD transfer BMG/RCA 09026 63001/2. Coates also recorded an abbreviated Brahms First Symphony on 2 and 9 December 1921 but this was not issued.

[120] Kenneth Morgan, *Fritz Reiner: Maestro and Martinet*, Urbana: Illinois University Press, 2005, p. 40.

tatively, however, Reiner fell under the spell of Toscanini in his La Scala and New York Philharmonic years and his relatively few recordings of the Brahms symphonies, distinguished as some of them are, betray little or nothing of Nikisch's alternation of almost reckless vigour and poetry.[121]

There remains but one, perhaps unpromising, line of investigation to retrieve some audible elements of Nikisch's otherwise untraceable Brahms. After his early training and career in both London and New York as an organist, and after he had taken his first steps in his immensely long and distinguished (if often controversial) career as a conductor, Leopold Stokowski (1882–1977) spent his summer months during 1905–08 in search of music making in Austria and Germany – as he put it without elaboration, 'for further studies'.[122] There is little doubt that at some stage during these vacational peregrinations Stokowski became in all but name a fully fledged pupil of Nikisch. Curiously, when asked about Nikisch in 1971, he spoke of Hans Richter as 'still greater', ascribing to him some of the very qualities more readily referable to Nikisch: 'Subtle, delicate, powerful, everything ... The greatest I ever heard.'[123] But Paul Donath, a Philadelphia Orchestra violinist in the years 1903–17 who attended Nikisch's master classes in the Leipzig Conservatory during the 1905/6 season, vouched for the fact that Stokowski was there 'in the same class with him'; his wife, also studying in Leipzig, 'confirmed that Stokowski was one of the studying conductors'.[124]

Many years later, one of the Philadelphia players present at Stokowski's first rehearsal with the Philadelphia Orchestra on 7 October 1912, Oscar Schwar, recollected the result of his first downbeat in the first work, Brahms's First Symphony:

> I could hardly recognize the men I had been playing with or the music that we thought we knew so well. It was as though we had been given some magic potion ... This man went straight to the heart of the music. He formed and moulded every phrase and with almost no physical effort. Everyone had heard that Nikisch achieved maximum precision with a minimum of bodily motion and that he was Stokowski's idol. It was immediately obvious.[125]

---

[121] *Ibid.* pp. 14–15; see p. 100. Recordings of Brahms: the Third Symphony with the Chicago Orchestra for RCA, rec. 14 December 1957, CD transfer LSC 2209; the Fourth with the Royal Philharmonic for *Reader's Digest*, rec. 9/10 and 12 May 1961, CD transfer Chesky CD6 (interpretatively one of Reiner's finest achievements and his own favourite: Morgan, p. 203); and the broadcast of the Second with the New York Philharmonic of 2 March 1960, CD in New York Philharmonic Broadcasts 1923–87.

[122] Oliver Daniel, *Stokowski: A Counterpoint of Views*, New York: Dodd Mead, 1982 (Daniel), p. 42. For information about this period of Stokowski's life, I am indebted to Edward Johnson.

[123] Daniel, interview with Edward Johnson, p. 12.

[124] Daniel, p. 42.

[125] Abram Chasins, *Leopold Stokowski: A Profile*, London: Dutton, 1979 (Chasins), pp. 70–1.

Questioned about the alleged Nikisch connection in 1931, neither Bruno Walter nor Weingartner could recollect Stokowski being around in Germany in the early days, but both were certain from his manner of conducting – until 1928, with a stick – that he had carefully observed and emulated Nikisch.[126] Boult approved of Stokowski's stick technique when he saw him in the early 1920s – 'he did use a stick and he used it jolly well', as he put it to me, a summation he would hardly have permitted himself unless he had perceived elements of the classic Nikisch technique.[127]

If the Nikisch connection seems reasonably well established, the task of tracing any stylistic reference to that conductor in Stokowski's ample Brahms discography presents almost insurmountable problems. In the first place, Stokowski always gave Richter precedence in his memory, even though Richter's classic Kapellmeister-style right-hand time-beating was the antithesis of his own: 'During his later years in particular, Stokowski talked of Hans Richter as exerting a powerful influence on his personal musical taste and on the development of his career. Richter was one of the men Stokowski chiefly wanted to emulate.'[128] On the other hand, no conductor in history was more enamoured of and, in his time, sophisticated in his manipulation of all the means of publicity for the enhancement of his musical (and physical) profile; and it would be entirely characteristic for Stokowski to have named Richter as the greatest in his pantheon as a smokescreen to divert anyone tempted to delve too deeply into his musical past.

If, however, there had been a strong Nikisch-influenced style in Stokowski's early Brahms performances, critics would probably have noted it – but such comparison is conspicuous by its absence. Commenting on his first LSO concert on 22 May 1912, the next day's *Times* went into considerable detail about Stokowski's way with the Brahms First Symphony, a Nikisch favourite familiar to London audiences, and specifically ruled out any close resemblance to other recent performances:

For good or ill, [the] work was [not] what it would be under a conductor who accepted the tradition of the players ... Both the first and last movements lacked continuity through the rhythm hanging fire a little at partial closes; the entrance of the three-note figure on the violas, *pizzicato marcato* [in the first movement], and the cadence in E minor just before the return of the big tune in the finale were cases in point. Some of the *tempi* too were not the necessary and inevitable ones; there seems to be no place for excited *accelerandi* in the middle section of the radiant third movement, but on the other hand one wanted more hastening where Brahms has given the direction *stringendo poco a poco* in the *pizzicato* passages in the introduction to the *finale*. Nevertheless, certain passages had remarkable power, the wonderful return in

---

[126] *Ibid.* p. 22.
[127] See Dyment interview, p. 42.
[128] Daniel, p. 11.

16. LEOPOLD
STOKOWSKI IN
1912 AFTER HIS
PHILADELPHIA
APPOINTMENT

the first movement, from [bar 293], was like the gathering of a great wave breaking at last into the principal theme. In general, whenever it was a question of working to a climax Mr Stokowski kept his goal well in view and arrived at it at precisely the right moment. This made the peroration of the last movement extraordinarily fine ...

The 'tradition of the players' was founded on the LSO's various performances under Richter, Steinbach and Nikisch; and the *Times* critic, in noting Stokowski's non- acceptance of that tradition, pointed rather to the conductor's individuality of approach.

In any event, Stokowski's approach to Brahms underwent many changes over the years and, had there at any time been a passing resemblance to some of Nikisch's ways in his earliest performances of the symphonies – which, to establish, would meet with the almost insurmountable difficulties noted in preceding paragraphs – it would surely have vanished by the time he came to record them. However, given Stokowski's early connection with Nikisch, it is worth discussing the recordings in brief, even if the outcome may well be largely negative.[129]

---

[129] Copies of the recordings examined for the purpose of this survey were kindly provided by Edward Johnson, who also made available copies of many reviews of both concerts and

The two early recordings of the First Symphony, dating from 1927 and 1936, show no great divergence of approach, save in the latter for the slower introduction to the first movement and an overloaded *Andante*; the 1936 recording does, however, cure the earlier version's distinctly *mezzoforte* end to the first movement's introduction (displaying, as Stokowski loved to do, the magnificent Philadelphia cellos) and the clunking, closely miked *pizzicati* which open the early recording's third movement. But this later recording does not quite possess the remarkable fervour of the first, the intensity of which carries it through some passages that in other hands would have sagged beyond redemption; here they hold the line – just. In particular, Stokowski subjects the first movement to a distinct *rallentando* from bars 113 and 386 onwards, the *tempo primo* not resumed in each case until the *pizzicato*, *marcato* three-note figure. It happens that Nikisch, as we know from the *Times* review extracted above, adopted precisely the same approach, diverging here from the Steinbachian groundplan. It seems, too, that Stokowski's *rallentando* in this 1927 recording was similar to his LSO performance in 1912, when the *Times* criticised him for the rhythm 'hanging fire' at just this point. Approval of Nikisch but disapproval of Stokowski suggests at least the probability that Nikisch must have been less extreme in his handling of the passage, although the distinction made between the two by the *Times* may well lie in their differing impact on successive critics, Fuller Maitland in 1906 and H. C. Colles in 1912.[130]

Whether Stokowski was inspired to do and dare what he did in 1912 as a result of hearing Nikisch conduct the Brahms First Symphony in Leipzig we do not know; given the frequency with which Nikisch programmed the work, it is perfectly credible that he did. So, optimistically, it is possible that elements of the Nikisch style, though no doubt fully absorbed into Stokowski's own interpretative vision, may still reside in the 1927 recording: at the very least, its volatile, rhythmically free but forward-driving approach is suggestive of Stokowski's teacher. As Flesch remarked of Stokowski – although not drawing the parallel with Nikisch that he might have done – his individuality lay in 'his mania for a maximum of expression and effect in life as well as in

---

recordings conducted by Stokowski. The recordings covered here are: *Symphony No. 1*: Philadelphia Orchestra, rec. 25–27 April 1927, RCA Victor 6658–62; Philadelphia Orchestra, rec. 15 January 1936, RCA Victor 8971–5; *Symphony No. 2*: Philadelphia Orchestra, rec. 29–30 April 1929, RCA Victor 7277–82; NYPSO, broadcast 2 April 1950 (PASC 215); Bavarian RSO, broadcast 16 July 1951; *Symphony No. 3*: Philadelphia Orchestra, rec. 25–26 September 1928, RCA Victor 6962–6; *Symphony No. 4*: Philadelphia Orchestra, 3/18 April 1931, unissued on 78rpm, M&A CD1173 (the first side did not survive and is therefore drawn from the 1933 recording); Philadelphia Orchestra, rec. 4 March and 29 April 1933, RCA Victor 7796–8. The Philadelphia Orchestra recordings of the four symphonies from 1927, 1928, 1929 and 1933 (second version) were transferred to CD, Biddulph WHL 017–18.

[130] See further p. 131, where the views of the various *Times* critics from 1902 until the Second World War are examined in the context of Abendroth's London performances of the Brahms symphonies and their possible comparison with Steinbach's.

art, his striving for the *ne plus ultra*, his perfectionism'.[131] And so, for the greater part, it goes in this recording.

In the other symphonies there is no evidence that Stokowski's early recordings approximate in any way to the Nikisch approach. The 1929 recording of the Second Symphony contains a Classically balanced first movement, succeeded by an overripe *Adagio* and two further movements markedly lacking in rhythmic lift and forward impetus – from all accounts, as far removed from Nikisch as could be. Latterly Stokowski drastically changed his approach to the last three movements: the 1950 New York Philharmonic and 1951 Bavarian Radio broadcasts replace the early somewhat turgid style with something altogether fleeter and, in the finale, with a drive that tests both orchestras to their limits.

Stokowski's early recording of the Third Symphony contains a bewildering number of tempo changes throughout. Here, at least, Stokowski's approach seemingly did not change, since the *Times* criticised him for this curious display in his London Festival Hall performance of the work some thirty years later, on 28 June 1960: 'almost every change of idea was accompanied by some change of tempo' – although the playing as such was 'incandescent'.[132] Whether Nikisch's account of the Third, so winningly but equivocally praised by Brahms in a Berlin performance, was similarly idiosyncratic we have no way of knowing. The two early accounts of the Fourth Symphony are very similar, both quite Classically, but flexibly, shaped save for the extreme *accelerando* that closes their first movements – an approach disliked by the composer; since Brahms was so full of praise for Nikisch in this work, presumably this device did not appear in his performances.[133]

With regret, the case for inferring the existence of some of his teacher's characteristics in Stokowski's Brahms recordings must, taken as a whole, be regarded as too weak to be of use in reconstructing Nikisch's style, although the early recording of the First Symphony may be suggestive of certain elements in it; on that account it is examined further in the next chapter. Save for that faint echo, the conclusion must be that there is no audible trace of Nikisch's way with Brahms in the legacy of his pupils. But what of other musicians who were never in any sense pupils yet stood in awe of Nikisch's accomplishments?

Others bedazzled

Nikisch's stature was attested by almost all who witnessed his methods and the results he obtained – a magician, they thought, who hypnotised his players with a consummate technique that appeared to make light of any difficulties. Carl Flesch's reaction

---

[131] Flesch, p. 287.
[132] See the *Times* review, 29 June 1960.
[133] See further p. 216.

was typical of the host of central European conductors who attempted to imbibe his example and technique, if not his wayward style.

Among the next generation's great conductors, such diverse eminences as Erich Kleiber and Wilhelm Furtwängler owed to Nikisch the revelation of the very sound it was possible to draw from an orchestra without apparent effort. In a memoir written in 1932, ten years after Nikisch's death, Kleiber wrote of the impact of Nikisch when at twenty-one he witnessed him take a *Tristan* rehearsal at Darmstadt in 1913:

> Nikisch rehearsed the *Liebestod* with orchestra alone. Our orchestra suddenly seemed transformed. We could none of us understand how Nikisch, with a single rehearsal could draw from them such beauty of sound and such ecstatic depth of feeling. The score rang out as it rings in the silence of one's work-room … Absolutely uncanny were the mighty crescendos: where other conductors flail away with both arms, Nikisch just slowly raised his left hand till the orchestra roared about him like the sea! Yet the melodic parts were never obscured.[134]

Notwithstanding this whole-hearted encomium, and whatever Kleiber then learned of conducting technique and the revelation of orchestral sound drawn so effortlessly, it is hardly necessary to add that in his maturity he owed little to the senior conductor in his handling of the symphonic repertoire, which in any case rarely featured works by Brahms.

Much the same conclusion may be drawn about Furtwängler, albeit perhaps with less unanimous agreement. After all, he and Nikisch are often bracketed together as the two greatest Romantic conductors of their respective generations, each recreating the symphonic repertoire with great freedom of tempo. And, as with Kleiber, the very sound of the orchestra under Nikisch came as a revelation to Furtwängler when in May 1912 he was persuaded to attend one of Nikisch's Hamburg concerts for the first time.[135] But the wide divergence from the basic pulse which characterised many performances of both conductors derived from different analyses. With Nikisch, as is plain from Carl Flesch's description, his aims in performance were entirely a response to the emotional force of the music from moment to moment, as he saw it and wished to project it. With Furtwängler there was also a process of long-pondered ratiocination that led him – it is true with all the emotional intensity at his command – to interpret each individual work in the symphonic repertoire as he did. Nikisch played his part in revealing the possibilities of orchestral execution, especially in the constant

---

[134] John Russell, *Erich Kleiber: A Memoir*, London, Andre Deutsch, 1957, p. 48. Erich Kleiber was at the time third conductor at Darmstadt.
[135] Riess, p. 46. The same event is also recorded in Sam H. Shirakawa, *The Devil's Music Master: The Controversial Life and Career of Wilhelm Furtwängler*, Oxford: Oxford University Press, 1992 (Shirakawa), pp. 19–20, with considerable embellishment and speculation.

singing line of the strings that Nikisch himself so admired in Wagner's conducting, and also in demonstrating a technique – in most respects as far removed from Furtwängler's as it was possible to be – depending not on time-beating but on a weightless grasp of phrase and contour that ignored the bar lines. However, Furtwängler had already experienced other and perhaps more powerful and fundamental influences that helped shape his mature interpretative stance.[136]

The Nikisch legend lived on but, sadly, the conclusion must be that his way with Brahms was virtually extinguished with him.

1859: A vintage year – Max Fiedler, Karl Muck and a lone American

Max Fiedler: a late developer

Among the few recording conductors who almost certainly witnessed Brahms himself conduct, (August) Max Fiedler (1859–1939), born on the last day of 1859, gained an immense reputation in Germany for his performances of that composer's works and was the first in seniority to leave a significant recorded legacy of the symphonies.[137] In his student years at the Leipzig Conservatory, when caricaturists lampooned him and his friend Karl Muck as Faust and Mephisto, Fiedler was introduced to Brahms and may well have witnessed the composer conducting the Gewandhaus orchestra in the Leipzig premiere of his Second Symphony on 10 January 1878 and the Violin Concerto with Joachim on 1 January 1879. Fiedler's early reputation was as a pianist, teaching piano at the Hamburg Conservatory from 1882. Very soon he got to know Brahms well during the composer's visits to Hamburg for the local premieres of major choral works conducted by Julius Spengel, who headed Hamburg's Cäcilienverein.[138] Brahms's familiarity with Fiedler's pianism induced him to suggest he take over from himself as soloist in a Hamburg performance of the Second Piano Concerto – a vote of confidence in him that Fiedler declined.

From 1887 onwards Fiedler was a devoted witness of Bülow's activities in Hamburg. As his biographer, Gaston Dejmek, put it:

> Fiedler was friendly with von Bülow and was greatly impressed by his personality ... [he] belonged to Bülow's admirers and spiritual disciples and was decisively

---

[136] See p. 135.
[137] See generally my two articles in *Classic Record Collector*: 'Apostle of Brahms?', Summer 2002, p. 26, and 'Pauses for Thought', Autumn 2002, p. 44 (Dyment 2002); the first article reviews his career and critical writing about his approach to Brahms, the second his approach to Brahms and other composers as revealed by his recordings, both studio and live.
[138] Julius Heinrich Spengel (1853–1936), whose choral conducting was esteemed by Brahms and Bülow.

17. MAX FIEDLER IN
HAMBURG

influenced by his conscious and alert way of phrasing, his ability to hit on the 'right' tempo for a piece, and above all by his intellectual approach to the masterpieces of German music. In particular, his [i.e. Bülow's] endeavour to polish everything down to the smallest detail had its effect on Fiedler's rehearsals later on: his conducting technique in Hamburg was to become a continuation of Bülow's work.[139]

Fiedler was slow in making a name for himself as a conductor, but, spurred on by his English-born first wife in the 1890s, by 1897, when he conducted the Brahms Fourth Symphony in Hamburg, he won praise for the 'absolute clarity' in 'the lyrical beginning of the first movement, the separation of the effective contrasts which appear here, the structuring of the development, and especially the manner of the composer's step-by-step calculation of the final increase in intensity' – a description which recognisably reflects some of the qualities present in his recording of the work.[140] In 1904 he was appointed – long after his due, according to many – conductor of Hamburg's Philharmonic concerts and the following years saw his fame as conductor spread

[139] Dejmek, pp. 28–30.
[140] *Ibid.* pp. 34–5, quoting the distinguished pedagogue and critic Emil Krause (1840–1916) in the *Hamburger Fremdenblatt* about Fiedler's concert on 8 November 1897.

18. FIEDLER CONDUCTS, C. 1935

throughout Germany and elsewhere in Europe, as well as on a fleeting visit to New York in 1905. There followed the invitation to take over the Boston Symphony Orchestra in 1908 in place of Karl Muck, who was doubtless instrumental in that invitation.

In the year before his crossing Fiedler made several visits to England; the incentive was to visit his brother Hermann Georg, newly installed professor of German language at Oxford, whose tenure lasted three decades. In the course of these visits Fiedler gave several concerts with the LSO and in the first of them, on 28 May 1907, he programmed Brahms's First Symphony. The next day's *Times* was full of praise:

> There were two main characteristics in Herr Fiedler's conducting; the first was the desire to maintain beauty of tone, and so to balance the instruments that even in the most rugged portions of the symphony the quality should never become hard or ugly; the second was a dramatic feeling which led him to emphasize climaxes and contrasts of mood with great skill, at the same time without allowing one to have the feeling that points were actually being made … The orchestra played magnificently all the afternoon.

In his four seasons with the Boston Symphony Fiedler gained great popularity with the public (rather less with the critics) for his forceful conducting of a wide repertoire; it seems his characteristic orchestral balance now tended to become blatantly brassy. Returning to Europe in 1912, his guest conducting in Berlin reinforced his already great reputation as a Brahms conductor – hailed indeed in 1916 as the greatest living interpreter (Richter and Steinbach were by then out of action). That reputation was enhanced during his years at Essen (1916–34), where he succeeded his junior, Hermann Abendroth, who had taken over from Steinbach in Cologne. The most 'authentic' Brahms, said the critics, on account of his performances' multi-faceted explication of Brahms's emotional world – but not, it is clear, on account of any laying on of hands from the composer: there is no evidence that Brahms saw him conduct and Fiedler's late development in that profession rules out the possibility.[141]

It was during his Essen years that Polydor recorded the septuagenarian Fiedler conducting Brahms in Berlin in the late 1920s: with the Berlin Staatskapelle in the Fourth Symphony and with the Berlin Philharmonic in the *Academic Festival* Overture and Second Symphony.[142]

Fiedler's Brahms style: the critics pro and con

Although a majority of German critics enthused over Fiedler's Brahms, others on both sides of the Atlantic were less enthusiastic. The *Musical Courier* complained frequently of his lack of poetry or subtlety. Richard Aldrich in the *New York Times* went well beyond that criticism in his reviews of Brahms in Fiedler's hands when the Boston orchestra visited New York. In his account of the conductor's style, as revealed by the First Symphony in a concert on 5 November 1908,

> There is vigor ... and there is an evident anxiety to be expressive, whereby the note is often forced – the pathetic, the dramatic or the sentimental. There is a tendency to an exaggerated modification of tempo, to retardation and acceleration and to the excessive modelling of the phrase, which destroy the repose, the continuity of line and disrupt the larger symmetry of outline without the production of deeply felt or emotional effect that is intended and is often at direct odds with the spirit of the music he is performing. And again there is a failure to appreciate the true value of other melodic elements, that leaves the listener cold, the music inexpressive ... The first and last movement of the symphony especially lost the breadth and dignity that belong to them, and the second movement suffered from the drag of an exceedingly slow tempo. The best results he obtained in the poco allegretto ... in which Brahms was allowed to have his own natural and flowing utterance. Mr Fiedler is fond of

---

[141] Dejmek, pp. 86–7, 154.
[142] Symphonies Nos. 2 and 4 are further detailed in Ch. 3, p. 167. The Second Piano Concerto with Ellie Ney as soloist was recorded with the Berlin Philharmonic on 1, 2 and 5 June 1939 and 29 April 1940. The 1939 parts amount to seven of the twelve sides and are conducted by Fiedler. The five remaining sides, recorded in 1940 after Fiedler's death, used an unknown conductor. All Fiedler's recordings are collected in a two-CD issue (PASC 363) engineered by Mark Obert-Thorn, whose note specifies the material in the Second Piano Concerto conducted by Fiedler.

using all the power of the brass instruments and of forcing them beyond the limits of euphony, so that many of his fortissimos sound coarse and blatant.[143]

Clearly, Aldrich thought differently from his London colleague and his demolition of Fiedler's approach to Brahms sounded a wholly different note from his equally penetrating account of Steinbach at work.[144] Two years later there was an improvement in orchestral balance, if not in interpretative approach, when Fiedler conducted the Third Symphony in a concert on 12 November 1910:

> Mr Fiedler elaborates his performances with painstaking care, and there is no doubt that they exactly reflect the conception of them he has formed in his mind. There is sometimes question as to the validity of this conception, especially as to some of his tempi ... there is a dissection of the structure of Brahms's symphony that is too obvious and that detracts from the splendidly passionate flow of the music. The Boston Orchestra has played the work here with a freer and more convincing utterance.[145]

Aldrich's views were closely reflected by a Hamburg critic of Fiedler's conducting there after his return to Germany. This account in Dejmek's biography must be quoted at length, not only because it demonstrates the divided nature of German critics' response to his performances of Brahms but because Berrsche, forever holding a candle to the memory of Steinbach, now comes into this picture:

> At a concert on 4 January 1915 at which Brahms's First was heard, the *Neue Hamburger Zeitung* published a comparison between the 'pre-American' and the 'post-American' Fiedler ... As 'prophet' [of Brahms], it claimed, he exhibited 'caprices' which were put down to a certain striving after effect: among these were counted 'pauses for breath at the bar-line, premature *accelerandi*, drawings-out and much blatant forcing (*viel forsches Wesen*)'. A few days later Fiedler conducted the same work, which was one of his showpieces, in Munich. There he ... would scarcely have been remembered from his pre-American period. The Munich press described him as 'the ideal of the reproductive artist, who knows how to immerse himself completely in the essence of each composer and to remain with it throughout that time and thereby to show its inmost nature off to advantage'.[146]

Berrsche, another member of the 'Munich press', dissented: attending this very performance, he reacted in terms similar to his Hamburg colleague. He was worried by

---

[143] Aldrich, pp. 231–2.
[144] See p. 42.
[145] Aldrich, p. 294.
[146] Dejmek, p. 85.

Fiedler's continual tendency towards excitability (by which he presumably meant noticeable and unmotivated changes of tempo, especially at any dynamic climax), which, with the all-pervading restlessness of his interpretative temperament, ignored the more sensitive and gracious aspects in which the music so abounded; what a pity, as he thought, Fiedler chose to end his concert with this disappointing performance.[147]

These descriptions, in particular the obvious distance between Steinbach's and Fiedler's approaches to Brahms so clearly to be inferred from Aldrich and Berrsche, are reflected in many of the characteristics present in Fiedler's recordings. The extravagant tempo variations of his interpretative approach, as also his excessive use of other expressive devices such as *Luftpausen*, were distant from the more Classically restrained conductors of his era and clearly bespeak his devotion to Bülow, even if he could scarcely command the latter's more comprehensive range of effects, both subtle and drastic. One example among many of Fiedler's habitual *Luftpausen*, bizarre in its placing and degree, occurs at bars 138–9 of the Fourth Symphony's scherzo: one is puzzled why Fiedler chose the moment, since it is far from a climactic point, and no more than a moment when *fortissimo* strings give way to equally *fortissimo* wind. Its effect is a self-conscious disruption of the music's pacing and flow, Brahms's 'holding back' carried to an alarming extremity. At the very least, this moment and others in the course of his recordings of the two symphonies provide vivid evidence of the kind of practice so deplored by Weingartner in Bülow's performances.[148]

To sum up, fascinating and valuable as Fiedler's recordings are for providing a probable echo of Bülow's approach, at least in broad terms if not in every detail, they also provide significant examples of those characteristics of the latter's performances that Brahms himself was reported to have found so irritating.[149] We can never know whether Brahms would on that account have had reservations about Fiedler's performances, but – courtesy Aldrich and Berrsche – it is beyond doubt that Steinbach's and Fiedler's performances of Brahms diverged stylistically to a substantial degree. Nevertheless, Fiedler's recorded performances stand as examples reflecting some of the characteristics habitual among certain conductors of Brahms's era, Bülow included. As such, they are a fascinating source of information about stylistic matters, some of which Brahms might well have approved, and others – well, perhaps not. The recordings of the two symphonies are therefore considered further in the next chapter relating to recorded material having a connection with the various stylistic approaches that probably received Brahms's approbation. But it must be emphasised that, as later recordings demonstrate, Fiedler, even more surely than was the case with Nikisch, could boast no successors looking to him as stylistic mentor in the conducting of Brahms symphonies: by the time he made his recordings, at least, he was too much the relic of a bygone age.

[147] Berrsche, p. 599.
[148] See pp. 24 and 82.
[149] See p. 21 above.

Karl Muck: a lost Brahmsian

Karl Muck, born on 22 October 1859 and dying in early March 1941, was, in contrast to his friend Fiedler, a lifelong and ardent Wagnerian, whose concert conducting virtually began and ended with works by Wagner's disciple, Anton Bruckner.[150] This Wagnerian immersion was, if not as all-conquering as Mottl's, sufficient to delay Brahms entering his repertoire with any regularity until his conductorship of the Boston Symphony Orchestra in the years 1906–8 and 1912–17. There he took up the cause with, it seems, enthusiasm and (unlike Mottl) great distinction. His Brahms was considered the finest ever heard in the city, and by the end of his first period in post all the symphonies except the Third had been played repeatedly; the Third at last came in 1915.[151]

The distinction of Muck's Brahms is apparent from Aldrich's response in the *New York Times* for 9 November 1917 to the previous day's performance of the Fourth Symphony by the Bostonians in Carnegie Hall, at a time when the controversy surrounding Muck's performance (or not) of the national anthem had already begun – he was interned four months later:

> Dr. Muck has more than once played Brahms's Fourth Symphony. And the beautiful rendering of it that he gives is well remembered – a reading full of life, of sinuous grace in the first movement, of immense vigor in the third and last movements, of lovely sentiment in the andante; everywhere of beautiful color and subtle adjustment of the instrumental voices, of finely turned and pregnant phrasing, of subtle nuancing of tempo.[152]

It hardly needs underlining that, for Aldrich, Muck's Brahms to all appearances came without the reservations concerning stylistic traits he felt obliged to make when assessing Fiedler and Nikisch.

After Muck's return from the USA he continued to programme Brahms in Hamburg, culminating in his participation in the 1933 Hamburg centenary festival, when, in three concerts on 7, 15 and 19 May, he conducted the First and Fourth Symphonies, the Second Piano Concerto, the Violin Concerto, the *Haydn* Variations and the Alto Rhapsody. These concerts marked Muck's exit from Hamburg and only his July 1933

---

[150] Muck gave five concerts as Kapellmeister in Graz, of which the '*Höhenpunkt*' was on 14 March 1886, featuring the Seventh Symphony in the composer's presence: Peter Muck, *Karl Muck. Ein Dirigentenleben in Briefen und Documenten*, Tutzing: Hans Schneider, 2003, p. 22. Muck's last concert was again of Bruckner, in Leipzig in July 1933: Sophie Fetthauer, 'Exkurs: Karl Muck', in Peri Arndt and others (eds), *Das 'Reichs-Brahmsfest' 1933 in Hamburg*, Hamburg: Bockel Verlag, 1997 (Brahmsfest), p. 90.

[151] H. Earle Johnson, *Symphony Hall, Boston*, Boston: Little, Brown, 1950, pp. 48 and 324.

[152] Aldrich, p. 550.

19. KARL MUCK, C. 1900

concert in Leipzig remained. It was an inglorious ending, for his support for the notoriously Nazified festival did not go unnoticed: thereafter senior Nazi officials marked
both his seventy-fifth and eightieth birthdays with extravagant congratulatory mes-
sages.[153] His imprint, save for his Wagner recordings, soon faded.

Why, then, is Muck worthy of mention? Other than through his friend Fiedler, he
had no known connection with Brahms nor with members of his circle, although in
the course of a long career he probably encountered many with such connections. Nor,
in the absence of recordings, can we further establish his credentials as a Brahmsian.
But that is indeed part and parcel of the point sought to be made: here is a conductor of the utmost distinction, contemporary with other distinguished musicians with
attested connections with Brahms, who, without any such connections, was nonetheless a great conductor of the symphonies. Had he been fortunate enough to make
more recordings than he did, including some of music by Brahms, his standing as
an artist and, specifically as a Brahmsian, would be immeasurably greater; and, with
the passage of time, his view of the composer might well have been retrospectively

---

[153] *Brahmsfest*, pp. 89–93.

accorded an authenticity which, on examination, would have been undeserved apart from its intrinsic and doubtless very substantial merits.

The Muck saga also suggests how fragile are the purported lines of authority having the Brahms imprimatur. Given Steinbach's intimacy with Brahms and the composer's frequently expressed admiration for him, no question arises about the importance of the Steinbach 'line'.[154] On the other hand, while, as we shall see, Weingartner was busy not conducting Brahms in the early years of the twentieth century, Muck was busy in Boston and New York conducting the symphonies to the acclaim of the authoritative Richard Aldrich. In this light, tradition or lines of authority look more like accidents of history. Muck's achievements in Brahms, such as they may have been, have been lost without remark; but, for once, a felicitous chance brought Weingartner and the Berlin Philharmonic to Vienna, and to Brahms's attention, on that day in 1895 and – hey, presto! – Weingartner's Brahms is hailed, one hundred and more years later, perhaps rightly, perhaps undeservedly, as having received the laying on of hands.[155]

The patina of time and, with it, the tendency to vest the recordings of certain conductors' views of Brahms's symphonies with an authority which on close examination they may well not deserve, is a phenomenon to be more closely examined later in this chapter and in the next.

Walter Damrosch: back to Bülow

By age the next musician in this survey, Walter Damrosch (1862–1950) had claims to be well connected with Brahms. His father, Leopold (1832–85), was acquainted with Brahms, as a violinist in Germany had toured with Bülow, founded what was to become the New York Symphony Orchestra and gave the first performances in the United States of the First Symphony and the complete *German Requiem*.[156] Walter himself studied conducting with Bülow in Frankfurt for some months in 1887, concentrating on the Beethoven symphonies and other German classics.[157] His later reputation in New York perhaps suffered, rather as Sir Henry Wood's did in Britain at the same time, on account of his omnivorous workload over a long period: a workhorse rather than the inspired teacher he aspired to be. Moreover, he was wholly outgunned by other and greater holders of the baton working in New York, in particular by Anton Seidl and the many distinguished guests later appearing with the rival to the New York Symphony, the New York Philharmonic Orchestra.

---

[154] See further p. 159.
[155] But see further p. 86.
[156] George Martin, *The Damrosch Dynasty: America's First Family of Music*, Boston: Houghton Miflin, 1983 (Martin), pp. 12, 46–8, 51, 159; Avins, p. 338; Birkin, pp. 118, 129.
[157] Martin, pp. 93–7; see also Birkin, pp. 331–2.

20. WALTER DAMROSCH
IN 1908

   Nevertheless, American Columbia evidently considered his Brahms to be worth
preserving, for on 4–6 January 1928 he recorded the Second Symphony for them with
the New York Symphony. This, Damrosch's only recording of a symphony, was made
just a few months before the merger of his orchestra with the New York Philharmonic.[158] Damrosch's reading has, in parts, an unequalled velocity among recorded
performances, particularly in the first movement's development. The influence of
Bülow's methods also seems to be evident in, for example, Damrosch's treatment of
Brahms's ambiguous *quasi ritenente* at bar 118 of that movement, which he marks
with a distinct break and an extreme change of tempo. In some respects Damrosch's
interpretation has substantial similarities with Fiedler's recording, pointing perhaps
to a common influence. He did not, however, achieve Fiedler's eminence as a Brahmsian. Their relative stature is suggested by the London *Times* report of 31 March
1912 about a recent Brahms festival in New York, which, adverting to the frequent
repetition of the First Symphony that season, remarked that it had been given 'with
positive inspiration by the Boston Symphony Orchestra under Mr Max Fiedler,
whose departure at the end of this season is deeply regretted by hosts of admirers.
Mr Walter Damrosch's performance [on 25 March] was on the whole a fine one,
despite some exaggerations of tempo changes and other blemishes of detail.' In the
same report, Damrosch's handling of the Second Symphony on 30 March 'took, as
he is inclined to do, certain liberties with its tempo gradations, so that the retarda-
tions sometimes disguised the fundamental rhythmic pulse; but on the whole he

---

[158] The combined orchestra was henceforth known as the Philharmonic-Symphony Orchestra
of New York (hereafter referred to by the usual abbreviations, 'New York Philharmonic' or 'Philharmonic'). This recording was issued in the USA on Columbia set M82, CD transfer, Biddulph
WHL 053.

gave an ingratiating and vigorous performance' – not dissimilar, it seems, to his recorded performance.

Damrosch's Brahms is not considered further in this study, since he had no known direct connection with Brahms; nor is there any evidence of influence upon his style of anyone connected with the composer, other than Bülow. In New York he may well have witnessed Brahms in the hands of visiting maestros such as Steinbach, Nikisch, Weingartner and Muck, but they did not appear to have made any mark on his own stylistic approach, crystallised long before their arrival.

Felix Weingartner: 'tradition' or felicitous accident?

That performance of Brahms's second symphony – and none other

For reasons already touched upon, this conductor is one of the most important witnesses in the context of this chapter's documentation of 'lines of authority'. In 1895, when Weingartner and Brahms exchanged courtesies over his performance of the composer's Second Symphony,[159] the conductor had – at the age of just thirty-two – already ascended to the premiere conducting position in Germany. In his young days he was a frequenter of the Liszt circle and was shown exceptional regard by his mentor. He attended the first performances of *Parsifal* in 1882, the conductor Hermann Levi forever his ideal and Wagner's music thereafter, if not as performed at Bayreuth, a guiding star. Subsequently Weingartner rose rapidly through the ranks in various German opera houses, including a stint in Hamburg under Bülow during 1887–89. Famously, they did not see eye to eye on interpretative matters, in particular on the performance of Bizet's *Carmen*, in which Bülow's treatment, for his supporters, transformed it into a great and grand opera, but for Weingartner induced mirth (was Bülow making a joke at the public's expense?) at these absurdly slow tempos, the 'nonsenses', 'tricks, pauses' and 'positively ridiculous procrastination'.[160] In 1891 Weingartner was appointed Hofkapellmeister at the Berlin Royal Opera, a post he retained until 1898; he continued to conduct the symphony concerts of the opera's orchestra until 1906.

Weingartner saw Brahms conduct on at least two occasions: in the Fourth Symphony, as already described,[161] and at the Leipzig premiere of the Third Symphony on 7 February 1884. On neither occasion did he understand the work: as he put it of the earlier occasion, '*Ich verstand wenig davon*.'[162] It was all the more remarkable that he

[159] See p. 22.
[160] See Birkin, p. 333; Weingartner, *Buffets and Rewards*, p. 162; Weingartner, *Lebenserinnerungen*, vol. 1, p. 304: 'Mätzchen, Luftpausen, Nuancen'.
[161] See p. 24.
[162] *Lebenserinnerungen*, vol. 1, p. 186. As in the case of the Hamburg Fourth Symphony, *Buffets and Rewards* omits this observation.

21. FELIX WEINGARTNER IN LONDON, 1898

felt in sympathy with the Second Symphony with the result that Brahms, in writing to Fritz Simrock about the landmark Berlin Philharmonic performance witnessed by the composer in 1895, extolled the conductor, whose

> healthy and fresh personality was uncommonly appealing. [The programme] began with my symphony which he conducted from memory and quite splendidly. Even after just the first movement, the whole orchestra had to rise in thanks. The third movement had to be repeated. The performance was quite wonderful.[163]

Weingartner's acquaintance with Brahms did not end with the already quoted words of praise in the Roter Igel. They spent time in each other's company, with other friends on an outing to Schönbrunn on the day following his concert. In Brahms's speech over lunch at Schönbrunn he:

> included that praise of my conducting of his Second Symphony, which has often been printed and which is a tribute to my work as a conductor of which I am very proud. Never, he said, had he heard that work so beautifully played as the evening before. Walking arm in arm with me in the Schönbrunn Park he said to me of his own accord that I really ought to be in Vienna.[164]

Later they corresponded about this very matter and Weingartner's acquaintance with Brahms continued with a convivial evening in Berlin in company with the Joachim Quartet. That was the last occasion on which they met.[165]

Notwithstanding the conviviality, Weingartner's lack of understanding of or sympathy with Brahms's other symphonies – indeed, the greater part of Brahms's output – persisted. In early editions of his *Symphony Writers Since Beethoven*, a book based initially on a lecture given in the year of Brahms's death in 1897, we find such remarks as:

> In many other works of Brahms, as in the last two symphonies, there is, to my idea, more reflection than true artistic feeling, more of that fanciful element of cunning which was peculiar to him … [after detailing negatively some of Brahms's rhythmic and harmonic characteristics] that melodic and harmonic complexity … which results from the above-mentioned mannerisms, and which, of course, destroys the clearness of the music, is the cause of so many of Brahms's compositions giving the impression of forced and anti-natural works, that all the technical skill in the world cannot make capable of warmth. It cannot be denied, either, that precisely this complexity engenders a monotony which is absolutely foreign to a real and true simplicity … Excepting

[163] Brahms's letter to Simrock, 5 April 1895, in Avins, p. 726; see also p. 23.
[164] *Buffets and Rewards*, p. 222; *Lebenserinnerungen*, vol. 2, p. 64.
[165] *Buffets and Rewards*, p. 224; *Lebenserinnerungen*, vol. 2, p. 69.

the works which I have mentioned particularly before, when I let Brahms's music act on me insensibly, I feel the same powerless frigidity that that doctor would feel in making himself try to put life back into the dissected corpse ... His works are of an unimpeachable technical perfection, but I have only discovered a warm, palpitating feeling in very few of them ... [Most esteemed by others are the Fourth Symphony and Clarinet Quintet] which to me are loud-sounding, empty hollowness.[166]

Contrast the foregoing, written when the Wagner–Brahms disjuncture was still a moving force in music, with his remarks in the last edition:

That Brahms belongs to the unassailables is no longer in doubt today. His works force their way triumphantly ... The last two symphonies of Brahms at first did not enjoy the great success of the first two. They even disappointed quite a few ... Who will easily forget the principal theme of the first movement of the F major Symphony, stretched out in an imposing arch, or that tender and most personal second theme? Musical thoughts like these are earthbound no more; they carry us into the realm of infinity ... In the Fourth Symphony the two middle movements, for my taste, are of lesser value. The outer movements, however, are of absolutely monumental grandeur, especially the final movement.[167]

In this edition, Weingartner reserved the criticisms made in the second edition for only 'very few cases'.

As will be clear, Weingartner could not bring himself to conduct Brahms's symphonies, other than the Second, until middle age, in the second decade of the twentieth century. Moreover, his performances of the Second varied greatly because, as Flesch put it,

The effect left by his interpretations depended above all on whether he found it possible to compel the orchestra to surrender its will entirely to him. Thus his art rested primarily on psychic foundations, whereas his pure craftsmanship, both in his baton technique and in rehearsing the orchestra, was on a comparatively primitive level. His state of mind was decisive for the achievement or failure of his intentions, since purely technically he was unable to produce, up to a point, a substitute for any missing inspiration.[168]

[166] Extracts from the second German edition (*Die Symphonie nach Beethoven*), Berlin, c. 1901, transl. Arthur Bles, London: William Reeves, [1907], pp. 50–61. The lecture on which the first edition was based was given in Berlin, Bremen, Munich and Hamburg; the third edition was a totally rewritten work, appearing in 1909, the fourth, with further changes, in 1926.
[167] From 4th ed. transl. H. M. Schott for *Weingartner on Music & Conducting*, New York: Dover, 1969 (*On Music*), pp. 272–5.
[168] Flesch, p. 151.

Flesch's analysis is not in some respects the whole truth: in his maturity Weingartner consciously refined his technique to avoid all unnecessary posturing and certainly, in doing so, it was calmed to a degree – but none of the many players interviewed about him suggested that the technique was primitive: rather, 'simple' was the watchword. But what Flesch termed his 'state of mind' was, indeed, crucial: Weingartner's boredom threshold was low; if for any reason he felt to some degree disengaged, the performance suffered.[169] That was the case throughout his career, as may be inferred from the *Times* account as early as 5 May 1902, reviewing his performance of Brahms's Second Symphony at the London Music Festival on 1 May:

> [it] had its moments of real dullness, so stolid was the tempo of the first *allegro*; and even the strenuously vigorous finale left one unmoved emotionally, though one admired intensely the outward spirit of the performance. It was all very sane and very sound, but also very serious ... Brahms's symphonies are not invariably almost ponderous as Herr Weingartner seemed to imply ... In his own work [the *King Lear* Overture] Herr Weingartner seemed to throw over some of his (apparently) recently acquired stolidity.

To sum up, the written evidence discloses warm words by the composer for a performance of one work by a conductor who at the time disliked most of the others and was very variable in his conducting of the single work he did like. It is a distinctly shaky foundation on which to erect anything so solid as a 'tradition', to be contrasted with other, competing, 'traditions'. By the time that Weingartner came to conduct a broader range of Brahms's works, a large number of conductors with a direct or indirect line to the composer were, as will be obvious from this chapter, busy giving their own interpretations of his works around the world.

Weingartner's style and his recordings: how close to 1895?

Given the outlined circumstances, what is the historic significance of Weingartner's legacy of Brahms recordings and how faithfully do they reflect the conductor at his best? Here are all four symphonies, the *Haydn* Variations and the *Academic Festival* Overture recorded in the short period 1938–40 (with earlier versions of the First Symphony dating from 1923 and 1928) by a conductor who knew the composer, if not intimately (as was the case with Steinbach), at least well enough to sustain a correspondence about musical matters and to be welcomed to his company on several occasions.[170] Brahms's

---

[169] See Dyment 1976 at e.g. p. 49. Weingartner's pupil Joseph Krips recounted to me in 1972 Weingartner's need for fresh stimulus to achieve of his utmost: a routine existence tended latterly towards routine performances.

[170] For details of the recordings, see p. 168 and Dyment 1976, 'Recording Sessions', pp. 72 *et seq.*

applause for Weingartner's handling of one of his greatest creations was the first and only instance of such a direct link with a conductor who later recorded it: as we have noted, nothing survives of the equally strong link with Weingartner's polar opposite, Nikisch, and no extant evidence links Brahms with Fiedler in the same way. Such gaps in the evidence may suggest that Weingartner's exceptional position is simply fortuitous and mere happenstance: if, say, Steinbach and Nikisch had been as long-lived as Weingartner (dying therefore in 1934), our knowledge of their stylistic approaches might well have been transformed through the medium of recorded sound; so, too, would their positions as standard bearers of Brahmsian 'traditions'. But whatever reservations there may be about the labelling of Weingartner as the representative of a distinct line of authority for his Brahms performances, the almost universal respect in which he was long held as *the* archetypal Viennese Classicist – a perception founded on his conductorship of the Philharmonic from 1908 to 1927 and many appearances thereafter – demands that the recordings, if regarded as reliable documents of Weingartner's lifelong approach to Brahms, be taken seriously as statements of the works which demonstrate a style having an attested link with the composer.

But, before assessing what it was that the composer heard in that performance of his Second Symphony, the essential elements of Weingartner's stylistic approach as a whole and possible changes to it during the course of his career need close consideration, a task not helped by Flesch's attention to psychological rather than musical factors. We have already noted the shock, and relief, of critics in London on their first encounter in 1898 with Weingartner's purity of style, an approach so clearly at odds with Mottl's ever-present, characteristic *tempo rubato*. A few years later it fell once more to Richard Aldrich to analyse that style, as he heard it during one of Weingartner's many visits to the United States before the Great War, on the occasion when the conductor led the New York Philharmonic on 10 February 1905:

> Weingartner has … the power of possessing himself of [the music's] spirit and of embodying it in a perfectly balanced, symmetrical and finished whole. With a keenly analytic power there goes hand in hand a warm, poetic feeling … His effects are fine and delicate, and there is the subtlest sense of proportion and of finish in the adjustment and the color of every phrase; and this he accomplishes without losing sight of the larger outlines of the whole … Everything is elaboration with the presence, almost, it might be said, the divination of one who has seen straight and seen clear to the bottom of it all – dynamic gradation, rhythm and accent, the plastic expression of theme, the delicate modification of tempo. But with this subtlety of finish there is withal the pulsing throb of life, a poignant intensity of spirit.[171]

---

[171] Aldrich, p. 94, 11 February; this programme contained various overtures and works by Liszt and Weingartner himself.

Aldrich's analysis suggests a more interventionist conductor than Weingartner was later to become, even if the essentials remained unchanged.

A more familiar picture starts to emerge with the portrait in the *Musical Times* in 1923 by Britain's foremost critic of the era, Ernest Newman. His close analysis marked the occasion of Weingartner's return to London after the Great War for a series of concerts with the LSO.

> Weingartner's readings are like himself – lean, taut, sinewy, sparing of gesture, contemptuous of mere peacoquetry – incomparably clear headed, with an intellectual lucidity that of itself [is] an emotional joy, as a fine demonstration in philosophy or science sometimes is, dignified, sincere, and enormously impressive for all his lack of ostentation … What Weingartner mostly does is to give the music its head, but with perfect control of it and the wisest guidance of it. So little does he interfere with the natural 'step' of the rhythm, that a superficial listener might be forgiven for believing his beat to be merely metronomic. But if you are curious enough to test him on this point over, say, a hundred bars, you will find that the pulse of the music is subtly varying its pace all the time. The steadiness is anything but dead uniformity. And the steadiness comes from that admirable intellectual control that, in any given bar, keeps in view the land so far traversed and the land still to be traversed; over the whole of the work – in a symphony especially, over the whole work, not merely each movement – runs that big containing line [that is] the ideal and the secret of good design.[172]

The picture of a conductor who was simultaneously immersed in the music but seemingly viewing it with a certain Olympian detachment became more obvious with the passage of decades, during which his London concerts frequently featured one or another of all the Brahms symphonies. His last Queen's Hall concert in February 1940, just before the hall was destroyed by wartime bombing, contained once more the Brahms Second Symphony on the eve of his recording of the work. Weingartner's pupil Stewart Deas summed up the qualities he heard in this concert:

> Weingartner has a peculiar power of becoming detached from a work even while he is in the midst of conducting it … This detachment is, of course, a quality which has become more pronounced in recent years, but … it is that which has always made his command over the orchestra so absolutely unquestionable. He never becomes entangled with the music. He is always its master but a kind and sympathetic master who has no need to assert his authority.[173]

---

[172] *Musical Times* vol. 64 1 July 1923 p. 503. Newman (1869–1959) was the *Sunday Times* music critic from 1921–58.
[173] Dyment 1976, Steward Deas, 'Weingartner as Teacher' p. 29. Deas attended Weingartner's conducting class in Basle 1928–9 and later was professor of music at Sheffield University.

22. WEINGARTNER
CONDUCTS, BASLE,
1935

Taking account, then, of the subtle changes of style noted by these eminent observers, to what degree is it possible to assert that what Brahms heard in 1895 was that which was later preserved by the gramophone? Indeed, how far do any of Weingartner's recordings, not just those of Brahms, reflect the conductor in concert? This last question raises a host of problems, some of them technical in character, which must all be tackled in order to arrive at a feasible answer about the Second Symphony. The first and most obvious problem: to compare Weingartner on record and in concert is impossible in the absence of an adequate number of live concert recordings. The one extant recording of value in this context is the off-air Vienna Philharmonic rendition of Beethoven's *Eroica* Symphony from the Salzburg Festival on 11 August 1935, which discloses several differences from his recording made with that orchestra in May 1936.[174] For example, the latter's sudden broadening of tempo at bar 45 in the first movement is less noticeable in concert, while the sequence of great chords near the end of the first movement's exposition, taken strictly *a tempo* in the 1936 recording, are in concert very slightly spaced out, more a matter of emphasis than tempo. In the second movement, in concert Weingartner ignores his own advice not to speed up the major section sequence starting with the oboe theme (bar 69) to a

---

[174] The EMI/Columbia recording was made in the Grosser Musikvereinssaal, Vienna on 22–23 May 1936 and issued on Columbia LX 532–7, frequently reissued on CD. The Salzburg Festival concert recording has some extreme pitch problems and has never been commercially issued.

markedly greater extent than in the Columbia recording.[175] If the live *Eroica* is typical
of differences between Weingartner in concert and in the recording studio, as these
two performances suggest, then the Columbia recordings of the symphonic repertoire
as a whole should not be taken to be a full portrayal of Weingartner in concert – and,
hence, not to be a consistently reliable guide to what Brahms encountered in that 1895
performance of his Second Symphony.

Secondly, Weingartner's changes of approach in the case of multiple recordings of
the same work also create problems: if, say, the differences of tempo taken for the
second movement of Brahms's First Symphony over the fifteen years separating his
first recording of this work in 1923/24 and his last in 1939 are typical of Weingartner's
developing stance – 7:27 in 1924, 8:52 in 1939[176] – how can we be at all positive in
asserting that his 1940 recording of the Second Symphony is a solid guide to what
Brahms heard forty-five years before? Again, no certain answer can be given. Only
Weingartner's conscious pride in the praise bestowed by Brahms can be called in aid
to suggest that major changes in his interpretation over the years would have been
unlikely – that, and the evidence supplied by reviews spanning the decades of his concert performances of the work.

Thirdly, another query lies in the restrictions imposed by the recording process,
where the conductor was aware that he had just four minutes per side to expound his
vision, fractured into several parts whenever a symphonic movement took more than
one 78rpm side. To the often-posed question whether this affected the results among
conductors recording symphonic movements spanning several 78rpm sides, one can
readily infer in Weingartner's case both in general and in particular that he was willing to make slight adjustments in his tempos for the recording studio to ensure that
the music occupied the requisite number of sides. Weingartner was very conscious of
his position as a premier exponent of the major symphonic repertoire and wished to
ensure that posterity, in the shape of the gramophone record, was aware of his stature.
His correspondence with EMI in the 1930s frequently shows him urging the completion of his Beethoven symphony cycle and the recording of other major specialities of
his, such as Schubert's Great C Major Symphony. As he remarked in a letter dated 29
July 1934 to EMI, 'Don't forget that I am 71 years old, and after my death you cannot
make records with me.'[177]

---

[175] See Weingartner's *On the Performance of Beethoven's Symphonies* in *On Music*, p. 103.

[176] The LSO recording of the First Symphony was made by Columbia on 28 November 1923
(first movement) and 21 March 1924 (movements 2–4) and issued on L 1596–1600; for details
of the 1939 recording, see p. 168. The space available on the original discs suggests that shortage
of time was not a factor leading to the differing tempos.

[177] EMI archives, which contain a substantial cache of Weingartner's mostly hand-written letters
to various EMI personnel, including F. W. (Fred) Gaisberg (1873–1951), HMV/EMI impresario
and recording manager, and Rex Palmer (1896–1972), then general manager of the International Artistes' Department. See further Dyment 2012 pp. 58–9.

23. WEINGARTNER AND EMI
IMPRESARIO FRED GAISBERG:
A PRESENTATION, PROBABLY
ON COMPLETION OF THE
CONDUCTOR'S BEETHOVEN
SYMPHONY CYCLE IN 1938

On occasion he considered whether tempos might be adjusted for recording purposes; for example, he rejected a suggestion that he record Beethoven's *King Stephen* Overture on one 78rpm side: with the score he had experimented with the fastest possible tempo but, he informed the EMI's artists manager Rex Palmer in a letter dated 9 August 1938, it 'came quite near to six minutes'. But once in the studio, he ensured by his rapid and co-operative method of working that the maximum was recorded in the time allowed. So, in one instance, when about to record the Brahms First Symphony in February 1939, the producer (in this instance Fred Gaisberg) invited him to rehearse; Weingartner replied: 'Rehearse! What we want to rehearse for? The orchestra know this symphony and I think I know it. We make a record.'[178] It is clear that Weingartner was an old man in a hurry: amazingly, he recorded both Mozart's Symphony No. 39 and Brahms's Symphony No. 2 in one day, 26 February 1940, and he worked intensively with EMI to make as many possible recordings in the limited time he probably thought would be available to him.

The technical evidence from Weingartner's recording sessions suggests that, if he made some compromises in relation to tempos for some of his recordings, especially

[178] Dyment 1976, p. 40 (recollections of Ralph Nicholson, LSO violinist).

in the early part of his recording career, latterly such compromises were not needed. The most obvious example of the early practice lies in his three electric recordings of Beethoven's Fifth Symphony, where we observe Weingartner expanding the time taken over the second movement as the recording process became more sophisticated, from a two-sided 7:32 in 1927, when the process and speed were erratic, via a more reliable 8:35 in 1932, to 9:47 in 1933, when engineers at last permitted the second movement to occupy more than two sides, with the beginning of the third movement included in the latter half of the third side; quite possibly this was the tempo Weingartner wanted all along.[179] This device was used in some of his late recordings, including Brahms's Third and Fourth Symphonies, to ensure that his recorded performance was aligned as closely as possible with his favoured tempos.

There is just one possible exception to that conclusion, unfortunately in the finale of the very symphony that Brahms heard Weingartner conduct. Stewart Deas remarked that his recording of the Second Symphony was for the most part characteristic, but he disagreed with the tempo of the finale as recorded: 'I find it difficult to believe that when he conducted it in Brahms's presence he took it at such a headlong speed ... I can honestly say I never heard him take it at such a hurried tempo.'[180] Possibly, therefore, the 78rpm time constraints may have played a part in Weingartner's mind when making the recording, which lasts a few seconds under eight minutes. There are, however, several arguments against that view. First, evidence about early performances of the work suggests an eight-minute span was not unusual, including Richter's in the premiere of the symphony.[181] As will be seen, Fritz Busch's first recording of the work took a precisely similar view, although the *Times* dissented from its pacing when he conducted the work in London a few years later.[182] So it may well be that, if Weingartner was in a hurry here, he was only marginally so.

Technical evidence also supports this view. On 29 February 1940, three days after recording the Second Symphony and in his last recording session, Weingartner, again with the LPO, recorded the *Academic Festival* Overture, an unhurried and superbly cohesive performance lasting nine and a half minutes, but fitted nonetheless on two

---

[179] Columbia recordings of the Beethoven Fifth Symphony (excluding the pre-electric version made with the LSO in November 1924): RPO, recorded 28–29 January 1927, issued L 1880–83; (?)British SO, recorded 17–18 March 1932, issued American Columbia 68078D–68081D; LPO, recorded 31 January–2 February 1933, issued DX 516–19. The conclusion about Weingartner's later recordings is supported by the timings of the *Allegretto* of Beethoven's Seventh Symphony in Weingartner's two electrical recordings: the recordings of the RPO in January 1927 (L 1898–1902) and the VPO in February 1936 (LX 484–8) are virtually identical in timing, even though the earlier recording used three 78rpm (actually widely varying around that mark) sides and the later one only two – the greater available time had no effect on Weingartner's tempo.

[180] Dyment 1976, Stewart Deas, 'Weingartner as Teacher', p. 28.

[181] See n. 21.

[182] See p. 142.

78rpm sides; there appears, therefore, to have been no time constraint in completing the symphony's last movement on two sides. In any event, had extra space and time been needed, it could have been found by reducing the recording space allotted to the third movement, the five minutes of which are spread extravagantly over two sides, thereby giving ample time for the start of the finale if such groove space had been required. These technical details suggest that, if Weingartner had wanted to take a slower tempo, that requirement could have been met quite readily.

That inference is underlined by a variety of accounts describing his performances of the symphony as a whole. For example, in 1922 Boult caught him in the Second Symphony, a January concert in Prague with Talich's orchestra, and the First Symphony, an April concert with the Vienna Philharmonic, of which he wrote in his notebook, 'he took the C minor fast, but the playing of the orchestra, who obviously knew it by heart, never let clearness be sacrificed, as was the case when he did the D major in Prague – they hadn't time to straighten out anything'; clearly too fast in the latter, if not in both, for Boult's taste.[183]

London critics, at least in the 1920s when the LSO was in far from its best estate, tended to agree with Boult.[184] A few examples from their assessments also provide an overview of Weingartner's stature as seen at the time. The day after an LSO concert in the Queen's Hall on 22 April 1926, the *Times* remarked that,

> It is not necessary to insist on the effortless fertility of the ideas in Brahms's No. 2, but their magical growth has never been more apparent than in [this] performance … It was not entirely ideal; it would take more rehearsal than London orchestras get to make everything sound clear and easy at the quick *tempo* which Herr Weingartner adopts for the first and last movements. But it was intensely alive …

In reviewing another performance ten years later, on 16 January 1936 – an all Brahms concert (the *Tragic* Overture and Symphonies Nos. 2 and 3) sponsored by the Royal Philharmonic Society with the LPO – the next day's *Times* showed a congruence with Stewart Deas's view:

> It was this command of line … that distinguished last night's performances, making Brahms's music as euphonious as it is coherent. The most obvious instance of the conductor's art was [Weingartner's] handling of the Allegretto in the Second Symphony, which was not only played with a consummate virtuosity, but was so exactly timed and so finely shaped in detail that one *tempo* merged into the next without any perceptible jolt, and in the pauses one could feel the rhythm carrying on. So it was in

[183] Kennedy, p. 87.
[184] See Dyment 2012, pp. 11–15.

all these unhurried, spacious performances, which were brought to a splendid and
fiery climax in the final movement of the Second Symphony.

The *Times* critics evidently heard in these two performances of the Second Symphony
something closely resembling what is to be heard in the recording, including that 'fiery'
finale. There is also some force in the far from conclusive view adumbrated above that
Weingartner's latter-day performances of the work would not have changed markedly
from the performance in 1895 on which Brahms bestowed his approval, because of his
first-hand and internalised knowledge of just what it was that the composer approved.
Further than that it is not possible to go.

The performance history of Weingartner's renditions of other works by Brahms is
shorter than that of the Second Symphony and one can at best do no more than guess
that these, too, might have had the composer's imprimatur had he ever heard them.
All this is slender material on which to found anything so grand as a 'tradition' or any
line of authority somehow in contrast to other modes of performance countenanced
by Brahms. At best, Weingartner's recorded performances of Brahms's Second Symphony in particular, and of the symphonies in general, stand as an example of just
one out of the range of performance styles that, more likely than not, the composer
would have been prepared to acknowledge as a valid interpretative approach. Given
Weingartner's considerable posthumous reputation as the embodiment of Classical
rectitude, that conclusion is of substantial significance and merits the more detailed
examination of his recordings undertaken in the next chapter.[185] Further, the posthumous stature of Weingartner's reputation and its standing today require at least a
summary investigation.

Posthumous Weingartner: pupils and a reawakening

Weingartner's pedagogic inclinations, manifest in the tracts from which quotations
have already been given, found their ultimate outlet in his annual conducting classes
at the Basle Conservatoire during his years with the Basle orchestra, 1927–35. Distinguished as some of his pupils in these classes were to become, one would look in vain
among them for any with a particular standing in the music of Brahms: such well-
known names as Paul Sacher (1906–99) and Alberto Erede (1909–2001), both alumni
of the 1928–29 class, founded their later reputations elsewhere. Andrzej Panufnik
(1914–1991) also took conducting lessons from Weingartner in 1937 but from 1956
until his death was known more or less exclusively as a composer.

Other well-known figures who could claim Weingartner as teacher before the
institution of the Basle classes did, however, achieve some distinction in the Viennese

---

[185] See p. 162.

classics, including the symphonies of Brahms. Ernest Ansermet (1883–1969) said that he had had only 'a few' lessons with Weingartner in his year of study in Berlin before his debut in 1910, but in that year he watched the methods of all the great conductors appearing there.[186] His recordings of the Brahms symphonies possess integrity, strength, directness and, nearly always, mobility, with a consistent aim to clarify the essential melodic line and avoid superfluous rhetoric; the first movement of the Fourth Symphony is a distinguished example, where Ansermet seems to draw on the Weingartner precedent. Elsewhere, although the qualities mentioned have their counterpart in Weingartner's performances, there is little or no evidence of a direct influence. If, for example, Weingartner's introduction to the First Symphony moves swiftly, Ansermet's is heavy in the extreme; a similar comparison may be made between their performances of the Second Symphony's finale.[187]

Josef Krips (1902–74) had far more prolonged contact with Weingartner, commencing in his years assisting the latter during his tenure of the Vienna Volksoper from 1919 to 1924. Krips's recordings of the First Symphony with the Vienna Philharmonic and the Fourth Symphony with the LSO, made when he was perhaps at the high point of his career, show some of Weingartner's rhythmic rectitude and freedom from eccentricity but, lacking Weingartner's driving tempos and rigour, suggest a more easy-going, quintessentially Viennese approach.[188]

More rewarding than these diluted specimens of their master's voice is the conscious return to Weingartner as one source for an historically informed approach to the composer adopted by some conductors from late in the twentieth century onwards. The first to do so was Roger Norrington, who commenced his recorded cycle of the Brahms symphonies with his period instrument orchestra, the London Classical Players, in 1990. By 2012 the Weingartner influence had extended to the modern symphony orchestra in the shape of Riccardo Chailly's performances and recording of the cycle with the Leipzig Gewandhaus Orchestra. These developments are further considered in Chapter 4.[189] At this stage it suffices to observe that, as a consequence of these developments, Weingartner's name and reputation are now more familiar to the musical public than they have been for half a century.

---

[186] See interview in the *Times*, 9 December 1963; in this Ansermet said that he was otherwise self-taught, although he had watched the rehearsals of, among others, Nikisch, Mottl and Richard Strauss.

[187] Symphonies Nos. 1–4 recorded in the Victoria Hall, Geneva, with L'Orchestre de la Suisse Romande in February 1963, CD transfer Decca Eloquence 480 0448.

[188] Symphony No. 1 recorded in the Sofiensaal, Vienna, October 1956, and Symphony No. 4 recorded in the Kingsway Hall, London, April 1950, CD issue Decca Eloquence 480 4325.

[189] See p. 230.

Arturo Toscanini: Brahms from Italy via Munich

Brahms in Toscanini's career: Steinbach as exemplar

With the witness of Arturo Toscanini (1867–1957), we leave behind those conductors who could claim a direct link with the composer. Yet, far from Vienna or Hamburg though Toscanini was in his younger days, Brahms's works virtually book-ended his career as a concert conductor. The *Tragic* Overture was among the works in his first ever full-length orchestral concert on 20 March 1896 with the orchestra of the Turin opera, which he led at that time; included at the suggestion of his Brahms-loving friend (shortly to become his brother-in-law), the orchestra's concertmaster, Enrico Polo,[190] this performance was its Italian premiere. He repeated the work in his first engagement with La Scala forces in a series of four concerts one month later. Toscanini's last concert was to have been a performance on 4 April 1954 of the *German Requiem* with Elisabeth Schwarzkopf as soprano soloist; his infirmity led him to substitute familiar Wagner orchestral excerpts for a formidable work he had not conducted since 1943.[191] As it was, once more the *Tragic* Overture was the final piece by Brahms programmed by Toscanini, with the NBC Symphony Orchestra, on 23 November 1953.[192]

Two years after his concert debut Toscanini conducted a gigantic series of forty-four concerts with his Turin orchestra at the international exposition in Turin, commencing on 28 May 1898 and ending, after a six-week break in July–August, on 31 October. The concerts contained over two hundred works, some repeated, by composers dead and alive, including the first performances in Italy of Brahms's Second and Fourth Symphonies. At that stage Toscanini was probably uninfluenced by anyone else in performing these works: he was, after all, the pioneer within Italy. He programmed the two symphonies and subsequently the *Haydn* Variations on several occasions in the series of orchestral concerts with which he ended each season during the years he was conductor at La Scala (1898–1903, 1906–08 and 1921–29). The First Symphony joined his repertoire in a series of New York Philharmonic concerts in November 1930 and the Third Symphony in a similar series in October 1929 (as, in that month, did the Double Concerto).

Here I digress to portray in outline Toscanini's engagement in musical and non-musical artistic matters since, even during his lifetime and more frequently in recent years, some portrayals have suggested a musician both unaffected by and unreceptive of any influence exterior to his native land and monomaniacally centred upon the study of the score, an 'idiot savant' unlettered in literature, with no eye for the visual

---

[190] See further Fig. 24 and n. 205.
[191] See Dyment 2012, p. 230, n. 56.
[192] In RCA's current (2015) complete CD edition of Toscanini's RCA recordings, vol. 7, 88697916312-07.

arts and almost wilfully ignorant of the musical practices of his Austro-German contemporaries.[193] Taking first arts other than music, in the course of a long life Toscanini
became immensely widely read in several languages. As his biographer Harvey Sachs
has explained, his knowledge of Classical and Romantic literature was profound. He
had learned most of Dante and a good deal of Shakespeare (in English) by heart, and
nineteenth-century Italian writers were his constant companions. He read in Italian,
Latin, English, French and, with greater difficulty, German, and his reading included
the French and Russian novelists. His letters to his many female admirers often quoted
from his vast memory of literature, and in one he described his current reading 'with
those dear spirits named Dante, Shakespeare, Shelley, Keats and [Benedetto] Croce'.
Toscanini was on friendly terms with H. G. Wells, Thomas Mann, Stefan Zweig and
many other writers among his contemporaries. His knowledge of the visual arts
was also substantial and he once said 'I don't know whether I like music or paint-
ing better'.[194] The conductor's large and passionately treasured collection of Italian
Divisionist painters, among whom their leader, Vittore Grubicy de Dragon, became
an intimate friend, was given a special exhibition in New York and Livorno in 2007.
While Toscanini had no claim to be an 'intellectual', his cultural baggage was clearly
as great as virtually all his musical contemporaries and, indeed, more weighty than,
for example, Nikisch's, whose sole interests apart from music lay in 'cards, women and
company'.[195]

   At the turn of the twentieth century some of Toscanini's literary and artistic passions doubtless lay in the future, but from his earliest days he evinced the same catholic
engagement in his musical explorations. By the time he crossed Europe to reach London for Mottl's *Götterdämmerung* in June 1900, as recounted above,[196] he had already
visited Bayreuth on at least three occasions: in 1894 to witness Levi's last performances
of *Parsifal*, in 1897 for Mottl's performances of that work and in 1899 to attend both
Franz Fischer's *Parsifal* and Richter's *Die Meistersinger*.[197] While he commended Levi's
Parsifal above all others he had ever heard (none of the others had Levi's 'elasticity'),
he was frustrated by the quality of some of the performances; this did not prevent him

---

[193] See, for a recent example, Brown, p. 320.
[194] This paragraph is based on Harvey Sachs, 'About That Man Toscanini', in Renato Miracco
(ed.) *Maestro's Secret Music: The Artworks Collected by Arturo Toscanini*, catalogue of the 2007
exhibition, New York and Livorno: Mazotta, 2007, pp. 24–6. An example of Toscanini's delight in
literature was his study of a volume of John Clare's poetry, hitherto unknown to him, just prior
to a picnic outing in countryside near London in the late 1930s; over the picnic, he declaimed by
memory and with huge enjoyment large chunks of the verse he had read just a few hours before:
Dyment 2012, p. 165.
[195] See Flesch, p. 148.
[196] See p. 51.
[197] The evidence for the two earliest visits to Bayreuth lies in taped conversations with Toscanini
during his retirement, discovered by Harvey Sachs.

from returning in 1902, probably for Muck's *Parsifal* and Richter's *Ring* cycle.[198] At the Turin expositions of 1904–05 he again encountered Richter, whose *Eroica* strongly influenced him in his early approach to Beethoven, and also other distinguished Austro-German conductors such as Max Fiedler and Felix Weingartner.[199] Later in the decade came Nikisch – 'was *good* conductor but sometimes unprepared' (an accurate observation) – Schuch in Dresden and, during his time with the Metropolitan Opera in New York (1908–15), Muck's Boston orchestra in Beethoven: the orchestra was good but Muck was 'Beckmesser of conductors', his tempos in Beethoven's First Symphony 'so slow'.[200] Such comments made later in life indicate that Toscanini took from the Austro-German exemplars only what he needed and was not afraid to remark on the emperors' apparent lack of clothing when he felt justified in doing so.

But there was one conductor among his seniors whom he never criticised and always praised. On vacation before returning to the Metropolitan Opera in the autumn of 1909, he visited Munich for Steinbach's Brahms Festival given on 10–14 September. After the first two of Steinbach's lengthy programmes on 10 and 11 September,[201] he sent a postcard dated 12 September to Polo: 'How I wish you had been here these [last few] days! I have enjoyed myself beyond words. Brahms is great. Steinbach marvellous (*meraviglioso*).' As his La Scala biographer, Guglielmo Barblan, posed rhetorically, when did Toscanini ever repeat that epithet about any colleague so eminent?[202] What is yet more remarkable was Toscanini's lifelong consistency. We have noted his awareness of the eminent Austro-German conductors senior to him in years; he heard them all and appraised them variously. Only for Steinbach did he always profess unqualified admiration to the end of his career. When, as already noted, Fritz Busch distanced himself from those seeking to denigrate Steinbach, he thought it sufficient answer to call in aid Toscanini's enthusiasm for Steinbach's Brahms performances, no doubt expressed when they were often together in the 1930s; according to Fritz, the Italian conductor considered some of Steinbach's readings the most beautiful he had ever heard.

During Toscanini's last visit to London in September–October 1952, to conduct two concerts with the Philharmonia Orchestra in what was to be his last Brahms cycle (the four symphonies, the *Tragic* Overture and the *Haydn* Variations), his admiration for Steinbach surfaced again in rehearsals, when he recollected Steinbach's brilliant pacing of the fifth *Haydn* Variation[203] and asked the orchestra for his own *bis* – evoking admiring applause from the Philharmonia players. In conversation with the orchestra's impresario, Walter Legge, Toscanini complained that, despite repeated

---

[198] See Dyment 2012, p. 5 and n. 10, and p. 7 and n. 13.
[199] *Ibid.* p. 236.
[200] *Ibid.* p. 238.
[201] See p. 36.
[202] Guglielmo Barblan, *Toscanini e La Scala*, Milan: Edizioni della Scala, 1972, p. 174.
[203] See p. 37.

24. ARTURO TOSCANINI IN TURIN, 1911. ON HIS LEFT ENRICO POLO;
ON HIS RIGHT HIS DAUGHTER WALLY AND WIFE CARLA (PARTLY
OBSCURED); ON THE EXTREME LEFT GIUSEPPE DEPANIS, DIRECTOR OF
THE TEATRO REGIO, TURIN

attempts, he could never bring off the Third Symphony as he had heard Steinbach do
– even though Legge thought his Philharmonia performance of that work the greatest
performance of anything he had ever heard.[204]

Still more significant than these expressions of view was an incident that occurred
only a couple of years after Toscanini's attendance at the 1909 Munich Festival. The
story starts in September 1911, when Steinbach came to Turin to conduct Brahms's
Second Symphony. Steinbach's concert was one of many, including five conducted by
Toscanini himself and others by such distinguished names as Debussy, Elgar, Kajanus
and Mengelberg, given at Turin's International Exposition.[205] In preparation for
Steinbach's arrival, Toscanini rehearsed the orchestra in the Brahms symphony and,
after playing it through with them, Steinbach remarked, 'I have nothing to do. Who

[204] Dyment 2012, pp. 221–2.
[205] Fig. 24 dates from this time. Enrico Polo (1868–1953), graduate, like Toscanini, of the Parma
Conservatoire, completed his studies under Joachim in Berlin (1893–95) and was instrumental
in enthusing Toscanini for the music of Brahms when the conductor was music director at
the Teatro Regio, Turin, 1895–97. Polo later devoted his career to teaching in the Milan Conservatoire. Giuseppe Depanis (1853–1942) was responsible for securing Toscanini's services as
conductor at the Teatro Regio in 1895; together with Arrigo Boito, who recommended Toscanini
as the music director at La Scala two years later, he boosted the conductor's already burgeoning
Italian career more than anyone else. He helped organise the Turin Exposition concerts in 1911,
inviting Toscanini to conduct.

is your conductor?' The answer, of course, was Toscanini, who quietly recounted this anecdote in response to Furtwängler when, on 16 June 1924, after a La Scala concert in Zürich, the latter berated him for mishandling the symphony.[206] Rudolph Serkin, who found the performance he had just heard an 'incredible revelation', was, with his equally enthralled musical partner Adolf Busch, an eyewitness to this exchange, describing Toscanini's meek submission ('like a little boy') to Furtwängler's 'violent and embarrassing' diatribe. Perhaps Toscanini would have been rather less polite had he been aware of recent Berlin comment criticising Furtwängler for taking un-Brahmsian liberties in this very work.[207]

A changing style

Toscanini's handling of Brahms did, of course, change over the years and, so inured are contemporary writers to the taut and austere style of the aged Maestro with the often harshly recorded NBC orchestra, it takes some effort to pin down his overall approach at the time of the events recounted here. Let two attempts suffice: one from the era of Steinbach's visit to Turin, the other from a later period, a few years after Toscanini's encounter with Furtwängler. Among early writers describing Toscanini's attributes, the American critic Max Smith was one of the most enthusiastic, making much of the Toscanini personality and methods in a long essay dating from 1913.[208] Of more permanent interest, however, he also attempted to convey a detailed analysis of the musical process he observed at the Metropolitan Opera, where Toscanini was principal conductor from 1908–15. Expanding at length on Toscanini's 'imaginative grasp of the movements best suited to express the emotional import of the score', Smith continued:

> His feeling for tempo, indeed, is one of Toscanini's most extraordinary gifts; for under his sway the metrical ebb and flow ... sweeping in waves now broad and placid,

[206] Robert Jacobson, *Reverberations: Interviews with the World's Leading Musicians*, New York: William Morrow, 1974, p. 203, cited also by B. H. Haggin, *Music & Ballet 1973–1983*, New York: Horizon, 1984, p. 227 (without attribution), and Potter, pp. 350–1. Adolf Busch relayed his impressions in a letter to his brother Fritz (see p. 146). No doubt he later told him of the exchange between Toscanini and Furtwängler – hence its inclusion (without reference to the latter) in Fritz Busch, p. 48, where Fritz mistakenly refers to the work in question as the *Haydn Variations*. See also Harvey Sachs, *Toscanini*, London: Weidenfeld & Nicholson, 1978 (Sachs 1978), pp. 115–16.

[207] See p. 137 and Shirakawa, p. 49.

[208] T. Max Smith (1874–1935), music critic for the *New York Press* (1903–16) and the *New York American* (1916–19 and 1923) and a foreign music correspondent for the *New York Herald Tribune*; latterly a friend and business associate of the Toscanini family. The extracts quoted are from Max Smith, 'Toscanini at the Baton', *The Century*, vol. 85 (1913), pp. 691–701.

now light and fluent, now wildly propulsive and turbulent, creates the impression of something inevitable. His rhythm is always articulate … Even the fluctuating and irregular pulsations of 'rubato' – and what a master of rubato Toscanini is! – rise and fall on a heaving groundswell of rhythm. The unity and cohesion of Toscanini's musical perspectives, the perfect adjustment of one part to another, is striking … the most clashing contrasts are dovetailed into a seamless and homogeneous whole. His crescendos are models of dynamic ascension, set at exactly the right angle from the outset, no matter how distant the summit, and beautifully graduated from start to finish; his accelerandos are as accurately calculated as though they were impelled by the force of gravity. In the most delicately interlaced network of tones … no meshes hang loose. Every filament is as closely related to those that are not yet disclosed as it is to the threads that are not already spun. And as the impressions roll by, vitalized by a temperament that spans the whole gamut of human feelings … one realizes that Toscanini has not been revealing merely a rapid succession of pictures … but a single gigantic canvas projected on the memory through the wide-angled lens of his mind.

Smith spared no adjectives, but the emerging musical portrait is a recognisable reflection of the conductor. Particularly relevant in the present context is Smith's emphasis on elements of Toscanini's style at the time, such as the mastery of a frequently used *rubato*,[209] which generations of those familiar with his work only through his late recordings would be less willing to acknowledge.

Smith was describing Toscanini in the opera house. For a view of him in the concert hall, let us fast-forward to Neville Cardus's portrait of the conductor (part of an obituary article written in 1957) as he remembered him at the time of the New York Philharmonic's four London concerts in June 1930, which concluded the orchestra's tour of Europe under the Maestro's direction:

Once upon a time, and within the memory of the present writer, it was Weingartner who represented a classic objectivity in conducting, while Toscanini was made the rallying-ground for young musicians eager for freedom of utterance and liberty to go adventuring among the masterpieces. We respected Toscanini's scrupulous regard for the blue-print of a composition … but we were [also] conquered by the passion of Toscanini that went into his conducting, the singing line, the Italianate nuances and flavours. London's first experience of Toscanini was in 1930, when he conducted the New York Philharmonic Orchestra … He enchanted us in the second symphony of Brahms by phrasing songful and elastic. There was as yet no rigidity. Here was the Toscanini *bel canto*. Brahms suffered a sea-change into music rich and evocative in the memory. In his period of increasing years and increasing American influence,

---

[209] What is meant by this term at that time is discussed further at p. 155.

25. TOSCANINI IN 1913

Toscanini began to harden the music of Brahms. The *gemütlichkeit* of Brahms went out of his interpretations.[210]

There we have the perception of change, again colourfully described – but Cardus was wrong about 'hardening' and American influence. Toscanini's changing view of Brahms and the rest of the Classical repertoire stemmed rather from his increasingly certain belief that the slow tempos favoured by his Austro-German coevals were simply wrong – a view now generally shared among 'authenticist' interpreters. Quickening tempos also reflected a passionate response, at least during the years 1933–40, to his deep emotional entanglement with his mistress Ada Mainardi.[211]

In addition, from 1937 onwards Toscanini felt himself to be under the overwhelmingly rigid pressure of NBC's timetabling of concerts – one second late and he would be cut off. Did he, one wonders, hear Fritz Reiner, Lotte Lehmann, Flagstad et al., who suffered that infamous broadcast cut-off in the last pages of *Die Walküre* Act 2 in San Francisco on 29 November 1936? At the back of his mind, operating on it in many a broadcast, was this fear, driving him to ensure that he never overran his time; nor did he.[212] So, irrespective of any loss of Cardus's *Gemütlichkeit* – probably never a component of Toscanini's Brahms and arguably not of Brahms's symphonies either – there is no doubt that his performances in general tended towards an increased velocity and austerity of approach, particularly during his NBC years (1937–54), although that tendency did not run in a straightforward line during the second half of his career (1920–54) as documented in recorded sound: there were many exceptions, byways and backward glances between one performance and another.

Toscanini's Brahms: critiques of his early performances

The evolution of Toscanini's style makes it inevitable that any search for traces of a Steinbach influence in his performances of Brahms must concentrate on his early performances, so far back as they may be documented. From this viewpoint, we do have some idea of the impact of Toscanini's Brahms from Richard Aldrich and his successor, Olin Downes, who evidently agreed on their lack of enthusiasm for Toscanini's performances of the Second Symphony in the 1920s.[213] When Toscanini toured the USA and

---

[210] Neville Cardus, 'Toscanini: Some After-thoughts', in Evan Senior (ed.), *The Concert-Goer's Annual No. 1*, London: John Calder, 1957, pp. 81–4 at p. 83. Sir Neville Cardus (1889–1975) was the *Manchester Guardian* music critic from 1927 to 1939 and again from 1951. For details of the London concerts and their reception, see Dyment 2012, pp. 21–30.

[211] For more about these aspects of Toscanini's interpretations, see Dyment 2012, pp. 39, 238–9.

[212] For this insight into this aspect of Toscanini's broadcasts, I am indebted to Richard Caniell for his detailed information.

[213] Olin Downes (1886–1955), music critic of the *New York Times* 1924–55, who became an enthusiastic but – as these extracts from his reviews demonstrate – not uncritical admirer of Toscanini.

Canada in his vast cross-continental tours with the orchestra of La Scala in the winter of 1920–21 (for the purposes of that tour the orchestra bore his name), his performance of the symphony in New York on 11 January 1921 met with Aldrich's ambivalent appraisal:

> Besides a somewhat deliberate opening tempo, there were to be noted all through the symphony that translucent clarity in the exposition of the voices, that perfect finish of the ensemble and in the turning and molding of each phrase, that flexibility of tempo that were to be noted [in the orchestra's previous concerts]. Certain portions seemed unsubstantial, lacking in weight, as in the adagio. The feeling of the whole was essentially lyric ... There were certain phrases that you will perhaps never hear played with such a golden concentration of musical beauty. There were others that needed a more rugged statement. On the whole, for all its beauties, the reading of the symphony seemed rather small, short-breathed and over-detailed.[214]

In Toscanini's first performance of the work with the New York Philharmonic on 26 January 1928, Olin Downes's reaction was strikingly similar:

> In general ... it emphasized the lyrical spirit which is the prevailing characteristic of the score ... The symphony suggests a fuller orchestral tone than he projected last night ... What was very beautiful was the tempo and the lovely flow of the melodic line in the opening movement. But as a whole this was Brahms ... with moments of haunting poetry, with a very admirable proportion and articulation of phrase, and a suitably brilliant finale. In general the orchestral tone was small and the conception somewhat miniature. It was a performance of exceptional beauty of tone; interpretatively it came nearer an Italian pastorale than the underlying force, and even, in pages, grandeur of [the work].[215]

Downes's view moderated a little by 1935, when Toscanini's Philharmonic performance of the work on 21 February 1935 drew tributes to the 'wonderful glow' of the orchestral playing and the 'unity of conception, the beauty and poetry of the music'; but now he complained that Toscanini's approach to Brahms's 'quasi ritenuto' [sic] in the first movement was insufficiently held back 'to confer the rugged power that is in the idea'.[216] By 12 February 1938, Downes was with Toscanini (now with the NBC Orchestra), all the way in a performance 'compounded equally of Brahms lyricism and Brahms vigor. It was not always so with this conductor ... The virility of the interpretation was properly its keynote but it only balanced the tranquillity of the beginning'.[217]

[214] *New York Times*, 12 January 1921.
[215] *New York Times*, 27 January 1928.
[216] *New York Times*, 22 February 1935; on this much analysed passage, see p. 203.
[217] *New York Times*, 13 February 1938.

The negative views expressed in the 1920s by Aldrich and Downes about Toscanini's approach to the Second Symphony seem puzzling, especially since in 1911
Steinbach and, in the 1920s, his pupil Adolf Busch clearly thought quite the opposite.[218] But partial explanations may be sought in the references to the slow start to the
work, the acute delineation of the melodic lines, the detailed moulding of each phrase
and the constant flexibility. These all seem to reflect Steinbach's approach, as to some
extent does Downes's 'miniaturist' and Aldrich's 'short-breathed and over-detailed'
critiques, for, from the very start of the work, short phrase markings are part and
parcel of expressive devices required by Brahms in certain places and reflected in the
approach of some of his interpreters, almost certainly including Steinbach; certainly,
too, at various points by Toscanini.[219] We have no recordings by him of the work dating
from the 1920s, but parts of the 1935 Philharmonic and the whole of the 1938 NBC
performances survive and are, along with other selected performances, examined in
more detail in the next chapter with these critiques in mind.

Downes's reviews of Toscanini's first (ever) performances of the Third and First
Symphonies contrast with those already quoted. That of the Third Symphony, on
10 October 1929, reported in the next day's *New York Times*, lacked specifics other
than the observation that the first movement had 'been taken more rapidly by some
conductors, and in a more virtuoso and dramatic spirit'; but it is clear that Downes
thought very highly of the result. The earliest extant recorded performance of this
work took place on 17 March 1935 as part of Toscanini's Brahms cycle with the Philharmonic in February–April of that year; that performance is examined closely in
the next chapter, together with a selection of his later accounts.[220] However, it should
be noted at this stage that Toscanini's final performances of the Third Symphony
in November 1952, including the RCA recording, were listless failures and are not
further examined.

Toscanini's first performance of the First Symphony, on 13 November 1930, was
met next day by Downes's critical parsing at great length, but his views are not on
the whole germane to the search for any Steinbach influence. It is, however, worth
noting some of his comments on details of the second movement, set out in the
next chapter.[221] Further, Downes had thought Furtwängler's 'colossal interpretation'
of this symphony at his Philharmonic debut in 1925 the 'last word', but Toscanini's
had 'a passion and profundity of feeling and an originality of approach which said as
much or even more'. In the first movement 'the introduction was a little faster than
some conductors take it, the following allegro a little slower, therefore more massive
… though suitably varied in pulse where there were lyrical lines or points of repose;

[218] As to Adolf Busch's view, see further p. 146.
[219] See further p. 203.
[220] See p. 167.
[221] See p. 190.

and it was dramatic to the last degree'. The earliest recording of the First Symphony is contained in Toscanini's opening concert of his 1935 Philharmonic cycle, dating from 17 February (a few bars are missing); this recording is to be heard only in the Rogers and Hammerstein collection in the New York Public Library of the Performing Arts (NYPLPA), containing all of Toscanini's Philharmonic/NBC concerts as preserved. The earliest performance publicly available is in the Maestro's first concert with the newly formed NBC Symphony Orchestra on Christmas night, 25 December 1937. Together with certain other Toscanini-led performances, these two performances are examined in the next chapter.[222]

And so to the Fourth Symphony: Toscanini's first Philharmonic performance on 10 December 1931 was greeted with unqualified praise by Olin Downes in the next day's *New York Times*. However, little is to be gleaned of details relevant to the current search, although it is worth noting his observations that 'this interpretation was Teutonic in breadth and ruggedness' and that Toscanini's 'sovereign faculty for clarity and significance of detail, subject to the proportions of a balanced and elaborate form, were never better displayed'.

The earliest complete recording of the Fourth Symphony is contained in the first two of Toscanini's concerts with the BBC Symphony Orchestra on 3 and 5 June 1935, captured (contrary to his wishes at the time) by HMV's engineers in London's Queen's Hall. These performances, in the very first concerts with a British orchestra conducted by Toscanini, were met with unalloyed praise by London critics. Neville Cardus, for example, virtually deserted his critical faculties: he pronounced Toscanini 'the world's master conductor', whose interpretation of the Brahms was the 'fullest conceivable', 'eloquent yet direct, beautiful in its balanced line and energy, but always human and many-sided' and ending with a passacaglia which recalled Nikisch in its 'explosive and generating energy'. For the *Times* (in the person of the habitually more sober H. C. Colles), the Brahms was 'so nobly proportioned that one … stands amazed by the inevitability of its shape', a performance that 'said exactly what Brahms meant it to say with extraordinary clarity and certainty'.[223]

The saga of Toscanini's capture by the BBC and his relations with the corporation and its orchestra has been recounted elsewhere.[224] In the present context, the significance of this performance of the Fourth Symphony lies in its revelation of the

---

[222] See p. 167.

[223] The writing of the anonymous *Times* critic H. C. Colles (1879–1943) was, according to successive editions of *Grove's Dictionary* (which he edited for its 3rd edition), admired 'for its admirable qualities of comprehensive taste, sure and fair judgment' and for 'an unfailing tact and humanity that tempered even his severest strictures'. From 1925 he was assisted by Frank Howes (1891–1974), who was the *Times* critic from 1943 until 1960; Howes probably covered the second performance on 5 June, further referred to in the text.

[224] See Dyment 2012, Chs 2–8.

conductor's approach in that concert, differing substantially from his later and more austere style and, to some extent, from his other pre-war performances of this work as preserved. Further, there are substantial grounds for claiming that this rendering, more than any other of Toscanini's extant Brahms recordings, may reflect aspects of his absorption of Steinbach's practice. Of course, it would be grossly simplistic simply to claim that, since this Brahms Fourth is the work of a master conductor and admirer of Steinbach still in his prime, it therefore reflects closely what Toscanini heard in Munich a quarter of a century before: that would be to set at naught the analytic intellect and unique temperament that Toscanini himself brought to bear in his own study of his repertoire. Moreover, a lengthy *Times* article about these 1935 concerts remarked pertinently that those who could remember how Richter, then Steinbach, Nikisch, Weingartner, Furtwängler 'and now Toscanini' handled the symphonies of Brahms, could trace the process of individual interpretation, producing a gradual revision of the estimate of Brahms. If the highest estimate was given to interpreters most faithful to the text, 'nonetheless if we could be given an absolutely accurate record of the Meiningen Orchestra's performance of the Symphony in E minor which Brahms found completely satisfactory, there can be little doubt but that we should receive something of a shock at the difference between it and those which we think of as being most Brahms-like today.'[225]

Necessary qualifications apart, this performance may nonetheless bear some degree of a Steinbach imprint. Steinbach's score markings, as handed down to us, are in substantial measure adverted to here, particularly in the second and fourth movements.[226] Perhaps more reliable than these markings is the witness of Adrian Boult, who, as we know, notated his score of the Fourth's passacaglia with Steinbach's manifold tempo modifications;[227] and the tempo relationships and proportioning of the movement in his finest recorded performance (LPO 1954) and Toscanini's (BBC SO 1935) mirror each other to a significant extent, particularly in the latter variations; the next chapter examines their respective approaches in more detail.[228] The evidential point to be emphasised here is that such an exact meeting of minds, which in both performances results in unsurpassed structural clarity and remarkably vivid characterisation of each variation, cannot be ascribed merely to coincidence or to the two conductors' exceptional musical penetration: the common influence is plain to hear.

Naturally, this Fourth Symphony is also refracted through the lens of Toscanini's overwhelming personal vision. There is here a continual subtle flexibility of pulse, in which scarcely a single phrase is conducted in precisely the same tempo throughout.

[225] The *Times*, 8 June 1935.
[226] See p. 217.
[227] See p. 41.
[228] See p. 220.

This characteristic is especially to be noted in the *Andante*, which contrasts strongly with Toscanini's later and more austere, taut style. Indeed, to revert to the speculative Steinbach shadow, this whole movement might serve as a checklist of the characteristics attributed to him in the detailed portrait given earlier in this chapter. Nevertheless, it is only if one consciously adverts to these fluctuations that they become noticeable, since here and throughout the work they follow with complete understanding the implicit character of the musical material, its alternate intensification and relaxation (or, in Brahms's words, 'pushing forward and holding back'); hence the impression conveyed of absolute architectural integrity and certainty of purpose.

With such superhuman demands in terms of flexibility, clarity and power, it was inevitable that, at what was the earliest stage of Toscanini's relationship with the BBC orchestra, the playing would betray its share of accidents. Nevertheless, despite minor shortcomings, the performance remains – in the author's view – an unrivalled experience for its intellectual grasp and emotional penetration of every corner of the score and for the conductor's overarching projection of a supreme masterpiece of symphonic logic. The recording must, therefore, be closely examined for possible traces of Toscanini's remembrance of things past at that Munich Festival in 1909. That analysis is a feature of the next chapter.[229]

Vittorio Gui: a Berrsche sidelight

To whom else did Toscanini enthuse and did he ever explain in detail what struck him about Steinbach's interpretative approach – in addition, that is, to his virtuoso handling of the fifth *Haydn* Variation noted above? It is surely remarkable that the only Brahms conductor whom Alexander Berrsche praised unreservedly in later years was an unexpected Italian. Berrsche did not witness Toscanini in Salzburg but, curiously, attended the Nazified 1938 Festival, when Vittorio Gui (1885–1975), not himself a fascist, nonetheless had little compunction in substituting for the missing Maestro. Berrsche reviewed two of his concerts, one with the Vienna Philharmonic in Salzburg including Brahms's *Tragic* Overture, the other in Augsburg containing the Fourth Symphony.[230]

Gui had already conducted Brahms in Salzburg: Walter invited him in 1933 for a programme including the Second Symphony[231] – perhaps the sprat to catch the

---

[229] See p. 215.
[230] Gui's Salzburg concert was on 31 July 1938 in the Mozarteum, review in Josef Kaut, *Festspiele in Salzburg*, Salzburg: Residenz, 1969, p. 446; the date of the 1938 Augsburg concert is unknown. Berrsche also praised Gui's Salzburg *Falstaff* (previously Toscanini's) as virtual musical perfection (*ibid.* p. 618).
[231] *Ibid.* p. 429.

26. VITTORIO GUI IN 1954

Toscanini mackerel, which was duly hooked the following year when, alongside Gui's Brahms First Symphony, Salzburg audiences heard Toscanini's *Haydn* Variations and Third Symphony.[232] Now, in 1938, Berrsche was startled by Steinbach redivivus. He detailed at length the many elements in Gui's Fourth Symphony where 'all was as it was when Steinbach lived', such as the oboe solo at bar 17 in the first movement given with 'penetrating force, a sudden glowing accentuation', and in the *Andante* the 'sensitive espressivo' of the first violins' semiquavers, the 'scrupulous weighting' of the highly expressive accompanying cello cantilena – two passages also unmistakeably characteristic of Toscanini. As in the symphony, so it was in the overture, the like of which Berrsche had not heard since Steinbach.[233]

Gui, wholly Italian trained, assisted Toscanini at La Scala for two years from 1923 and began his long association with Florence in 1928. He could hardly have avoided Toscanini's concert work with La Scala's orchestra, which often featured Brahms's Second Symphony, and he may also have heard his La Scala *Haydn* Variations in October 1925 and Fourth Symphony in October 1927; perhaps in addition he discussed the music with the Maestro. Certainly Gui went on to become the most important Italian

[232] Toscanini's performances of all four Brahms symphonies with the Vienna Philharmonic 1933–37 were major successes with Vienna and Salzburg audiences: see Herbert Peyser in the *New York Times*, 14 November 1937. Gui's 1934 Brahms First Symphony at Salzburg was on 2 August, Toscanini's *Haydn* Variations on 23 August, his Third Symphony on 30 August.

[233] Berrsche, pp. 620 and 623. In Toscanini's BBC SO performances the recording fails to capture the oboe solo; it is best heard in two later concert performances from 1948 and December 1951. See further pp. 168 and 217.

Brahmsian of his generation, recording the Second and Third Symphonies with his Florence orchestra in June 1946 and, again with that orchestra, choosing the Fourth Symphony for what turned out to be his last concert a few weeks before his death.[234]

To have reproduced Steinbach's characteristics without linkage of any kind would have been almost uncanny, but the putative Toscanini connection provides a possible solution to the mystery, to which Gui's recorded Brahms adds substance. His 1975 Fourth Symphony suggests a rather gentler, plainer facsimile of Toscanini's 1935 BBC SO performances and in particular his passacaglia is indistinguishable in structure from Toscanini's. This performance is described further in the next chapter.

Sir Henry Wood: sometimes successful

Henry Wood (1869–1944) is at first sight an unlikely witness in the search for the holy grail of the true Brahms: his reputation is hardly commensurate with those of the other conductors whose styles are examined here in detail. But – and there are many buts about his career – Britain's first fully professional full-time conductor was taken seriously when he appeared abroad. It is true that in England he became known as a trusty workhorse for the safe delivery of a huge range of the repertoire, conducted (particularly in the annual Promenade Concerts at the Queen's Hall each summer over several decades) with a minimum of rehearsal time – meticulously organised though that had to be. But musicians abroad were aware of his worth: after both he and Walter Damrosch appeared as guests with the Concertgebouw Orchestra in 1903, Mengelberg wrote to a friend that Damrosch was not a good conductor, having neither individuality nor spirit – in a word, a time-beater. Wood, on the other hand, he liked much more: he was a real conductor, with his own personal conceptions and fresh musical ideas.[235] In the following year, Wood was hailed by critics in New York as a masterful guest conductor with the Philharmonic.[236] And as Wood himself later recounted, he was 'wooed' intensively to succeed Muck in Boston after the Great War and only the pleadings of those charged with organising his Promenade concerts and

---

[234] Gui's Brahms recordings: Symphony No. 2: Parlophone/Cetra BB 25171–74, LP transfer Tempo MTT 2074; Symphony No. 3: BB 25163–66, LP transfer Tempo MTT 2040; Symphony No. 4: see p. 167 below. The Cetra recordings were made in June 1946, the Third Symphony on 12 June, the Second a few days later. The LP transfers were released in the USA in August 1951 (Symphony No. 3) and August 1952 (Symphony No. 2) but were neither advertised nor reviewed. Courtesy Michael H. Gray and Pennsylvania College, I have been able to confirm the clean, Classical character of Gui's recorded performance of the Third Symphony.

[235] Zwart, p. 150.

[236] Arthur Jacobs, *Henry. J Wood: Maker of the Proms*, London: Methuen, 1994 (Jacobs), pp. 96–7.

27. HENRY WOOD IN 1903

English festival appearances succeeded in changing his mind.[237] So, forever after it was to those institutions that his name became indissolubly attached.

As Wood also recounted, he was a devout follower of Steinbach. He missed the London concerts of the Meiningen Hofkapelle in 1902 but, shortly after, as he recollected, he was introduced to Wüllner in Cologne, who in turn introduced him to Steinbach. Wood expressed his sorrow at having missed those London concerts; thereupon Steinbach invited him to join him on his imminent tour with the Meiningen Hofkapelle:

> I readily accepted his wonderful invitation and heard, during those three memorable weeks, Brahms's works played many times over – as it were by Brahms's own orchestra and Brahms's chosen director of it. From that day to this I do not think my interpretation of Brahms has varied one iota ... I moulded my Brahms on Steinbach and the Meiningen Orchestra.[238]

Such unequivocal devotion would seem to settle the matter – Wood consciously and, it would seem, conscientiously, followed Steinbach's Brahms. Moreover, he later complained that, while Steinbach filled the London halls for his Brahms, for his own purportedly identical readings the halls were half empty.[239] But the details of Wood's

---

[237] Henry J. Wood, *My Life of Music*, London: Gollancz, 1938, pp. 304–5.
[238] *Ibid.* pp. 166–7.
[239] Pearton, p. 32n.

account of his Cologne visit and its outcome do not match the facts. The Meiningen Hofkapelle's London concerts took place in November 1902 but Wüllner had already died by then (on 7 September).[240] The Hofkapelle did indeed undertake several post-London tours under Steinbach up to the end of February 1903, including visits to Basle, Berlin and Leipzig, after which the conductor took up Wüllner's posts in Cologne; but the towns which Wood said he visited in the course of the tour he attended included Wiesbaden and Freiburg – which did not figure in the Hofkapelle's post-London tours, nor had done for some years before.[241]

Whatever the truth behind Wood's errant narrative, he was clearly a devotee of Steinbach's Brahms, but his success in following Steinbach's style was evidently mixed. In the *Times* report on 5 December 1910 about Wood's concert with his Queen's Hall Orchestra on 3 December, the critic lambasted Wood's 'singularly incomplete under-standing' of Brahms's Third Symphony:

> Almost throughout a rate of speed was adopted which made it impossible to bring out all the beauties of any of the movements. Some of these were, indeed, realised by slackening the speed considerably, but at a sacrifice of the unity of design which is essential. On many occasions the extreme degree of slowness attained in some of these *rallentando* passages was quite fast enough for the normal pace of the move-ment. The exquisite *poco allegretto* was played more nearly at the usual rate; but much of the ethereal grace seemed to have evaporated. The *finale* was so rushed through that the coda, that most inspired moment ... made no effect whatever. The great conductors of Brahms, like Richter and Steinbach, have insisted on the purely logical treatment of certain phrasings, represented by the usual signs for increase and decrease of tone, but requiring the place and force of each note of the phrase to be accurately calculated, so that the climax of the phrase comes with irresistible conviction. Mr. Wood brings out points, but they are nearly always points, not the culminating moments of a symmetrically designed means of effect.

Not only is this evaluation of Wood's efforts quite precise, but it also shows clearly wherein Richter and Steinbach – significantly, bracketed together for their stylistic approach in relation to the aspects mentioned – differed from Wood and thereby, in

---

[240] Wood refers specifically to Franz rather than his son, the singer Ludwig (1858–1938).

[241] See Goltz 2009 (see n. 15 above). If it be assumed that Wood gave his apologies to Steinbach *before* the London visit because he was to be engaged elsewhere, and when Wüllner was still alive, the last preceding Meiningen Hofkapelle tour before London was in March 1902, again leaving Wiesbaden and Freiburg unvisited; it is doubtful that Sir Edgar Speyer's plans for the Hofkapelle's London visit would have been public knowledge so early in 1902 as to make sense of Wood's narrative. As the cited footnote indicates, Goltz 2009 is not quite complete, but it is extremely unlikely that significant events on the scale related by Wood could have been omitted.

the critic's view, made them great interpreters of Brahms: no speeding, nor exaggerated tempo changes, nor misplaced emphases in phrasing.[242]

Still, Wood evidently took the strictures to heart, to judge by the *Times* report three
years later, when on 17 November 1913 it reviewed Wood's concert two days before:
this time, Wood's account of Brahms's Fourth Symphony

> was a performance to be classed with the best that have been heard under Steinbach,
> Nikisch and Richter. It was distinguished by faithfulness to the text and imaginative
> intelligence in interpreting it. To take one example, the passage leading to the *reprise*
> of the first movement, where wind and strings pass a fragment of the theme to and
> fro antiphonally, was exquisitely balanced because the marks of crescendo and
> decrescendo were impressed without a suggestion of artificiality. There were many
> examples of the same careful judgment in the slow movement, particularly in the
> passage which shows the second theme growing out of the episode which precedes
> its appearance.

These evaluations would matter little if Wood's approach to Brahms were adequately
documented in recorded sound: one could then test the results against the available
information about the acknowledged great Brahms interpreters. Unfortunately, apart
from a couple of Hungarian Dances issued in 1916, the only recorded Brahms by
Wood is the *Haydn* Variations made for Decca in 1935.[243] Suggestively, this recording
is so lively that it was for a time mistakenly attributed to Toscanini and transferred to
CD as such.[244] There were some grounds for that misattribution: the performance is
throughout brisk and well played, if not up to Toscanini's standards; but what is most
germane is the very rapid pacing of the Fifth variation, outpacing even Toscanini and
Weingartner. To that extent, Wood corroborates Toscanini's memory of Steinbach's
very fast tempo in this variation and, hence, the Italian's own practice.[245]

Of the symphonies under Wood's baton, however, we are left only with reviews
such as those quoted above and comments by other contemporaries. Fortunately,
an unlikely source for such comments presents itself in the *Gramophone* reviews of
Stokowski's earliest recordings of the symphonies, discussed earlier in this chapter

---

[242] Although for a contemporary assessment of Steinbach's performance of this work, see p. 46.
[243] Brahms Hungarian Dances, issued in September 1916 on Columbia L 1054; *Haydn* Variations with Wood's 'New Queen's Hall Orchestra', recorded on 29–30 April 1935, issued on Decca
K763–4. See outline discography in Jacobs, pp. 427–9.
[244] Pearl GEMM CDS 9922, included in a set of little known or unissued performances with the
New York Philharmonic.
[245] See p. 98. Any suggestion that 78rpm side-lengths necessitated Wood's tempo here is coun-
tered by the fact that his four sides occupy the same as virtually all pre-tape recordings of the
work, save only Furtwängler's and Casals's, each occupying five sides: see Francis J. Clough and
G. J. Cuming, *World Encyclopaedia of Recorded Music*, London: Sidgwick & Jackson, 1952, p. 86.

in the context of Nikisch's possible influence upon him.[246] Wood was very much in
the reviewer's mind: in the course of the review of the First Symphony, he remarked
that 'the great Brahms conductors are very few. Wood gave us rich satisfaction at
the Proms. in the four symphonies, in spite of his under-rehearsed orchestra.' In the
review of the Second Symphony's finale, 'I prefer the pace set by Stokowski to Wood's
faster rate. This on the whole is about Boult's pace, who takes nine and a quarter
minutes, to Wood's eight.' In the review of the Third Symphony, 'I like the change of
spirit for the *Allegretto* [i.e. the change of pace for the 'trio' at bar 54], though I think
Sir Henry Wood's scheme of contrast in pace here the best I have found.'[247] According
to these reviews, then, Wood's pacing for the Second's finale equated with both Weingartner and Fritz Busch, while his contrast of tempos within the third movement of
the Third was, it must be inferred, significantly less extreme than Stokowski's. These
comments are further examined in the next chapter,[248] but at this stage it is sufficient
to note their significance if Wood was here following Steinbach's practice – even if
the quoted *Times* reviews suggest that this inference might rest on sometimes shaky
foundations.

Willem Mengelberg, Oskar Fried and Bruno Walter: tradition-free?

Three conductors so rich in the traditions they inherited (with Mengelberg always
insistently vocal about them) would seem odd candidates for the above subtitle;
but in this study 'tradition' or lines of authority refer specifically to those strands of
conducting style or styles plausibly connected with Brahms's practice or preferences.
Mengelberg has been referred to as one of those conductors whose broad-brush
extravagances in matters of tempo change and phrasing might provide indications of
the approach with which the composer himself was most familiar and, further, probably reflected the practice of his most favoured conductor, Fritz Steinbach.[249] It is this
type of loose but perhaps ill-founded claim that must now be tested in more detail:
will Mengelberg emerge as a sound witness to Brahmsian performance traditions or
was he witness simply to his own development as a virtuoso conductor, a journey that
his recordings strongly suggest became increasingly individual and, in some critics'
views, ultimately over-ripe?

---

[246] See p. 68 and n. 129.
[247] Review extracts from the *Gramophone*, vol. 7 (December 1928), p. 303 (First Symphony),
vol. 9 (February 1931), p. 440 (Second Symphony), vol. 8 (July 1930), p. 81 (Third Symphony).
[248] See pp. 206 and 214.
[249] See Ch. 1, n. 3.

Mengelberg and ancestral traditions

> Talk, talk, talk. That was Mengelberg. Once he came to me and told me at great length what was the proper, German way to conduct Beethoven's *Coriolanus*. He had got it, he said quite seriously, from a conductor who supposedly had got it straight from Beethoven. Bah! I told him: 'I get it straight from Beethoven, from the score.'[250]

Although correctly pinpointing Mengelberg's endless loquacity, Toscanini's impatient summing up hardly did justice to either of them. As already demonstrated, Toscanini readily imbibed the practice of others when he was musically convinced by them, while Mengelberg's point was that, since he was a pupil in composition and conducting of Franz Wüllner during 1888–92 and since the latter was a pupil of Anton Schindler (1795–1864), he could (and always did) claim a direct line of succession back to Beethoven himself.

Schindler acted as amanuensis for Beethoven in his last years and saved some 136 of Beethoven's Notebooks, which in 1845 he sold to the Prussian state. That sale was indicative of Schindler's penury by that time; his career as pedagogue was modest, for all his claims as the one true prophet of his master against hosts of alleged misinterpreters. He believed that by the 1860s the performance of Classical works for both orchestra and piano (that is, works by Mozart and Beethoven) had been wholly traduced. Principal targets of his ire included Brahms's most treasured friend, Clara Schumann, 'the celebrated, infinitely over-rated artist' according to Schindler, and, in the execution of orchestral works, Mendelssohn and his followers, with their characteristic rapid tempos and consequent glossing over of detail and insensitivity to tempo change.[251] His prize pupil was, in fact, Wüllner, whose teaching he took upon himself over a period of six years, between 1846 and 1852. But Wüllner ultimately disappointed him because he later fell under the influence of Schumann and Brahms: Schindler thought 'he had failed to fulfil all the conditions of an arduous education'.[252] Thus any claim to be treading the true path via Wüllner meets with this immediate difficulty.

Mengelberg's biographer attributes many of the characteristics of his conducting of Beethoven's symphonies to Wüllner, even though there seems to been no direct comparisons made between pupil and teacher. When conducting the symphonies, Zwart says, Mengelberg always referred back to his personal acquaintance with his teacher (as Toscanini was so painfully aware):

[250] Howard Taubman, *Toscanini*, London: Odhams, 1951, p. 180.

[251] Anton Felix Schindler, *Biografie von Ludwig van Beethoven*, 3rd ed., Münster: Aschendorf, 1860, transl. Donald MacArdle as *Beethoven as I Knew Him*, Chapel Hill: University of North Carolina, 1966, repr. New York: Norton, 1972, pp. 434–7.

[252] *Ibid.* pp. 397n, 445–6.

There are ... striking resemblances between the characterisation of Wüllner's conducting and descriptions of Mengelberg's interpretations: flexible tempo, tempo
choice and colour separation towards the key moments of a movement (meaning,
tempo choice determined by form), a surprise stressing of certain motifs and an
endeavour at clarity in performance.[253]

Further, 'many of Mengelberg's scores contain remarks and directions that can be
traced back to Wüllner's teachings'.[254] It must here be pointed out that other observers contradict accounts of Wüllner's flexibility; Levi's view has been noted and Bruno
Walter's will be hereafter.[255]

But, assuming these descriptions of Wüllner and Mengelberg to be broadly correct, how did the latter's memory of his teaching help him in the interpretation of
Brahms? In assessing Mengelberg's reliance on this line of authority, one cannot avoid
discussion of both Schindler's reliability and Wüllner's limitations. In Mengelberg's
era there was still a tendency to regard Schindler as holy writ, even though his claims
had been contested by Carl Czerny (1791–1857), Beethoven's early pupil and lifelong
friend, whose book on the performance of Beethoven's piano music was admired and
approved by Brahms.[256] In any event, since the 1970s any high estimation of Schindler
has been strongly in question; indeed (without discussing here the whys and where-
fores[257]), one authority has gone so far as to assert that 'anything reported by Schindler
must be assumed to be doubtful or false, unless supported by independent evidence
(in which case, Schindler's contribution is redundant)'.[258] If that assertion is even partly
justified, a fatal weakness must lie at the heart of Mengelberg's insistent appeal to the
existence of the line of succession from Beethoven to himself – and to his further
reliance on the application of similar performance characteristics to other composers,
in particular to Brahms. His sometimes extreme 'pushing forward and holding back',
affecting major sections of symphonic movements, may – but, with equal weight, may
not – gain some validity from the practice of his teachers: the performance style, so far

[253] Zwart, pp. 87–8.
[254] Booklet note by Frits Zwart with 'Willem Mengelberg/Concertgebouw Orchestra, Live
Radio Recordings', 10 CD set, 97016, p. 35.
[255] See pp. 14 and 122.
[256] Brahms–Schumann, vol. 2, p. 29, letter of (?)March 1878: 'I certainly think Czerny's large
pianoforte course is worthy of study, particularly in regard to what he says about Beethoven and
the performance of his works, for he was a diligent and attentive pupil ... In fact I think that
people to-day ought to have more respect for this excellent man.' Brahms was here referring to
Czerny's On the Proper Performance of all Beethoven's Works for Piano of 1846.
[257] For a full summary of all the issues and also pleas in mitigation, see Theodore Albrecht's
online essay 'Anton Schindler as Destroyer and Forger of Beethoven's Conversation Books: A
Case for Decriminalization'.
[258] Barry Cooper, Beethoven, Oxford: Oxford University Press, 2000, p. ix.

28. WILLEM MENGELBERG TALKS,
TOSCANINI PERFORCE LISTENS,
ITALY, N.D.

as it may rely at one remove on the teaching of Schindler, has too little evidential value as precedent or justification for his very personal approach.

As for Wüllner, we have noted already this distinguished pedagogue's poor reputation as conductor among some of the foremost musicians of his era – Wagner, Bülow and also Levi, who as the then foremost champion of Brahms regarded Wüllner as incapable of conducting the composer's works adequately.[259] These opinions date from the late 1860s and early 1870s and subsequently Brahms himself took a rather different, albeit measured view of Wüllner's capabilities. He entrusted him with early performances of his *Haydn* Variations and First Symphony but thereafter he himself took good care to conduct early Cologne performances of the later orchestral works (Symphonies Nos. 2–4 and the Double Concerto) with either the Gürzenich Orchestra or the Meiningen Hofkapelle.[260] Furthermore, while he was preparing the first version of Schumann's Fourth Symphony for public performance in 1888, his letter to Clara in July of that year praised Wüllner, who had undertaken the detailed editing of the work, as having 'more insight and better judgement' than others, but 'unfortunately, I do not like the Gürzenich [under Wüllner] for the production of the piece'. When in

---

[259] See p. 14.
[260] Symphony No. 2, 7 January 1880 and 15 May 1883; Symphony No. 3, 12 February 1884; Symphony No. 4, 23 November 1885 (Meiningen Hofkapelle) and 9 February 1886; Double Concerto, 18 October 1887: Bass, pp. 113–22.

1891 he decided to have the work published – a decision that endangered his almost forty-year friendship with Clara – he again praised Wüllner's editing: 'I regard [him] as one of the soundest and most cultured musicians, who has an excellent orchestra at his disposal'.[261] Ample respect, then, for Wüllner's musicianship, but, it seems, only a guarded respect for him as a conductor.

Mengelberg and Brahms

Mengelberg's first contact with Brahms came at a very early age: his parents got to know the composer and he stayed with them on his visits to Amsterdam.[262] On one of these occasions the teenaged Mengelberg played Brahms's *Handel* Variations for him, to which the composer responded that the boy understood the piece and should play his other works.[263] In his years with the Concertgebouw Orchestra (1895–1945) Mengelberg conducted the Brahms's symphonies regularly, if with less frequency than some of his specialities such as Beethoven, Strauss and Mahler; that pattern was reflected also in his years with the New York Symphony and Philharmonic (1919–30). Mahler festivals came and went in Amsterdam, but Brahms had to wait for his birth centenary in 1933 before Mengelberg celebrated him in similar style. His recordings of all four symphonies, dating from 1932 to 1944, have tended to enjoy less fame than his astonishing performances of Tchaikovsky's symphonies and Strauss's orchestral works.

It is evident from most of Mengelberg's recordings of the Brahms symphonies that he applied principles and practices to the performances similar to those he applied to Beethoven's symphonies, which, as noted, derived from ancestral influences – almost fatally shaky in their foundations – that reflected his understanding of Beethoven's own stylistic approach. In a typical and obvious example, the *Andante* of the Third Symphony (available in two corroborative recordings[264]), the range of tempo change is extreme whenever the full orchestra is engaged and plays at dynamic levels above the opening *piano*: bars 24–32 and particularly bars 62–80 provide vivid examples of extravagant manipulations of tempo that, in their seemingly unstoppable, almost

---

[261] Brahms–Schumann, vol. 2, pp. 137 and 204, letters to Clara Schumann of July 1888 and 16 October 1891.

[262] Brahms visited Amsterdam on two occasions, to conduct his Third Symphony on 27 February 1884 and to conduct his Fourth Symphony on 13 November 1885 (with the Meiningen Hofkapelle) (Bass, pp. 118 and 120; Hofmann, pp. 237 and 252). Mengelberg's encounter with him therefore took place on one or other of those visits.

[263] Zwart, p. 29, citing H. E. Weinschenk, *Künstler plaudern*, Berlin, n.d., 'Willem Mengelberg. Artzrechnung durch Muzik bezahlt', p. 207.

[264] Recordings with the Concertgebouw Orchestra: Columbia recording of 10 May 1931, issued on LX 220–3, CD transfer Naxos 8.110164; and the broadcast of 27 February 1944 in Willem Mengelberg, Live, The Radio recordings, 97016 (CD2). In all four movements the latter is markedly slower, but the climactic changes of tempo are remarkably similar in character.

29. MENGELBERG
CONDUCTS BRAHMS

frenzied, rush towards climactic points (bars 32 and 80), sacrifice all other consid-erations, such as clarity in enunciating string figurations accompanying the principal melodic lines and, frequently, a smooth transition from one section of the movement to another. There is no evidence that this approach approximates that of any other among the most eminent of Brahms conductors to whom the composer gave his approval, Steinbach in particular, and much that, as the foregoing pages of this chapter have aimed to analyse, suggests otherwise.[265]

Throughout his career Mengelberg had many contacts with very different con-ductors of Brahms's symphonies, such as Felix Weingartner, who had a substantial number of engagements with Mengelberg's orchestra; thus he had ample chance to compare approaches sharply diverging from his own. He may even have witnessed the Meiningen Hofkapelle under Steinbach in their Amsterdam concerts, when Steinbach conducted the Second Symphony:[266] their concerts took place on 4, 5 and 7 Novem-ber 1900 and Mengelberg himself conducted concerts with his orchestra on 4 and 11

[265] See e.g. pp. 26 and 48.
[266] See p. 35.

November; he was in town and quite probably sampled the opposition.[267] Mengelberg's recorded performance of the Second Symphony is, as it happens, extremely continent by comparison with his other Brahms symphony recordings; it contains little that is extravagant by way of tempo modification save for the race to the finish, in which, in that era, Mengelberg was far from alone.[268] Whether he took note of Steinbach's approach back in 1900 is an interesting question to which there can be no answer. On the whole, it is probable that Mengelberg's approach was fashioned only by his own study and inclinations and that, to take but one example, his Classically 'correct' playing of Brahms's *quasi ritenente* in the first movement of this symphony was his interpretative decision alone.

Ultimately, the conclusion from this account must be that, whatever may have been the lines of authority that Mengelberg might have sought to invoke in order to explain his idiosyncratic interpretative style in much of Brahms, he alone was responsible for it. As we now see, the weakness of his favoured traditions of performance precludes treatment of the recordings as representing a link, whether direct or indirect, to any style having the composer's approbation. Accordingly, his recordings of the Brahms symphonies are not considered further in this study.

Oskar Fried: the Mahler influence?

In chronological order, it is appropriate to glance briefly at Mahler's friend and disciple Oskar Fried (1871–1941), who left a highly individual pre-electric recording of Brahms's First Symphony.[269] Fried's musical ancestry was distant from Brahms and his circle, involving composition lessons from Wagner's disciple Humperdinck, further encouragement from Hermann Levi (in his Wagner years) and the overwhelming example and personality of Mahler, who coached him for the Berlin premiere of his Second Symphony in November 1905.

As might be expected, Fried's approach to Brahms's First Symphony bears only a passing resemblance to any of those by the conductors hitherto traversed, although it

---

[267] Steinbach's only engagements with the Concertgebouw Orchestra were on 18 and 19 April 1914, both including the Fourth Symphony, but Mengelberg was, it seems, elsewhere: he had no engagements with his Amsterdam orchestra between 5 April and 22 May.

[268] Recorded by Telefunken on 4 April 1940, issued SK 3075–9, CD transfer Naxos 8.110158.

[269] After enjoying guest appearances with a wide selection of ensembles throughout Germany, Fried fled to the Soviet Union when the Nazis took power, although he continued to guest conduct in the UK and elsewhere in the rest of Europe until the late 1930s. He recorded the Mahler Second Symphony in 1924, Polydor 66290–300, 69681–91, CD transfer Urlicht UAV-5980 (The Music of Gustav Mahler: Issued 78s, 1903–1940). His recording of Brahms's First Symphony with members of the Berlin State Opera Orchestra, made in August 1924, was issued on Polydor 69701–05/66304–8, LP transfer Past Masters PM 32 with notes by the author. It is noted further in Frisch, p. 166, and Musgrave and Sherman, Ch. 10 (Frisch), p. 279.

30. GUSTAV MAHLER AND OSKAR FRIED,
NOVEMBER 1905

is noteworthy that his fluctuations of tempo in the first movement are to some extent paralleled by the descriptions of Nikisch's performance given at page 60 – very probably, however, outdoing Nikisch in extravagance. Further, Fried's extreme acceleration in the last movement after the initial statement of the *Allegro*'s main theme is, as will be seen, similar to the approach adopted by Hermann Abendroth, albeit with marginally less extravagance.[270] Contemporary accounts of Fried's concert performances of the symphony are, in this light, of some relevance. In November 1908 the Berlin critics were puzzled after Fried conducted the work with the Bluthner Orchestra: 'Fried has an original conception ... a conception that differs materially from the traditional one, especially in point of tempi and nuances'.[271] Who conducted Berlin's 'traditional' performances of the work is unstated, but presumably the reference encompassed giants such as the Philharmonic's conductor, Nikisch, as well as Steinbach and perhaps Weingartner. Twenty years later, when Fried conducted the symphony in the course of a couple of concerts with the New York Symphony, Olin Downes[272] in the *New York Times* was less equivocal: in his report on 17 March 1928 he thought 'the interpretation of that familiar work was as a whole mannered and superficial'; the finale met with an ovation at the close but that movement 'tells anyway, even when played less precipitately and at a pace more just to its form and content than the prevailing tempi of the conductor'.

---

[270] See p. 194.
[271] *Musical Courier*, vol. 47 (8 November 1908).
[272] See further p. 103.

Once again we find a style distant from conductors with a direct connection to Brahms and his world. It is more likely that, in the outer movements of the symphony, their clear segmentation into paragraphs at differing tempos reflected or was influenced by Mahler's way with the Classical repertoire, but it is not necessary to pursue that issue further in the present context. Similar considerations make it superfluous to examine the recorded Brahms performances of the much younger Otto Klemperer (1885–1973), very fine though some of them are.

Bruno Walter: a free agent in Brahms

The early days of Bruno Walter (1875–1962) were spent in a musical culture in which Brahms was worshipped and Wagner's name never mentioned.[273] As he remarked, his later love of Wagner simply took its place unobstructed beside the love of all great music, including Brahms's. His early musical memories were dominated by Bülow conducting the Berlin Philharmonic. Walter's first experience of him (he is a little hazy about dates in his memoirs, but this probably occurred early in 1889) determined his own future: he could be nothing other than a conductor. Thereafter he attended all Bülow's increasingly rare appearances with this orchestra until his last in 1893. In that period he heard works by all the major German masters under his baton (save for Wagner), including all four Brahms symphonies, the Third of which Bülow programmed repeatedly, as well as one of his famous 'double' performances of Beethoven's Ninth.[274] At that stage, however, Walter had no other yardstick for comparison: Bülow was simply 'the undisputed ruler of German orchestral music' and he accepted Bülow's characteristic treatment of detail by means of extreme variations in tempo merely as 'a personal charm and fascination'. Other conductors in his teenage years failed to measure up and, in his early posting in Cologne (1894), 'nowhere near me did I see a musician I considered superior to myself ... Concerts in the *Gürzenich*, led by Franz Wüllner ... seemed to me dry and stiff'.[275] This judgement is all the more significant in memoirs dispensing so many words of admiration to a host of musicians met on his journeys and postings.

It was only in 1894, when Walter reached Hamburg and there came under Mahler's influence, that he met with a musical experience as overwhelming as Bülow had been, one which indeed was the dominant factor in his years with Mahler in Vienna and in his music-making for the rest of his life.[276] Although Walter fought for his musical independence, the Mahler influence was such that during his brief

---

[273] Walter memoirs, pp. 27 and 44.
[274] See Birkin, pp. 679–99, Walter memoirs, pp. 49–51. Walter's experience of Bülow's 'double performance' of Beethoven's Ninth Symphony took place on 6 March 1889 (Birkin, p. 670).
[275] Walter memoirs, p. 77.
[276] *Ibid.* p. 84.

tenure in Berlin in 1900–01 he observed with relative coolness the achievements of many of his senior colleagues. He witnessed a *Tristan* under Strauss which was 'subjectively fiery, but musically super-*rubato*', in contrast to a powerful performance under Mahler in Vienna a few weeks earlier; an impressive *Götterdämmerung* under Muck lacking in 'spontaneous dramatic impetuosity'; and a Nikisch concert most notable for an 'admirable' conducting technique that produced an 'overwhelming' Tchaikovsky *Pathétique* and a 'perfect and romantically conceived' *Euryanthe* overture.[277]

Since Walter had been brought up from his earliest days in a place and at a time of Brahms-worship, it was understandable that this composer should figure significantly in his later orchestral concerts, but he had little to say about Brahms's music and the part it played in his life. In his memoirs he limits himself, in relation to the orchestral music, to two remarks praising others: the 'excellent' performance of the Third Symphony given by Koussevitsky and his orchestra in Moscow before the Great War and the 'superlative rendering' of the Second Symphony by Toscanini and the Vienna Philharmonic which he said took place at a Salzburg Festival concert.[278] In his *Of Music and Music-Making*, he makes some pertinent remarks about performing the opening of the First Symphony's *Andante* – but that is all.[279] Nor do Walter's career and his many observations about other conductors senior to him suggest that there were any particular influences that might have been brought to bear at the time he studied the works – Bülow excepted, but, as already mentioned, that youthful influence occurred at a time when Walter had no yardstick for comparison and long before he reached maturity of outlook.

Walter reached a peak in his career on becoming Generalmusikdirektor at the Munich opera in January 1913 in succession to Mottl and Franz Fischer, and the seasons there offered him for the first time the opportunity to conduct a substantial number of orchestral concerts on a regular basis.[280] These were given by the Musikalische Akademie, his opera orchestra, with which he gave eight concerts each season. It is possible that around this time he encountered Steinbach's few concerts in Munich during 1914–15, but there is no evidence of this and, given Walter's hectic schedule

[277] *Ibid.* p. 140.

[278] See Walter memoirs, pp. 204 and 341. Walter's memory was at fault here: Toscanini conducted the First, Third and Fourth Symphonies and other works by Brahms at various Salzburg Festivals between 1934 and 1937, but not the Second Symphony. He did, however, conduct the Vienna Philharmonic in this work on 17 October 1937, the last work in two concerts undertaken at Walter's special request, which opened the orchestra's 1937/38 season; it was to be the last work Toscanini ever conducted with the orchestra: see Sachs 1978, p. 261.

[279] Bruno Walter, transl. Paul Hamburger, *Of Music and Music-Making*, London: Faber, 1961, New York: Norton, 1961 pp. 73, 129.

[280] See further Erik Ryding and Rebecca Pechefsky, *Bruno Walter: A World Elsewhere*, New Haven and London: Yale University Press, 2001, pp. 103–4.

31. TOSCANINI,
BRUNO WALTER
AND STEFAN ZWEIG,
SALZBURG, 1934

at the time, it seems unlikely. In any event, his Brahms performances seemed to have taken their time to settle: his attempt with the Second Symphony in February 1913 was 'driven by nervous haste' and lacked depth.[281] Over time, however, Walter's Brahms attained a rare distinction throughout Europe and the USA and, unlike Karl Muck for example, he left a legacy that includes many recordings of the symphonies, dating from 1934 until the end of his career.

In Walter's early Berlin years he no doubt met many individuals familiar with Brahms and his ways.[282] As an interpreter of his music, however, it is impossible to pinpoint the influence on the mature Walter of anyone who was known to have had either a direct or indirect link with the composer. His interpretations of the symphonies, particularly the pre-Second World War versions with the BBC Symphony and Vienna Philharmonic Orchestras, are, nonetheless, widely regarded as possessing great distinction. They may therefore stand as exceptional examples of Brahms interpretations disclosing particular characteristics that contrast with those recorded performances where direct or indirect links with the composer may suggest a reflection of the composer's preferred range of stylistic approaches. Some of Walter's earliest

---

[281] *Ibid.* p. 107, quoting the *Allgemeine Zeitung*, 15 March 1913.
[282] One example whom Walter mentions is Brahms's friend and biographer Max Kalbeck; see p. 22 and Walter memoirs, pp. 150 and 263.

recorded performances of the symphonies are examined in the next chapter with these considerations in mind.

The Mottl acolytes: Hermann Abendroth and Wilhelm Furtwängler

Adhering to chronology, the next two witnesses are eminent recording conductors having an immediate connection with Felix Mottl: Hermann Abendroth (1883–1956) and Wilhelm Furtwängler (1886–1954). At first sight that connection with a conductor widely regarded as disastrous in his handling of Brahms's works might suggest that these conductors are unlikely witnesses in the present pursuit of authentic Brahms performance styles. Nevertheless, as was noted at the outset of this study, the first has been upheld as a probable exemplar of the Steinbach style, while the second stands among that band of eminent conductors (Mengelberg is another example) whose reputation in their intensely individual performances of Brahms's works has stood so high and for so long that the aura of authenticity – a probable closeness to the Steinbach outlook – has attached itself to them without the necessary close consideration of the evidence.[283] That task must now be undertaken in relation to both conductors.

Abendroth's early career

The Frankfurt-born Abendroth received his musical education in Munich during 1901–05, where his teachers were Ludwig Thuille and Anna Hirzel-Langenhan.[284] Here without doubt he also witnessed and absorbed Mottl's 'authentic' Wagner presentations, among them *Die Meistersinger* and *Tannhäuser* in May 1904 and the *Ring* in August that year during the Summer Wagner Festival, held each year in the Prinzregenten-Theater.[285] As the reigning Hofkapellmeister at the summit of a

---

[283] See Ch. 1, n. 3 and p. 27.

[284] Ludwig Thuille (1861–1907), German composer and teacher, professor of theory and composition at the Munich Akademie; Anna Hirzel-Langenhan (1874–1951), Swiss pianist and teacher, pupil of Theodor Leschetizky and resident in Munich from 1898.

[285] Abendroth's biographer, Irina Lucke-Kaminiarz, *Hermann Abendroth. Ein Musiker im Wechselspiel der Zeitgeschichte*, Weimar: WTV, 2007 (Lucke-Kaminiarz), p. 17, suggests that Abendroth also assisted Mottl at Munich and Bayreuth during his studies, but this is questionable: after five months as guest conductor in the United States, Mottl did not arrive as Munich Hofkapellmeister until May 1904 and took over as director of the Akademie der Tonkunst only in October that year (that late arrival also makes it unlikely that he taught Abendroth). During his Munich years Mottl conducted at Bayreuth in 1906 (*Tristan und Isolde* – his last appearance there, on the eve of his break with Cosima Wagner and the Bayreuth musical establishment) and Abendroth is not listed among the Bayreuth musical assistants and répétiteurs for that year: Käte Neupert, *Die Besetzung der Bayreuther Festspiele*, Bayreuth: Edition Musica, 1961, pp. 64–5.

32. HERMANN ABENDROTH
IN 1909

distinguished career, Mottl's approach to the repertoire in his Munich concert and opera presentations would necessarily have impacted deeply on the young conductor. Subsequently, his studies concluded, Abendroth was appointed Mottl's assistant conductor for the Munich Wagner Festivals of 1907–10, when he helped him prepare the *Ring*, *Die Meistersinger* and *Tristan*.[286] At that time, too, Abendroth befriended Mottl's assistant, Wilhelm Furtwängler; beyond doubt the two young conductors were thoroughly soaked in the Mottl style and method.

After early conducting experience in Munich before graduating, Abendroth was appointed Kapellmeister for concerts and opera in Lübeck, followed by his appointment in 1911 as Kapellmeister in Essen, a post he kept until May 1916. During these years he guest conducted in virtually all major German-speaking centres, including Berlin, Hamburg, Munich, Frankfurt, Vienna and many others.

Did Abendroth find time in such a busy schedule to attend any of Steinbach's Brahms concerts in Cologne, just 70 kilometres distant from Essen? It is quite possible, but a definite answer would require the most intensive investigation of Abendroth's early

[286] The Festivals began in 1901; see Haas/Mottl, pp. 265, 309 and 328. Abendroth's appointment was noted in biographical details in EMI files, presumably compiled from material supplied by Abendroth or his agent. Other than details of his HMV recording sessions, nothing more about Abendroth survives in EMI's archive.

career, which at that time was, as noted, peripatetic in the extreme. In any event, his opportunities to hear Steinbach's Brahms would have been limited because, during the relevant period (1911–1914, after which Steinbach left Cologne), Steinbach gave, as was his custom, just one all-Brahms concert each year: on 15 March 1912, featuring the Third Symphony; on 28 March 1913, the First; and on 6 February 1914, the Fourth.[287] As will be seen from the next chapter, the recorded evidence from Abendroth's own performances is far too thin to suggest that he attended any of these concerts save (just possibly) the second, containing the First Symphony;[288] moreover, Steinbach did not conduct Brahms's Second Symphony at all in Cologne during Abendroth's Essen period. Abendroth may, of course, have heard Steinbach conducting Brahms at one of the latter's geographically more distant Brahms festivals or when he himself was on tour elsewhere, but again the evidence is wholly lacking.

Less speculatively, in his Essen years Abendroth was already forging his own way with the repertoire, which necessarily bore the imprint of the wide and emphatic tempo changes typified by Mottl's practice, and by the end of his tenure in Essen he was 'already counted as a Brahms conductor of stature'.[289] Contemporary critics enjoyed comparing the differing Brahms styles of Steinbach, Abendroth and his successor in Essen, Max Fiedler:

[Fiedler's] style of conducting happily accommodates the composer's ruggedness and forward-storming temperament. There is a fundamental difference between Fiedler's Brahms and that of his predecessor, Abendroth, who gave more emphasis to the architectural element, allowing the melodic aspect to sing out more profoundly, and sought to refine the sound of the Brahmsian orchestra ... Fiedler ... pays more attention to fullness than to nobility of sound, and moves forward in a great urgent wave without giving particular attention to more far-seeing structural organisation.[290]

Given the critical outlook and language of the time in Germany, the comparison is apt and makes clear that the extremes of tempo to be heard in Abendroth's recorded performances were, in this critic's view, part of the conductor's attempt to organise musical structure, an emphasis on the 'architectural element'.

---

[287] See concert listing in Scharberth, pp. 215–27. Steinbach's last Cologne performance of Brahms's Second Symphony was on 9 March 1909, before Abendroth moved to Essen.

[288] See pp. 198 and 231.

[289] Dejmek, p. 149.

[290] Excerpt from an article by Max Hehemann (1873–1933), the leading Essen critic for the Essen *Allgemeine Zeitung*, quoted in Dejmek, p. 149, written on 8 October 1916 on the occasion of Fiedler's first Essen Musikverein concert, in which he conducted Brahms's Fourth Symphony. Dejmek later briefly compares Steinbach and Fiedler in Brahms's First Symphony: see further p. 201.

Abendroth in Cologne

As a forceful personality and, at thirty-two, already a greatly experienced conductor, Abendroth was, with the additional help of Richard Strauss,[291] chosen unanimously from among several distinguished candidates as best qualified to succeed Steinbach in Cologne after the latter's flight.[292] On learning that Abendroth had accepted the post, Steinbach regretted that his favourite, Fritz Busch, had not gained it: from his Munich retreat he wrote to Adolf Busch in January 1915, 'if they wanted a young man they could ... have taken Fritz'.[293] In fact, Fritz had been approached for the Gürzenich post but felt that, just five years out of the Conservatoire, he could not tactfully step into his master's shoes and, shortly after, his call-up for war service ended that possibility.[294] Abendroth conducted in Cologne for twenty years, his first full season (1915/16) in tandem with the Essen concerts.

Although Brahms's First Symphony featured in one of Abendroth's earliest Cologne concerts, in March 1915, and eventually became one of his calling cards as guest conductor in and outside Germany, in his Cologne repertoire Brahms was just one of many featured composers stretching from Bach to Schoenberg and Bartók, with Beethoven and Bruckner perennially and much to the fore.[295] Abendroth was evidently a master conductor of his generation who, as was noted in Essen, already had decided ideas about the interpretation of Brahms which were almost certainly grounded in his experience of Mottl's stylistic approach in an extensive repertoire. It cannot therefore be suggested with any credibility that his Cologne players would have passed on to him any specific interpretative information about performing Brahms: this was the era of the domineering conductor and Abendroth's job was to drill his players with his own ideas and approach rather than accept ideas culled from players about how best to perform the Brahms symphonies. Whether Abendroth inherited the orchestral score parts from Steinbach we do not know; in any event, Steinbach's score parts gave few clues about his

[291] Lucke-Kaminiarz, pp. 35–6.

[292] *Ibid.* p. 36. Abendroth's rivals included Max Reger, who was about to leave Meiningen, and Gustav Brecher (1879–1940), at the time first conductor of the Cologne Opera, who shared the 1914/15 Gürzenich season with Abendroth: Scharberth, p. 227. The latter's later postings included the Frankfurt Opera and later the Leipzig Opera before dismissal by the Nazis and losing his life at sea in a torpedoed vessel crossing the Channel towards refuge in England; see further, Jürgen Scherbera, *Gustav Brecher und die Leipziger Oper 1923–1933*, Leipzig: Edition Peters, 1990, pp. 31–50.

[293] Busch-Serkin, p. 115.

[294] Fritz Busch, p. 99.

[295] Lucke-Kaminiarz, pp. 44 and 51, and see concert listing in Scharberth, pp. 227–45. The listing shows five Brahms First Symphonies (1915–33) and four each of the Second (1918–33), Third (1924–31) and Fourth (1916–33), plus five *German Requiems*; but the number of Brahms performances is dwarfed by the sheer quantity of Beethoven.

approach.[296] There is no known evidence of a direct connection between Abendroth and Steinbach and, from the latter's correspondence quoted above, some suggestion to the contrary. If, therefore, Abendroth was aware of his predecessor's approach to Brahms, his knowledge would most probably have stemmed only from witnessing one or more of the three Gürzenich Brahms concerts noted above.

Abendroth in London

Abendroth introduced himself to London audiences with an all-Brahms concert in April 1926; in the next season there followed Beethoven's Ninth Symphony and more Brahms. So impressed was the LSO that the orchestra urged HMV to place him under a major contract.[297] The company contented themselves with recording Brahms's Fourth Symphony in 1927 and the First in 1928 (there was also an unissued Bach Third Brandenburg recorded at the latter session).

If the LSO was impressed, the critics were not. In particular the *Times* was as unimpressed with Abendroth as it had earlier been full of praise for Steinbach, his predecessor in Cologne. That first LSO concert, on 23 April 1926, including the Second Piano Concerto (soloist Franciszek Goldenberg) and First Symphony, was slated the next day in the following terms:

> It … seems to us definitely wrong to make a radical change of *tempo* in the introduction to the first movement of the symphony; and, if there is a tune which requires above all things to be announced at a steady pace, it is the great swinging melody of the final *Allegro*. To start it Andante and work it up to its proper speed, as was done by Herr Furtwängler some time ago[298] and by Herr Abendroth last night, is to take all the *brio* out of it and to substitute a cheap dramatic effect … [I]t was the accumulation of such things which deprived the works played last night of their true impulse, and broke them up piecemeal. [After strong criticism of the orchestral playing] It is fair to add that the performances were received with great enthusiasm.

Worse was to follow a couple of years later, on 20 February 1928, with an LSO programme that included the Brahms Second Symphony, which was:

---

[296] See p. 37. Steinbach's Cologne scores have, it seems, not survived: Musgrave and Sherman, p. 276. See further p. 229 and n. 22. Abendroth's scores disappeared in the 1970s and only his working parts for the First Symphony survived; these disclose nothing relevant to this study: information courtesy of Irina Lucke-Kaminiarz, December 2009.

[297] Hubert Foss and Noel Goodwin, *London Symphony: Portrait of an Orchestra*, London: Naldrett, 1954, p. 120.

[298] In his London debut concert at the Queen's Hall with the orchestra of the Royal Philharmonic Society on 24 January 1924; see p. 137.

overdriven in the way which has become too customary with Brahms ... Brahms is suffering nowadays from the breakdown of the old illusion that he was a rather phlegmatic composer. Modern conductors have discovered that his music can be exciting. They turn his symphonies into one long rant, pull out his broad melodies, wallow in sentiment over his cadences, and hurry his *finales*. This performance was one of the most glaring examples of the modern vulgarization of Brahms which we have heard, but it pleased the audience enormously.

The *Times* critic could have saved his effort by quoting *Hamlet*: doubtless Abendroth was no 'robustious periwig-pated fellow', but he had clearly torn Brahms 'to tatters, to very rags, to split the ears of the groundlings'.[299]

A month later the same critic was at it again the day after Abendroth's LSO concert on 19 March 1928, not this time Brahms but instead Weber, Strauss and Beethoven's Fifth Symphony; the import must be quoted to complete the critic's views about the conductor:

It appeared from the performance of various familiar German works ... that Herr Hermann Abendroth labours under a confusion of thought which four times out of five is disastrous to the music he conducts. He mistook exaggeration for interpretation, caricature for illustration. His variations of *tempi* in the 'Freischutz' [*sic*] overture were grotesque, so that simple, romantic Weber was inflated into the swaggering figure of Strauss ... and the overture simply became an incoherent series of highly coloured fragments. When minims in one bar are equated with quavers in the next rhythm is destroyed; for unless the mind can feel a constant pulse as a standard of reference for the minute variations which differentiate vital rhythm from mechanical sequence, music falls to bits ... Herr Abendroth squeezed [a Handel concerto grosso] as from a collapsible tube and made unrecognizable nonsense of it ... [M]eans and ends are confused in Herr Abendroth's mind, so that it is only when the composer gets into a stride from which nothing will shake him (as in the *finale* of the [Fifth] symphony) that virtuosity subserves the music.

Which other eminent twentieth-century conductor had ever been skewered so mercilessly by the *Times* at such length? To provide the necessary perspective about the critical assessments of Steinbach and Abendroth already set out in these pages, one needs to disentangle the personalities and musical tastes of the various *Times* reviewers in the period 1925–30. It is clear enough that the reviews just quoted were not written by the critics who adhered to the respectful language typifying reviews of the pre-Great War Brahms concerts conducted by the LSO's outstanding Brahms interpreters

---

[299] Act 3, scene 2.

of yesteryear – Richter, Steinbach and Nikisch. The anonymity of its writers was carefully guarded by the *Times*, but those pre-war reviews were almost certainly the work of its music critics of the period, A. H. Fuller Maitland and H. C. Colles. Both wrote books about Brahms.[300] Colles, who for some years assisted Fuller Maitland before the latter's retirement in 1911, took over from him that year and remained in post until his death in 1943. It is evident that Colles had a long memory, reaching back to Steinbach's London concerts and probably also to those with the Meiningen Hofkapelle in November 1902. But his generous, balanced writing, tactful even when serious criticism was needed, was clearly not in evidence in the reviews quoted above. They must therefore have been the work either of his assistant since 1923, Dyneley Hussey, or of his newly appointed assistant, Frank Howes; their relative youth probably meant that they had few memories of Brahms performances by the LSO's pre-Great War luminaries.[301] It seems more likely that these important concert reviews would have been written by Hussey rather than the new arrival and, if Hussey's views on the proper performance of Brahms's symphonies had been influenced by the rather different experience of Weingartner's post-war LSO concerts, it is not altogether surprising that Abendroth's Brahms received such a drubbing at his hands during 1926–28.

For reasons that will appear, it is probable that Abendroth's concerts were reviewed by Colles from 1929 onwards: the sting is accompanied by sufficient emollient appraisals to suggest a different pen. The reasons for the change are speculative, but it appears that Abendroth had his admirers in London who probably thought that the *Times* reviews had failed to do him justice. As the *Musical Times* remarked after a Weingartner Brahms concert on 2 April 1928, 'there are conductors who go too far in assuming that it is necessary to contradict the letter in order to attain the spirit. Weingartner is not one of these. Probably to a strong advocate of Dr. Abendroth he appears somewhat prim.'[302] So, with what was in all probability Colles's pen, Abendroth's next concert on 11 February 1929, containing the *Oberon* Overture, *Ein Heldenleben* and Brahms's First Symphony, was met next day by the observation that he:

[300] John Alexander Fuller Maitland (1856–1931) was the *Times* music critic 1889–1911. He 'worshipped' both Wagner and Brahms according to his *Times* obituary, unusual in his generation. He numbered books about Joachim (1905) and Brahms (1911) in his output, was regarded as having good judgement save in regard to his younger contemporaries such as Elgar and Delius, but was found to have falsified some facts in certain writings and his integrity was seriously questioned by Elgar in 1905. For H. C. Colles, see further n. 223; his book on Brahms was published in 1908.

[301] Hussey (1893–1972) wrote for the *Times* between 1923 and 1946, and was known, according to the *New Grove*, for a well-informed balanced judgement and an urbane style. For Howes, see p. 106, n. 223.

[302] *Musical Times*, vol. 68 1 May 1928, p. 450.

is a strong conductor who gets from his men what he wants, and wants a great deal
… the playing of Weber showed the value of his discipline. 'Ein Heldenleben', too, was
one of the clearest performances heard in recent years … But our complaint of his
'reading' of Brahms made last year must stand … To make every stroke tell is the aim
of the tone-poem, and Herr Abendroth achieves the aim. To make every stroke tell in
the symphony is to disintegrate the structure. That began with the *pizzicato* dropping
seventh in the introduction. A slower time dragged it from its context, and if a conductor does these things in the first movement, what shall be done on the *finale*? Many
things, too eccentric to be catalogued. There were fine moments, that magical second
theme of the slow movement, for example, but continuity gave way to emphasis.

To complete the survey of Abendroth's Brahms concerts with the LSO in these
years, his concert on 10 March 1930 containing the Fourth Symphony was greeted by
next day's *Times* with strictures about the first movement, where 'there were several
places where a needless alteration in the *tempo* sounded very uncomfortable and inef-
fective. But later Herr Abendroth steadied himself' and the rest of the performance
was highly praised.

A few days after the February 1929 performance of the First Symphony came the
extended essay in the *Times* on 16 February 1929 about conductors' approaches to
Brahms, which has already been quoted in the pages devoted to the evolution of Steinbach's style in his later concerts.[303] Its burden was the change in that style towards
a certain over-emphasis during Steinbach's last appearances in London, especially,
according to contemporary reviews, in the two inner movements of the Third Symphony and the opening movement of the Fourth. Was there, the columnist asked, any
validity in the notion of a similarity between Steinbach's and Abendroth's approach to
Brahms, that in his interpretative liberties Abendroth was 'following the example' of
Steinbach? The essay was clearly by Colles, with its memories stretching back to Steinbach's concerts with the Meiningen Hofkapelle in 1902. His conclusion was that the
comparison had an element of validity only in relation to Steinbach's 'late' style, as distinct from the subtler style with which Brahms would have been familiar in Steinbach's
Meiningen years. Moreover, Abendroth ventured beyond any interpretative gloss by
the latter-day Steinbach towards liberties that contradicted Brahms's clear markings
and intended effect. Colles instanced the *pizzicato* passages in the introductory bars of
the First Symphony's last movement, with a *stringendo* marking in the third bar:

The process of gathering impulse is very attractive to the virtuoso conductor. There
are only six bars of the *pizzicato* in which to do it. Herr Abendroth says, Let us begin
it so slowly and end it so quickly that everybody's breath is taken away by such a rapid

[303] See p. 47.

getting up of steam. Mr. Stokowski, on the contrary (to judge by his recent gramo-phone record[304]), says, Let us begin the *stringendo* sooner than Brahms has written it in order to display its effect over a larger space.[305] Both are equally destructive of the force of the passage in its context, because two slow bars of the rigid ticking figure are needed to establish the normal time from which the restless *stringendo* makes a bid for freedom and to which the music is ruthlessly brought back, with the words *in tempo* in the score.

Colles concludes a long piece by quoting Clara Schumann: a conductor should at least 'play what is written as it is written; it all stands there'. Virtuosity had, he said, moved on since her day, but 'we may at least ask the virtuoso conductor to see what stands there before deciding what else he will put into the symphony'.

From this somewhat detailed tour of the late 1920s, rendered necessary by the claims made for Abendroth's Brahms recordings of the time,[306] it is sufficiently clear that the major and extreme fluxes of his Brahms style in those years – sometimes contradicting the composer's text – strayed very substantially beyond the more subtle flexibility of Steinbach's Meiningen period, the Steinbach with whom Brahms was so content. Abendroth veered towards an interpretative stance more consonant with descriptions of Bülow's idiosyncrasies or, far more likely (given that Abendroth never heard Bülow, nor had any special bond with his immediate successors), with that line of conductors influenced by Wagner's most extreme performance practices: in par-ticular, Abendroth's teacher, Felix Mottl, disastrous in his performances of Brahms.

In this light, any resemblance between Steinbach's later approach to Brahms and Abendroth's style (as perceived by the *Times* and recorded at the time by HMV) would have been at best fortuitous. Put another way, Steinbach's latter-day Brahms (if correctly described) represented a fundamentally Classical approach with its flexibility in nuance and detail slightly going to seed; Abendroth's probably Mottl-influenced approach decorated Brahms's symphonic framework with a Baroque extravagance. Their musical ancestry differed to a degree that in our own era is perhaps difficult to comprehend and any formative influences in their early careers would have led to quite different formal analyses in the performance of the Classical repertoire, including for that purpose the symphonies of Brahms. And once more let it be borne in mind that the recording conductors who readily acknowledged Steinbach's influence in their approach to Brahms – Busch, Boult and Toscanini – encountered him only in the last few years of his career, at a time when, as we have seen, the stylistic features of his Brahms performances were by some accounts metamorphosing into something

---

[304] See p. 69.
[305] Nikisch also altered the composer's directions here: see p. 61. Whether Stokowski's approach was modelled on Nikisch's is not known. See further Ch. 3, p. 191.
[306] See p. 4 and n. 4; see further Ch. 3, p. 198.

more emphatic – eminently neither a development of which these conductors were aware nor a factor inhibiting their appreciation of what they heard. It is a matter of simple deduction to conclude that these noted Classical conductors heard nothing in Steinbach's performances that approached the extreme emphases and changes of tempo featuring in Abendroth's Brahms. And would the three of them have admired Steinbach as they did if such extremes had been present in what they heard? To paraphrase a British politician of recent memory, the answer must be 'No, no and again no!'

Abendroth's later career: a summary and a conclusion

Resuming in brief the principal facts of Abendroth's later career, it is sufficient to note that, because local politicians could not stomach his left-wing views, he left Cologne in 1934. Moreover, despite those views, after Walter fled the Nazis in Leipzig, Abendroth then took over his position with the Gewandhaus Orchestra. With that orchestra and the Berlin Philharmonic he recorded quite extensively, including further versions of Brahms's First and Fourth Symphonies which replaced the HMV recordings for German distribution. His post-war career in Soviet-occupied Europe, from which derive most of his broadcast recordings later issued on CD, is detailed elsewhere.[307]

The conclusion reached above about Abendroth's Brahms interpretations makes problematic any claim of 'authenticity' for his recordings. There is no question of their approximating to performances with claims to touch a strand of authority reaching back to Brahms himself: any influence that Abendroth may have imbibed at an early age was derived from other sources. The best that may be deduced from the documentary evidence is that Abendroth's stylistic approach might have been one of those that Brahms would have been willing to countenance, had he ever heard performances of this character – but that conclusion applies to any number of performance styles among those already traversed, including those of Fiedler, Muck, Mengelberg, Fried and Walter. Furthermore, this conclusion is purely speculative, with no foundation in any documentary source. It would be tempting to leave Abendroth at that, but, given the detailed examination of some of his recordings by proponents of his close stylistic and other connections with Steinbach, a representative selection of his recordings of the four symphonies is further discussed in the next chapter.

Furtwängler: early influences and controversial Brahms

The career of Abendroth's friend Wilhelm Furtwängler is important in the present context only for the significance of his period as assistant to Mottl in Munich during

---

[307] Lucke-Kaminiarz, pp. 107–51.

1907–09, a reward for his remarkably accomplished performance of Bruckner's Ninth Symphony with the Kaim orchestra early in 1907. Whatever his posts in Breslau and Zürich prior to that experience gave him by way of practical knowledge, their significance was dwarfed by the richness of this Munich period, hearing an array of the great singers and witnessing techniques of first-rate stage management. But by far the most important aspect of this engagement was his experience of a wide repertoire of Wagner, Strauss and Beethoven under Mottl, who, whatever projectiles were aimed at him, was still regarded as among the greatest conductors working in Germany.[308] During this two-year period Furtwängler can hardly have failed to absorb some at least of Mottl's interpretative characteristics, such as his broad, and broadly fluxed, tempos, especially in Wagner's music dramas.

As third conductor under Pfitzner at Strasbourg from 1909, Furtwängler encountered in him another conductor who, to judge from his recordings, presented (at least in some of them) characteristics somewhat similar to Mottl's performances; Pfitzner indeed had a close relationship with Mottl.[309] Furtwängler also fully absorbed that composer-conductor's views on the exalted place of the artist in society and the more misty concepts of German identity. In his next post as music director in Lübeck, appointed in succession to the Essen-bound Abendroth in 1911, he encountered Nikisch, with the results already described;[310] and in those years he also found in the writings of Heinrich Schenker a further guide to his interpretative development.[311]

The diverse influences identified here helped develop a style quite distinct from the Brahms–Steinbach line, with (like Mottl and Abendroth) structural signposts underlined by wide distensions of tempo and in later years (like Mottl but unlike Abendroth) a further admixture of inflated tempos often manipulated for expressive effect. His style had matured by the 1920s, when his rapid progress to the top saw him succeed Nikisch in both Berlin (the Philharmonic in 1922) and Leipzig (the Gewandhaus Orchestra in the same year).

Over time, and as political events in Germany in the 1930s unwound so tragically, Furtwängler came to regard himself as a musician who alone was capable of

---

[308] See pp. 52–3. For an accessible and more detailed account of Furtwängler's early career, see Holden, pp. 204–7.

[309] Although he was a prolific recording conductor in the 1920s, Pfitzner's stature as a composer has since overshadowed that aspect of his career. As a Munich resident in the early 1900s, he had substantial contact with Mottl, who programmed his music with some frequency, e.g. in his debut concert with the Vienna Philharmonic in November 1904 which included a work by Pfitzner preceding the *Eroica* Symphony: Haas/Mottl, pp. 274 and 302. Pfitzner's interpretative approach (e.g. his extreme changes of tempo in Beethoven) may therefore have owed something to his experiences of Mottl. See Dyment 2012, p. 243, for suggestions as to the character of Mottl's interpretation of the *Eroica* Symphony.

[310] See p. 71.

[311] Schenker (1868–1935) was a Viennese musical theorist.

33. WILHELM FURTWÄNGLER
IN 1924

divorcing his art from political realities and alone was capable of saving the soul of German music from its despoliation by the Nazi regime. According to Bruno Walter, this supreme egotism had deleterious effects on his performances: in a letter dated 4 February 1938 to Toscanini concerning Furtwängler's attempt to muscle in on the 1938 Salzburg Festival, Walter explained his feelings about his German colleague:

> Furtwängler's atmosphere is – at least for me – politically, personally, and artistically intolerable; and particularly at Salzburg. You want nothing but art, and you know, that I too have nothing in my heart but the same; thus the pure spirit of artistic work reigns until now in Salzburg. But Furtwängler has one sole idea: himself, his glory, his success; he is a man of talent, of personal weight but bad-hearted, which expresses itself even in his music-making. I have now in Vienna had new proofs of how bad he is because of his 'intrigues' against me.[312]

As will be seen, those closest to Steinbach's milieu had much to say in the same spirit.[313] This narrative diversion – no doubt unpalatable for some – is necessary for a full

---

[312] Harvey Sachs, *Reflections on Toscanini*, New York: Grove Weidenfeld, 1991, Ch. 7, 'Toscanini, Hitler and Salzburg', pp. 123–4. Toscanini realised that the Nazis were about to take power in Austria; in February 1938, in advance of that takeover, he cancelled his participation in the 1938 Festival. That festival thus became a Nazi showpiece with full participation by Furtwängler.
[313] See p. 147.

understanding of certain traits in Furtwängler's Brahms, as preserved, which are as distant as could be imagined from Steinbach's probable handling of the symphonies, but which are sometimes upheld as typical of the spirit of the times: 'they all did that sort of thing' and so Brahms expected it[314] – a flip judgement actually contrary to the evidence about the performance practice of Steinbach's line of authority as distinct from the line from which Furtwängler's sometimes extremely wayward performance characteristics are descended.

Comments on Furtwängler's Brahms performances in the 1920s make clear the distinction proposed here between his interpretations and those of the Brahms–Steinbach line. His first performance of Brahms's Second Symphony as conductor of the Berlin Philharmonic on 22 October 1922 was criticised by one writer with a long memory for 'preciously stretched tempos' that 'Brahms himself never had taken', to which he himself could testify.[315] It is also significant that, in his London debut with the Orchestra of the Royal Philharmonic Society in the Queen's Hall on 24 January 1924, the next day's *Times* – in a period when Steinbach's Brahms was, as we have seen in the case of Abendroth, still in the memory of some critics – praised his total command in a 'striking' performance of Strauss's *Don Juan*, but as to the Brahms First Symphony complained, as the critic (most probably Colles) was to complain in the case of Abendroth, that 'a bigger head would not have made the climax of Brahms like the climax of Strauss, a thing of such intense physical excitement'. Moreover, in the second movement, 'this and that detail stood out sometimes with remarkable beauty, but also sometimes at the expense of continuity. As the symphony progressed, one longed for a lighter treatment, especially in the ending of the allegretto, and felt rebellious against the fevered climax of the finale.' Clearly, for this critic, the performance was a long way from Steinbach's more coherent approach.

Berrsche's strong reservations about Furtwängler's Brahms Fourth Symphony in a performance given in Munich in 1922 were rather different from his Berlin colleague's strictures about the Second Symphony. He admired the clarity and the masterly logic of his structure (Berrsche is here presumably referring to the emphatic distensions of tempo which sought to clarify structure) but objected to his Beethovenish brio and dynamics which rode roughshod over the more sensitive inflections revealed in earlier times by Steinbach.[316] The *Haydn* Variations in 1928 were better in these respects, although the *crescendos* in the seventh variation were exaggerated and the fourth variation was far too slow. Here, again, Berrsche pined for Steinbach's agogic inflections[317]

---

[314] See p. xi of the Preface.
[315] Leopold Schmidt (1860–1927), in the *Berliner Tageblatt*, 24 October 1922, quoted in Shirakawa, p. 49.
[316] Berrsche, p. 609.
[317] *Ibid.* p. 611.

– doubtless similar to those to be heard with great clarity in Toscanini's performance of the work which opened his 1935 Brahms cycle with the New York Philharmonic on 17 February 1935.[318]

It must be concluded that 'authentic' Brahms, either in the Meiningen way or in any other way traceable to performance styles having the composer's approbation, cannot be looked for in Furtwängler's interpretations any more than in Abendroth's. The kind of rhythmic freedom that Brahms undoubtedly wanted in the performance of his symphonies, which Steinbach gave him as abundantly as he needed, tended more to the finer nuances of detail than to Furtwängler's characteristic broad swathes of substantial departures from basic tempos. Nevertheless, it must be emphasised here that, as with so many of the conductors encountered in this study, the absence of authenticity affects neither the merits nor demerits of the performances in themselves: they must be judged solely on whether they solve interpretative problems in a convincing manner, provided always that they do not in their course contradict the composer's stated wishes.[319] Given the importance widely attributed to Furtwängler's recordings of Brahms's symphonies, a selection of them is examined in the next chapter.

Sir Adrian Boult: always 'Steinbach for Brahms'

Adrian Boult (1889–1983) was the most significant British witness of Steinbach's performances. It was, however, Hans Richter who dominated his early years and subsequently Weingartner provided extra illumination and vitality in Beethoven. A few years later Steinbach set new standards for Boult in the interpretation of Brahms. Quite how many Steinbach concerts Boult attended is not clear: he was present at several of Steinbach's Brahms concerts in London and witnessed him in other works, including Beethoven's Fourth and Ninth Symphonies, during his travels as a student in Germany before the Great War. But, although Boult's memoirs say much of Richter, Wood and, in particular, the revelation of Nikisch's conducting methods, they are virtually silent about Steinbach, about whom he was forthcoming only in later interviews, including my own in 1972. Yet consistently and throughout his career, in his non-autobiographical writings Boult always gave Steinbach as his conductor of choice for the Brahms symphonies. His reasons have been quoted above, along with the musical benefits received from observing Steinbach's methods in performing

---

[318] This performance can only be heard in the New York Public Library for the Performing Arts: see p. 106.

[319] Frisch, pp. 183–4, in the course of a panegyric about Furtwängler's Brahms, comes close to suggesting that various passages in the Second Symphony's first movement, as performed by Furtwängler, have interpretative problems better solved by him than by the composer.

34. SIR ADRIAN BOULT IN 1937: LIKE NIKISCH, ARMS AT SHOULDER HEIGHT

35. THE BRITISH STEINBACHIANS: WOOD AND BOULT INTERVIEWED BY THE BBC'S FREDDIE GRISEWOOD IN 1942

Brahms.[320] Like Toscanini, Boult retained his memories of and respect for Steinbach throughout a remarkably long career.

In time, especially after he became chief conductor of the BBC Symphony Orchestra on its formation in 1930, Boult became a highly respected interpreter of the Brahms symphonies, without doubt Britain's finest. He recorded two studio cycles of the symphonies after the Second World War, of which the first, with the LPO in 1954, is the stronger and more firmly characterised. This cycle is examined in the next chapter, together with another recording of the First Symphony from 1959, which differs in some respects from its predecessor.

Fritz Steinbach's pupils: the Busch brothers and others

As pupils of Steinbach, the Busch brothers, Fritz and Adolf, are obviously two of the most important witnesses in the present context, both for any influence he exerted upon them – if such influence is observable in their recorded legacy – and for what they had to say about his musical character and interpretative stance. It is fortunate that Fritz at least had somewhat more to say about these matters than did Boult in his memoirs.

Fritz Busch: Brahms direct

Fritz Busch (1890–1951) entered the Cologne Conservatoire in 1906 and in October 1907 joined Steinbach's conducting class. More than any other recording conductor he had the chance to observe and absorb the Steinbach method and style and was unsparing in his praise for this fearsome character who nonetheless showed him 'remarkable sympathy … on every sort of occasion'.[321] Ultimately Steinbach hailed him when he first conducted the Conservatoire orchestra as 'the conductor of the future!' and, although they had their differences over stick technique – quickly forgotten – they remained in close contact after Fritz left Cologne.[322] Steinbach wrote to him frequently in the following years, including a heartfelt letter about Max Reger's experiments with Brahms at Meiningen, and in 1914 became godfather to Fritz's first child, Hans Peter.[323]

In later years Weingartner and possibly Toscanini also left their marks of influence upon Fritz – so much so that Berrsche, who never favoured Weingartner's tempos in

---

[320] See pp. 40 and 107.

[321] Fritz Busch, p. 56.

[322] *Ibid.* p. 62. Fritz records their quarrel over stick technique at p. 65.

[323] The Busch Brothers Foundation's archive contains sixteen letters from Steinbach to Fritz Busch and five from Fritz in reply. For the letter about Reger, see p. 173.

Beethoven, saw in Fritz's own Beethoven (a 1919 *Pastoral* in this instance) a 'wein-gartnerisch' haste, albeit tempered by an intense musicality.[324] Fritz, however, never disavowed his indebtedness to his teacher. Others, too, recognised this invaluable connection, even if in Flesch's case (as ever with him) it was clothed in words which expressed a minimal tribute to Steinbach's stature: Flesch regarded Fritz as 'profoundly musical, frank and honest, an enemy of all pose, straightforward, uncomplicated and unsentimental', who in his exile years in America 'continued in the style of Fritz Steinbach, though his conducting was far more flexible and universal in taste'.[325] Once more Flesch here confirmed the general view of European musicians about Steinbach's fundamentally Classical approach to the repertoire and, in emphasising what he saw as, by comparison, Fritz's extra flexibility, threw a spotlight on the nature of Steinbach's style in general.

Fritz's memory of Steinbach's performances of Brahms was lifelong. A fascinating example of the persistence of memory occurred in 1937 when, taking a day's leave of his work at Glyndebourne, he slipped away to hear Toscanini's concert with the BBC Symphony Orchestra in Oxford's New Theatre on 8 June 1937, the Maestro's only concert outside London. The concert, which included the *Pastoral* Symphony and Brahms's First, was given by Toscanini as a consolation (and with all proceeds) to the University for its unconsummated desire to clothe him in a 'funny hat' (his words) at an honorary doctorate ceremony.[326] Afterwards, in a letter dated 27 July 1937 to his brother Adolf, whose admiration for Toscanini was more whole-hearted than Fritz's, he remarked that '[the concert] was very lovely, of course, but … the Brahms I still have in my memory *even more warmly and convincingly as a whole by Steinbach*'.[327] The significance of this assessment cannot be overestimated because, as must be obvious, had Busch retained in his memory the fancifully extreme pecu-liarities of tempo change attributed by some to Steinbach, his praise would have been less whole-hearted – indeed, given Busch's musical personality, not forthcom-ing at all.

By the late 1940s, when Fritz came to write his memoirs, he was content to cite Toscanini's approval of Steinbach's Brahms without comment of his own,[328] noting only that Brahms was regarded as his teacher's speciality.[329] Perhaps by then he felt a greater independence of view; if so, Fritz's earlier recordings would be more likely to bear any surviving traces of the Steinbach imprint. Unfortunately, only one of his Brahms symphony recordings dates from pre-war days. His post-war recordings of

---

[324] Berrsche, p. 136.
[325] Flesch, pp. 324 and 343.
[326] See further Dyment 2012, pp. 93–6.
[327] Busch-Serkin, vol. 2, p. 370, emphasis added.
[328] See p. 98.
[329] See letter from Fritz to Adolf Busch, 13 June 1949, in Busch-Serkin, vol. 2, pp. 512–14.

the Second and Fourth Symphonies adhere closely to a pure Classical ideal, but the broadcast of the Second Symphony with his Dresden Staatskapelle from Berlin on 25 February 1931 shows him in a rather different light. Although the Classical line is here upheld, it is married to a free-flowing spirit which bends the tempo seemingly spontaneously and momentarily without interrupting the forward impetus. It was that symphony that Fritz chose to programme in a Queen's Hall concert with the LSO on 28 November 1938, of which the *Times* – clearly Colles once more – remarked the next morning:

> His performance of Brahms's Second Symphony reminded us of Steinbach and what was said of Steinbach in the days when Brahms was still a stumbling-block to the simple-minded, that he always told his audiences where the essential tune lay. From the first motive in the basses the tunes were sung and did not lose their continuity by being passed from strings to horns and thence to wood-wind. Only in the finale, but here very definitely, did we feel the movement to be overdriven. We do not believe that 'Allegro con spirito' meant to Brahms the pace that it means to Mr Busch.

Whether, indeed, it did, has already been considered in other contexts, including Weingartner's similar approach on record; a final judgement must await the next chapter.[330] But at least we have this significant comparison between Fritz and his teacher only seven years after the remarkable 1931 performance of the same work.

About three years after Fritz's London concert containing the Second Symphony lies the broadcast recording of the First Symphony drawn from his concert with the New York Philharmonic on 1 February 1942. In many ways this performance is as remarkable as the 1931 broadcast performance of the Second Symphony and is also immensely valuable in demonstrating just what Fritz may have meant in holding up his teacher's performance of the work as 'even more warm and convincing' than Toscanini's. All his recorded Brahms symphony performances – that is, the broadcast performance of the First Symphony, the two versions of the Second Symphony and his late recording of the Fourth Symphony – are examined in the next chapter for any evidence they may disclose of Steinbach's influence.[331]

---

[330] See pp. 92 and 206.

[331] I am indebted to Peter Aistleitner, Kevin Mostyn and Aaron Snyder for the opportunity to hear the recording of the First Symphony. Recording details of Fritz Busch's post-war Brahms are set out at p. 166 below.

36. FRITZ BUSCH IN FEBRUARY 1931

Adolf Busch: beloved pupil

Adolf Busch (1891–1952) entered the Cologne Conservatoire at the age of eleven and, in addition to his tuition in violin with Bram Eldering and piano, eventually joined Steinbach's composition class.[332] His closeness to Steinbach cannot be overemphasised: he was the chosen protégé of the Director, who oversaw his progress in detail. Not long after graduation Steinbach enjoined him to 'Du' familiarity and to address him as 'Onkel'.[333] Their correspondence, before and after Steinbach's fall from grace (about which Adolf was the first to comfort his mentor), was copious. Nevertheless, Adolf left few observations about Steinbach's Brahms style – he was simply too close to and continuously familiar with it to need further comment. In one letter he said to Steinbach 'no-one does [the Second Symphony] as beautifully as you do', but his correspondence reveals little more.[334] Significantly, however, after leaving the Conservatoire Adolf played the Brahms concerto at least eight times under Steinbach and thereby, with his help, achieved supreme mastery in it; his robust, eloquent and unmannered recorded performances of it are living testament to the Steinbach legacy. Adolf's mentor also conducted him in Brahms's Double Concerto and the Beethoven and Reger concertos. Clearly, he was as happy to play under Steinbach's direction as he was later under Toscanini's, choices which have a musical significance further explored below.[335]

It is also significant in the present context that Adolf had no hesitation in passing on to other conductors his knowledge of Brahms's wishes gained from this experience of playing the Brahms concertos under Steinbach. Potter's biography has an illuminating example from 1937, when, in rehearsal for the Brahms Double Concerto with Adolf and his brother Hermann, the conductor, Adrian Boult, seemed to an observer (the composer and writer Harold Truscott) to be happy for Adolf to pass on insights gained from Steinbach and his associates: 'Boult was definitely being guided by Adolf. He stopped Sir Adrian several times and … I remember hearing him say: "Brahms would have it so". The performance that evening was superb.'[336]

---

[332] Eldering was formerly Steinbach's Meiningen Hofkapelle lead violinist, who followed Steinbach to Cologne – see p. 37.

[333] Busch-Serkin, vol. 1, pp. 68–9. letters between Steinbach (1 September 1913) and Adolf (8 September 1913).

[334] *Ibid.* vol. 1, p. 87, letter of 3 February 1914 to Steinbach.

[335] See p. 146. For the occasions on which Adolf played the Brahms concerto under Steinbach, see Potter, vol. 1, pp. 115, 118, 119, 120, 140 and 199; also Busch-Serkin, vol. 1, pp. 32, 37 and 38–9. Adolf's performance of this concerto is best heard in the recording of 18 July 1943 with the NYPSO conducted by William Steinberg, Music & Arts CD 1107. His performance on 18 December 1951 with the Basel SO, conductor Hans Münch, together with his performance of the Double Concerto on 21 June 1949 with his brother Hermann and the French National Radio Orchestra, conductor Paul Kletzki, are on Guild GHCD 2418.

[336] Harold Truscott (1914–92). See further Potter, vol. 1, p. 646.

37. ADOLPH BUSCH
AND TOSCANINI,
SALZBURG, 1936

Adolf's comments on conductors

If Adolf left few comments on Steinbach, he did leave illuminating, if (with one nota-ble exception) brief, comments about other conductors. Starting in 1915, in a letter to Fritz dated 4 February of that year he wrote about Artur Bodanzky – just before this conductor left to take over the Metropolitan Opera musical direction in succes-sion to Toscanini – and in the same letter about his first experience of playing with Abendroth: 'I played in Mannheim with Bodansky [*sic*] (*very* competent)'. In Cologne in January 1915 to play the Mendelssohn Concerto with Abendroth, he thought him a 'fine, serious musician, who is concerned about the work and not himself', but he 'did not have a *profound* impression' and he was 'not *yet* at the *top* though with his serious way of working he has hope of *getting* there. However, that is by no means certain, I still know him too little.'[337] A few weeks later, after playing the Brahms Concerto with Abendroth in Essen, Adolf remarked that 'it was very nice, and we understood each other very well – he is also a good person.'[338]

---

[337] Busch-Serkin, vol. 1, p. 120, letter to Fritz dated 4 February 1915.
[338] *Ibid.* vol. 1, p. 121, letter to Fritz dated 13 April 1915.

Not all conductors were so cooperative: still reporting to Fritz in the same letter about a Brahms Concerto performance that month, 'I ... played with Nikisch in the Gewandhaus – with very considerable success – unfortunately the orchestra was a little loud in the accompaniment and the tutti were somewhat arbitrary on Nikisch's part – but his performance of the D major symphony was wonderful and also his *Tragic Overture!*'[339] Nikisch's antithesis, Karl Muck, was, by contrast, 'good but frightfully boring' as accompanist in two works in 1927.[340]

Of Toscanini's Zürich Brahms Second Symphony in 1924 (the performance which so incensed Furtwängler[341]) Adolf remarked that 'Toscanini was wonderful – in the Brahms Second Symphony, thank God, there was even something *happening* for a change', although he thought the second movement a trifle fast.[342] Here it is germane to underline the close relationship that developed around this time between violinist and conductor: Adolf and Toscanini were frequently present at each others' concerts in the 1920s and 1930s and among violinists of the time it was to Adolf that Toscanini turned for a soloist with whom he felt he could work in the major works of the violin repertoire (at least until his later cooperation with Jascha Heifetz). Further, it was Adolf's profound knowledge and patent, often fierce, integrity that gained a respect from Toscanini that the Maestro hardly ever (indeed, perhaps never) gave to any other musician: 'Adolf is a saint!' he is reported to have remarked.[343] Obviously, Steinbach and Toscanini came from distinct musical cultures but, given that Adolf clearly admired both in equal measure and that his musical outlook always demanded a Classical integrity of approach, it is not difficult to deduce that Steinbach, too, must have possessed that approach at least to the extent that Adolf felt as much at one, musically speaking, as with the other.

Notwithstanding this mutual admiration between the era's most famous conductor and its foremost Classical violinist, Adolf's single most remarkable encomium about another conductor was his contribution to the *Mengelberg Gedenkboek*, published in 1920 to mark the conductor's twenty-five years with the Concertgebouw Orchestra. Surprisingly, in this tribute dated 1919, two years after he first played with Mengelberg and two years before he first witnessed Toscanini in action, Adolf describes a conductor in terms hardly recognisable to those familiar with his recordings: a conductor who '*did not want* anything different from the composer himself',

[339] *Ibid.* p. 122.
[340] *Ibid.* vol. 1, p. 251, letter to Fritz dated 6 November 1927.
[341] See p. 100.
[342] Busch-Serkin, vol. 1, p. 240, letter to Fritz Busch, undated.
[343] See Potter, pp. 308–10. The friendship terminated in 1947 after Adolf married his second wife – too soon, in Toscanini's estimation, after the death of his first, thereby infringing the Italian's highly idiosyncratic views on the sanctity of marriage vows: see generally Dyment 2012, pp. 39–40.

who 'can sense the composer's ultimate, most secret thoughts', with 'an empathy ... astounding in its many-sidedness ... with him, a composer's work remains pure, clear and great ... He does without any so-called "personal touch"' – and much more to similar effect.[344]

After a few years Adolf became impatient with Mengelberg's outsize podium manner and his interpretative evolution towards increasingly wilful and broad fluctuations of tempo. In the letter to Fritz commenting on Muck, Adolf included both Mengelberg and his principal bête noire, Furtwängler ('Furti' to the brothers), in his strictures:

> Toscanini was *very unhappy* with M. [in New York] when he talked with me ... on account of the crazinesses. Furtwängler is doing a lot of damage in this regard, and his success will diminish accordingly until he has perhaps learned ... to develop his tendencies towards precise music making and everything that has to do with good, 'impersonal' music making.[345]

Of course, Furtwängler never did develop in the direction espoused by the Busch brothers; hence Adolf's never resolved musical differences with him, although he did admit in the same letter that the Berlin Philharmonic was '*much* better than before'. But Adolf continued to be deeply troubled by Furtwängler's style: the following month in an undated letter he again wrote to Fritz on the subject, remarking that Furtwängler was 'hopelessly corrupt' in his manner of music-making, 'but the public is beginning to smell the stench and occasionally notices the fresh air' of his own music-making, whether with Rudolph Serkin or with his quartet.[346]

Adolf's reservations did not stop him from playing concertos with Furtwängler, usually with unsatisfactory results, as witnessed by Paul Grümmer, Adolf's Busch Quartet cellist in the years 1919–30:

> I witnessed Furtwängler being unpleasant only when he was working with Adolf Busch. An accommodation between these two seemed impossible. They had absolutely no confidence in each other and made music next to each other but not with

---

[344] Paul Cronheim (intro.), *Willem Mengelberg. Gedenkboek 1895–1920*, The Hague: Martinus Nijhoff, 1920, section on 'Der Dirigent', Adolf Busch, 'Mengelbergs Einfühlingsvermögen' ('Mengelberg's Powerful Empathy'), pp. 65–7, emphasis in original; the extracts from this article are taken from the translation in Potter, vol. 1, pp. 215–16.

[345] Busch-Serkin, vol.1, p. 253, letter to Fritz of 6 November 1927, emphasis in original.

[346] *Ibid.* vol. 1, p. 254; Potter, vol. 1, p. 216. See also Potter, vol. 1, p. 160, for Adolf Busch's relations with Furtwängler.

each other ... Busch was a pure Classicist but Furtwängler was likewise a Romantic [and] a nervous tension regularly resulted.[347]

If Adolf was tart enough about Furtwängler, the latter in turn claimed that Adolf had 'no feeling for Brahms'.[348] Here is the clearest possible evidence, if more were needed, of the gulf between the Steinbach and Mottl lines, which is in any event implicit in all the material extracted here. Clearly, for Adolf, Steinbach and Toscanini stood on the peak, Nikisch sometimes did, while Muck and Abendroth took their places on the slopes; but, for him, Furtwängler had barely set foot on the upward path to the peak – he simply did not see the point of what, to him, were Furtwängler's musical extravagancies. As Potter puts it, 'these two mountain-climbers [Adolf Busch and Furtwängler] shared a lofty view of music but it was a view seen from separate peaks' – peaks, it may be added, labelled respectively 'Brahms' and 'Wagner'.[349]

Berrsche did not, it seems, hear Adolf in the Brahms Concerto but referred to his performance by repute as placing him in the Joachim tradition. Moreover, he praised the Busch Quartet especially for its mastery of *adagio* movements, for its musical spirit and for its elasticity of tempo, from all of which he concluded that Adolf was the most interesting and musical of German violinists, as well as the most expressive and musically full-blooded.[350]

To sum up, Adolf Busch's tutoring by Steinbach and Eldering in the Brahms Violin Concerto, as well as his comments on the conductors mentioned in previous paragraphs, provide evidence that places him centrally within the Steinbach line of authority. The presence of this strong background gave him the confidence to inform others about Brahms's wishes (as transmitted by his teachers) in the performance of the Violin and Double Concertos.

Hans Knappertsbusch: 'no talent for conducting'

Hans Knappertsbusch (1888–1965) joined Steinbach's conducting class in 1908. Steinbach did not hesitate to tell him, as (with the exception of Fritz Busch) he did many

---

[347] Paul Grümmer, *Begegnungen. Aus dem Leben eines Violoncellisten*, Munich: Bong, 1963, p. 110, cited in Potter, vol. 1, p. 160.

[348] Elly Ney, *Elly Ney. Briefwechsel mit Willem von Hoogstraten*, vol. 1: 1910–26, Tutzing: Hans Schneider, 1970, p. 296, letter dated 4 June 1926, quoted in Potter, vol. 1, p. 367. Ney witnessed Adolf Busch with Paul Grümmer in the Brahms Double Concerto at the concert on 4 June in the 1926 Heidelberg Brahms Festival, in which Furtwängler conducted Adolf 'even in the solo passages and said to me afterwards, Adolf has no feeling for Brahms. That was the evening of the Third [Symphony]. He conducted it insanely slowly but beautifully.'

[349] Potter, vol. 1, p. 161.

[350] Berrsche, pp. 660–5.

38. HANS KNAPPERTSBUSCH IN 1929

another class student, that he had no talent for conducting.[351] Perhaps he resented Knappertsbusch's already well-developed Wagnerian sympathies, which were confirmed when his pupil left Cologne to assist Richter at Bayreuth. After succeeding Walter in Munich in 1922, Knappertsbusch frequently came under Berrsche's gaze. Apparently he never invoked Steinbach's name in connection with Knappertsbusch's Brahms performances, but he did praise his rendering of the Third Symphony in 1933 for carefully reconciling its formal and expressive problems, commending in particular the 'glowing and exuberant impetus' given to the transition back to the first movement's recapitulation.[352] Unfortunately, the mantle of *Parsifal* in most of Knappertbusch's post-war Brahms recordings, especially those derived from broadcasts in his old age, weighed him down in some bizarrely slow tempos which almost certainly had nothing to do with Steinbach.[353] Accordingly, his Brahms recordings are not further examined in this study.

Heinz Bongartz: some affectionate Brahms

Finally, another Steinbach pupil, Heinz Bongartz (1894–1978), attended the conservatories of Krefeld and Cologne between 1908 and 1914. He conducted the Blüthner

[351] Friedrich Herzfeld, *Magie des Taktstocks*, Berlin: Ullstein AG, 1953 p. 107.
[352] Berrsche, pp. 281–2.
[353] E.g. Symphonies Nos. 2 (27 November 1959) and 3 (4 November 1956) with the Dresden Staatskapelle, Tahra TAH 303–04: the outer movements of No. 2 are, respectively, 16 minutes (without the repeat) and 11 minutes, those of No. 3 (without the first movement repeat) 11 minutes each; compare the timings in Table 1, below, p. 169.

39. HEINZ BONGARTZ (CENTRE)
WITH NIKOLAI ANOSOV (LEFT)
AND YAKOV ZAK (RIGHT) IN 1955

Orchestra in Berlin during 1924–26, and then, uniquely among Steinbach's pupils, went to Meiningen for four years (1926–30) as conductor of its orchestra, reconstituted under the Weimar Republic. His appointment as music director of the Saarbrücken Opera in 1933 lasted until 1945. He became conductor of the (East German) Dresden Philharmonic in 1947 and held the post until retirement in 1964, returning as a guest thereafter. Bongartz made warm, dignified but not otherwise outstanding recordings of the two Brahms Serenades with his Dresden orchestra in 1962.[354] It is not possible to glean from them any clues about what particular influence his master may have had; by then, Bongartz was approaching the end of his career.

Walter Blume: dedicated to both Steinbach and Fritz Busch

We come to the last witness examined in this chapter in the quest for authentic Brahms. Like the first, Alexander Berrsche, he won distinction for what he wrote, even though his main career was as a conductor. Walter Blume (1883–1933) was another pupil of Mottl in the latter's Munich period but he achieved no great distinction: his principal posts were at Koblenz, probably at the time of Steinbach's Cologne tenure; with the Konzertverein Orchestra in Munich during the First World War; and with the Württemberg Tonkünstler from 1931. His claim to fame lies in his book, published from the manuscript typescript in 1933 by Ernst Surkamp, entitled *Brahms in der Meininger Tradition. Seine Sinfonien und Haydn-Variationen in der Bezeichnung*

---

[354] Berlin Classics CD 0013592BC. Other distinguished pupils of Steinbach, such as Karl Elmendorff (1891–1962), left no recordings of Brahms's works and are not, therefore, further considered here.

von Fritz Steinbach.[355] Jonathan R. Pasternack's complete English translation has been mentioned above; it also contains a valuable contextual introduction.[356]

Dedicated to Fritz Busch – but why?

Like Berrsche, Blume was convinced that Steinbach's Brahms was uniquely authoritative and that, before all memory was lost, his interpretative approach, as Blume himself heard it, should be described in all possible detail. As the introduction to his book shows, it was a task he carried out with commitment and passion. Given that context, the book's dedication to (*'gewidmet'*) Fritz Busch assumes indisputable significance. It is not known whether the two conductors knew each other and it seems that no correspondence between them survives; there is nothing in the Busch Brothers archive. It is, however, inconceivable that Blume would have dedicated his book to Fritz unless at the time of compilation he had heard something of Steinbach's voice in the Brahms performances of his pupil. Perhaps, indeed, he heard Fritz's 1931 broadcast of the Second Symphony as he worked on his text. Fritz's exile in the year of publication, as well as Blume's racial origins and his death in that year, are sufficient explanation of the book's extreme rarity in its original form. Internal evidence suggests that it was compiled in considerable haste. Perhaps the author, whose cause of death is as yet unknown, was aware either that he did not have long to carry out his task or that political developments would soon make its publication impossible.

Blume watches Steinbach – but how often?

Blume wrote and compiled his work in the early 1930s, principally from his notes made during and after Steinbach's Brahms performances. His main opportunity to witness the conductor would almost certainly have been during his Koblenz years: the town is about 80 kilometres from Cologne. In his introduction, Blume also says with emphasis that he obtained the score extracts with Steinbach's markings in Munich during 1914–15, when he came into personal contact with Steinbach and became his student, also attending his 'frequent' concerts there.

Blume's introductory observations, his detailed advice and his claims for the absolute authenticity of the reproduced score markings need critical assessment. There is no reason to doubt that he observed Steinbach's Brahms performances in Cologne during his Koblenz years, but that period ended nearly twenty years before he made his compilation. As earlier noted, because of ill-health and other factors Steinbach apparently conducted very few concerts in Munich; they were rare occasions and far

---

[355] Page references hereafter are taken from Schwalb/Blume.
[356] Pasternack/Blume, pp. vi–xx.

from 'frequent' as Blume maintained.[357] The concerts during 1914–15 were seemingly limited to a couple of charity events, after which Steinbach informed Adolf Busch that he was giving up concert work in Munich because of unsatisfactory orchestral playing. Of course, Blume may also have witnessed Steinbach at the 1909 Munich Brahms Festival or later festivals, but he does not say so; he confines his prefatory remarks to post-Cologne concerts in Munich. In any event, Steinbach was incapacitated from early December 1915 until his death. If, as he often complained, he lacked paying engagements in his post-Cologne period in Munich, he may well have accepted the thirty-year-old Blume as a student; but, in the absence of live performances, what he could have imparted with due accuracy about nuancing and phrasing by words alone remains at best speculative.

Those annotations – originating where?

Of greater significance, it is not clear how far Steinbach annotated his desk scores of the complete symphonies – as distinct from his score parts for the orchestra – which Blume says he saw and copied. It is normal practice for a conductor to mark his own score of a work with his individual requirements concerning expression, dynamics and so forth. From that score a librarian or copyist marks up the orchestral parts as necessary. As we know, Steinbach's orchestral parts of the Brahms symphonies did not contain 'anything special' by way of annotation and for that reason he did not bother to take them with him on his travels; he simply relied on his stick technique and his rehearsals to get the response he wanted from whichever local orchestra he was conducting.[358] In so far as his desk score markings would have been the source of any material for his librarian to copy into the orchestral parts, there is a peculiar disjunction here between what may be implied from Steinbach's remark – that his scores, whether his desk copies of the complete scores or the orchestral parts, contained 'nothing special' by way of annotation – and the many markings that Blume says he saw and copied into his script: it is surely unlikely that Steinbach would have made detailed annotations on his desk copies of the complete scores purely for himself, since he had been conducting the symphonies all his musical life. Or perhaps he did annotate these scores just for himself. We do not know and can only guess – and guesstimates are hardly secure enough foundations for any musicological exercise, whether the present study or Blume's parsing of Steinbach's way with Brahms.

An insuperable obstacle to the solution of the major difficulty here outlined is the complete disappearance to date of Steinbach's scores, both his desk copies of the complete scores and those orchestral parts with 'nothing special' by way of marking

[357] See p. 38.
[358] See p. 37.

up. Searches in Cologne have so far been unproductive.[359] Nor are any of Steinbach's privately owned scores and parts that he might have used in Meiningen held in the Meiningen collections.[360] In the absence of any corroborative information, the question mark over the source of Blume's annotations must, unavoidably, be borne continuously in mind whenever he illustrates his 'advice' on any point of detail by reference to what he claims to be Steinbach's own score markings.

How much Steinbach, how much Blume?

Whatever the source of Blume's advice, how helpful or reliable is it as an indicator of Steinbach's approach? As will be seen in Chapter 3, a number of Blume's precepts reflect common currency among more sensitive later Brahms interpreters, with or without such further explication. And are Blume's written observations sufficiently precise to be more than a general indication? The tempo of the fifth *Haydn* variation, he says, should always be 'very lively'[361] – hardly a helpful gloss on Brahms's *vivace* and conveying nothing of the virtuoso spirit with which, through Toscanini and Henry Wood, we know that Steinbach addressed it. Where by contrast Blume is more explicit, his link with Mottl raises questions: Mottl's style, unsuited to Brahms, was quite distinct from Steinbach's, but it cannot be assumed that Blume himself remained wholly uninfluenced by his master's tendency to extremes. 'Make a strong *crescendo*' with the 'greatest possible tone', he says of the *crescendo* in the second part of the seventh *Haydn* variation;[362] but, as noted above, Berrsche – forever conscious of Steinbach's shadow – thought it a misplaced exaggeration when Furtwängler did just that.[363] Was Blume here invoking Steinbach or Mottl (who had the work in his repertoire and performed it in Vienna)?

If such advice is doubtful, so also on occasion are Blume's references to Brahms's scores, where he relies on a faulty memory rather than the scores themselves; for example, in Variation 17 of the Fourth's passacaglia he refers to the descending strings' *fortissimo* as a triple *forte*, a typical error of a kind footnoted in other instances by Pasternack. To take but one example of the latter, Pasternack notes an error as early as bar 9 of the First Symphony's introduction, where, in place of Brahms's *forte* marking, Blume substitutes a *fortissimo*. And so such mistakes proliferate – well over a dozen

---

[359] See Musgrave and Sherman, p. 276, and p. 129 and n. 296.
[360] Information courtesy of Dr Maren Goltz, May 2014. The Meiningen collections hold first editions of the Brahms symphonies formerly belonging to the Hofkapelle Music Library, some of which are heavily marked and amended, but the handwriting is unknown. For the Brahms scores as amended by Max Reger at Meiningen, see p. 173.
[361] Schwalb/Blume, p. 86.
[362] *Ibid*. p. 87.
[363] See p. 138.

of them. The errors are evidence of the pressures likely to have been acting on Blume at the time of compilation. But in a work concerned with the minutiae of expressive annotations, such lapses, minor though they may be, must raise queries about the complete reliability of Blume's memory elsewhere.

Furthermore, it is unclear how far Blume's annotations reflect his own opinions as distinct from Steinbach's opinions and markings: there is much comment throughout the work that appears at first sight to reflect what Blume heard Steinbach say, but on closer examination suggests Blume's own extrapolations from the master, perhaps justified, perhaps not. The lack of clarity about the authorial voice is underlined by Blume's unexplained habit of 'quoting', from time to time, some of his pithiest advice. Do such quotations signify – as seems likely – Steinbach's very words, imparted personally to Blume? If so, with what degree of authority is the remaining advice – by far the greater part – to be treated?

That query can only be repeated *a fortiori* in relation to those passages in Blume's advice that without doubt reflect his own views rather than Steinbach's, a feature that adds to our difficulty in assessing the authenticity of the rest. For example, Blume's extensive advice about performance of upbeats in a strong fashion in certain contexts, a practice about which he is almost obsessive, strays far and wide in his discussion of the First Symphony, eventually citing the performance practice of both Steinbach and Nikisch – clearly an instance in which the authorial voice is Blume's alone. Other examples achieve less prominence but serve to reinforce doubts about the directness of input from Steinbach himself.[364]

The strange uncertainties and unanswerable questions outlined above lead unavoidably to the conclusion that, as Pasternack puts it, 'in relationship to Brahms's work, Blume's text must be designated as a tertiary source'.[365] The contradictions concerning the source of Blume's annotations – from Steinbach's scores even though these may well have carried little by way of comment – constitute a substantial barrier to a straightforward acceptance of the verity of Blume's annotations, a barrier reinforced by the other shortcomings cited, such as his errors, the inextricable mixing of the views of his master and himself and his unexplained habit of 'quoting' his source. Other than even closer analysis of the published typed text of 1933, it is doubtful that there now exists any scope for further investigation of the questions raised here about

---

[364] Pasternack/Blume, pp. 44–5; Schwalb/Blume, p. 32. Further examples are given in the text. An instance which shows Blume wholly in error is where he states that Brahms's inspiration for the Fourth Symphony's scherzo lay in the 'well-known bas-relief by Thorwaldsen, "*Der Alexanderzug*"': Pasternack/Blume, pp. 111–12; Schwalb/Blume, p. 78. Pasternack shows that this ascription was without foundation: see Pasternack/Blume, p. 112, n. 9. This is also an example of the presence of the authorial voice that may throw doubt on the authenticity of the rest. See further p. 199.
[365] Pasternack/Blume, p. xix.

Blume's text. At best, those issues must be borne continuously in mind if Blume's text is to be relied on at all for guidance as to Steinbach's practice; at worst, the plausibility of Blume's text must be questioned rigorously for any light it purports to throw on that practice. With some reluctance to rely on the quality and reliability of Blume's evidence, the present study assumes that, given his evident commitment to his task, it is more likely than not that a substantial part of his annotations reflects Steinbach's practice. But his observations must be assessed critically and supplemented from other reliable sources whenever possible. For these reasons Blume is treated hereafter as an aid towards reconstructing the Meiningen way, but certainly not as an infallible guide.

The critical language: whose 'rubato'?

The completion of this documentary survey permits further consideration of the issue raised on several occasions during its course: how do we know that a seemingly detailed description of one or another performance of a Brahms symphony a century or more ago is couched in language that conveys to the modern reader a meaning similar to that conveyed to its contemporaries? That question received a provisional answer in the context of descriptions of what were clearly some very marked distensions of tempo as practised by Arthur Nikisch. There I suggested that the meaning of the words used had probably not changed but that the critical tolerance of Nikisch's practices almost certainly had: some instances of those practices would very probably have been found unacceptably extreme today, to the point (as Boult confirmed) of eccentricity.[366]

The problem concerning critical nomenclature is undoubtedly a major issue about which much has been and could be written. In the present context, however, it is necessary to focus only on usage during the period immediately preceding the Great War, from which date many of the reviews quoted in this study. In that limited context, confirmation sufficient to attest the validity of the provisional answer offered in the preceding paragraph is to be found in an extended feature article, almost certainly by Fuller Maitland, in the *Times* dated 16 April 1910. The article was stimulated by Padarewski's contribution (his only published writing to that date) in H. T. Finck's book, *Success in Music and How It Is Won*, published in New York in 1909. The *Times* critic's most difficult task concerned nomenclature – what terminology was most accurate as a description of the ebb and flow necessary for the enlivening performance of all music? As Fuller Maitland pointed out, *'tempo rubato'* in its literal sense, of 'lingering repaid by hurrying', whether within a bar or a phrase, would, if consciously attempted, result in nothing but an uncomfortable rigidity without the 'satisfying steadiness' of

---

[366] See pp. 10, 41 and 61.

the metronome. Equally unsatisfactory was '*tempo rubato*' in the meaning ascribed
to Chopin: the combination of free time in the right hand and strict time in the left.
Better, thought the critic, to refer simply to 'free' or 'flexible' tempo: '*rubato*' in the
sense of flexibility was needed as a natural and inevitable extension of the principle
applicable to 99 per cent of compositions; that is, 'humanized expression' normally
necessitates some measure of *rubato*.

Using this terminology interchangeably, the critic attempted to analyse what was
meant by a 'fine, flexible rhythm' and found that possible only in terms of negatives:
there had to be breadth of phrasing with no chopping of the notes; there could be no
hysterical gulps or gusts of feeling 'to break the vividly pulsating general flow'; and
there could be nothing to stand in the way of structural homogeneity and the steadiness of the 'crests of the accentuation'. Ultimately, however, the essence of *rubato* is that
'it is too subtle to be indicated in musical notation': all formulae are too clumsy for
'its imperceptible gradation and swing. Excessive attention to rhythmic niceties may
very easily lead to their exaggeration', a characteristic of those reprehensible performers 'whose chief emotional stock-in-trade consists of *ritardandi* so huge as entirely to
upset the organic unity of the music'.

Fuller Maitland acknowledged that many of his comments were more referable to
solo performers or chamber music: he gave detailed descriptions of the Joachim Quartet's Classical stance which nonetheless encompassed their use of *rubato* (in his loose
sense) 'very subtly present in some form or another in nearly every bar'. But, rounding
off with comments on orchestral practice, the critic remarked that:

> A good deal of attention has been given of late years to orchestral rubato, and conduc-
> tors so diverse as Herr Nikisch and Mr. Sousa have acquired special fame in that line.
> But the Meiningen Orchestra under Herr Steinbach was *hors concours*; their Brahms
> playing, *absolutely non-metronomic and absolutely unified* [emphasis added], was a
> unique revelation. Of course, perfection of this kind implies infinite rehearsing, for
> which orchestras usually do not have the time … [hence] the very frequent lack of viv-
> idness in orchestral rhythm … strike[s] us much more strongly; a certain atmosphere
> of military discipline still seems to hang over most of our bands. Some day, perhaps, a
> successor to the Duke of Meiningen will arise who will subsidise an orchestra which
> can spend its whole time studying the problems of free rhythm *en masse* … [for] in
> the proper subtle sense of the words, free rhythm applies to all music.

While I readily acknowledge the detailed studies elsewhere about the meaning in
different eras of terms such as '*rubato*', 'flexible' tempo, 'free rhythm' and the like,[367]

---

[367] See e.g. Musgrave and Sherman, Ch. 13 (Philip), pp. 360 *et seq.* There are also valuable quotations by conductors and other musicians in Robert Philip's *Early Recordings and Musical Style*,
Cambridge: Cambridge University Press, 1992, Part 1, 'Rhythm'.

it appears that the foregoing *Times* column provides sufficient evidence for deducing that, in the era with which this study is primarily concerned, the terminology in common critical parlance has not undergone such change as to render the reviews quoted throughout – which necessarily contain much of the material from which this study draws its conclusions – an unreliable vehicle for conveying a meaning understandable to the modern reader. The acceptability of degrees of *rubato*, flexibility of rhythm and freedom of tempo may well have changed, but not their inherent meaning – at least in that period before the Great War on which this study has concentrated to a substantial degree.

It is, however, noteworthy that Fuller Maitland was concerned that, even in 1910, orchestral technique had, at least in London, by no means fully achieved the means of effecting 'free rhythm *en masse*'. His comments are in themselves a measure of the degree to which orchestral playing has improved over the last century, in the training of players, the improvements in instruments and, in some respects, a developing sophistication in the technique of conducting – so much so that the problems encountered in achieving an immediate response to fine adjustments of phrasing and nuance do not now meet with the degree of difficulty that seems to have been the case in the pre-Great War period of which Fuller Maitland spoke. At that time, Henry Wood, for example, might on occasion achieve sophisticated results in terms of nuance and flexibility but, as demonstrated by reviews of his concerts, on other occasions the result was crude. It was left to the great foreign artists to show what could be done in terms of refinement and flexibility of response, sometimes to the delight of London critics, but at others with results that again went beyond the boundary of what those critics (much more to be feared, as Boult put it, than their German counterparts) found acceptable on grounds of both taste and structural coherence – operating, as now demonstrated, within an accepted critical vocabulary that can be understood today, even if our taste would not always see eye to eye with theirs. Of course, the great foreigners differed sharply in character among themselves: Fuller Maitland places Steinbach in a category of his own as regards the use of *rubato* by his Meiningen Hofkapelle. The reference to Nikisch having acquired fame for *rubato* – but not by comparison with Steinbach – shows that the critic was concerned, not with the major deviations of tempo characterising Nikisch's general approach in all his music-making, but with the subtle changes of pulse so readily achieved by Steinbach with his forces, on display in London in 1902.

These explications of critical vocabulary appear satisfactory as far as they go, but they are not sufficient to clarify all aspects of Berrsche's appraisal of Steinbach's approach to Brahms, fully set out above, nor certain remarks of Blume.[368] Berrsche noted Steinbach's 'loving cultivation of details', his 'agogic refinements' and the 'great

---

[368] See p. 41 and also p. 186.

expressive power of the cantilena' – clear enough references to the way in which, as other critics pointed out, Steinbach practised incessant minor fluctuations of tempo in order to heighten the expressivity of the line at appropriate moments. Berrsche also refers to Steinbach's 'iron rhythm', through which the conductor achieved an 'overwhelming effect'. Again this chimes exactly with observations by London critics.[369] But Berrsche mentions Steinbach's 'rarely used but so natural rubato' as well. Fuller Maitland's essay demonstrates that '*rubato*', as a term used by London critics, indicated simply the expressive fluctuations to be heard at every turn in Steinbach's Brahms performances with the Meiningen Hofkapelle. Berrsche, by distinguishing his use of the term from Steinbach's constant 'agogic' refinements of line, clearly means something else, especially since he adds that *rubato* was rarely used by Steinbach.

Berrsche's use of the term '*rubato*' is not easy to explain: he surely did not have in mind the pianistic devices with which Fuller Maitland opened his explanatory essay, 'lingering repaid by hurrying' within the bar line or the freedom of the right hand as against the strict time of the left. It seems likely that, given the rarity which Berrsche ascribes to Steinbach's use of the device, he had in mind more major and obvious fluctuations of pace, which in Boult's account was a feature that Steinbach used infrequently: 'he wasn't always doing that', but in the Fourth Symphony's passacaglia 'he did express himself very freely'.[370] If that conclusion is accepted, it seems clear that Berrsche's analysis of Steinbach's art was on all fours with that of his London colleagues.

Blume sets a similar problem: in the context of the First Symphony's introduction, he warns that, regarding the *tenuto* signs with which the musical examples in his texts are littered, 'in no case should the impression be given that the note values … become lengthened'; where that was needed, the word *rubato* has been added to the musical example. And by *rubato* he clearly means the 'paying back' within the bar line that Fuller Maitland rejects as an expressive device – and which that critic clearly implies was not to be heard in Steinbach's Brahms performances.[371] As with Berrsche, the anomaly cannot readily be explained, save perhaps by its being subsumed in the London critic's more general remarks about the interchangeability of critical vocabulary to describe what he heard in the constant flexibility of the Meiningen Hofkapelle's Brahms under Steinbach.

Interim conclusions

Given the range of London's critical vocabulary as explained above, what conclusions remain to be drawn about the principal players featured in this chapter? We

[369] See p. 44.
[370] See p. 41.
[371] See Pasternack/Blume, p. 13; Schwalb/Blume, p. 12.

have noted the brickbats hurled at that archetypal 'tempo rubato conductor', Felix Mottl, who apparently had no difficulty in securing from London orchestras of the 1890s the broad, fluctuating emphases so typical of his style;[372] we have noted, too, the untrammelled delight of the critics in welcoming to London Mottl's antithesis, Felix Weingartner. Four years later, Fritz Steinbach's Brahms performances came as a revelation for the subtlety of their constant but never self-regarding flexibility (as compared with any symphonic performance by Mottl). Nikisch's Brahms, by contrast, came as rather a shock to those (including Boult) for whom Steinbach had said the last word on the composer. But it must be recollected that even Steinbach's handling of part of the First Symphony's first movement, if much less extreme than Nikisch's treatment of the same passage, was notable for a certain amount of tempo flexibility regarded by the critics as unorthodox – in its turn, a measure of how far the 'orthodox' (presumably in the shape of Hans Richter) cleaved to the straight and narrow, to a degree that today might well be regarded as stiff-jointed. After a few years of Nikisch, however, many critics simply viewed his extreme flexibility as casting fresh light on Brahms; familiarity had bred acceptance within contemporary critical terminology, so much so that Max Fiedler's probably not dissimilar degree of extreme flexibility in handling Brahms – if with far less poetic results – was not considered by the London critics to be unacceptable.

Arthur Nikisch, Felix Weingartner and Fritz Steinbach: these conductors could all draw on their personal memories of Brahms's approbation in their handling of his symphonies. No other conductor among those examined in the present chapter could do so in the same, direct way. Max Fiedler, by way of example, lived in the north German milieu to which Brahms was accustomed until the composer moved, beyond the power of persuasion to recall, to the Vienna that became his permanent home. This conductor's contacts with the Hamburg Brahms circle were intimate to a degree, while his attachment to Bülow was similarly close. But Brahms never saw Fiedler conduct and, given the latter's open attachment to the Bülow way, we can only speculate about the composer's possible reaction to his performances – even though many German critics in the second and third decades of the twentieth century regarded Fiedler's handling of Brahms as the most authoritative around.

So many other conductors forced in this chapter through the sieve of historical accountability have failed to demonstrate any connection with Brahms or any connection with those who had Brahms's direct approbation. Karl Muck, Willem Mengelberg, Bruno Walter – all conductors of great repute in the performance of Brahms and the last two with distinguished recordings of the symphonies to their name – had formative influences hailing from afar, in the shape of Wagner, Bruckner and (overwhelmingly for Mengelberg and Walter) Mahler. Similarly distinguished

---

[372] See p. 51.

– or at least distinctive – in their Brahms recordings were Hermann Abendroth and Wilhelm Furtwängler, again both heirs to influences as far removed as could well be from Brahms and his circle: specifically their revered senior, Felix Mottl, swimming in Wagner, uncomprehending of Brahms and forever incompetent or indifferent in his handling of him. Suggested resemblances between the Brahms performances of the composer's most direct heir, Fritz Steinbach, and those of Abendroth are, so far as may be documented, not substantiated, save to the extent that there may have been a few fortuitous, unidentifiable similarities in some of Steinbach's later and most emphatically stamped performances. But even this concessionary glance is rendered null by the testimony of Steinbach's pupils and admirers, who heard nothing so wayward in his Brahms as Abendroth's performances of the Brahms symphonies subject to the extreme critical skewering in post-Great War London.

And so we return to the three anointed heirs: Nikisch, Weingartner and Steinbach. Nikisch exercised a magnetic influence on all who came directly under his spell, a uniquely refined technique used to create the most suggestive nuances, the most expansively stretched departures from *tempo primo* and the most exciting, sometimes fevered, climaxes, all quite independent of the bar line. But few conductors were in any real sense his musical heirs: they came, saw and were conquered but then went their own way musically. Of the many considered in these pages, only Stokowski survived to tell – just possibly – something of the Nikisch legend in his 1927 recording of the First Symphony.

Weingartner had better luck. Coming just a few years after Nikisch, he survived to make recordings of the Brahms symphonies with, as the material set forth in this chapter has demonstrated, some claim to authenticity of utterance – even if assessments now sometimes made of him claim more than can be strictly justified by the documentation. But again, his direct musical heirs, at least in the performance of Brahms symphonies, are thin on the ground. His influence lives on today in those now seeking to return to a Brahms shorn of the accumulated history of conflicting traditions and attendant performing accretions. Sensibly handled, the Weingartner example can still provide the groundwork, a *Grundnorm*, for a renovated and continuing validity – and vitality – in the performance of Brahms's symphonies.[373]

That leaves Fritz Steinbach. This conductor's practice, as viewed both through available documentation and through the word of mouth of his musical heirs, remains central to any discussion of the possibility of a continuing tradition in the performance of Brahms's symphonies. It is to be hoped that the documentation in this chapter both informs the reader why he remains important – his prolonged, close and mutually beneficial contact with the composer, the lessons he learnt from him – and

---

[373] A *Grundnorm* is a 'basic norm' in Hans Kelsen's jurisprudential theories, denoting a foundational norm for a legal system; see further Hans Kelsen, *Pure Theory of Law* (transl. from 2nd German ed. by Max Knight), Berkeley and Los Angeles: University of California Press, 1967.

also articulates and analyses the particular attributes of his stylistic approach. If my analysis of that approach differs from assessments made by others, I can only pray in aid the appraisals of critics, eyewitnesses, other performers and (crucial for today's listeners) those who explicitly accepted his influence, whose words are set forth as fully as may be in the course of these pages – expressed, moreover, in a critical or descriptive currency whose meaning has changed little over the years.

The witness of the critics, commencing with Berrsche's close analysis of Steinbach's Brahms performances and continuing on both sides of the Atlantic until the outbreak of the Great War, is sufficiently firm to amount to virtual unanimity: Steinbach's constant and subtle shaping of rhythm and nuance ventured relatively infrequently in the direction of an exceptional degree of freedom, as Boult and Berrsche agreed, and never endangered the fundamentally Classical coherence of the whole. That conclusion is bolstered in no uncertain terms by the conductors and other musicians who in their different ways founded and developed their own musicianship in the performance of Brahms upon the rock (or, again, *Grundnorm*) of Steinbach's example: Adrian Boult, Fritz and Adolf Busch and, perhaps most eloquently, albeit with *multum in parvo*, Arturo Toscanini.

It is left to the next chapter to analyse the recorded legacies of various noted conductors who, by virtue of their differing stylistic approaches to the performance of the Brahms symphonies, may properly be regarded as providing a genuine link with the composer – and, also, those alleged to have had such a link, albeit without any demonstrable documentary evidence of such lines of authority. Given the centrality of the Steinbach legacy to this history, it will come as no surprise that those who acknowledged his influence tend to dominate the course of the narrative; but others, also, must have their (recorded) say.

RECORDED EVIDENCE:
TRADITIONS TRACED OR LOST

The chosen recordings: an overview

Selected early recordings of the Brahms symphonies are examined in this chapter with the aim of isolating those characteristics in them that may be attributable, in whole or in part, to the influence of those conductors who received some form of approbation by the composer for their stylistic approach. In one case only, that of Felix Weingartner, there is no intermediary: his approach to the Second Symphony received the composer's direct approval in 1895. If one accepts, as Chapter 2 suggests may plausibly be the case, that Weingartner's recorded approach preserved at least a sufficiency of the characteristics that Brahms himself heard, the analyst's task is relatively straightforward: it is enough to draw attention to how Weingartner performs one or another passage by comparison with his coevals and invite the inference that such handling is at least one solution that might well have had Brahms's approbation. Chapter 2 does, however, signpost possible difficulties in any such straightforward acceptance.[1]

In the other examples covered by this chapter, attribution of a particular influence by one conductor having the composer's approval upon another conductor is far less straightforward. We are dealing here with the performance characteristics of non-recording conductors (at least in the works of Brahms) who had the composer's blessing for their approach and who exercised an audible influence upon others who did record. Such identification and attribution poses formidable difficulties. All the conductors with whom this study is concerned had their own highly developed performance characteristics, and to home in on this or that passage as suggesting the interpretative influence of someone else risks a misleading and simplistic manner of dealing with a subject too obviously littered with booby traps for the credulous.

Where the recording conductor seemingly rejects the possibility of any influence by another, the difficulties outlined are all but insurmountable. In the case of Stokowski,

---

[1] See pp. 86–94.

for example, we know that the conductor invoked only Hans Richter as an influence on his music-making, even though on the face of it the sturdy Hans had almost nothing in common with Stokowski's evolved style (or, as vividly demonstrated by his early and late performances of the Second Symphony, styles). Nevertheless, it is worth including Stokowski's 1927 recording of the First Symphony in this chapter's comparative exercise for any light it may, just, throw on the interpretative ways of Arthur Nikisch, who, as the documentation attests, was without doubt Stokowski's teacher in Leipzig, circa 1906.

In the case of Steinbach, ever central to this study, the difficult task of ascertaining recorded influences deriving from his example is alleviated to some degree by the openly expressed admiration of pupils and other conductors. Again, however, it would be a snare to suggest that the work of the band of great Steinbach witnesses further examined in this chapter – Fritz Busch, Adrian Boult and Arturo Toscanini – can be conveniently pillaged for examples of Steinbach's way: their very different and powerful personalities as they developed to full maturity and the long decades of experience elapsing between Steinbach's performances and their own recordings of the Brahms symphonies suggest the need for the most sophisticated degree of sieving through their recorded legacy for any signs of Steinbach's stylistic approach. While acknowledging the difficulties, it is indeed necessary to examine with due care all of Fritz Busch's Brahms symphony recordings, together with selected recordings by Toscanini and the earliest Brahms recordings (1954 and also the First Symphony of 1959) by Adrian Boult. The Fourth Symphony conducted by Vittorio Gui in his last concert in 1975 is also included, because of Berrsche's description of an earlier performance of that work under Gui.

There remains a miscellaneous band of conductors whose recorded performances of the Brahms symphonies need further examination, if only to act as musical foils to the aforementioned conductors whose attachment to the Steinbach way is securely founded on traceable connections. The two conductors labelled in this study as the Mottl acolytes – Hermann Abendroth and Wilhelm Furtwängler – require inclusion. In Abendroth's case that inclusion is merited because some regard him as having a close connection with Steinbach, a conclusion based, it seems, on a few of his recordings that are thought to reflect Steinbach's probable approach – although there is an almost complete absence of written documentation to support this view. In Furtwängler's case, inclusion is necessitated because of a belief, loosely expressed by some, that his interpretative stance, an illustrious example of the licence taken in the early part of the twentieth century in the performance of symphonic literature, illustrates the kind of approach that Steinbach himself probably adopted – again, a suggestion not only without documentary support but also quite contrary to every musical and critical view commonly expressed by contemporaries. Notwithstanding these formidable obstacles to their acceptance as forming a continuous line of authority connected to the composer, a selection of Brahms symphony recordings by both of these conductors is examined further in this chapter. Bruno Walter's Brahms is also further scrutinised because his recordings typify those by conductors over whose performances of the Brahms symphonies there began a slow accretion through many decades of a patina of respect and admiration, even though there existed no evidence of a solid musical link between them and the composer.[2] If the conclusions reached in the documentary evidence set out in Chapter 2 are on the right lines, it is to be expected that the Brahms recordings of these three conductors will exhibit clear differences from those of the Steinbach witnesses.

As suggested in Chapter 2, the Brahms recordings of Max Fiedler are useful to illustrate a probable contiguity with the style of Hans von Bülow, whose close collaboration with Brahms suggests the need to examine these recordings in further detail, even though they cannot be connected unequivocally to a stylistic approach having the composer's known approval. Chapter 2 also dealt with the Brahms performances of several other early recording conductors, but the conclusion there drawn was that their recordings had no links with the composer – direct or indirect – sufficient to merit their further analysis in the present chapter.

Most of the conductors whose performances have been selected for further examination in this chapter recorded the works more than once and, in several cases, live performances, both early and late in their careers, throw further light on their interpretative approach. Where there is a choice between earlier and/or live performances as against later 'official' recordings, as is the case especially with Toscanini, the former are preferred because a live performance (as opposed to studio recordings on 78rpm discs or tape) is more likely to reflect actual performance practice and, by its closer proximity to the Steinbach era, might be expected to display his influence, if any, more explicitly. Abendroth's and Furtwängler's Brahms symphonies are likewise preserved in several versions of each; choice was dictated by the foregoing criteria and also by ready availability. Walter's pre-war Brahms recordings are here preferred since they are free of the possible contentions concerning 'New World' influence or the undue relaxation of tension in old age sometimes raised against his late American recordings. For these reasons, too, the Second Symphony, not recorded in the 1930s, is represented

---

[2]   An example illustrating how this 'patina' is transmuted into unverified fact is to be observed in the online MusicWeb review of Tahra CD 452 containing Walter's concert with the Berlin Philharmonic on 25 September 1950 (Mozart's great G minor Symphony and Brahms's Second, the latter also chosen for further analysis in this chapter: see p. 168). Referring to the way in which the cellos phrased the opening of Brahms's second movement, the reviewer remarks: 'It's as though they are carrying on their shoulders a whole tradition, one that stretches back to the composer; one Walter was as qualified as any conductor who has ever lived to represent, too.' At the time of Walter's performance the Steinbach admirers, Boult, Fritz Busch and Toscanini, were all alive and conducting Brahms.

by his Berlin performance on 25 September 1950, at a date before the relaxed Brahms in the latter years of that decade somewhat changed his approach.

A word is needed about the public availability of some of the chosen recordings. At the time of writing the recording of Fritz Busch's Carnegie Hall concert performance of Brahms's First Symphony on 1 February 1942 remains in private collections. Toscanini's earliest recorded performance of that symphony, dating from February 1935 in the same hall, is likewise locked away in the vaults of Toscanini's legacy of sound recordings in New York, to be heard only via the New York Public Library of the Performing Arts.[3] Non- or limited availability, however, must not be a bar to their detailed consideration, the more so since, as will become evident, both of them are among the most important aural documentations pinpointing the likely character of some of Steinbach's performance characteristics in this repertoire.

Recording details and tabular analyses

The following pages set out in tabular form the details of the chosen recordings. As mentioned, a few are not publicly available; it is to be hoped that this shortcoming will be rectified. Further tables set out the timings of most of these recordings, movement by movement. The final set of tables looks more closely at these recordings with the perhaps doubtful aid of the metronome. The purpose of these exercises is further explained below, but it may be remarked here immediately that, in the course of compiling these tables, in very many instances the mastery of the chosen conductors showed dramatically how useless the metronome is as a device called in aid to analyse the performances in any detail. None of the conductors adhered to the metronome values at any point for more than a couple of bars and, of course, the two Mottl acolytes added some abrupt and/or extreme fluxes of tempo that a (necessarily) highly selective use of the metronome could not catch. Surprisingly, however, it was often the Classical conductors – Weingartner and Toscanini in particular – who offered the greatest challenges to the machine: Ernest Newman's remarks in 1923 about the former were vindicated in no uncertain fashion, with the machine demonstrating how easy it is to forge a negative view of Weingartner's style if ears are not fully attuned to what is actually happening in these ancient grooves.[4] Similarly, in the recordings selected, Toscanini proved to be the antithesis of his reputation among careless listeners as the metronomic Maestro: the heart was, of course, beating as passionately as any on record, with a resultant and ever constant – but usually slight – change of pace in

---

[3] See pp. 166 and 167, below. It should be noted that in this recording bars 66–71 of the second movement and bars 167–70 of the last movement are missing, each containing an estimated fifteen seconds of material. These estimates are used for the timings of each movement in Table 1.

[4] See pp. 24 and 88.

almost every musical phrase. The characteristics of the chosen conductors, as revealed by their Brahms recordings, are further considered in the context of each symphony.

In the following details all recordings are of concert or broadcast performances, save where the date appears in italics; selected commercial releases are identified (in CD format unless otherwise stated).

Hermann Abendroth

No. 1	London SO	*20 Mar 1928*	78: HMV D 1454–58 Biddulph WHL 052
	Bavarian State Orchestra	16 Jan 1956	Tahra TAH 490 Memories MR 2045/46
No. 2	Breslau RSO	15 Apr 1939	Music & Arts CD 1099
	Leipzig RSO	*3 Mar 1952*	Memories MR 2045/46
No. 3	Leipzig RSO	17 Mar 1952	Berlin Classics 0094332 BC Memories MR 2045/46
No. 4	London SO	3 Mar 1927	78: HMV D 1265–70 Biddulph WHL 053
	Leipzig RSO	8 Dec 1954	Berlin Classics 0094332 BC Memories MR 2045/46

Adrian Boult

No. 1	London PO	*Nov 1954*	Nixa NIXCD 1002
	London PO	*21/23 Oct 1959*	CRQ CD 022
No. 2	London PO	*Nov 1954*	Nixa NIXCD 1002
No. 3	London PO	*Nov 1954*	Nixa NIXCD 1002
No. 4	London PO	*Nov 1954*	Nixa NIXCD 1002

Fritz Busch

No. 1	NYPSO	1 Feb 1942	
No. 2	Dresden Staatskapelle	25 Feb 1931	Profil Hänssler PH 07032 Guild GHCD 2371
	Danish State RSO	*20/21 Oct 1947*	78: HMV C 4006–09 EMI/IMG 724357510325
No. 4	Vienna SO	Oct 1950	Arlecchino ARL 77

Max Fiedler[5]

No. 2	Berlin PO	*1930*	78: Gramm. 95453–7
			PASC 363
No. 4	Berlin Staatskapelle	*1929*	78: Gramm. 95357–61
			PASC 363

Wilhelm Furtwängler

No. 1	Berlin PO	10 Feb 1952	Virtuoso 2699072
No. 2	Vienna PO	28 Jan 1945	DG 4353242
	Berlin PO	7 May 1952	Virtuoso 2699072
No. 3	Berlin PO	18 Dec 1949	Virtuoso 2699072
No. 4	Berlin PO	24 Oct 1948	Virtuoso 2699072

Vittorio Gui

No. 4	Orchestra del Maggio	5 Oct 1975	Warner Fonit 50467 12012
	Musicale Fiorentino		

Leopold Stokowski

No. 1	Philadelphia Orchestra	*25/27 April 1927*	78: RCA V 6658-62
			Biddulph WHL 017

Arturo Toscanini

No. 1	NYPSO	17 Feb 1935	
	NBC SO	25 Dec 1937	PASC 275
	NBC SO	6 May 1940	Naxos 8.110806
	NBC SO	*10 Mar,*	78: HMV DB 6124–28
		14 May,	78: RCA Victor M 875
		11 Dec 1941	RCA GD 60277
			RCA 88697916312–26
No. 2	NYPSO	24 Feb 1935	
		(excerpts)	
	*NBC SO	12 Feb 1938	Pristine Audio PASC 283
	BBC SO	10 Jun 1938	EMI 7233342

[5]   The exact dates of Max Fiedler's recordings of Brahms Symphonies Nos. 2 and 4 are unknown, but the nearest approximations based on known data about surrounding matrices give the Autumn of 1929 for Symphony No. 4 and 1930 for Symphony No. 2.

No. 3	NYPSO	17 Mar 1935	IPCD 1025
	NBC SO	15 Oct 1938	Guild GHCD 2211/12
	NBC SO	8 Feb 1941	Naxos 8.110827
	Philharmonia	1 Oct 1952	Testament SBT 3167
No. 4	NYPSO	7 Apr 1935 (excerpts)	IPCD 1025
	*BBC SO	3/5 Jun 1935	EMI 72333442
	NYPSO	15 Mar 1936 (excerpts)	
	NBC SO	27 Nov 1948	EMI/IMG 724356293922

* References in the analysis below are to this performance, except where otherwise stated.

Bruno Walter

No. 1	Vienna PO	3/4 May 1937	78: HMV DB 3277–81 Opus Kura OPK 2022
No. 2	Berlin PO	25 Sept 1950	Tahra TAH 452
No. 3	Vienna PO	18/19 May 1936	78: HMV DB 2933–36 Koch 3-7120–2
No. 4	BBC SO	21 May 1934	78: HMV DB 2253–57 Koch 3-7120–2

Felix Weingartner[6]

No. 1	LSO	16/18 Feb 1939	78: Col. LX 833–37 CHS 7642562 PASC 281
No. 2	LPO	26 Feb 1940	78: Col. LX 899–903 CHS 7642562 PASC 281
No. 3	LPO	6 Oct 1938	78: Col. LX 748–51 CHS 7642562 PASC 334
No. 4	LSO	14 Feb 1938	78: Col. LX 705–9 CHS 7642562 PASC 334

[6]   Timings in Table 1 are drawn from the latest transfers from 78s to CD, Pristine Audio PASC 281/334.

A table of timings for each complete movement of the above recordings is given in Table 1. As noted above, such timings have limited value, since they give no hint of the extremely wide range of tempo variations within movements, while in the outer movements of the First Symphony the varying tempos taken for their introductions disguise the overall timings of the main Allegros. Table 1 therefore includes (bracketed) timings for these introductions while Table 2 provides the metronome markings for the tempos taken at various equivalent points within specified movements.

Table 1: Timings of recordings

Symphony No. 1	I	II	III	IV	*Total*
Abendroth 1928	13:18 (2:54)	8:46	4:25	15:07 (4:47)	41:36
Abendroth 1956	12:58 (2:52)	9:00	4:19	15:04 (5:08)	41:21
Boult 1954	12:40 (2:26)	9:11	4:49	16:26 (4:44)	43:06
Boult 1959	12:58 (2:31)	8:49	4:51	16:52 (4:48)	43:30
Busch	13:14 (2:34)	10:20	4:44	16:05 (5:13)	44:23
Furtwängler	14:36 (3:15)	10:37	5:17	17:02 (5:10)	47:32
Stokowski	12:32 (2:35)	8:22	4.13	15.10 (4.14)	40:17
Toscanini 1935	12:38 (2:28)	9:19*	4.48	16:42 (5:07)*	43:27
Toscanini 1937	12:20 (2:30)	8:40	4:19	16:36 (5:00)	41:55
Toscanini 1940	12:24 (2:30)	8:37	4:25	16:21 (4:39)	41:47
Walter	12:53 (3:01)	8:52	4:21	14:49 (4:12)	40:55
Weingartner	11:39 (2.16)	9:00	4:18	14:35 (4:05)	39:32

* Estimated timings: see p. 170, n. 7.

Symphony No. 2	I	II	III	IV	*Total*
Abendroth 1939	14:13	9:13	5:06	7:55	36:27
Abendroth 1952	13:58	9:02	4:58	8:12	36:10
Boult	15:01	9:24	5:05	9:40	39:10
Busch 1931	14:12	10:17	5:10	7:34	37:13
Busch 1947	13:24	8:41	4:44	7:53	34:42
Fiedler	14:49	9:18	5:01	8:52	38:00
Furtwängler 1945	14:07	10:05	5:44	8:21	38:17
Furtwängler 1952	15:28	10:37	5:51	8:56	40:52
Toscanini 1938/NBC	14:21	8:31	5:26	8:28	36:46
Toscanini 1938/BBC	14:08	8:15	5:20	8:22	36:05
Walter	14:21	10:22	5:24	8:47	38:54
Weingartner	13:54	8:16	5:02	7:51	35:03

Symphony No. 3	I	II	III	IV	Total
Abendroth	11:52<	8:25	5:56	7:34	33:47<
Boult	13:35	8:33	5:46	8:36	36:30
Furtwängler	13:09	9:36	6:17	9:09	38:11
Toscanini 1935	12:30	8:46	6:16	8:15	35:47
Toscanini 1938	12:04	8:02	6:03	8:11	34:20
Toscanini 1941	11:28	7:42	5:45	7:54	32:49
Toscanini 1952	12:29	8:32	6:18	8:35	35:54
Walter	11:22^	7:19	5:27	7:46	31:54^
Weingartner	11:14>	7.26	5:35	7:53	32:08>

<Repeat omitted; includes addition of a notional 2:56 (actual totals: 8:56 and 30:51)
^ Repeat omitted; includes addition of a notional 2:45 (actual totals: 8:37 and 29:09)
> Repeat omitted; includes addition of a notional 2:38 (actual totals: 8:36 and 29:30)

Symphony No. 4	I	II	III	IV	Total
Abendroth 1927	11:58	12:24	5:43	10:23	40:28
Abendroth 1954	11:33	12:30	5:48	10:04	39:55
Boult	12:33	9:45	6:28	10:30	39:16
Busch	10:57	10:50	5:50	9:49	37:26
Fiedler	12:29	11:53	6:13	10:53	41:28
Furtwängler	12:38	12:15	6:21	9:40	40:54
Gui	11:38	11:33	6:23	9:46	39:20
Toscanini 1935	11:35	11:33	6:04	9:18	38:30
Toscanini 1948	11:36	10:47	6:05	9:25	37:53
Walter	11:39	11:51	5:26	9:55	38:51
Weingartner	11:21	9:21	6:33	9:40	36:55

Table 2: Metronome marks[7]

Symphony No. 1	I (♩. =)			IV (♩ =)		
bar	42	150	184	62	106	120
Abendroth 1928	100	69	120	104	160	160

[7]   In this table, Toscanini's 1937 performance of the First Symphony has been chosen in preference to his 1935 performance documented in the table of recordings and Table 1, primarily on grounds of the former's wide availability, so permitting other researchers to test the figures and conclusions reached. The figures for the 1935 performance for the most part differ little; where they do differ significantly, the discrepancies are noted in the text.

Abendroth 1956	104	58	120	104	168	160
Boult 1954	100	84	104	112	132	126
Busch	92	72	100	126	140	144
Furtwängler	104	72	100	108	144	138
Stokowski	108	60	120	126	132	138
Toscanini 1937	96	72	112	104	132	138
Walter	100	84	108	112	132	144
Weingartner	102	92	116	126	138	144

Symphony No. 2	I (♩ =)				III (♩ =)	
bar	1	50	136	212	1	120
Abendroth 1939	104	120	126	126	92	69
Boult	96	108	108	116	84	72
Busch 1931	104	116	120	132	92	76
Busch 1947	104	116	120	126	96	88
Fiedler	96	132	126	138	88	84
Furtwängler 1945	108	130	126	136	88	66
Furtwängler 1952	100	120	108	120	84	60
Toscanini 1938/NBC	100	112	112	132	84	69
Walter	108	116	112	126	84	72
Weingartner	96	116	116	126	88	72

Symphony No. 3	I (♩ =)		III (♪ =)	
bar	3	112	1	54
Abendroth	104	56	72	120
Boult	76	50	84	96
Furtwängler	88	46	84	84
Toscanini 1935	92	42	84	88
Toscanini 1938	80	48	88	92
Toscanini 1941	92	56	96	100
Toscanini 1952	84	44	84	92
Walter	96	69	88	92
Weingartner	88	52	88	104

Symphony No. 4	I (♩ =)					IV (♩ =)			
bar	1	88	91	130	433	1	97	129	253
Abendroth 1927	112	160	132	160	176	84	72	108	168 (+accel.)
Abendroth 1954	116	184	132	168	184	104	72	132	168 (+accel.)

Boult	132	144	126	144	152	104	66	112	160
Busch	152	176	144	168	168	104	80	112	168
Fiedler	104	168	120	160	168	76	63	120	168
Furtwängler	112	152	126	160	184	88	84	138	184 (+accel.)
Toscanini 1935	108	152	126	160	160	96	88	96	168
Walter	126	152	120	160	176	104	69	120	184 (+accel.)
Weingartner	138	152	132	164	152	108	84	108	152

Although the tables have limited utility, some features stand out. First, in broad terms the performances by the Steinbach witnesses – Boult, Busch and Toscanini – fall in the median range of overall timings in all the symphonies. In particular, Toscanini's pre-war performances include some of the slower examples among the great Brahms conductors. The Mottl acolytes Abendroth and Furtwängler tend, with some exceptions, towards a greater expansiveness of tempo and longer overall timings. Even so, the tables also provide ample evidence of the preponderance of quicker tempos in the performance of the symphonies before the Second World War. Performances by Walter, Weingartner and, in the First Symphony, Stokowski are cases in point here, as well as many of the performances by the Steinbach witnesses – although it may also be noted that Fritz Busch tended towards considerable breadth in live performances of second movements marked *Andante* or *Adagio*. Timings elsewhere point unequivocally to the post-war 'slow Brahms' phenomenon of which, again, there is plentiful recorded and other evidence.[8]

Again, the range of tempos within those movements selected for comparison in Table 2, which include some of the structurally most complex and expressively diverse, is at its widest in many of the movements conducted by Abendroth and Furtwängler; on the other hand, that range is at its narrowest in virtually all of Weingartner's recordings. In broad terms the Steinbach witnesses fall between these extremes, although it may be noted that Toscanini's range of tempos is the widest among them. This observation concerning the Steinbach witnesses connects directly to another significant conclusion: among them, Table 2 discloses a distinct convergence in structural and expressive emphases signified by modifications of tempo. These conclusions are considered further in the context of the analysis of each symphony, to which most of this chapter is devoted.

---

[8]   See Musgrave and Sherman, Ch. 4, Bernard D. Sherman, 'Metronome Markings, Timings, and Other Period Evidence Regarding Tempo in Brahms', pp. 115–19. See also Reinhold Brinkmann (transl. Peter Palmer), *Late Idyll: The Second Symphony of Johannes Brahms*, Cambridge, MA: Harvard University Press, 1995, pp. 29–31, 60–1.

A pure text?

So, then, Adolf is going to Vienna! I had, and have still, great misgivings, but he knows so well how to dispel and disprove them that I can't do other than wish him good luck. There is something uncommonly pleasing for me about his devotion and affection, which are a great joy to me. In the same way, your assurances of gratitude and affection are a pleasure to me, and for a serious man who takes his pupils seriously that is the best reward. And therefore I hope too that you will emerge as a successor to me in the interpretation of Brahms. For the outlook is really awful as far as Brahms conductors are concerned. In Wiesbaden I had a serious argument with Reger about his arbitrary changes of instrumentation and so-called 'improvements'. Finally I told him: if someone wishes to 'improve' Brahms, he has to be greater than Brahms. And if one day someone should come who is greater, he will have such an enormous respect for Brahms's work that he definitely won't change a *single* note. 'Touching-up' won't get one far with Brahms. I found it doubly interesting that you and Adolf had words with him about this too. The awful thing about it is simply that he *does not understand* Brahms and doesn't see that it matters. I imagine he'll come to realise it some day.

This letter (here omitting irrelevances) from Steinbach to Fritz Busch dated 20 August 1912 was addressed to 'My dear Busch' and signed off 'Your old friend'.[9] It is important on three counts. First, it shows how close the relationship was between him and the Busch brothers. Secondly, it shows how fearful he was for the future of Brahms conducting – presumably in the knowledge that what he offered was unique in its direct relationship with the composer – but that he hoped also that Fritz would follow in his footsteps.[10] Finally it demonstrates Steinbach's detestation of 'improvements' to Brahms's orchestration, especially as so radically changed by Max Reger, at the time his successor in Meiningen.

A closer look, however, suggests that not all is as it seems. Reger's Brahms scores, in the Max Reger Archive of the Meiningen Museum, do indeed disclose a substantial number of 'improvements' to a degree that would probably be rejected in contemporary circumstances; but they also show Reger's preoccupation with voice leadings and changes of dynamics in instrumental details to ensure that the music sounded as he wished.

The concerns over balance and voice leadings are shared equally by Blume, where many of his (or perhaps Steinbach's) suggestions focus on this problem. Occasionally,

---

[9] From the Bruder Busch archive. Translation courtesy of Nicholas Chadwick. Steinbach was on vacation at Ober-Engadin at the time.

[10] The extent to which Fritz did so is given at least a partial answer here: see pp. 141 (Flesch) and 151.

HOTEL MARGNA

SILS-BASEGLIA

OBER ENGADIN.

PETER A. BADRUTT, Propr.

Archiv-Nr.

B 220 V

Sils, den 20 Aug. 1912

Telegramm-Adresse: MARGNA

Mein lieber Busch!

[handwritten message in German Kurrent script]

Dein
Fritz Steinbach

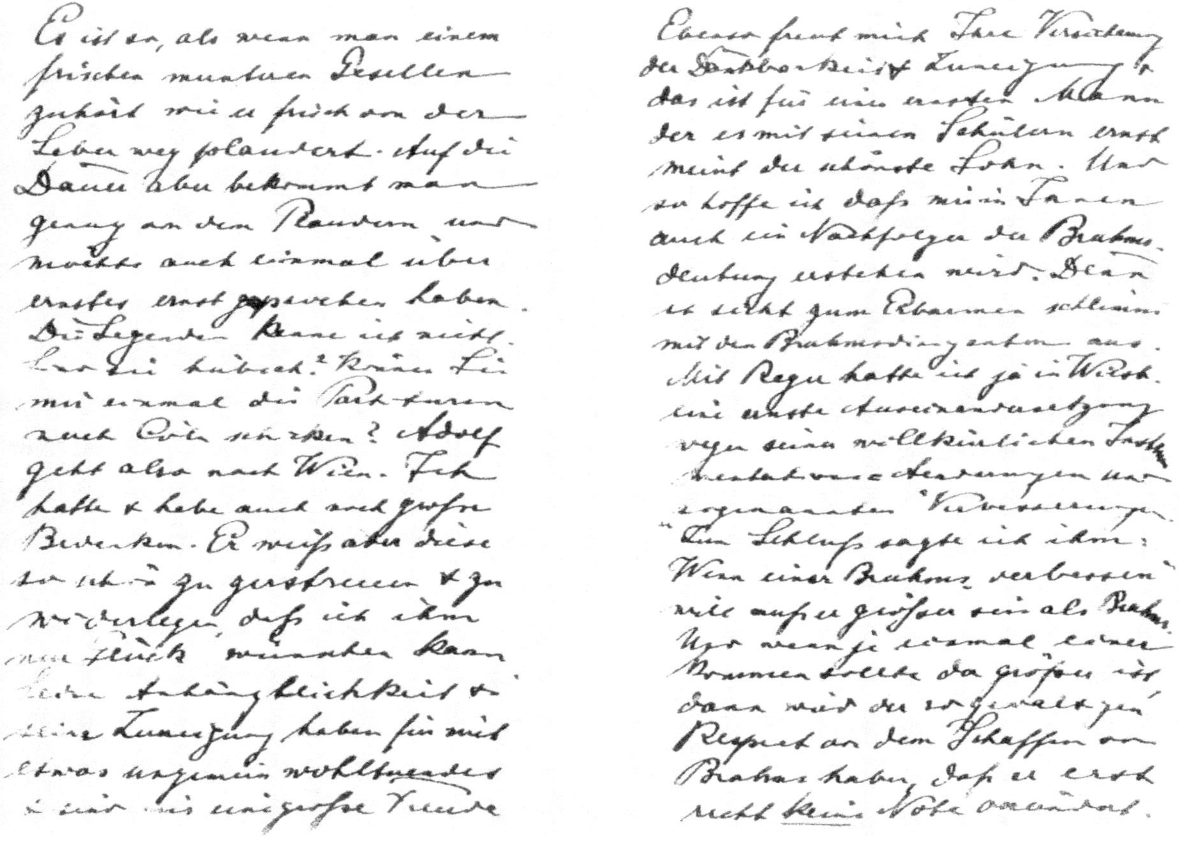

Es ist so, als wenn man einem frischen munteren Gesellen zuhört wie er frisch von der Leber weg plaudert. Auf die Dauer aber bekommt man genug an den Rändern und möchte auch einmal über ernstes ernst gesprochen haben. Die Legenden Kranz ist nicht [illegible] hübsch. Können Sie mir einmal die Partituren nach Cöln schicken? Adolf geht also nach Wien. Ich hatte & habe auch noch große Bedenken. Er weiß aber diese so schön zu zerstreuen & zu widerlegen, daß ich ihm nur Glück wünschen kann. Seine Anhänglichkeit & seine Zuneigung haben für mich etwas ungemein wohltuendes & sind mir eine große Freude

Ebenso freut mich Ihre Versicherung der Dankbarkeit & Zuneigung & das ist für einen ernsten Mann der es mit seinen Schülern ernst meint der schönste Lohn. Und so hoffe ich daß mir in Ihnen auch ein Nachfolger der Brahmsdeutung erstehen wird. Denn es sieht zum Erbarmen schlimm mit den Brahmsdirigenten aus. Mit Reger hatte ich ja in Wiesb. eine ernste Auseinandersetzung wegen seiner willkürlichen Instrumentationsänderungen und sogenannten "Verbesserungen". Zum Schluß sagte ich ihm: Wenn einer Brahms verbessern will muß er größer sein als Brahms. Und wenn je einmal einer kommen sollte der größer ist dann wird der so gewaltigen Respekt vor dem Schaffen von Brahms haben, daß er erst recht keine Note verändert.

40. STEINBACH'S LETTER TO FRITZ BUSCH, 20 AUGUST 1912

Blume suggests minor changes in instrumentation. For example, in the last movement of the First Symphony, he recommends that the contrabassoon be omitted from bars 20–21 'since it is likely to endanger the *piano* dynamic'.[11] In the Fourth Symphony's second movement he recommends the addition of a contrabassoon at the low C in bar 114 until the end; this would 'augment the bass' and 'the organ-like sound intended here would be brought out well'.[12] In two places Blume recommends the use of reduced forces: from the beginning of the third movement of the Second Symphony up to the *presto* 'in order to maintain the chamber music style of the *Allegretto*, have only the two uppermost cello stands, or even just two players';[13] and in the second movement of the Fourth, bars 64 onwards, 'the theme in the violas should be played with great tenderness and by only two solo players', the latter, as Pasternack remarks, 'an interesting deviation' from the printed score.[14] Even for Steinbach, then – if one places faith in Blume – the printed score was not sacrosanct. However, Blume must, as ever, be treated with caution: in the context of the First Symphony's introduction, he remarks that the conductor 'may even introduce retouchings to the score, if these are made in the spirit of the composer's intentions'.[15] Given Steinbach's emphatic and unequivocal remarks to Fritz Busch, this question-begging gloss is an obvious example of Blume's own views tacked on to others having a possible origin in Steinbach's voice.[16]

Acknowledging the problems outlined above makes it easier to understand some conductorial emendations, particularly Toscanini's adjustments of the scores of the First and Third Symphonies. Toscanini first conducted the Second and Fourth Symphonies in 1898 but delayed his first performances of the First until 1930, and of the Third until 1929. In the latter two he had problems in making the lead voices at certain moments sound as he wished and his recordings show evidence of his continued experiments to achieve what he heard in his mind's ear. One example from the first movement of the Third must serve for many quite similar; here I quote the late Harris Goldsmith, who studied Toscanini's scores and described his changes in some detail.

> At bars 21 and 22 in the first movement … Brahms answers the first violins' upward triplet arpeggios with similar ones begun by the cellos and completed by the second violins. Toscanini, finding that these answers are invariably inaudible … remedied [this] by having his cellos continue upward along with the second violins. [He] knew from experience that cellos playing in the high register would produce a sonority almost indistinguishable from that of the violins, but that the added stress and strain

[11] Pasternack/Blume, p. 39; Schwalb/Blume, p. 28.
[12] Pasternack/Blume, p. 110; Schwalb/Blume, p. 78.
[13] Pasternack/Blume, p. 68; Schwalb/Blume, p. 49.
[14] Pasternack/Blume, p. 108; Schwalb/Blume, p. 76.
[15] Pasternack/Blume, p. 10; Schwalb/Blume, p. 10.
[16] See further p. 154.

from their effort would introduce the definition needed to bring the passage into the foreground.[17]

Steinbach seems to have encountered a similar problem, for at this point Blume requires 'all instruments [to] make a *crescendo*' at bar 22.[18]

It is unnecessary to multiply such examples aimed, fundamentally, at ensuring that the voice lead or other details are heard. But Toscanini's tinkerings with the timpani parts in the finales of the First and Third Symphonies introduce a prominent and perhaps disturbing effect, particularly at the reappearance of the chorale theme at bar 408 of the First's finale. Fritz Busch, however, adopts precisely the same emendations, for reasons which cannot now be clarified: his teacher, Steinbach, apparently left these bars without amendment. Busch's Carnegie Hall performance on 1 February 1942 came as a last-minute substitute for Adolf as soloist in Reger's Violin Concerto, which the latter had played at the otherwise identically programmed concerts on 29 and 30 January. Very probably Fritz had relatively little rehearsal time for the Brahms and possibly accepted emendations in the Philharmonic players' parts that had remained there at least since Toscanini's February 1935 performance, when he last conducted them in the work. That possibility, however, faces the difficulty that the work had been played a dozen times in the Barbirolli years, 1936–42. Perhaps they all accepted Toscanini's extra timpani amendments.

In the Third Symphony's finale Toscanini sometimes added timpani at one or another point but abandoned these changes in favour of the score as written in his Philharmonia performance.[19] Such changes seem to reflect the spirit of the times, since Abendroth in 1956 added timpani rolls at bars 413–15 of the First's finale and Furtwängler freely added timpani in the Third's finale (bars 44–5 and 86 and in the recapitulation). Further pursuit of these questionable amendments seems unprofitable; they do not impinge on the central issues at stake in this chapter.

Repeats

Whether Brahms wanted the first movement repeats in the first three of his symphonies always to be observed is an issue that has spawned a considerable literature which, for

---

[17]   See further Goldsmith's notes to the first RCA CD issues of the RCA recording of Symphony No. 3, 4 November 1952, GD 60259. See also my review of Symphony No. 3, Toscanini's 1938 NBC SO performance, Guild GHCD 2011–12, *Classic Record Collector*, Autumn 2002, p. 81.

[18]   Pasternack/Blume, p. 79; Schwalb/Blume, p. 57.

[19]   Toscanini added timpani in bars 172–7 of the 1952 RCA recording but omitted them in his 1938 NBC performance, which, however, included similar timpani amendments in bars 188–93. Some later performances, in 1941, 1942 and 1948, included both these additions.

present purposes, need not be examined in detail. It is sufficient to note here, first, that in the 1880s omission of those repeats was an exceptional course. So much may be deduced from Bülow's specific request to Brahms for his assent to the omission of the repeats in the First and Second Symphonies in October 1884 to enable him to programme all three symphonies then written in one concert; without such omission, Bülow feared that his Vienna concert agent (the music publisher Albert Gutmann) would reject the programme as over long.[20] Kalbeck's biography seems to support this view as late as January 1895, when he recorded Brahms as saying in response to a query about repeats in sonata-form movements, 'I want the repeats in my movements to be observed'.[21] It is, however, worth noting that the query came from Karl Heinrich Barth, pianist and professor in Berlin, who may therefore have been referring to Brahms's early piano sonatas.

We do not know whether Steinbach observed the first movement repeats in the first two symphonies when he conducted them with the Meiningen Hofkapelle for Brahms's entertainment during the 1890s. We do know that Weingartner very probably omitted the Second Symphony's first movement repeat in that Vienna concert in November 1895 which pleased Brahms so unambiguously. Stewart Deas noted that the repeat bars were crossed out in Weingartner's score and thought it most unlikely that he ever observed the repeat.[22] Steinbach was at that time, or possibly post-1897, evolving his own practice, which, if Blume is to be regarded as reliable on the point, omitted the repeat in the first two symphonies. As Pasternack observes in relation to Blume's direction to omit the repeat in the First, 'It is unfortunate that no reason is given for the omission of the exposition repeat', and pertinently queries whether this was 'a practice begun during Brahms's lifetime, presumably with the composer's sanction' or 'a decision made later by Steinbach' – a query that, unfortunately, it is impossible to answer in the absence of Steinbach's scores. In similar terms, Blume directs omission of the repeat in the Second Symphony but in the Third says quite simply 'the first part should be repeated'.[23]

Against this somewhat uncertain background, it is relevant to note the practice of the chosen conductors in Table 1, which discloses a uniform omission of the First and Second symphonies' first movement repeats, whether or not the conductors were Steinbach witnesses. In the Third Symphony, however, Toscanini reflects the Blume direction to include the repeat, as does Boult; this seems to have been their usual practice throughout their careers unless, as in Toscanini's NBC broadcasts, there were

---

[20] See p. 21. Even so, Gutmann rejected the programme.
[21] Kalbeck (see p. 21, n. 60), vol. 4, pt 2, p. 380. See also that note regarding Kalbeck's general reliability.
[22] Information to the author, 1972.
[23] See Pasternack/Blume, p. 20, and Schwalb/Blume, p. 16 (First Symphony); Pasternack/ Blume, p. 59, and Schwalb/Blume, p. 42 (Second Symphony); Pasternack/Blume, p. 83, and Schwalb/Blume, p. 59 (Third Symphony).

possible time constraints.[24] Walter, however, omitted the repeat in the Third Symphony because of his lifelong aversion to repeats in general. Weingartner's concert practice in this symphony is unknown but his omission of the repeat in the Columbia recording was clearly a consequence of the need to fit his performance on eight 78rpm sides. Abendroth presumably faced no such constraints in his concert and other performances of the Third; so his omission of the Third Symphony repeat was, like Walter's, a personal decision – and a curious one, if it were to be believed that he was in some way close to Steinbach's practice.

Some preliminary (and personal) observations

Any scholar, musical or otherwise, must stick closely to his or her last; the intrusion of personal preferences into the analysis of data might well compromise the whole exercise. In the present instance it is of the essence that assessments of how each conductor manipulates the musical line and all such related matters are made in a manner as objective as can be. But in the nature of such things, the exclusion of personal preferences cannot be wholly avoided: given an honest pair of ears, one may describe the little less or the little more without fear of contradiction, but judgement of the outcome necessitates the expression of a personal point of view. The reader is, therefore, entitled to know where, metaphorically, the author comes from.

Many years ago, indeed from my earliest serious listening and critical analysis in the 1950s, the foundation stone – the *Grundnorm* again – for the appreciation of great Brahms conducting was shared between Weingartner and Toscanini: as well as their expressive character – never overboard – both, it then seemed, held the key to the legitimate approach to Brahms in terms of structural integrity and coherence of argument. How to express that superiority was not always easy, especially as eloquent admirers of other Brahms conductors, in particular Furtwängler, came on stream in the 1970s with seemingly authoritative judgements.

A particularly attractive explanation of Weingartner's distinction of rhythm and phrasing was offered by Peter Rabinowitz in 1993:

> What is most important about rhythm in Weingartner's performances ... is not its steadiness or subtlety, but its rhetorical function ... Weingartner conceived of rhythm as a source of progression rather than a means for emphasis, a way to link details rather than highlight them ... [R]hythm (which Weingartner saw in terms of

---

[24] In Boult's final Brahms symphony cycle, recorded in the 1970s, and also in his concert performances in that decade, he reinstated the repeats in the first two symphonies. However, no rationale seems to have been offered by him save for his remark to the effect that, since the composer wrote the second-time bars, they should be heard.

articulation and phrasing as well as tempo) was the key to formal structure, the key
to the relation between parts and whole.[25]

But if that assessment is correctly understood, it perhaps claims too little, since
much the same might be remarked of Toscanini's pre-war Brahms performances. Let
the *Times* (probably Colles) speak of Toscanini's performance of the First Symphony
on 26 May 1937 with the BBC Symphony Orchestra in the Queen's Hall, just seven
months before the 1937 Christmas night performance of that work, his first concert
with the NBC Symphony Orchestra and chosen for inclusion in the foregoing Tables
and analysis below. Toscanini was, said the *Times*, supreme in his capacity to keep the
whole in mind while working over the detail. Throughout the symphony the critic was
constantly hearing things which generally escaped attention, 'particularly those little
overlappings of the ends of phrases, notably in the second theme of the first movement, which often fade away into one another. It would be easy to make such things
too prominent, but they never were; they were just present.' By contrast with the virtuoso conductor bent on dynamic effect (no names here, but at the time Stokowski
and Koussevitsky were probable candidates), this characteristic demonstrated the way
in which Toscanini 'always finishes a phrase through'. Although the entry of instruments was the primary care of a conductor, their exit was too frequently left to look
after itself while he attended other entries – but that was not Toscanini's way: his
'power of carrying through … often gives the impression that he is not only playing on the
orchestra … but that he is really playing each instrument. And just as the single phrase is
carried through, so is the group of phrases, the period, the movement, so that ultimately
the whole symphony is modelled to completeness.'[26] In other words, Toscanini's underlying rhythmic tautness is forever present to aid the moulding of the phrase, from the
smallest to the largest musical cell: a function differing little, if at all, from Rabinowitz
on Weingartner. And Toscanini's ferocious downbeat in bar 42 of the first movement
on that Christmas night NBC performance in 1937 has such intensity that it seems to
bear aloft the whole movement.

What, then, were Weingartner's unique qualities? The key surely lies in the
observations of his pupil Stewart Deas, set out in Chapter 2, which home in on his
'peculiar power of becoming detached' from the works he is conducting, which
'always made his command over the orchestra so absolutely unquestionable'.[27]
He never becomes 'entangled' with the work conducted, but is 'always its master'.
This Olympian quality was often to be observed in his performances of both the
Beethoven and the Brahms symphonies: in 1972 a veteran violinist from the LPO
observed to me in an unscripted moment in the Royal Academy of Music that, in

---

[25]   Liner notes for CD transfer on Centaur CRC 2124, p. 5, quoted by Frisch, p. 179.
[26]   See further Dyment 2012, p. 86.
[27]   See p. 88.

playing the Brahms Third Symphony in the 1930s, one felt that 'the whole work was laid out as if it one was viewing a map'. How Olympus was made audible in this way is a complex matter, involving acute balances, observance of particular dynamic markings, sometimes a rock-steady tempo (the Second Symphony's third movement is a prime example), articulation of accompanying figuration (hear the first violins and violas from bar 52 in the Third's finale) and elastic but masculine phrasing, all of which contribute to a sense of infallible 'rightness' in forward motion – as if Weingartner were expounding the music from a lofty vantage point, yet infusing it with an inner vitality.[28] At one time these many qualities led me to estimate Weingartner's Brahms as pre-eminent, a view reinforced by the knowledge of Brahms's expressions of approval back in 1895.

Ultimately, however, the even greater achievement of Toscanini in some at least of his early recordings of the Brahms symphonies could not be ignored. That achievement may be illustrated by reference to the final pages of the Fourth Symphony, from bar 129 to the end, in Weingartner's 1938 recording and in Toscanini's concert performances of the work in the Queen's Hall on 3/5 June 1935.[29] Here one finds in essence a reasonably close concordance of view between the two conductors on overall pacing and architectural proportioning: see Table 2. In Weingartner's case the architecture is immaculate, each variation slotted into its seemingly pre-ordained position, with, for the listener, 'an intellectual lucidity that of itself [is] an emotional joy', as Newman put it, a cosmic jigsaw solved in terms that preclude argument.[30] With Toscanini, however, there comes in addition a sheer sense of drama that lifts the whole, if not to another plane, at least to a more complete realisation of the music's possibilities: a titanic struggle of the gods whose resolution leaves the listener – and, surely, the players and the Queen's Hall audience at the time – emotionally exhausted. Strangely, however, it is Weingartner who, in his *Symphony Writers Since Beethoven*, so accurately describes the music in terms redolent of Toscanini's achievement – 'an impression of implacable fate', he says, 'which imposes an ineluctable downfall on a great man or a great people. In spite of all struggle ... destruction is foredoomed; it approaches with inexorable steps. The conclusion of this movement seared with deeply moving tragedy is a veritable orgy of destruction, a frightful counterpart to the paroxysm of joy' that ends Beethoven's Ninth.[31] Precisely so; but Weingartner's dramatic instinct in his own conducting was not his strongest attribute.

---

[28] See further Christopher Dyment, 'Weingartner: Eastern Approaches', *International Classic Record Collector*, Spring 2000, p. 14.

[29] See pp. 219–21.

[30] See p. 88.

[31] In *On Music*, pp. 275–6.

If these twin pinnacles of the conductor's art gave me the greatest satisfaction, what of the competition? Adrian Boult was always *there* (in much the same way as, for him, Richter was ever present), giving unadorned and fundamentally honest Brahms performances in terms of their architectural propriety. But how close were the results to the well-documented link with Steinbach and Brahms? The answer must now await the analysis that follows.

Max Fiedler seemed to offer a Brahms at 180° from Boult and my early assessment of him was, perhaps to one's regret, immortalised by the distinguished Brahms scholar, Walter Frisch, by his quoting my summing up in his fine book on the four symphonies: 'flabby' and 'advanced in years'.[32] My more detailed consideration of his style followed in 2002, to which is now added the description in Chapter 2 and further references hereafter.[33] Without doubt the recording of the Second Symphony with the Berlin Philharmonic in 1930 is, one must insist, the work of a conductor 'advanced in years', with the shortcomings or at least characteristics attendant on age;[34] but it also preserves a unique and beautiful sonority touched frequently by Fiedler's reliance on the heavy brass to thrust home his interpretative points amidst the golden tones of the orchestra. Of course, Fiedler had countless such points to thrust home, some of them disruptive in character; herein lies both the weakness of the architectural element in his performances and his fascination for contemporary listeners in observing at least one of the interpretative approaches current in the last years of the nineteenth century, seemingly reliant on the spirit and example of Fiedler's hero, Hans von Bülow.

Fritz Busch as a Brahms interpreter lacked presence in the second half of the twentieth century, since some of his most important performances were not unearthed until quite recently. There was always his fine Second Symphony from Copenhagen in 1947 – but this seemed to be a slightly pale precursor of the Toscanini manner heard more dramatically and vividly in the Maestro's magnificent 1952 RCA recording, the only example of his late, 'official' Brahms that has claims to stand comparison with his pre-war concert performances.[35]

I came to the other interpreters represented in this chapter more recently, in part because some of these performances, too, were unearthed or reached CD transfer relatively recently; and in part (leaving aside the often convincing Bruno Walter) because of a reluctance to engage with interpretative approaches that seemed deeply flawed and sometimes offensive to ears attuned to the architectural propriety of Weingartner, Toscanini and Boult. Was one meant to take Abendroth's recordings from the 1920s seriously? Why drop the opening tempo of the First Symphony so suddenly when

---

[32] Frisch, p. 182, with citations.

[33] See p. 72; also Dyment 2002.

[34] See p. 76 for comments on Fiedler's performance characteristics after his return from the USA.

[35] Recorded 11 February 1952, latest RCA transfer 88697916312-7.

the *pizzicati* arrive? And what of the outlandish and abrupt tempo changes in this symphony's last movement? Could this finale ever have been on the same planet as Steinbach's own, achieved, as his pupil Fritz Busch straightforwardly remarked, 'even more warmly and convincingly' than Toscanini's? Fortuitously, these initial personal reactions to Abendroth's strange contortions equated closely with those of the London critics in the 1920s described in Chapter 2, still waiting to be unearthed at the time.[36] Further analysis of Abendroth's recordings must determine whether his approach may, after all, be justified on historical grounds.

And Furtwängler? Some, perhaps many, regard him as the ideal and revelatory Brahms interpreter. For Walter Frisch, for example, he 'emerges as the finest Brahms conductor of his generation, perhaps of all time … [H]is glorious 1945 recording of the Second … displays many of the same qualities that have made him a legend in this repertory'.[37] For me, on the contrary, one hearing of Furtwängler's opening *poco sostenuto* in the First Symphony was sufficient to mentally defenestrate the perpetrator of this leaden-booted trudge, utterly alien (so it seemed) to the real Brahms and as far from *poco* anything as it could possibly be. Incidental beauties and subtly handled transitions (but often from one questionable tempo to another[38]) could not rescue these performances, which evoked pained astonishment when encountering the steep *accelerandi* at the end of that vaunted 1945 concert recording of the Second Symphony and the outer movements of the Fourth Symphony – in the first movement of the latter almost off the metronomic map (see Table 2). Was one obliged to accept these frenzied passages, characteristic examples of Furtwängler at work and worshipped as such by his admirers, as reflecting a legitimate approach to Brahms, let alone an approach related by some unknown route to Steinbach's own? In pursuit of those lines of authority connecting us with the composer, further analysis of his recordings must again tell, but, as Chapter 2 has shown, available documentation does not support any such claim.[39] In any event, I was content to note the similarity of the views expressed here to those of Steinbach's beloved pupil Adolf Busch, whose extreme and negative reaction to Furtwängler's style was noted in Chapter 2.[40] Clearly, however, as remarked at the outset of this digression, readers are entitled to know the analyst's antecedent predispositions.

And so to the analysis. In the following examination of recordings a number of passages are compared, many of them using Walter Blume's description of the

---

[36] See p. 129.
[37] Frisch, p. 183.
[38] For examples, see pp. 192 and 193.
[39] See p. 138.
[40] See p. 147. It should be noted that Walter Frisch considers Furtwängler's Brahms style to be unrelated to Steinbach's: Musgrave and Sherman, Ch. 10, p. 282; but compare this with Musgrave and Sherman, Ch. 8 (Pascall and Weller) (see Ch. 1, n. 3).

Steinbach way as a guide – but not, for reasons given in Chapter 2, as an infallible observer.[41] Other important elements in assessment include any observed consistency of approach among the Steinbach witnesses, other possible influences on the chosen interpreters and the distancing effect of the passage of time between the date of Steinbach's performances and the chosen recordings. In any event, Blume is hardly relevant to authoritative Brahms performances clearly unconnected with the Steinbach tradition, such as those of Weingartner, Fiedler and also Stokowski in his 1927 recording of the First Symphony. Nevertheless, inclusion of these recordings here is a convenient means of assessing either their contiguity with or remoteness from Steinbach's unassailable line of authority connecting him to the composer – assuming, that is, that the recordings to be examined disclose sufficient of Steinbach's practice to enable such comparisons to be made with reasonable certainty.

Comment on all of Blume's observations relating to every movement would require a study of inordinate length. This study is therefore limited to some obvious and vital elements, such as the tempo variation and nuancing for which Steinbach was peculiarly noted, with examples drawn from the majority of movements in each symphony.[42] In what follows, the brief extracts in English from Blume's book draw on Pasternack's translation (to which reference has already been made), with in some cases possible alternative meanings and, where extra illumination is needed, the German language original.

Symphony No. 1 in C minor Op. 68

First movement: *Un poco sostenuto – Allegro – Meno allegro*

<u>Bars 1–33</u>: In the first movement's introduction Blume is insistent on the *un poco* qualification of the *sostenuto*, beaten with fairly hard drumsticks in six but not slow, with a hint of a *Luftpause* between *forte* and *piano* at bar 9 to avoid hall resonance covering the first *pizzicato*. These *pizzicati* are to be 'stiff and rigid' and 'strictly in time', compared with the 'sighs' which follow, although whether that 'time' should be precisely the *tempo primo* Blume does not specify; but had he not meant *tempo primo*, his observation would hardly have been worth making.[43]

Toscanini, Busch and Boult (his 1954 performance save where otherwise stated) agree on the meaning of *un poco*, the tempo made plain by their evidently quite hard drumsticks; they leave minimal pauses between *forte* and *piano*, although Toscanini

---

[41] See p. 154.

[42] Examples are omitted from the third movement of No. 1, the finale of No. 3 and the third movement of No. 4 for reasons given below: see pp. 214 and 219.

[43] Pasternack/Blume, pp. 9–11; Schwalb/Blume, pp. 9–10.

in 1935, Busch and Boult (1959) are slightly more flexible in this respect. By 1937 Toscanini omitted all hint of a *Luftpause* at bar 9 and, given the constricting acoustics of his infamous Studio 8H, it may have seemed natural to him to forgo the flexibility hinted at in his earlier Carnegie Hall performance; but he held to this omission in all subsequent performances, wherever they took place. All three Steinbach witnesses keep the *pizzicati* virtually in tempo, although Toscanini in 1935 affords the barest hint of reverting to his *tempo primo* at the very outset of the work, while in 1937 he slackens the tempo very slightly second time round (bars 13–14) in anticipation of the repeated 'sighs'. His achievement in both these early performances is to meld continuity with expressivity; later he always adopted a strict tempo for the *pizzicati*.

Among the other conductors, Weingartner, despite ill-defined timpani, is remarkably similar to the Steinbach witnesses throughout this opening passage: no hints of *Luftpausen* nor slackening for the *pizzicati*. Stokowski begins in similar tempo but the Romantic spirit soon breaks through: the *pizzicati* slacken the tempo as soon as they appear and the pulse is distended at the end of the introduction to accommodate gorgeous massed cellos after bar 33. Still, at a basically brisk tempo little harm is done to the structure. Abendroth starts more slowly than the foregoing conductors but at a plausible tempo, the timpani indistinct in 1928 (probably the aged recording), with *Luftpausen* clear in both his recordings but more distended in 1956. In both, more so in 1928, he drops sharply in tempo for the *pizzicati*, a feature much disliked by the *Times* in its reviews of his Queen's Hall performances of the First Symphony in the late 1920s.[44] The sudden change cannot avoid breaking the musical line and, certainly, departs from Blume at the very outset. By Blume's standards, Walter and more especially Furtwängler adopt implausibly slow opening tempos with much lingering later on; the latter also droops noticeably during the *pizzicati*.

To sum up, Toscanini, Boult and Busch, and, fortuitously, Weingartner, are fully consonant with Blume, although the minimalist tendency in regard to *Luftpausen* in some of their performances suggests a more modern approach. Abendroth, particularly in his (here very powerful) 1956 version, has a tendency to sectionalise and linger; Walter and Furtwängler go their own late Romantic ways.

Bars 42–6, 51–3, 57–60: In the Allegro's main theme, bars 42–6, the non-slurred crotchets must be shortened and played *marcato*, says Blume. Toscanini (all versions but particularly in 1935 and 1937), Boult and Busch agree entirely, all other conductors less conspicuously so. Blume is further insistent on the accents on weak (last) beats in bars 51 onwards, a cross-accenting effect of which, as he correctly remarks, Brahms was very fond and frequently used.[45] Toscanini reflects this advice in full with characteristic attack, abetted here by Busch and Boult but rather less forcibly by

[44] See p. 132.
[45] Pasternack/Blume, p. 15; Schwalb/Blume, p. 13.

Abendroth and Furtwängler. Walter and Stokowski downplay the accentuation; but in any event the latter drives ahead here at a highly athletic tempo that leaves all others panting in his slipstream.

Bars 101–30: Moving to the lyrical passage commencing at bar 101 which includes the oboe's second subject from bar 131, Blume expands on the need for 'our refined microscopic (*elektroskopisches*) feeling for tempo to prevail'. He demands *inter alia* fleet playing of bars 101–2, broadening at 103–4, resuming as before at 105 until 114 where the tempo is to broaden again, resuming *tempo primo* at 121 and slowing at bar 130 in anticipation of the oboe's broadened second subject.[46] Some of these expansions and contractions are obviously implied in the nature of the music itself and may sometimes be heard in performance today. It is in any case worth emphasising once more that, for Blume, any changes here in tempo as per Steinbach had to be so slight as to be virtually unnoticeable; these were instances where any 'pushing forward and holding back' was eminently not of the obvious character so often bestowed on such passages by Bülow. Blume's reluctance even to advert to the nature of his comments for fear of exaggeration by others is characteristic and will be noted again in the context of the Third Symphony's first movement;[47] his comments do, though, tend to confirm the documented observations on the characteristics of Steinbach's style detailed in Chapter 2.

Of the chosen conductors, Busch is the model in this passage: he observes the expressive moments distinctly, although the listener is barely conscious of the fact that he is doing so – '*elektroskopisch*' indeed. Before the solo oboe enters, Busch also makes the prescribed slowing down in the preceding bar (129) to allow a broader tempo for the solo ($\mathbf{J}$. = 80, compared with his basic 92). In 1935 and to a lesser extent in 1937 Toscanini also very clearly reflects the slight changes of tempo urged by Blume; in addition, in anticipation of the oboe's entrance, he greatly expands the lyrical phrase commencing at 125, a consistent feature of all his performances but at its most distended and intense in 1935, and allows the oboe's second subject only a marginal relaxation from *tempo primo* ($\mathbf{J}$. = 88, compared with 96). The expressive range of Boult compared with these two is more reined in, although he recognises similar changes of mood. Abendroth in 1928 virtually ignores the expressive requirements until slowing at 128 in extended anticipation of a substantially broadened oboe theme; in 1956, like Toscanini, he is expansive from bar 125 onwards.

In the passage just analysed, Weingartner and Stokowski offer interpretations at each extremity. The former acknowledges the change of mood from bar 101 only by sensitive changes of dynamics and barely acknowledges a shift in tempo for the solo oboe, although it must be borne in mind that, even so, Weingartner never binds himself

---

[46] Pasternack/Blume, pp. 17–18; Schwalb/Blume, p. 15.
[47] See p. 211.

to the metronome; here, nonetheless, is Classicism personified. Stokowski begins a major shift in tempo starting at bar 104 and intensifying at 110 – his tempo will not recover until bar 157. As noted in Chapter 2, the *Times* critic described an apparently similar approach in these very bars by Nikisch in 1906 without disapproval, although in 1912 he condemned as too extravagant what seemed to be a similar approach by Stokowski in his first concert with the LSO.[48] The analyst now can do no more than describe these different reactions and invite the listener to consider whether something of the Nikisch spirit survives here in Stokowski's recorded approach; to my ears, it seems likely, particularly in the light of Stokowski's fire elsewhere, but others may regard this conclusion as too optimistic.

Bars 137–57: These bars, after the broadened oboe subject, include the whole of the passage which has always in living memory been subject to some broadening of tempo up until the final octave drops in the horns at bars 155–6. Surprisingly, Blume has little to say here about tempo variation and limits himself to what seem to be subsidiary matters: thus he advises the string chords from bars 145–6 be not 'connected together' (the 'disconnect' that distinguishes some performances from others, what Pasternack describes as 'a brief stopping of the bow between each tied chord'[49]) and the dialogue between horn and winds be shaped with freedom, the final octave drop to be slightly separated and accented, until the tempo is 'revived' with the subsidiary theme at bar 157.[50] Such 'revival' implies an earlier broadening of tempo, but it must also be recollected that Steinbach's manipulation of the tempo here was the subject of comment by the London critics in 1905, who regarded this feature as unorthodox as compared, presumably, with Richter. It is fair to deduce from this comment that Steinbach's broadening of tempo was here probably quite modest in character, certainly by comparison with Nikisch; that could well explain Blume's own absence of comment: the tempo change in this passage would be no more than would be needed to characterise the new material.

If it is correctly inferred that Steinbach's change of tempo here was modest, it also readily explains the differing approaches of the conductors under review. Toscanini reflects Blume's injunctions in full, with the disconnect at bars 145–6 just audibly observed and with a fairly modest change of tempo thereafter.[51] Busch at his slightly broader tempo responds still less generously but with a clear disconnect and also with

---

[48] See pp. 60 and 67.
[49] Pasternack/Blume, p. 18.
[50] Pasternack/Blume, pp. 18–19; Schwalb/Blume, p. 15–16.
[51] Toscanini's practice was not consistent here: in later performances he made no particular effort to 'disconnect'; his earlier practice is most clearly audible in the NBC performance of 17 January 1943, part of his finest of all complete recorded Brahms cycles in December 1942/January 1943, M&A CD995.

clear emphasis on the final octave drop in the horns as Blume advises. Boult is also very contained (with disconnect), as is Weingartner (without disconnect). All these modest tempo changes are confirmed by Table 2.

Table 2 also shows how, by comparison with those in the preceding paragraph, Abendroth slows extravagantly (with disconnect), an approach obviously inconsistent with Blume and more akin to the maximalist Stokowski (also with disconnect). Furt-wängler is less extravagant (without disconnect) but, again, his broadening of tempo is more marked than the others.

Bars 157–85 onwards: At the 'revival' marked by the violas' *marcato* subsidiary subject at bar 157, Blume asks for 'much more energy', but initially contained to allow for a later increase in tempo up to 185; thereafter the chords are to be very 'chopped' or 'incisive'.[52] Once again, in his early performances Toscanini's incisiveness and rhythmic emphases on the weak beats as marked in the score stand out, as does his grappling at a broadened tempo with the entry into the development (from bar 190), which, for Blume, 'cannot be played too brilliantly or lushly'. His unusual term for this last word, '*vollsaftig*', translates literally as 'extremely juicy'; perhaps 'tonally saturated', in which Toscanini excels, best conveys the sense. Busch, Boult and also Weingartner, with their slightly more contained response to the preceding broadening of tempo, need rather less of an acceleration from 157 to reach the mark – but, even so, they do not quite command Toscanini's energy here, nor do battle as he does with the entry into the development. Abendroth's extravagant response to the broadening of tempo needs a correspondingly steep acceleration to bar 185, bringing with it a doubtful effect on structural coherence; Stokowski likewise, yet his wild energy here is akin to Toscanini's, although (at its steepest point) reaching a significantly faster tempo. Again, one may wonder whether there is something here of Nikisch's sheer abandon.

Bars 197–222: Of the quiet passage near the start of the development, Blume requires a 'strict tempo at first' (applying up to 215), with 'very small' *crescendi* in the strings and the tempo becoming 'calmer' – that is, dropping slightly below *tempo primo* – as the double bar at 215 is approached. The tempo 'revives' at 225 as in bar 157.[53]

A slightly different description of Steinbach's approach in these bars is given by Berrsche in an article dated 1929, referring to a Steinbach nuance 'completely forgot-ten today', which he regarded as 'absolutely authentic'.[54] He heard a 'slowing down' of the tempo in bars 203–5 and a similar slowing down at the parallel place at 212 con-tinuing up to 225, a passage in which Steinbach slowed from 'note to note' and, from

[52] Pasternack/Blume, p. 19; Schwalb/Blume, p. 16.
[53] Pasternack/Blume, p. 20; Schwalb/Blume, pp. 16–17.
[54] Berrsche, p. 279, and see also Musgrave and Sherman, p. 284 (Walter Frisch's translation and commentary).

the *diminuendo* at 216, played 'almost at the limits of audibility' in order to create a 'truly oppressive, ghostly hush'. This remarkable feat of memory coincides with Blume so far as concerns the 'calming' of the tempo just before 215, although not elsewhere; but that coincidence does provide some corroboration of Blume's indication at this point.

None of the conductors under consideration reflect Berrsche in their entirety, although some do mark Blume's advice to calm the tempo towards 215. Of the Steinbach witnesses, Boult in 1959 contains vestigial, slight deviations of pace up to bar 225. Busch starts to slow from bar 212 onwards and keeps the pace down very slightly until the revival; his players here succeed in creating a particularly hushed atmosphere after 215. In all his performances Toscanini decelerates near the end of the exposition (from bar 185) and again after bar 197 to a pace slightly broader than his *tempo primo*; he is alone in slowing here. Thereafter in most performances he makes no further change of pace – obviously, to him, it was already slow enough to await the revival at bar 225. However, in some of his performances, notably in 1935, 1940 (see Table 1) and once more in December 1942, he seems to have been in a more relaxed mood and permits himself to indulge in a slight broadening of tempo in the bars preceding the revival. A relaxation in the last couple of bars before 225 is more clearly audible in Abendroth's 1928 recording. Of all the conductors, Busch reflects the spirit of Blume's advice most completely and convincingly.

Second movement: *Andante sostenuto*

<u>Bars 21–50 onwards</u>: Again, we have here two competing sets of instructions, from Blume and from Berrsche's memory in 1917, not so long after Steinbach's death.[55] Blume's directions in this passage are many. So, bars 21–31 are to be 'performed with pathos' and so, too, are bars 34–8. Blume adds detailed directions over certain note values in these sections, most notably the '*quasi legato*' oboe at 39 and the clarinet's '*rubato*' effect from 45, with increased note values here for the top note of each phrase. These solo wind passages are to be followed by an increase in tempo from bar 48 towards the *sforzatos* in bars 51–3, the 'main tempo' resuming thereafter (presumably at the end of bar 55). Notably, among Blume's many injunctions his only indicated change of tempo throughout this passage occurs at bar 48; his advice to perform most of bars 21–38 with 'pathos' may suggest, if anything, a slight broadening of pace.

Berrsche waxes lyrical, but refers to bars 27–39 as a transitional passage in a contrasting mood requiring a flowing *andante* tempo; Steinbach, he said, would become imperceptibly faster from 27 up to (presumably) 39, after which the darkening mood was expressed only by the accents and dynamics. Thereafter the oboe played 'in

---

[55] Pasternack/Blume, pp. 28–31, and Schwalb/Blume, pp. 21–3; Berrsche, p. 278, and see also Musgrave and Sherman, pp. 283–4 (Walter Frisch's translation and commentary).

a dreamy manner' in contrast with the clarinet, which played with 'agitated accent patterns like the frightened fluttering (*das verängstigte Flattern*) of a bird'. From bars 47–50 there was a 'deep breath', after which the *sforzato* bars were taken with 'savage determination', perhaps implying some increase in pace. Thus Berrsche observed Steinbach taking a slight *increase* in tempo in the great majority of those bars which Blume required to be performed with 'pathos', thereby inferring a slight *decrease* of tempo. However, Berrsche's memory of the oboe and clarinet solos equates well enough with Blume's description, as does his implied increase of pace in bars 51–3 containing the 'savage' *sforzatos*.

None of the chosen conductors offers a reading coinciding fully with either Blume or Berrsche. Toscanini has in all listed versions a bare increase in pace from bar 29, continuing up to 37 with an increased intensity, which reaches its maximum in the *sforzato* passage. The oboe solo in the 1935 Philharmonic performance (Bruno Labate) is dreamy enough and, significantly, the subsequent clarinet solo (Simeon Bellison) has slight changes of pace and a hairsbreadth 'leaning' on the top notes of each phrase that do suggest the persistence of memory from that Brahms festival in 1909, effects eliminated in all of Toscanini's later performances. His way in this whole passage was singled out by Olin Downes on the occasion of his very first performance of the work in 1930: it was played, said Downes, with a 'blazing intensity and sweep' with the strings 'rushing downwards, preparing for the entrance of the solo oboe, followed in turn by the clarinet'. Who, asked Downes, 'could have imagined this new efflorescence of melody, this new torrent of feeling, in music played every season ... by justly renowned interpreters?' That, at any rate, was the Toscanini of 1930 and Downes's words well describe, too, the astonishing intensity still present in the 1935 Carnegie Hall performance. Intensity is, as ever with this conductor, present at this point in his later performances but not to that extraordinary degree, nor with such breadth: the 1935 version of this movement takes an extra half-minute compared with the 1937 NBC performance. Moreover, the latter, remarkable enough though it is, has to cope with Studio 8H's fatal drainage of colour and grandeur.[56]

Busch, who takes a broader tempo then the other Steinbach witnesses, fluctuates gently throughout with intensifications of tempo where stated or implied by Berrsche; however, although his solo clarinettist was still Bellison, there is no suggestion of the *rubato* or emphasis audible in his solo passage as they were seven years before. Boult is here similar in pace to Toscanini, although he does not match his intensity. As might be expected, he, like Busch, refrains from refinements of pacing in the oboe/clarinet solos, although in other respects his progress fits more or less loosely with Berrsche.

Weingartner's approach to the passage contains many subtle variations of tempo (not, however, matching Berrsche's description) – but his observance of the *sforzato*

---

[56]   See also p. 105.

passage is the most ferocious of all. Walter, too, fluctuates, although not in accord with Berrsche, but he indulges the greatest increase in tempo from bar 50 onwards. As one might expect, these two conductors, uninfluenced by Steinbach, go their differing ways effectively enough.

Abendroth holds the tempo steady until bar 29, after which it increases slightly, but this increase is sustained throughout the passage so that, when the unrelieved darkness at bar 51 onwards arrives, there is correspondingly little sense of an increased intensity; his handling of the passage is therefore one of the least effective among those chosen. From the start of the movement Furtwängler phrases voluptuously. Although the passage under consideration is played without any noteworthy fluctuation of pace, it does gain considerably in its intensity; but the conductor's initial manner of phrasing is confirmed throughout, making of this passage (for this listener) a Wagnerian rather than a Brahmsian experience.

This study now passes to the fourth movement, where interpretative problems are even more copious than they are in the first.

Fourth movement: *Adagio – Allegro non troppo, ma con brio – Più Allegro*

Bars 1–12: According to that February 1929 *Times* article quoted extensively in Chapter 2 both Stokowski and Abendroth erred in the opening bars of the fourth movement's introduction, the first by initiating the *pizzicato* increase in pace virtually from the outset at bar 6 instead of, as marked, at bar 8, while the latter commenced the *pizzicati* so slowly – in order to effect a greater increase of pace – that the tempo failed to match the opening bars.[57] Stokowski's 1927 recording and Abendroth's 1928 recording indeed show the *Times* critic to have been correct in every word. What, then, was the correct course? That critic would, no doubt, have been pleased to hear Weingartner's 1938 recording (his third of the work), which sets matters aright with eminently just results, even if it hardly sets the Thames on fire.

Blume, as usual, has his gloss on the printed page – although, it should be noted, his glosses for the most part consist of additions to the printed page rather than contradictions. Here he asks for a very slow basic tempo, with the first two bars of *pizzicato* in an 'absolutely rigid stillness' (one may infer that this means *a tempo*), with the *stringendo* at first very moderate (unstated, this refers to bars 8–9), intensifying in bars 10–11, hastening to the abruptly cut-off chord (bar 12).[58]

How, then, do the conductors under examination fare alongside Blume's detailed glosses? After his slower-than-basic-tempo start to the *pizzicato* passage, Abendroth retards several times in bars 8 and 9, reflecting also the hairpins (*crescendos* or *diminuendos*) in his tempo, before a downplayed, very modest *stringendo* in bars

---

[57] See pp. 47 and 132.
[58] Pasternack/Blume, pp. 38–9; Schwalb/Blume, p. 28.

10–12. There appears to be no authority for this curiously contrived approach, which manages to combine deliberate misreadings of the score with (unlike Stokowski) little return in terms of exciting effect.[59] Furtwängler here outdoes his friend. He interprets the *diminuendo* in bar 4 as meaning also a marked *ritardando* which brings the music to a halt by the beginning of bar 6, where the *pizzicato* passage commences. If one has reached stasis, there has to be a way out; Furtwängler, like Stokowski, takes the illegitimate course of ignoring the score and accelerates immediately from bar 6 – with gradual effect, it is true, but this merely illustrates the earlier observation that this conductor's famed subtle transitions are frequently used to smooth the path from one questionable tempo to another, a feature to be encountered elsewhere in this work.[60] After bar 3, as with Abendroth, the *stringendo* rocks back and forth with the hairpins before picking up, correctly, in bars 10–11. Some may applaud the passage as an inspirational reading between the notes that is justified by its results. Others will look for Brahms *come scritto*, without such interesting but questionable solutions testifying to Furtwängler's apparent belief that the composer's clear instructions should be no bar to his own preferences.

Fritz Busch meets the need for undecorated Brahms, although his introduction is taken generally at an exceptionally slow tempo with much poetic insight. Nevertheless, he demonstrates beyond any scintilla of doubt that Brahms is best taken neat: after commencing the *pizzicati* at a broad tempo equating with the opening bars, he makes a modest and slightly wavering *stringendo* in bars 8–9; but he then accelerates ferociously in bars 10–12, ending with a real and startling *fortissimo* cut-off in bar 12. So compelling is the result, one feels it must be Steinbach's own (and indeed Brahms's) voice, a reaction reinforced as the movement progresses. Toscanini in 1935 virtually matches Busch note for note – their introductions to this movement in these performances pan out within a few seconds of each other with similar poetic results. Both are indubitably magnificent in this passage and, as it happens, accord with Blume. The other Steinbach witness, Boult, is by comparison straightforward (not, however, straight-laced), the *stringendo* strongly marked from bar 10 onwards, just as Blume would have it. It is worth noting that Toscanini's later performances, from 1937 onwards, although still remarkably fine and in accord with Blume, do not achieve quite the breadth and intensity of his achievement with the New York Philharmonic, perhaps a demonstration once more of Studio 8H's notorious acoustics embedding themselves too deeply in the Maestro's consciousness.

Bars 30 *et seq.*: The horn theme is, Blume remarks, 'like a phoenix arising from the ashes', now emerging 'from the C minor darkness'.[61] Again, in this and the bars that

[59]   But see Musgrave and Sherman, Ch. 10 (Frisch), pp. 288–9.
[60]   See pp. 183 and 193.
[61]   Pasternack/Blume, p. 39; Schwalb/Blume, p. 29.

follow, Busch is supreme – in part because he has a great orchestra, strong in the wind
section. Not only this: he responds fully to Brahms's direction for the horn and flute
solos, *forte sempre e passionate*, in a way no other conductor matches (save perhaps,
as noted hereafter, Toscanini in 1935): Bruno Jaenicke's horn and John Amans's flute
outdo anything of which, say, the NBC SO's counterparts were capable or, indeed,
the soloists of any of the other orchestras under examination. Busch's handling of the
passage reminds us that one of Steinbach's signal strengths was, according to contemporary commentators such as Aldrich and Carl Flesch, his clear delineation at all times
of the melodic line, a feature with which, as noted above, *The Times* also credited him
in a London performance of the Second Symphony in 1938.[62] Here the effect, taken at
Busch's slow tempo, is one of exceptional wonderment – again, surely a direct legacy
from his master. It should be added that Toscanini in 1935 once more matches Busch
very closely in this passage – indeed, one could substitute one for the other without
damage to either, with Jaenicke and Amans again given remarkable prominence; it is
hardly necessary to point to the common ancestry here.

Bars 62 *et seq.*: At the start of the main theme (bar 62) Blume dilates extensively on the
length of the upbeat with which it commences, which requires full value and weight
to be given to the crotchet, a 'slight broadening'.[63] This much-discussed feature is
conducted by Abendroth in 1928 as a full minim, which sounds quite natural, but in
1956 he distends it to the equivalent of a full bar's length, self-consciously contrived
and with disruptive effect. The prize here is Toscanini's treatment in 1935: the first
note is just short of minim length (that is, Toscanini extends it somewhat beyond
the score's crotchet) and proclaimed with such tonal resonance, extending also to the
next notes of the theme, that one cannot for a moment dream of dissenting from this
distinctive approach. In the 1937 NBC performance the note's distension is similar in
length but less emphatic in character, while in later performances Toscanini conducts
more or less in tempo, as do Busch and Boult. Apart from Abendroth, the only other
non-Steinbach witness to distend this note (fairly slightly) is Furtwängler, who apparently adopts this feature in order to effect a proper transition from the preceding bars,
where once more he has decelerated his orchestra to a halt over the preceding three
bars of *diminuendo*.

The theme itself should, says Blume, have internal variations of tempo in both its
first and second statement, the latter accelerating towards the *animato* at bar 94, where
the theme must be 'felt either as alla breve or 4/4'.[64] Busch alone at a faster tempo
than the other Steinbach witnesses treats the theme with the fluxes of tempo suggested
by Blume, with a barely contained rise of tension throughout the theme's statement

---

[62] See p. 142.
[63] See Pasternack/Blume, pp. 41–5; Schwalb/Blume, pp. 30–2.
[64] Pasternack/Blume, pp. 45–6; Schwalb/Blume, pp. 32–3.

and restatement achieved by a very gradual rise in tempo, swaying backwards and forwards: an effect that builds the tension in a way with which no other conductor competes. Stokowski's *non troppo* tempo, like Busch's, is faster than the competition and, like him, he anticipates the *animato* by several bars; however, he does not build in the tension to Busch's unique extent. Toscanini's approach in 1935 is extremely broad in character with the richness of orchestral colour already noted; there is flexibility here, if without quite the fluxes felt in Busch's treatment. Later Toscanini versions retain much of his characteristic breadth but do not match the Philharmonic's unique intensity of tone.

Neither Toscanini nor Abendroth make any acceleration until the restatement at bar 78. From the first *animato*, however, Abendroth's treatment in 1928 and 1956 is singular: as Table 2 shows, he increases his basic tempo by an astonishing two-thirds. Among the recordings here considered in detail only Furtwängler remotely competes, but he is far less extreme. Abendroth's sole parallel elsewhere is with the similarly extreme performance by Oskar Fried in his pre-electric recording, a reading that was seen as remote from the tradition in Berlin where the recording was made.[65] The observance of the *animato* by Toscanini (in all versions listed), Busch and Boult is more modest, which has the virtue, in the case of Toscanini and Busch, of enabling them to set a faster tempo for the second *animato* at 118 as the music seems to require and where, as Blume now says unequivocally, there should be a genuine *alla breve* tempo. In addition, Toscanini in 1935 and Busch are the only conductors to observe very slight changes in tempo from bar 94 onwards, where the emphasis on the spaced chords in bars 94 and 97–8 contrasts with the *sforzato*-marked bars at 95–6 and 99–100; both conductors here accord with Blume, who requires the spaced chords to be conducted in four, the rest in two.[66]

Illogically, Abendroth, Furtwängler and Boult feel obliged to slow slightly for the second *animato* at 118, surprisingly so in the last-named case, since Boult's proportioning elsewhere, as Table 2 indicates, is in line with his Steinbach witness colleagues.

Bars 106 *et seq.*: Abendroth's treatment of tempo in the rest of the movement right through to letter Q (bar 367) continues to be uniquely extreme in its extraordinarily rapid pace. For those who would have it that Steinbach was, in effect, the avatar of Abendroth in the latter's lonely eminence (so far as recorded sound is concerned), the immediate and obvious question arises as to whether Abendroth could conceivably be following memories of that avatar in a manner that no other conductor among

---

[65] See p. 121.

[66] Pasternack/Blume, p. 46; Schwalb/Blume, p. 33. It is noteworthy that, in Toscanini's televised performance (3 November 1951, Testament SBDVD 1006, a performance very much in his 'late' style), he conducted the theme throughout in four, although the accelerated material later in the movement he takes in two (or one!) according to the pace and shaping required.

those examined here could access – parallel, however, to Oskar Fried's similar drive to untraditional extremes in his pre-electric recording.[67] For this last-named conductor, the inspiration for the unorthodox might have lain in the general treatment of the late Romantics by his mentor, Gustav Mahler, but there is no evidence of a similar connection in Abendroth's case.

In any event, for several reasons Abendroth's singular approach in the main body of this movement almost certainly does not reflect Steinbach's practice. In the first place, Abendroth's orchestras find it impossible to play many of the notes at his forced tempos. In 1928 there are frequent scamped passages, such as those following bars 257 and 356; in 1956, when his approach was still more extreme, strings slither from bars 102 and 234 onwards, while from bar 352 the woodwind triplets are a mere confused blur since they cannot be played audibly at such a furious pace, which at bar 356 reaches $\,\mathtt{\downarrow} = 176$. It must be remembered that the Meiningen Hofkapelle was outstanding in its day for its precision and readiness to follow the minute changes (under Bülow probably not so minute) of phrasing and tempo demanded by its conductors.[68] In the decades following its disbandment in 1914 the general standard of orchestral playing gradually rose and to some degree that improvement applied even to the LSO in the latter years of the 1920s, particularly under the enforced subjugation by Mengelberg at the end of that decade. True, the LSO was subject to pungent criticism by London critics,[69] but those attending Abendroth's concerts at the time also remarked that, as a powerful conductor, for the greater part he got his way with the players.[70] Making full allowance for these changing standards, styles and expectations of what was possible in terms of orchestral execution, if the LSO in 1928 and more especially the Bavarian orchestra in 1956 could not meet the finer details of the score's demands at Abendroth's tempos, it is scarcely credible that the Meiningen players or Steinbach's Cologne and Munich players could have met them either. It would be wholly unrealistic to credit Steinbach with conducting in such fashion, scamping and slurring so many details – and yet giving immense satisfaction to the composer.

Again, Blume is insistent on the need throughout the movement to conduct with a mixture of *alla breve* and common time according to the character of the music, for example, from bar 168 onwards (letter G).[71] Abendroth's wholesale rush makes such differentiation all but impossible, in contrast to the Steinbach witnesses, who throughout vary the pace appropriately.

The strongest reason for rejecting any authenticist view of Abendroth's approach, however, lies in the contrast between his and Busch's finale. Leaving aside the propulsive

[67]   See p. 121.
[68]   See p. 20.
[69]   See Dyment 2012, pp. 12–13.
[70]   See p. 132.
[71]   Pasternack/Blume, pp. 48–9; Schwalb/Blume, pp. 34–5.

accounts of Stokowski, Walter and Weingartner, whose recordings of the movement have no audible connection with Steinbach, Table 1 shows the overall timing for Busch and Abendroth in the main body of the last movement to be quite similar (there is less than a minute between the quick Busch and the even quicker Abendroth), indicating a somewhat faster approach by these two conductors to the main body of this movement by comparison with other recordings. But, as shown by Table 2, Busch is exceptional among the Steinbach witnesses in his quick basic tempo for the finale's big C major theme; thereafter, although moving consistently faster, structurally his shifts of tempo throughout reflect the integrated approach of the other Steinbach witnesses. In the resulting combination of irrepressible impetus and structural coherence, the music surges forward with unrivalled conviction while, in striking contrast to Abendroth, permitting all details to be properly executed. Steinbach's finale was by all accounts one of his great triumphs; for example, the *Musical Times* thought his performance with the LSO in October 1912 'the sensation of the evening … a great interpretation, the playing of the final movement unforgettable'.[72] Busch, too, triumphs in recreating with supreme mastery what is surely his mentor's voice.

Bars 279–301: In the passage leading up to letter N, bar 285, extending to the lead back to the *alla breve* theme at bar 301, Blume is insistent on the need to conduct bars 279 onwards in two, bar 285 (alone) in four – that is, slower – then in 286 to resume the previous tempo until relaxing at the *calando*.[73] Many conductors slow both before and after the cataclysmic chord at bar 285, so losing the force of Brahms's *calando* at bar 297. Among the conductors chosen here, Stokowski, slowing slightly from 279 at ♩ = 96 lowers the tension needlessly. Weingartner at a sensible ♩ = 120 also slows very slightly from 279 but, unusually, returns to a quicker tempo in bar 285 (the bar to be slowed in Blume's scheme) to allow for the subsequent *calando*. As might now be expected, Furtwängler's *calando* is more extreme than any other.

Toscanini, Busch and Abendroth all preserve Blume's scheme of things here, although, with his faster initial tempo at bar 279, ♩ = 160, as compared with Toscanini's 132 in 1937 (very slightly slower in 1935), Abendroth's treatment of the ten bars following 286 sounds the more radical. Toscanini's treatment is clarified in his 1941 recording, where the various textual strands, including in particular the changing tempo of the timpani from bar 289 onwards, are clearly audible. Busch, at ♩ = 144 from bar 279, faster than anyone else save Abendroth, maintains clarity and remarkable impetus while preserving absolute structural coherence: his *animato* at bar 301 resumes again at the identical ♩ = 144. Altogether, Blume is vindicated in this passage: the Steinbach witnesses follow his indications far more closely than any other conductor, save only for Abendroth at his extreme tempo.

[72] See Ch. 2, n. 20.
[73] Pasternack/Blume, p. 51; Schwalb/Blume, p. 36.

Bars 383 *et seq.*: For the transition into the coda from the *stringendo* at bar 383 through the *ben marcato* marking at 395, Blume advises no *ritardando* before 390, but at 395, to reinforce the *ben marcato* character, the tempo is, in Pasternack's translation, to be held back 'slightly'; Frisch's earlier translation has 'somewhat', a significant difference. Blume's term is '*etwas*', which bears both meanings but, as will be seen from his usage elsewhere, Pasternack's choice seems to be the more appropriate.[74]

Dealing first with the various approaches to the *stringendo*, Toscanini's increase in pace from 383 is modest, reaching ♩ = 96 at 390, a pace continued through the transition without change. Busch once again heightens the drama with an increase of pace to ♩ = 120 at 390, maintained steadily but very incisively until the return of the chorale theme. Among the other conductors, Stokowski approaches at a relatively fast ♩ = 120 but thereafter his treatment of the text is extremely free. A pointer to Nikisch? Optimistically, yes – but opinions will differ. Furtwängler at the same pace is more steady, more concerned on this occasion with the longer view. Weingartner's pacing is an unsensational ♩ = 108 and he continues with a rather stately view of the final pages.

Turning now to the specifics of that *ben marcato* marking at 395, the second instance within five bars of this instruction: none of the conductors so far mentioned mark this bar with any special emphasis. There remains, however, the odd man out. Abendroth's *stringendo* is extreme, reaching in 1928 ♩ = 144, in 1956 ♩ = 152, at bar 390; but at bar 395 he pulls back in both recordings to ♩ = 112, causing complete disjuncture from one note to the next. It may be added here that he also stretches the returning chorale theme in extraordinary fashion in contrast to the modest expansion of tempo by the three Steinbach witnesses; Blume merely asks for the brass chords to be 'broad and strongly sustained'.

Blume's brief suggestions for the coda transition, and in particular for holding back slightly (or somewhat) at the second *ben marcato* marking (bar 395), pose considerable problems for those seeking the meaning behind the words. It seems clear that, whatever Brahms may have applauded in Steinbach's approach when listening to his performances of the symphony at Meningen, his score intended no change of tempo: at bar 391 the first *ben marcato* applies only to the cellos and basses, but that, surely, is because the timpani's rhythm in bars 391–5 supports the other instruments and provides the necessary *marcato*. When this rhythmic underlining ceases at bar 395, the *ben marcato* is then marked for all the strings with extra accents in compensation; the term *ben marcato* has the same meaning in both instances and implies no change of pace on the second occasion.

Most of Blume's suggestions augment what is in the score but do not contradict it. How, then, should one interpret his 'holding back' at bar 395, which, if regarded as signalling a change of tempo, implies a different meaning for *ben marcato* in the course of

[74] Pasternack/Blume, p. 51; Schwalb/Blume, p. 36; Musgrave and Sherman, p. 275 (Walter Frisch's translation).

five bars? In my view, Blume's advice is simply meant as a warning that the conductor should not give into the temptation to accelerate – a frequent course, as illustrated by Stokowski – but to hold back *in tempo*. That option is clearly audible in Toscanini's performances, most magnificently in 1935 where the strings' incisive bowing, digging deep into the rhythm, gives full value to the *ben marcato* marking; a similar incisiveness but with rather less energy is to be heard in his 1941 RCA recording. Boult is very similar at this point. Although adopting a faster tempo throughout, Busch's approach is in structural terms the same, the articulation again distinct.

Another possible interpretation of Blume's advice at this point is an emphasis combined with a very slight modification of tempo, an option to be heard in Max Fiedler's handling of a somewhat analogous passage in Brahms's First Piano Concerto.[75] Blume's advice is, however, unlikely to signify an abrupt reduction in tempo by one-third as heard in Abendroth's recordings; this sudden change of gear wholly disrupts the structure and musical line, a result inconsistent with virtually all reports of Steinbach's general approach. Moreover, Abendroth's wild tempo for the transition into the *più allegro* as far as bar 395 precludes any observance of the *ben marcato* where it is first marked at bar 391; thus his performance here combines misconceptions about both the score and Steinbach's likely approach – if, indeed, Abendroth ever heard him conduct it.

Preliminary conclusions

Abendroth's recordings of the First Symphony have been examined in detail elsewhere, with the proposal that they shine a unique light on the Steinbach tradition as described by Blume.[76] Hence the detail provided here, which suggests an alternative view that takes into account the interpretative approach of the proven Steinbach witnesses. This examination makes clear that, in the typical passages chosen for comparison, Toscanini's and Boult's earliest recordings and in particular Fritz Busch's 1942 concert performance reflect far more closely the (then unknown) precepts of Blume than do any of Abendroth's recordings.

Abendroth's strongest suit as a Steinbach witness seems to lie in his particular treatment of two places in the score. The first is what is termed above as the 'disconnect' at bars 145–6 of the first movement, which in his hands is a clear example of the brief stopping of the bow between the tied chords. Among the examined conductors, such

---

[75] At bar 9 before B in the first movement; performance on 26 October 1936 by Alfred Hoehn, piano, and the Hamburg Radio Symphony Orchestra: CD ARBITER160 and see Dyment 2002 (Autumn), p. 47. A similar, slight holding back at bar 296 is to be heard in Vladimir Jurowski's performances of the First Symphony: LPO 0043, 25 May 2008, which he repeated subsequently at a BBC Henry Wood Promenade Concert in 2009.

[76] See p. 4, n. 4.

treatment varies: some, including Busch, Boult and Stokowski (two followers of the Steinbach way and one obviously not), clearly observe the disconnect; one of them, Toscanini, sometimes allows the disconnect but at other times is less clear. The other conductors examined do not permit the disconnect. Among conductors beyond the scope of this study, those observing a disconnect include an entirely miscellaneous bunch of distinguished practitioners: 'Szell, Horenstein, Abravanel, Klemperer, Munch … Rowicki'.[77] In the absence of any evidence of a link between these conductors and the Meiningen way, beyond any real doubt the conclusion must be that the 'disconnect' practice extended well beyond Steinbach and his followers and was not unique to them.[78] Abendroth's practice seems unremarkable in this light and gives no support to the view that by some unspecified route he must have absorbed it from Steinbach himself.

Another place in the score where on the face of it Abendroth reflects a particular Steinbach practice as per Blume lies in the extended crotchet upbeat commencing the main theme of the fourth movement *Allegro*, clearly observable in his 1928 recording and likewise in Toscanini's 1935 Philharmonic and 1937 NBC SO concert performances. As the examination of this practice in these pages points out, Furtwängler also makes use of the device here and, along with others, in the opening of the Fourth Symphony.[79] Blume discusses at length the need for a prolonged emphasis on such upbeats, much of his explanation being in the mode of what conductors 'should' do, rather than attaching his guidance specifically to the Meiningen way. Further, he remarks that the 'intensity of the music-making of a Steinbach or a Nikisch was due in part to their having seized upon the strengthening of weaker notes as a correct approach to phrasing'.[80] It appears, therefore, that Blume's prescriptions here are not limited by him to Steinbach's example or to any explanation Steinbach might have given to him, but speak more generally of what he, Blume, conceived from the great masters was best practice. Given that this treatment of the upbeat in certain contexts was not confined to the Meiningen way, Abendroth's approach neither proves nor disproves a knowledge of or attachment to Steinbach's practice.

As a Steinbach witness in this work, Abendroth remains possible but far from proven or likely: the evidence of a few coincidences with Blume's advice is counterbalanced by many departures and also by fundamental differences between his approach and that of proven Steinbach witnesses.

Two further conclusions are obvious. First, quite clearly the Steinbach witness conductors do not always accord with Blume. In approaching the First Symphony, they took only what they wanted from their memories of Steinbach, selecting what they

---

[77] Gunther Schuller, *The Compleat Conductor*, Oxford: Oxford University Press, 1997, p. 306.
[78] Compare Musgrave and Sherman, Ch. 10 (Frisch), pp. 297–8.
[79] See p. 193.
[80] See p. 154.

needed to shape their own experience of the work. Sometimes, it seems, either they ignored seemingly vital points underlined by Blume or Blume must have misremembered Steinbach or read his own views into his description of the Steinbach way, which were not reflected in Steinbach's actual performances. For example, at the climactic point of the first movement (bars 470–5) Blume advises that the tempo be pushed ahead up to bar 473 but that the (slower) *tempo primo* be resumed in the climactic bar 474 in preparation for the distinct 'jolt' ('*Ruck*' – a sudden start or shock) at bar 475.[81] Of the conductors here examined, only Furtwängler, a Meiningen 'outsider', does anything approaching this, although there is a distinct trace of holding back in Boult's 1959 recording. Abendroth and the two other Steinbach witnesses take bar 474 in their preceding accelerated tempo and wait for bar 475 and after to commence their deceleration. It is possible that Steinbach did adopt the course remembered by Blume, and Boult's 1959 recording may bear some weight in this context; but, given the uniform course adopted by all other recordings by the Steinbach witnesses, the matter remains altogether uncertain. This short but crucial passage illustrates both the danger of treating Blume as gospel and the relevance of other aural and comparative evidence.

The foregoing analysis also affirms the importance of factors other than the Meiningen way in shaping the interpretative approaches of these recording conductors. For Boult, Richter's prolonged influence was probably as significant as his relatively few experiences of Steinbach. With his observant and balanced temperament, and also on occasion his tendency to a somewhat phlegmatic outlook, it is therefore hardly surprising that Boult's interpretation in its high maturity, fiery though it is, contains its expressive effects within closer confines than those of other Steinbach witnesses.

Abendroth, developing his independent interpretative approach during his Essen years, could not escape his background in the ultra-Wagnerian practices of Mottl, to whom both he and Furtwängler were indebted; and the grand fluxing of tempo which features in their approach to wide swathes of the repertoire, including Brahms, is more likely to be linked to that source than to the subtleties of Steinbach. This background must also account for the exaggerated response in Abendroth's recordings of Brahms's First Symphony to certain elements which might possibly have had their origin in his memory of Steinbach in Cologne.

Fritz Busch is a unique source of information, not only in his direct relationship with Steinbach but more especially because we know that he treasured the memory of Steinbach's performance of this work, which, just five years before his own New York performance of it, he invoked as preferable to Toscanini's in its warmth and overall conviction. In his interpretation, much of the first movement and the whole of his electrifying finale for the most part ring true as remarkable recreations in the spirit of his teacher; so, too, do his broad, flexible but never inflated *Andante* second movement

[81] Pasternack/Blume, p. 24; Schwalb/Blume, p. 19.

and his free-flowing but never pressurized *Allegretto* third movement (the latter not examined further here). But other long-term influences, such as Weingartner, who in his earlier years Busch greatly respected, may have contributed to the formation of his later conducting style; nor should one ignore the constant development of his independent interpretative viewpoint. Such factors may account for his sometimes more sober response to the expressive requirements of the first movement's *Allegro* than, say, Toscanini and also for his divergence from Blume's lengthy plea for an extended upbeat commencing the finale's C major theme; here one may recall that Flesch regarded Busch as Steinbach's heir, albeit conducting in a more 'modern' fashion.[82] Nevertheless, Busch's Brahms First Symphony must be counted among the prime documents available in the task of reconstructing the Meiningen way.

As for Toscanini, his capacious memory doubtless enabled him in the 1930s to recall in every detail what he heard in Munich in 1909. It seems clear that he deeply admired Steinbach, an admiration which helped ground his pre-war Brahms with a quite extraordinary expressive variety: in the 1935 and 1937 performances of the First Symphony the metronome finds it difficult to pace more than any two bars in the same tempo, a characteristic also to be found in Weingartner's 1938 recording. That admiration, however, did not preclude Toscanini going his own way whenever he felt the letter of the score took precedence, even if, as Fritz Busch implied, that sacrificed some of Steinbach's warmth. Notably, in the finale Toscanini's broad pacing probably differed in some degree from Steinbach; here Busch is a significant guide. But the dangers of the opposite extreme are only too vividly demonstrated in the scrambled incoherence of Abendroth's performances of this movement.[83] In any event, the 1935 Philharmonic performance, demonstrating the Maestro at the peak of his powers as a symphonic conductor, contains multiple reminders of the Steinbach way as explicated by Blume.

Despite Fritz Busch's example and Blume's guidance, exactly how Steinbach himself interpreted the finale will always be surrounded with some uncertainty, but it is worth pointing out that his approach did not meet with universal approbation. In contrast to the London critic quoted above,[84] the foremost contemporary Essen critic who witnessed Steinbach in a Cologne rendering of the work thought that 'at the end of the last movement he needed to resort to purely dynamic effects which can certainly

---

[82] See p. 141.

[83] Günter Wand's interpretation of the finale has elements of Abendroth's approach, without the scramble, and in the film of his 1997 Kiel performance with the NDR SO he can be seen to conduct the *animato* themes freely – sometimes in two, sometimes in four (24 August 1997, TDK DVWW-COWAND7). Wand studied in Cologne (though not conducting, in which he was largely self-taught) when Abendroth was still in post there and he probably witnessed Abendroth conduct the work. However, nothing else in his interpretation bears signs of an Abendroth influence.

[84] See p. 196.

be read into the score but are hardly in accordance with its spirit. There occurred there a *stretto* with piling up of the brass, which may have been Steinbach but was certainly not Brahms.'[85] The composer, as we know, took a different view, but that was two decades earlier. We also know how Steinbach's interpretations of Brahms changed somewhat between the time of his appearances in London in 1902 with the Meiningen Hofkapelle and his final London appearances in 1913–14. Perhaps by then the Essen critic's negative reaction to the final pages of the First Symphony under Steinbach had some justification – although in his parting shot on this symphony Blume remarks that the final bars should indeed 'be taken like a stretto'.[86] Was that what Brahms himself heard from Steinbach? We shall never know.

Symphony No. 2 in D major Op. 73

In this symphony we know that Brahms approved Weingartner's performance in 1895 and that there is some probability that his performances of the work remained substantially unchanged over the years between 1895 and 1940, the date when he recorded the work. We also know that Steinbach fully approved Toscanini's preparation of the work for him in 1911; Toscanini's approach (here principally his 1938 NBC Symphony performance) may therefore provide corroborative evidence of Steinbach's practice. Also noteworthy is the structuring of the first movement suggested by Table 2, in which both Weingartner (who, along with Boult, is the minimalist) and the Steinbach witnesses calibrate the fluctuations of tempo towards a point of maximum tension and resolution in the development, differing in this respect from the more varied treatment of all the remaining conductors.

First movement: *Allegro non troppo*

Bars 2 *et seq.* and 82 *et seq.*: According to Blume, both the first theme from bar 2 and the second at bar 82 require slight 'separations' or 'breaths' at the end of the short phrases (in the second theme at 85).[87] Toscanini reflects this advice and, indeed, in his February 1951 performance the degree of separation in the second theme's reprise is more marked than in any other: only his careful observance of the dynamics prevents an inappropriate swooning.[88] The other Steinbach witnesses are less consistent: Busch in 1931 is inaudible at the outset and on the second time round at bar 10 his horn

---

[85] Max Hehemann, quoted in Dejmek, p. 150. This was probably the performance in March 1913, noted above at p. 127.
[86] Pasternack/Blume, p. 52; Schwalb/Blume, p. 36.
[87] Pasternack/Blume, pp. 55 and 57; Schwalb/Blume, pp. 38 and 40.
[88] Performance of 10 February 1951, NBC SO, Carnegie Hall, Pristine Audio PASC 157.

is too rocky for one to form any judgement. In 1947 his horn makes no inflection at the start but does so second time round. Meiningen 'outsiders', such as Weingartner, Fiedler and Furtwängler, opt for less inflected phrasing. This specimen is the first of the 'short breathed' phrases of which Aldrich complained when he heard Toscanini conduct the work – strangely so, since he did not complain about Steinbach who, if Blume is to be trusted, followed this practice here and elsewhere in the movement.[89]

Bars 118 *et seq.*: At this much-discussed *quasi ritenente*, Brahms was unhelpful in response to requests for elucidation. 'The *quasi-rit.* … could just as well be left out', he remarked in a letter to Otto Dessoff, who had suggested four bars of preparatory pulling back from bar 114 onwards – even though he himself had changed his mind more than once over inclusion of the *quasi rit*.[90] According to Blume, the passage should be 'prepared' – presumably with a slight *ritenuto* beforehand, which many conductors insert – but should not be too broad: the emphasis should be on the '*quasi*', meaning that it should remain 'internally proportional' (Blume's quotes) to the main tempo.[91] Taking first the 'preparation', all the conductors who maintain a certain reserve in their emotional response – that is, Weingartner, Toscanini, Boult and Busch (both versions) – take care to include a very modest *stringendo* in the bars preceding 114, to be heard distinctly in their treatment of the *pizzicato* bassline up to the *crescendo* starting in that bar. This practice enables these conductors to draw back the tempo very slightly by the time they reach the *quasi rit*. Here once more they all agree that only a modest expansion is required. Remarkably, Fiedler, who until this moment has signally abjured any adrenalin control, also refrains from over-inflation. Lest one should connect him here with the practice of his hero, Hans von Bülow, one must note that the Bülow pupil Walter Damrosch adopts the most massively inflated *quasi ritenente* of all. Less pronounced but still all too obvious, Abendroth in both 1939 and 1952 emphatically distends; Furtwängler, especially in 1952, does likewise.

Bars 134–6 and 402–3: If the most convincing in the last-mentioned passage are those holding a leash on their emotional response, so also are they at two noteworthy points which follow. In the *fortissimo* climax at bar 134 Blume requires the trombones and bass tuba, which alone are marked *forte*, to commence *fp* with a *crescendo* to the *fortissimo* specified for the rest of the orchestra.[92] Busch, Boult, Toscanini and Weingartner,

---

[89] See pp. 42 and 104.
[90] See Musgrave and Sherman, Ch. 2, Styra Avins, 'Performing Brahms's Music: Clues from His Letters', p. 25; and Ch. 8 (Pascall and Weller), p. 228. The quotation is from Brahms's letter of 28 October 1878 to Dessoff.
[91] Pasternack/Blume, p. 57; Schwalb/Blume, p. 40.
[92] Pasternack/Blume, pp. 57–8; Schwalb/Blume, pp. 40–1. Blume's text and example do not match here. The text requires all the winds to observe this dynamic change, his example only the

so far as can be heard, ignore this here and in the recapitulation, following the score with a consistent *forte/fortissimo* through the two bars in question, complete with the emphasis supplied by the composer in 134 (Brahms marks no emphasis at 402 since he adds *fortissimo* timpani instead). The treatment by Abendroth in 1939 and Furt-wängler in 1945 is, by contrast, curious: Abendroth imposes a *crescendo* by the whole orchestra at this point in both exposition and recapitulation, a practice he rejects in 1952 in favour of the score as written; Furtwängler in 1945 makes a sharp, full orches-tra *crescendo* in the recapitulation (only) but follows the score in 1952. None of these full-orchestra *crescendos* has any authority either in the score or in Blume; it is not only Wagnerian in effect (compare the start of the Third Symphony below) but at these focal points in the structure virtually inverts the composer's own dynamic marking, with fatal effect.

Bars 137–40: In this passage Blume prescribes a 'slight break' after each slur.[93] This is another direction which would tend towards the 'short breathed' effect already men-tioned at the start of this movement; it would seem to have been part and parcel of the expressive devices current at the time. In 1931 Busch makes clean breaks, rather less obvious in 1947 where his treatment parallels Toscanini, who, while not ignor-ing the slur breaks, relies more on dynamic shading that favours greater continuity. That course is also Weingartner's choice, where one observes the cunning with which he follows the score: minimal breaks which are nonetheless there. Fiedler also breaks distinctly, but without exaggeration. Furtwängler gives no hint of breaks. The joker in the pack here is Abendroth who not only exaggerates the breaks (hardly 'slight') but in 1939 adds *crescendos* to each phrase, with self-consciously disruptive results; this effect is toned down in 1952. Who is closest here to the Meiningen way? One's response depends on the degree of reliance placed on Blume but the differing extremes of Furtwängler and Abendroth at this point are both doubtful solutions.

Bars 224–7, 230–3: Blume's direction for these passages is short: 'the trombones should make a *crescendo*' in bars 226–7, and similarly in 232–3; since the trombones are already playing at *forte*, one must assume he expected them to reach *fortissimo* before the *fortissimo* down beat from the rest of the orchestra (horns and trumpets excepted) in bars 227 and 233, which would emphasise continuity of presentation. This direction is reflected best in Toscanini's performances – he is not shy of ensuring prominent snarls from the trombones – and is particularly clear in his 1952 RCA recording. Most of the other recordings, including the Steinbach witnesses, make little or no *crescendo* and preserve continuity by means of a slightly damped down *fortissimo* entry in bars 227 and 233. Furtwängler in 1945 produces an unambiguous *fortissimo* in accordance

---

trombone and bass tuba, the only instruments not marked *ff*. I have relied on the latter.
[93] Pasternack/Blume, p. 58; Schwalb/Blume, p. 41.

with the score but with no change of dynamic level in the preceding trombones; the result sounds somewhat disruptive. Most disruptive of all is Fiedler, who introduces unambiguous *Luftpausen* before the full orchestra *fortissimos*. These examples are by no means the first such pauses in his performance of the first movement but they are without doubt by far the most disturbing to contemporary ears. Furthermore, they are decidedly superfluous in so far as they are placed well before the ultimate climax of the development at bar 282.

Second movement: *Adagio non troppo*

Bars 55 and 60: In these bars Blume left no advice save the suggestion of a short *fermata* on the first beat, returning to the main tempo on the second, an instance where, when observed, the result is likely to seem so natural as to be unnoticed.[94] The interest thereafter is the degree to which the little swells on tuba and trombone, each starting piano, are highlighted (or not); in the absence of comment from Blume, it may be inferred that he expected no special emphasis at these points. Toscanini is alone in ensuring that the rest of the orchestra is audible throughout, achieved by swells that barely reach a dynamic level of *mezzoforte*, which in the context seems the right course. Other conductors – Busch, Weingartner and Abendroth among them – do little to ensure the orchestra's audibility (although in some cases the recordings are perhaps too limited to make a certain judgement); but the swells themselves remain at a fairly low dynamic level. Furtwängler is alone in producing swells that reach a *forte* level and beyond, not only ensuring that other instruments are inaudible but introducing a Wagnerian element reminiscent of an angry Fafner slithering towards his nemesis. There is an imagination at work here but not, for this listener, one focused on the likely intent of the composer in this context.

Bars 87–96: Blume suggests that from bar 87 the conductor must lead energetically back to the 4/4 at 97, relaxing the tempo before the double bar at that point.[95] Toscanini relaxes slightly at 96, Busch (1931) a little more. By contrast Abendroth holds on to the last note of bar 96, extending the subsequent rests. These conductors illustrate two different ways of achieving the same aim, Toscanini and Busch better maintaining continuity, Abendroth bringing the music to a lingering halt. The one is Brahmsian in character, the other imports Wagnerian licence, reflected also in Furtwängler's 1945 recording.

---

[94] Pasternack/Blume, p. 66; Schwalb/Blume, p. 47. None of the conductors covered here follows this suggestion.

[95] Pasternack/Blume, pp. 66–7; Schwalb/Blume, p. 48.

Third movement: *Allegretto grazioso (Quasi Andantino)*

Bars 1–26: In the *Allegretto* Blume continues to advise, as he did with so much of the first movement's material, characteristic separations in the phrasing of the first (oboe) theme, particularly distinctive in opening up the E–D intervals in bars 8–11. Further, he advises that the major–minor distinction in bars 25–26 be highlighted by urging forward and pulling back.[96] Busch (1931) is the most forceful in articulating the oboe as per Blume and, indeed, his principal's distinctive tone begins to sound under strain from his demands here. Toscanini clearly articulates at least some of the separations and suggests, perhaps vestigially, the major–minor contrasts in tempo. His BBC SO soloist a few months later does not follow his NBC colleague. Other conductors, including Abendroth, Furtwängler and Walter, largely bypass these sophistications.

Bars 114–24: In bars 114–17 the three Steinbach witnesses once more accord with Blume's suggestion of separated downbeat crotchets, another instance where Abendroth, Furtwängler and Walter choose an alternative course. All conductors anticipate by several bars the *ritardando* at bar 124, commencing usually at 120; as is apparent from Table 2, the Steinbach witnesses do so to a modest extent, the Mottl acolytes (Abendroth and Furtwängler) to an extreme. Brahms wanted this movement to sound 'quite peaceful, especially at the end'[97] and Toscanini, particularly in his 1952 RCA recording, is here the most relaxed in tempo, adding a further modest relaxation for the *poco sostenuto* towards the close. Furtwängler's longer timing is a consequence of the dying fall he imposes on the closing bars, a habit of his in so many of Brahms's quiet endings – possibly one of the points occasioning the critical reception given to his first Berlin Philharmonic performance of the work in 1922.[98]

Fourth movement: *Allegro con spirito*

Bars 1–97: The question of tempo is, as the discussion in Chapter 2 indicated, a central issue in this movement. Without reiterating the arguments put forward there,[99] it seems fairly unlikely that Steinbach himself went to the extremes of Busch (both versions) and Weingartner. As Steinbach's prize conducting pupil, Busch's tempo must command respect, even if *The Times* dissented in 1938. But there may have been pressures and influences at work on him about which it is now impossible to make an informed judgement; perhaps in 1931 he thought the time allowance for the broadcast would place him under pressure, causing him in turn to put pressure on the tempo.

---

[96] Pasternack/Blume, pp. 68–9; Schwalb/Blume, p. 49.
[97] Musgrave and Sherman, Ch. 4 (Bernard D. Sherman), p. 118.
[98] See p. 137.
[99] See p. 92.

In making his post-war recording, he may have been over-conscious of the pressures to complete the finale on two 78rpm sides: certainly his much quicker tempo for the *Adagio* in 1947 would point in that direction. In any case, he may have long ago heard Weingartner and liked the result – assuming that Weingartner himself indulged in such a racing tempo at the time, as to which, again, there must be some doubt.

If any of the aforementioned pressures were present, they may also have led the two conductors to underplay the *largamente* at bar 78 as they do. Blume here asks for this subject to be 'prepared through a *ritardando*' and in the subject itself he places a *tenuto* sign to indicate a break at each slur.[100] Most conductors, to a greater or lesser extent, make such preparation for bar 78 in any event, minimalised, however, among most of the present recording conductors, Furtwängler and Walter included. Blume's prescription here indicates that *largamente* signifies not only warm phrasing but a modification of tempo. Of the conductors here examined, Fiedler provides the maximum contrast but without audible breaks. Toscanini runs him close in warmth in both his 1952 recording and in fragments of an aircheck of his Philharmonic broadcast in 1935; in the latter especially, his observance of the breaks is clearly audible, less so in the later performances.

<u>Bars 387–end</u>: Our concern in this final passage is the degree of acceleration towards the close indulged by the conductors under examination. Those already setting a fast pace (Busch and Weingartner) do not alter their tempos appreciably; other non-Steinbach witnesses, Walter and Fiedler, increase the pace to a modest extent. It is left to Furtwängler to display his unique attitude towards Brahms, which in the 1945 performance shows itself in a pressure on the tempo reaching as far back as the start of the recapitulation. That pressure sacrifices the *largamente* in the reprise, which is barely acknowledged, and by the end of the movement the pace is such that the heavy brass in the final bars are unable to articulate with clarity. For this listener the resulting effect has elements of naked hysteria wholly inappropriate to the performance of any of Brahms's music. Of course, at the time of the performance the conductor may well have felt himself to be in a dangerous situation vis-à-vis Nazi officialdom and, indeed, a few weeks later he sought refuge in Switzerland; his personal circumstances may therefore have weighed too heavily on this occasion. It would be tempting to take these extra-musical pressures into account when judging the result were it not that the conductor's admirers do not themselves do so and apparently regard the performance without qualification as the Brahmsian ideal.

Those who are unpersuaded of the divine status accorded by some to Furtwängler's 1945 performance may turn to Blume to shed some light on how Steinbach may have invigorated the final pages of the last movement. Blume's advice is, in brief, that bar

---

[100] Pasternack/Blume, pp. 73–4; Schwalb/Blume, p. 53.

387 be played 'heavily and holding back' (his own quotes once more – surely the voice of Steinbach himself here) and that there be a gradual acceleration from 391 to 405 to what amounts to a *molto allegro*; however, at bars 408 and 412 a *crescendo* should lead to an abrupt cut-off at each rest, and the closing horns and trumpets at 421–4 must 'above all' be clear and not rushed.[101] These directions suggest multiple changes of tempo which must at all costs avoid rushing the final bars, from which one may infer that any preceding increase of tempo should be modest in extent. Save in just one instance, none of the conductors examined – nor any other among the early record-ings – reflects the complexity of this approach. The one exception – in this instance the true reporter of the Meiningen way – is Toscanini: in his 1938 broadcast performance, and also, at a more leisurely pace, in the surviving fragments of his 1935 Philharmonic broadcast, he, in lonely eminence, reflects virtually all of Blume's prescriptions and thereby demonstrates in this instance the accuracy of Blume's reportage.[102] For this listener the result is, as Steinbach's must also have been, both noble and transcenden-tally thrilling, notwithstanding the constricting acoustics of NBC's Studio 8H in 1938.

Preliminary conclusions

As will be apparent from the foregoing analysis, the Toscanini broadcast performance from 1938 offers multiple insights into many of the Steinbach practices he heard thirty years before. The BBC SO performance only four months later disappoints expecta-tions in this respect and others: the playing, save for some wind solos such as Aubrey Brain's horn, is unfocused by comparison with the NBC Symphony; Toscanini was, it seems, thoroughly exhausted at the time.[103] It must, however, be borne in mind that the 1938 NBC performance itself marks a transition to Toscanini's later, less inflected style: reference has already been made to fragments of a New York Philharmonic aircheck from 24 February 1935 (encompassing the third movement from bar 110 and a complete finale), which are still more flexible, inflected and broader in tempo. On these counts, they may perhaps afford even closer insights into the performance practices of Steinbach which Toscanini by his own admission (to Furtwängler in 1924) had somewhere in his mind when conducting his own performances. That is not to imply a conscious effort by Toscanini to imitate, although his frustration with his, as he thought, unsuccessful performances of the Third Symphony by comparison with Steinbach's has been noted in Chapter 2.[104] But by the mid- to late 1930s, some elements of Steinbach's practice in the Second Symphony had clearly embedded

---

[101] Pasternack/Blume, p. 76; Schwalb/Blume, pp. 54–5.

[102] Mackerras, in his recording of the cycle, also here follows Blume closely, but with his Mein-ingen-size forces cannot emulate Toscanini's intensity; see further p. 235.

[103] See Dyment 2012, pp. 145–8.

[104] See p. 99.

themselves so deeply in Toscanini's consciousness that they emerged spontaneously in his own extraordinary re-creations of the Brahms symphony he cherished above all others.

Fritz Busch (1931) deserves the closest scrutiny, despite the remote and confusing sound. He conveys many notable Steinbachian insights in his spontaneity and freedom of approach within a Classical framework; the framework was retained in his 1947 recording but less of the freedom. By contrast, as may be inferred from the timings in Table 1, Boult's performances of the Second Symphony, and also the Third, do not have the fire of his First, although, in his observant but phlegmatic way, there is much insight in his Second in regard to matters of phrasing and significant detail.

It is unlikely that Abendroth heard Steinbach conduct this symphony. Steinbach did not perform it in Cologne during Abendroth's Essen tenure and the recorded evidence is still less persuasive than in the case of the First Symphony. In any event, the scattering of eccentricities, Wagnerian idiosyncrasies and exaggerations limits the value of Abendroth's 1939 performance either as a possible documentation of the Meiningen way or as constituting a Brahms performance of the highest quality. His later version, which has also been examined in this context, has conspicuously less energy and rather less individuality.

Walter, in his performance from Berlin in 1950, shows much wisdom: his refusal to accelerate unduly in the first *tutti* and later in that movement accelerating only to a moderate extent in the development are just two examples. He demonstrates that great Brahms performances do not depend on observance of the prescriptions of any tradition, whether from Meiningen or elsewhere. The same might be said of Weingartner, whose Second Symphony, perhaps the fastest ever recorded, nonetheless shows for the greater part how in the most judicious manner it is possible to combine a strong forward thrust with acute sensitivity to the music's ebb and flow. Sometimes his solutions to interpretative problems coincide with those of the Steinbach witnesses; but that is, indeed, pure coincidence and, as such, surely helps identify what is good practice in the performance of Brahms and what is not.

Symphony No. 3 in F major Op. 90

It is unfortunate that Fritz Busch did not record this symphony, the more so because his First Symphony and his 1931 reading of the Second yield multiple insights into the Meiningen way. Boult did record it on two occasions but, as Tables 1 and 2 disclose, the earlier of the two, the one chosen for further examination, lacks the fire he brought to his earliest recording of the First Symphony.

Among the Steinbach witnesses, we are left, then, with Toscanini's multiple versions, excluding from consideration here his RCA recording of 4 November 1952,[105] a curious exercise in broad tempos and dutiful, albeit listless, execution by the NBC SO – although I find this Toscanini failure musically more interesting than many another conductor's success. In the circumstances it is fortunate that documentation of his approach to the Third Symphony dates back to the Philharmonic performance of 17 March 1935, his earliest extant complete recording of a Brahms symphony. In this work his repeated experiments, already noted in regard to textures, extended also to tempos and proportioning, from the lightness of his NBC broadcast of February 1941 to the uninspired, extreme breadth of the RCA recording. As mentioned in Chapter 2, his constant searching also signified his long-term dissatisfaction in failing to recreate with his customary conviction some of the elements he heard in Steinbach's evidently persuasive way with the work in 1909. Tables 1 and 2 both indicate that in his last great performance of the work, with the Philharmonia Orchestra on 1 October 1952, he returned quite closely to the spirit of his 1935 reading.

First movement: *Allegro con brio*

Bars 1–14: The opening *Allegro* is notoriously full of traps for even the most complete conductor. Blume advises that the two opening bars are simply distinct *forte* chords without 'heroic "thunder resounding"' (his quotes again) and *a fortiori*, it would seem, without *crescendo*. In the following theme, the pairs of crotchets, marked as phrased and staccato in bars 4, 6 and 8 must, he says, be played *portamento*, by which in this context he probably means distinct but joined (Pasternack suggests *portato*, on the same bow stroke); only in the unphrased pair in bar 10 should there be space between them.[106] The theme's other notes, Blume continues, should be shaped sonorously rather than short and energetically. Every one of these precepts is reflected in all of Toscanini's performances, sometimes at a quicker tempo (as in the 1935 New York Philharmonic and 1952 Philharmonia performances) at other times in slightly more solid fashion (as in 1938). Boult at his slower tempo is similarly heedful.

In extreme contrast to the Steinbach witnesses, Abendroth swells the second chord in an ear-splitting, distended *crescendo* which would be vastly more at home in a Wagnerian *Trauermusik*; Furtwängler in these two bars, alas, does likewise, if in a somewhat less distended manner. Thereafter each note of Abendroth's opening theme, at headlong tempo, is articulated *staccato* without discrimination, heedless of Brahms's careful differentiation, with or without Blume's admonitions. Clearly, this conductor never heard Steinbach in this work – or, if he did, ignored him completely. At least after the two opening bars Furtwängler differentiates himself from his friend,

[105] CD transfer, Sony 88697916312-08.
[106] Pasternack/Blume, pp. 78–9; Schwalb/Blume, p. 56.

with a broad tempo taking account of Brahms's own scansions. Walter is similarly heedful in his surprisingly up-tempo reading of the opening pages.

It will be remembered that a veteran player received the distinct impression – evidently vivid, considering that nearly forty years failed to erase it – that Weingartner's performance of the work in the 1930s sounded as if a map had been laid out for players and listeners.[107] His 1938 recording corroborates that impression: it has a fine impetus from first bar to last, making it, among the chosen recordings, second only to Walter in total timing. His opening and first theme are admirably balanced and straightforward in following precisely what is in the score, enhanced by that rhythmic propulsion of which he was such a master.

Bars 35–42: The rest of the exposition is subject to Blume's frequent micro-management, but it is noteworthy that he suggests no change of tempo for the new theme at bar 36. When he does suggest such a change at bar 42, he is seemingly scared even to make the suggestion for fear of being misunderstood and requires *tempo primo* to return at bar 44. Having regard to the portrait of Steinbach's general approach painted in Chapter 2, which stresses that on the available evidence his tempo fluxes in Brahms were usually slight in character, it is worth quoting what Blume has to say about the nature of tempo change here, given in Pasternack's translation: 'if one speaks about this single small, subtle change of tempo, it is almost a foregone conclusion that it will become crude'. Blume goes on to stress that such places 'should not have the feeling of two distinct tempos but should only give the impression of slower and quicker characters within a single tempo'.[108] He is seemingly reluctant to draw attention to the possibility of tempo modification because of the likelihood of misunderstanding; Steinbach himself, it seems, would handle such passages, here and elsewhere, with such subtlety that the listener would scarcely be aware of any change of pulse. That approach is to be compared with, say, Walter's too audible change to a lower gear for the 9/4 theme, an apparently lifelong habit to be heard in all his recordings of the Third Symphony.

None of the conductors under examination reflects Blume's advice in the passage last considered and, indeed, one has to struggle to pinpoint anything in the rest of the exposition that accords with his micro-management, whether from the two Steinbach witnesses or others. Toscanini, by way of example, sometimes reflects what we read in Blume, sometimes not. Two examples suffice: of Blume's various suggested 'separation' marks in the 9/4 theme,[109] in his early performances Toscanini clearly lifts the phrasing at the *pianissimo* in bar 38 but not elsewhere. Others are no more heedful. And

[107] See p. 181.
[108] Pasternack/Blume, pp. 81–2; Schwalb/Blume, pp. 57–8.
[109] Pasternack/Blume, pp. 81–2; Schwalb/Blume, pp. 57–8.

at bar 46 Blume suggests an *accelerando* to allow a longer rest at the end of the bar.[110] Toscanini in 1935, like Abendroth in 1952, actually slows here but by 1938 takes it exactly in tempo, as he does in all later performances. The effect is startling enough. Others make no special preparation in either direction.

Bars 112 *et seq.*: In the much-analysed passage before the recapitulation, Blume advises a small *poco rit.* before H (bar 112) with the conducting thereafter taken *alla breve*, thus not too slowly.[111] As Table 2 shows, Toscanini interprets this as virtually half-tempo in some performances and something rather quicker in others, especially in 1941. Abendroth also halves his tempo, likewise Furtwängler. Here, of the two Stein-bach witnesses, only Boult – at a slower basic tempo – represents moderation; among the rest Weingartner and more especially Walter adopt a moderate change of gear.

Bars 183 *et seq.*: In the coda Blume wants a 'slight acceleration' at bar 183 continuing to the second beat of bar 194 with, after a distinct rest, an abrupt, downward, change of gear thereafter.[112] No conductor among those examined precisely reflects this, the closest being Toscanini in 1935, although at bar 194 his change of gear is only slight. Boult rather placidly declines to do anything not indicated in the score. Abendroth markedly accelerates his already headlong tempo at 183, resulting in an incoherent scramble before 194, where he continues virtually without change.

Second movement: *Andante*

Bars 36–41: These bars constitute the first of several passages in this movement which invite the temptation to tamper to an excessive degree with the tempo; the invita-tion is accepted by Mengelberg and also by Furtwängler, who brings his orchestra to a virtual halt yet again at bar 40. Blume suggests only that the theme starting at bar 41 should be slightly slower, with the original tempo resumed at bar 51.[113] These tempo changes are reflected in all the performances examined to a greater or lesser extent but, Mengelberg and Furtwängler apart, none of them sounds unbalanced. The inter-est in the opening pages of the movement perhaps resides more in the extent to which conductors emphasise the frequent hairpins: Weingartner responds very noticeably; Toscanini in 1935, too, but with less emphasis.

Bars 57–62: Once more Blume requires the tempo to be 'slower' (which, from the discussion above, one may infer means audibly slower, as distinct from the 'slightly'

---

[110] Pasternack/Blume, pp. 81–2; Schwalb/Blume, pp. 57–8.
[111] Pasternack/Blume, p. 84; Schwalb/Blume, p. 60.
[112] Pasternack/Blume, pp. 84–5; Schwalb/Blume, p. 60.
[113] Pasternack/Blume, p. 86; Schwalb/Blume, p. 61.

that appears to require a mere half-audible shading of tempo); all the notes are to be played *tenuto*, but unslurred, the 'flowing tempo' (that is, *tempo primo*) recommencing in bar 62.[114] Again, all conductors are sensitive to the obvious need for some modification of tempo and most of them keep the *tenuto* within bounds, avoiding thereby any hint of slurring; only Furtwängler comes close to joining up the notes in his dreamlike approach.

Bars 71–80: These bars contain a prolonged *crescendo* from *piano* to *forte*, continuing with *sforzando* chording in bar 78–9 and ending at bar 80 with a *staccato fortissimo* figure based on the opening bar of the movement's first theme; no change in tempo is indicated. It will be recollected that this is the passage in which Mengelberg accelerates sharply before pulling up at bar 80.[115] Blume suggests only that the tempo should increase slightly ('*etwas*' again) as the climax at 80 is approached, after which it should slow down.[116] Among the performances examined here in detail, it is a pleasure to encounter all conductors resisting the call for a precipitate *accelerando* so notably answered by Mengelberg: none exceeds the bounds of what is, in Steinbachian terms, stylistically appropriate.

Third movement: *Poco allegretto*

Bars 1–11: Like the first movement, the third movement *Allegretto* is full of traps for the unwary, albeit less widely acknowledged. For example, the reaction of the conductors here examined to Blume's suggestions for these bars highlight the care needed in choosing an appropriately relaxed but not too sleepy basic tempo. He asks for the first theme to move 'forward a bit' at bar 8, relaxing again for the peaceful ('*ruhig*') quintuplet at bar 11. In all the noted Toscanini performances, faster or slower, these adjustments are finely judged, with the quintuplet exquisitely realised. Boult is more straightforward. By contrast (how often that phrase is appropriate for this conductor), Abendroth, after a drowsy start, accelerates too much and fails to relax the tempo in time for the quintuplet, which is therefore (as recorded) indistinct. Furtwängler's basic tempo is also fairly slow, on a par with Toscanini's broadest, but he avoids the muddy effect of his friend's approach.

Bars 54 *et seq.*: Blume characterises the 'Trio' as '*scherzando*', at a tempo 'slightly (*etwas*) quicker';[117] the *scherzando* character is to be achieved in each bar by playing the second quaver rather short and emphasising the third, thereby suggesting that note

[114] Pasternack/Blume, p. 87; Schwalb/Blume, pp. 61–2.
[115] See p. 118.
[116] Pasternack/Blume, pp. 87–8; Schwalb/Blume, p. 62; for '*etwas*', see further p. 197.
[117] Pasternack/Blume, p. 90; Schwalb/Blume, p. 64.

values rather than increased tempo should contribute most to the musical effect. The answering string phrase at bar 69 is to be 'slightly held back'. This distinction between the *Allegretto* and 'Trio' is another instance in which Blume's description broadly reflects later practice, whether by Steinbach witnesses or not: it is quite usual to move this section forward at a faster pace.[118] The question is, as always, by how much – in other words, did Steinbach adopt a very distinct change of tempo or was the change modest in character? Blume's text, as analysed above, suggests a modest change of pace. That result seems to be confirmed by other evidence presented in Chapter 2.[119]

The Steinbach witnesses here adopt a distinctly moderate change of pace, as Blume implies: Toscanini and Boult interpret the section as slightly quicker with modest distensions for the answering phrase. As Table 2 indicates, Toscanini modified his practice from one performance to another; the forward-pressing 'Trio' is most explicit in his 1941 NBC and 1952 Philharmonia performances. Other conductors are varied in approach. Walter's handling is similar to Toscanini and Boult, whereas Abendroth almost doubles his tempo for the start of the section, thereby making it impossible to characterise each note in the way suggested by Blume; he then distends each answering phrase very markedly, all of which one can only characterise as un-Steinbachian in outcome. Furtwängler alone does not change tempo but distends both the answering phrase and the end of the movement in Wagnerian fashion.

Blume saw no great difficulties in the last movement and this study therefore does not discuss it further, save to observe that, among the examined conductors, it gives rise to less divergence of treatment than the other movements.[120]

Preliminary conclusions

Among the conductors examined, it is, once more, Toscanini's approach to this work that sheds substantial light on Steinbach's practice but, if Blume is to be trusted (which is not always), that illumination is fitful indeed. Boult's solid temperament displays its limitations most obviously in its dogged, if textually illuminating, adherence to the score: the architecture is immaculate, the Brahmsian fire stoked too low, especially for a first movement *allegro* marked *con brio*, while evidence of the Steinbach legacy is at best intermittent. But this is honest Brahms by the book and for that one should be grateful enough in the light of some of the competition. In particular, Abendroth's overheated first movement and his alternately sluggish and exaggerated *Allegretto*

---

[118] e.g. the distinct change of pace adopted by Stokowski with the Philadelphia Orchestra in their otherwise stylistically wayward recording of 25–26 September 1928 (see p. 70) and Gui in his disciplined 1946 recording (noted above at Ch. 2, n. 234).

[119] See p. 114 for Sir Henry Wood's practice compared with the Stokowski recording referred to in n. 70.

[120] Pasternack/Blume, p. 92; Schwalb/Blume, p. 65.

suggest a kinship with Mottl's much criticised way with the work, described in Chapter 2.[121] As noted earlier in this chapter, in this symphony alone Blume advises the first movement repeat, presumably following Steinbach's practice and, perhaps, the composer's own preference by the 1890s. Toscanini made the repeat whenever he felt unpressured by broadcasting restraints, Abendroth seemingly did not, while Walter resolutely never made it – responses that reflect their relationship more generally with the Meiningen way.

Symphony No. 4 in E minor Op. 98

All proven Steinbach witnesses left recordings of the Fourth Symphony, including Toscanini's 1935 BBC SO rendering examined already in some detail in Chapter 2.[122] Brahms also left his own performance advice on the Fourth in the form of those later cancelled score notations earlier referred to and it is necessary to consider how far his advice corresponds with Blume's and with the practice of the Steinbach witnesses.[123]

First movement: *Allegro non troppo*

Bars 1–12: The opening of the first movement presents a paradox in Blume's presentation of the opening theme with what he describes explicitly as Steinbach's markings – extended upbeats with a *diminuendo* on each downbeat;[124] but that advice seems virtually to nullify the effect of Brahms's own *diminuendos* in bars 4 and 6. Most conductors, including Abendroth, Boult and Busch, simply play as written, although Abendroth starts with a lengthened first upbeat, exaggerated (as in the equivalent instance in the First's finale) in his later recording. Toscanini's solution in the BBC SO recording is a lengthened first upbeat, followed by even stresses with slightly lengthened upbeats until the two *diminuendos*, where the upbeat is distinctly stressed. Could Steinbach really have ignored the significance of the composer's own score markings here, as Blume implies, or was Toscanini's recollection of him more accurate than Blume's? His indelible memory has to be compared with Blume's quite frequent minor inaccuracies: I place my faith in the former. Here it is also appropriate to note Fiedler's unprepared increase of pace by one-half in bars 8–12, which occasioned both my early exploration of the issues raised by this study and Boult's sharp remarks about a proffered explanation of the Fiedler effect.[125]

---

[121] See p. 52.
[122] See p. 106.
[123] See pp. 16 and 23.
[124] Pasternack/Blume, p. 94; Schwalb/Blume, p. 66.
[125] See p. xii.

<u>Bars 45–9, 57 et seq.</u>: In the rest of the exposition none of the conductors reflects Blume's frequent advice at all meticulously. In its moment-to-moment flexibility and full observance of the many hairpins, however, some may regard Toscanini's reading as coming close to the spirit of Blume's advice and at certain points he undoubtedly coincides with Blume's reproduction of Steinbach's score. For example, he observes fully the *staccato* separation of crotchets in bars 45 and 49 – although Blume here is merely reinforcing Brahms's own marking.[126] However, like all the other conductors, Fiedler included, Toscanini prefers a barely inflected singing line for the cello/violin theme from bar 57 rather than the frequent separations suggested by Blume.[127] This unanimity may again be thought to throw some doubt on the reliability of Blume's memory.

<u>Bars 131–3</u>: Blume requires the stress on the final upbeats in these bars[128] and this is a feature incorporated in any event by most conductors; Toscanini, in his almost savage pouncing on the feature, in this instance backs Blume to the hilt.

Perhaps of more interest than the various conductors' coincidence with Blume's advice in this exposition, best characterised as occasional, is the range of tempo variations within it. Table 2 affords no more than a glimpse, but the reaction to the arching phrase beginning at bar 91 is illustrative: this is a point at which Romantic conductors indulge themselves, while the those of a Classical bent are more continent. As the table shows, Abendroth, Fiedler and to some degree Walter are at one end of the scale; at the other lie Boult (at his slower overall tempo), Busch and Weingartner – precisely what would be expected. Unusually, Toscanini and Furtwängler at this point are in broad agreement, although their divergence later in the movement, to which we now turn, is extreme.

<u>Bars 387–end</u>: In the coda the composer's own markings, pencilled in for Joachim's benefit and later cancelled,[129] conflict with Blume. At 393 Brahms marked *pesante* under the double bass line and directed 'no pressing forward right up to the end'.[130] Blume advises an intensifying of pace from bar 387, reining back emphatically in tempo at 393, with a 'gradually more flowing' (*'allmählich flüssiger'*) tempo from 398, kept at an uninterrupted (*'zügiges'*) pace from 408 until broadening for the penultimate bar's timpani strokes.[131] Brahms therefore wanted no *accelerando*, while Blume

---

[126] Pasternack/Blume, p. 96; Schwalb/Blume, pp. 67–8.
[127] Pasternack/Blume, p. 96; Schwalb/Blume, p. 68.
[128] Pasternack/Blume, p. 99; Schwalb/Blume, pp. 69–70.
[129] See p. 16.
[130] *'Nicht eilen bis zum Schluss!'* (see Musgrave and Sherman, p. 223).
[131] Pasternack/Blume, pp. 102–3; Schwalb/Blume, p. 72.

prescribes something gradual, although his 'uninterrupted pace' is capable of a variety of interpretations.

To accelerate or not? All conductors rein back in tempo at bar 393, with a quite similar effect in every case; that is, save only for Fiedler's giant *Luftpause*, which surely exceeds by far what Brahms, or even Blume, had in mind. Further, contra Brahms, Fiedler then accelerates rapidly to the end. After bar 393 the rate and consistency of acceleration by the other examined conductors varies, as shown by Table 2, from Boult's sane intensification to Abendroth's 1954 race towards a doubling of pace; Furtwängler in his hysterical rush here equals his friend's achievement. Although the metronome cannot readily measure Toscanini's bar-by-bar changes of tempo in the coda, in general terms he adopts the *via media*, with maximum tempos permitting clear articulation (still clearer, at a similar pace, in his incomplete 1936 Philharmonic performance).[132] In some of his later performances, such as those of 1948 and 22 December 1951, both of greater breadth and intensity than his RCA recording, Toscanini virtually eschews an *accelerando* altogether and thereby adheres all the more closely to Brahms's expressed wishes;[133] Gui's treatment is very similar. Table 2 once more suggests structural similarities between the Steinbach witnesses and their marked differences from the other tabled conductors – save, as ever, the continent Weingartner, whose change of pace is minimal. Given the degree of unanimity among the Steinbach witnesses as to the rate of acceleration, it seems highly unlikely that Steinbach himself indulged in a rush to the finishing line.

Second movement: *Andante moderato*

In Chapter 2 Toscanini's performance of this movement in June 1935 was described as containing all the elements ascribed to Steinbach's performances in the evidential literature. This perhaps bold claim referred to the characteristics of the movement at large rather than its every detail: the constant and generous flexibility which nonetheless cleaves to its basic tempo, so ensuring that the architecture is unharmed. But the claim must be put to a more detailed test; the next paragraph therefore refers to some of Blume's prescriptions which seem to be reflected in that 1935 traversal. It should be noted, however, that Blume's haste to finish his work is more than usually evident in these pages, with necessary minor corrections being provided by Pasternack in his translation.

---

[132] See the table of performances at p. 168.
[133] See the table of performances for the 1948 performance. The performance of 22 December 1951 is on Hunt (CD) 706. RCA's recording dates from 3 December 1951, its Sony/RCA transfer on 88697916312-9.

The theme first heard in the clarinet, <u>bars 4–10</u>, is 'given suspense and allure through a slight delay', with *tempo primo* to be resumed.[134] There is certainly a prolonged first note in the clarinet in Toscanini's 1935 traversal, giving a very strong lyrical quality to what follows. At the *forte* restatement, performed more '*marcato* and energetically', the clarinet must play his descending motif 'with pathos': <u>bars 16 and 18</u>.[135] In the 1935 recording there is both the emphasis and, in these bars, the pathos, projected dynamically rather than by an audible change of tempo. Beginning at <u>bar 30</u> and continuing through to <u>bar 36</u>, the music is to be performed with a 'singing tone' and the violins should become 'more animated and urgent in expression' in <u>bar 33</u>.[136] In this passage Toscanini requires several strong yet smooth manipulations of tempo, just below *tempo primo* at the start, at bar 33 pressing forward – as per Blume – and easing back at 35 in preparation for the following *forte* passage. Both Fiedler and Walter are also persuasive here with rather less pronounced distensions of tempo; the effect in their performances is fine and beautiful – but Toscanini's insight and intensity of expression are, simply, deeper and more perceptive. <u>Bars 87–91</u> are to be played 'as sonorously as possible' with basses in 88 and 90 given 'a *crescendo* in imitation of the melody'.[137] Toscanini's resonance in these very bars is remarkable and more than reflects this direction. At <u>bars 96 *et seq.*</u> the tempo should 'increase' with the *crescendo* (bar 96) and then 'proceed uninterrupted' with the theme at bar 97 – Blume does not say whether at *tempo primo* or faster.[138] In his 1935 version Toscanini first slightly increases and then slightly broadens the tempo within bar 96, the better to resume at *tempo primo* in the next bar; this hairsbreadth change ensures utmost continuity. Walter reacts similarly in his persuasive performance with the same orchestra made in the studio the previous year. Were they, rather than Blume, right? That, now, can be no more than a matter of preference, but what cannot be gainsaid is the remarkable range of expression achieved throughout this movement by Toscanini in his very first concerts with the BBC Symphony Orchestra.

If my preferences are perhaps made too clear for many in the context of this movement, that is a consequence of the lack of real competition. Fiedler, Abendroth and Furtwängler have their own style of flexibility here and achieve much without disrupting the movement's architecture too radically – at any rate if one can put up with Furtwängler's usual dreamy reluctance to come to the close of any Brahms symphonic movement that ends quietly. But the others are rather less eloquent: Weingartner makes clear from his ultra-austere, albeit observant '*Andante molto moto*' that, as he confirms in the last edition of his *Symphony Since Beethoven*, this movement (and

[134] Pasternack/Blume, p. 103; Schwalb/Blume, p. 73.
[135] Pasternack/Blume, p. 104; Schwalb/Blume, p. 73.
[136] Pasternack/Blume, pp. 105–6; Schwalb/Blume, p. 75.
[137] Pasternack/Blume, p. 109; Schwalb/Blume, p. 77.
[138] Pasternack/Blume, p. 109; Schwalb/Blume, p. 77.

the next) fail to attract him.[139] Among recording conductors, probably only Yevgeny Mravinsky and, among those examined here, Boult are runners-up to Weingartner in the *Andante* stakes.[140] Boult and, more especially, Busch are nonetheless admirable Classicists, combining sensitivity and robustness; but they do not here possess the blazing conviction of their fellow Steinbach witness, Toscanini, nor his acute sensitivity to at least some of the very minor tempo changes that Blume assures us typified the Steinbach way.

Blume remarked of the third movement that 'there should be no problem whatsoever in its interpretation';[141] accordingly, we move straight to the passacaglia, where the problems multiply.

Fourth movement: *Allegro energico e passionato*

As shown by Table 2, the Steinbach witnesses, together with Gui, agree on the structure of this movement to a remarkable degree. They set a similar pace for the 'exposition' variations, a moderate drop in tempo for the central variations (for example, in the flute solo – though here Boult reduces more markedly), resuming at or close to *tempo primo* as the score specifies at bar 129, with a proportionate increase in tempo for the coda at 253, maintained without acceleration to the end; the ever-continent Weingartner adopts the same ground plan. By contrast, Fiedler, Abendroth, Walter and Furtwängler adopt a radical increase in pace at the *tempo primo*, bar 129, and all of them save Fiedler accelerate markedly in the coda.

Among the directions Brahms gave in his later withdrawn advice, he wanted variation 8 (bar 57) slower and *pesante*, with variation 9 back in tempo, variation 20 (bar 153) also *pesante* and variations 25–27 faster.

Blume's advice differs from Brahms's. And, once again, it is Toscanini in June 1935 who, out of his capacious memory of Steinbach's performance of the Fourth Symphony in 1909, bears witness to the accuracy of at least some of Blume's recollections, together with an instinctive response to Brahms's own preferences. Following through his annotations with Toscanini and the BBC SO reveals many striking similarities to Blume and Brahms of which a few include: the *marcato* timpani at <u>bars 25–32</u>, variation 4; the violins' *marcato* and *largamente* in <u>bars 33–40</u>, variation 5; the extreme precision of rhythm in <u>bars 57–64</u>, variation 8 (which with Toscanini also has something of Brahms's desired *pesante*); and the flute solo, <u>bars 97–104</u>, variation 13, where, as Table 2 indicates, Toscanini alone approximates to the specified equivalence of pace on which Blume insists; not only that, but, again *per* Blume, he slows down 'slightly in

[139] In Weingartner, *On Music*, p. 275; see further p. 85.
[140] As will be seen from Table 1, Boult is within 20 seconds of Weingartner; Mravinsky, in his performance of 28 April 1973 clocks in at exactly 10 minutes: BMG/Melodiya BVCX-4003.
[141] Pasternack/Blume, p. 111, Schwalb/Blume, p. 78; but see also p. 154, n. 364.

the last bar',[142] where London's premier flautist, Robert Murchie, broadens his tone to accommodate precise responses to the preceding bar's *crescendo* and the minute swells in that last bar.[143]

At the *tempo primo*, bar 129, variation 17, Blume, despite the obvious meaning of Brahms's marking, wants the music 'faster' than the opening.[144] Boult and Busch disclose a barely perceptible increase while Toscanini waits until the following variation to step it up – logically so, since variation 17 largely replicates in outline the opening theme. Blume's advice here doubtfully reflects Steinbach, given that Boult marked his score with Steinbach's changes of tempo in this movement and that Brahms, in his pencilled directions for Joachim, chose not to elaborate on his *tempo primo* marking. As mentioned, all the other conductors save Weingartner choose a marked increase of pace at this point, as indicated by Table 2.

Reverting to Blume, Toscanini once more reflects his 'energetic accented staccato' at bar 153, variation 20, hinting again at Brahms's desired *pesante*. Further, he accords with Blume's 'slightly (*etwas*) broader' tempo at bars 169–76, variation 22, where the annotator's demands for 'resounding and well-sustained' trombones with 'short and energetic' chording could not better describe the effect Toscanini secures.[145] Boult here broadens his tempo a little more, Busch a little less, whereas Abendroth presses on regardless at the increased basic tempo in the second half of the movement adopted by him and other conductors specified above. In general terms, those who adopt this increase in tempo – Fiedler, Walter, Abendroth and Furtwängler – thereby fail to characterise each variation effectively. The following variation 23, bars 177–84, is, Blume exclaims, '*scherzando!*' and, uniquely, Toscanini increases the tempo a little to achieve precisely that effect.[146] The tempo in bars 209–16, variation 27, should be 'flowing', says Blume, and here and in the following two unannotated variations, Toscanini moves the tempo gracefully forward. The *Più Allegro* coda (from bar 254) says Blume, 'speaks for itself' as from bar 281, implying no further change of tempo; and that is indeed the scheme to which all the Steinbach witnesses adhere.[147] Other conductors, save for Fiedler and Weingartner, intensify the pace up to the final bars. There is excitement and a rush of blood to the head in this approach – but there is none of the enormous breadth and weight, the sense of finality, conveyed by both the Steinbach witnesses and Weingartner.

---

[142] Pasternack/Blume, pp. 115–17; Schwalb/Blume, pp. 80–2.
[143] Murchie was to leave the BBC SO in 1937 after an unfortunate contretemps with Toscanini: see Dyment 2012 p. 133.
[144] Pasternack/Blume, p. 117; Schwalb/Blume, p. 82.
[145] Pasternack/Blume, p. 118; Schwalb/Blume, p. 82.
[146] Pasternack/Blume, p. 118; Schwalb/Blume, p. 82.
[147] Pasternack/Blume, p. 120; Schwalb/Blume, p. 84.

Preliminary conclusions

There are a few differences between Toscanini's rendering of the passacaglia and Blume's advice about that movement. In general, however, the reflection of one in the other is remarkably close. Further, Toscanini's scheme of things, as well as much of the detailed handling of the variations, is corroborated by the other Steinbach witnesses. By contrast, in the movements of this symphony scrutinised above there is little evidence that Blume's advice is reflected in any of the other performances, whether Abendroth's, Furtwängler's or Walter's; the first two, in particular, have between themselves much in common in their search for the maximum of auditory excitement in the shorter term. In any event, the lesson to be drawn from these pages is not merely that it is in the highest degree unlikely that Abendroth heard Steinbach performing the Fourth Symphony. Of greater significance, the degree of similarity between the Steinbach witnesses, and the elements in their performances of the work which do suggest absorption of key elements in Steinbach's performances, stand as a vindication of the search for the true Meiningen way – and hence the composer's own wishes – as it has been undertaken in this study. The three conductors, each differing in temperament, in their own way took what they needed from Steinbach and internalised those elements to produce in each case recognisably different results in accord with their individual personalities: Boult imperturbably the Classicist *par excellence*; Fritz Busch with an added exuberance; and Toscanini with an incendiary fire and, it may be added, a depth of feeling that outmatch all competition. Steinbach's common influence upon them, however, remains indelible.

CHAPTER 4

CONCLUSIONS

A synopsis with caveats

There is not now, nor will there ever be, some kind of Holy Grail awaiting discovery, its contents disclosing the true gospel of the interpretation of Brahms's orchestral music. We can never know precisely how, in audible terms, Brahms conducted his symphonies or wanted them to be performed. This strong caveat to the conclusions reached in this chapter – which will already be obvious to those familiar with the preliminary conclusions scattered throughout preceding chapters – is an inevitable reflection of what was termed at the outset the 'tantalising' period in which Brahms lived: the era which saw the birth of the virtuoso conductor but failed for the most part to preserve his work in recorded sound.[1] Who among Brahms lovers, would not wish to hear the performances of those conductors with whom the composer was familiar, among them Hans von Bülow, Hermann Levi, Hans Richter, Fritz Steinbach and Arthur Nikisch? And, if that wish were granted, how near to the mind of the creator would we place their interpretations? As it is, we are necessarily reliant on the printed word to bring us near to the spirit of conductors contemporary with Brahms. The second best, with which this study has also been concerned, is to trace, through everything reported about Brahms's own performances, together with his favoured conductors and their disciples and admirers, what it was that attracted the composer and, where the disciples left recordings, to isolate those characteristics which are most suggestive of their silent predecessors.

Chapters 2 and 3 undertook the task of tracing the lines of authority of the conductors known to have received Brahms's blessing, through their disciples (if any), and so, by means of recorded sound, to those performances which may have preserved for us something of the spirit and characteristics heard and approved by the composer. That task has been an inextricable mixture of detective work and a monstrous jigsaw puzzle, although in just one instance there is, on the face of it, a direct and uncomplicated line of authority linking us with the composer: Brahms strongly approved the

---

[1] See Preface, p. xiii.

performance of his Second Symphony conducted in Vienna by Felix Weingartner in 1895 and Weingartner went on to record the four symphonies in the studio in later years. These performances would at first sight seem to have an excellent pedigree.

Other strands of authority connecting certain performance styles to the composer, initially of some strength, have been broken beyond repair: with the perhaps doubtful exception of Max Fiedler's hearty, rather unsubtle and, in terms of rhythm, highly manipulated interpretations on disc, we have no exact means of determining the precise character of performances by Brahms's contemporary Hans von Bülow, whose interpretations of the symphonies were, if sometimes with mental reservations on Brahms's part, nonetheless readily accepted by him.[2] Of their frequently changeable tempo and nuancing there can be no doubt; nor can there be any doubt about an equal degree of extravagance, albeit in structural terms of a very different character, in Arthur Nikisch's Brahms performances, some of which again secured the composer's approval – with, once more, evident hesitation. As Chapter 2 concludes, Nikisch left no musical successor, although if one is in an optimistic turn of mind there is one possible recording from an unlikely source that may, just, have caught some of the Hungarian's poetic abandon.[3]

In such a depopulated landscape, there can be no surprise that the principal focus throughout this study has been on Fritz Steinbach, the conductor who gained the composer's entire confidence as Bülow's successor with the Meiningen Hofkapelle, an orchestra of just forty-eight players whose renderings of the symphonies brought complete satisfaction to Brahms. Much has already been written about the Meiningen way under Steinbach but he can never be brought back to us fully alive – in the sense that, faced with interpretative difficulties about the works of the master he held most dear, we would know with certainty precisely how he would solve them. But at least some progress has been made, in so far as the surveys of documentary evidence uncovered in Chapter 2 and the recorded evidence examined in Chapter 3 bring us close to an informed portrait of Steinbach's music-making. Further, each group of recordings of individual Brahms symphonies examined in Chapter 3 shows, to a varying degree, the likelihood of some Steinbach influence in performances by the eminent recording conductors whom we know witnessed, took note of and were consciously influenced by his performances – namely, Adrian Boult, Fritz Busch and Arturo Toscanini. Other distinguished conductors of the Brahms symphonies examined in this study remain distant from the Meiningen way, as will be clear in the following pages from the more detailed consideration of the methodology and evidence on which this study is based. Separating the one group from the other is essential for a deeper understanding of Brahms's mind and intentions, a fundamental purpose underlying this entire work.

[2]   See p. 21.
[3]   See pp. 69 and 163.

Following the trails

The summary conclusions reached in preceding pages do not touch on the difficulty, the conundrum even, that provided one of the incentives for undertaking the present analysis of documentary and recorded evidence, to which it is necessary to revert here in more detail: the strange paradox of Steinbach's Classicist disciples, Fritz Busch, Boult and Toscanini, ranged against the sometimes extreme stylistic idiosyncrasies of Hermann Abendroth, upheld elsewhere as an exemplar of the Steinbach tradition.[4] That conundrum is yet more obvious in claims made about other and obviously extreme Romantic conductors such as Furtwängler and Mengelberg, whose styles, it has again been suggested elsewhere, provide at least some echoes of Steinbach's own approach.[5] The prolonged exposure of fresh evidence presented throughout this study demonstrates that no conundrum exists and that claims made for the authenticity of approach of conductors beyond the identified Steinbach disciples are without foundation.

The necessary first steps taken towards that conclusion lay in a close examination of documentary evidence about the conductors who were most prominent in championing the performance of the symphonies in Brahms's latter years, exposing as thoroughly as possible the traits which attracted the composer and following through the performance histories of these conductors, including their musical parentage and the influence they exerted on their pupils and coevals at the time, to their various conclusions. Without such building from the ground upwards (or, rather, forwards in time), and securing evidence from all available quarters about these conductors – from critics, other commentators, fellow musicians and fellow conductors – any conclusions about their stylistic traits, especially in the absence of recorded sound at this critical time (roughly 1880–1914), are liable to be no more than shots in the dark or, what is worse, actively misleading. It is not enough to analyse particular stylistic attributes common to performers in the period and likely to have been approved or used by the composer himself in performance: without the wider picture, and an exact delineation of the performers and their interconnections with others, conclusions may well be misguided and may thereby distort the ultimate message concerning the composer's expectations.

Documentary evidence in the round has in the present study led ineluctably to examination of lines of authority and affinity – from Wagner onwards, from Brahms onwards – which in the field of orchestral performance indicate how the fundamental division between those two camps separated interpretative outlooks in the late nineteenth and early twentieth centuries almost as much as it did creative and critical

---

[4]   See pp. 4 and 133.
[5]   See p. 4, n. 3.

endeavours. Wagner's advice on conducting – in particular his prescriptions for the frequency and extent of tempo modifications – had a near-universal influence. But in treating the performance history of the critical period before the Great War, the temptation to conflate the approaches of all conductors of the time as being subject to that influence in one omni-German-Austro-Hungarian 'Romantic' tradition has, at times, not been avoided; nor has a parallel misconception, leading some to maintain that the more bizarre the treatment of Brahms by certain recording conductors, the more likely this was to have reflected – by routes unexplained – the kind of performance style known to and approved by the composer. This study has attempted to disentangle fact from supposition (although gaps in the historical record do not completely eliminate the latter) and thereby to elucidate solid musico-historic lineages hitherto sometimes disguised by these misapprehensions.

The conductors subject to close observation in these pages commenced, after Brahms himself, with the composer's earliest champions, including in particular Hermann Levi and Hans von Bülow, both products of the 1830s by birth.[6] After a necessary overview of Hans Richter, born in 1843, the survey continued with the two conductors born in the mid-1850s who, as Bülow informed Brahms, were the finest among his juniors: Fritz Steinbach and Felix Mottl.[7] Thereafter came a group of conductors, among them Arthur Nikisch and Max Fiedler, whose individuality expressed itself with an extravagance that, as recorded sound came on stream, can be identified as possessing the characteristics we now label as Romantic.[8] Felix Weingartner and Karl Muck were both Wagnerians of the highest repute, but resisted the call to extravagance of gesture and manipulations of tempo found among some of Wagner's immediate entourage.[9] The former had the good fortune to be heard by Brahms conducting one of his symphonies; the latter – by all accounts, just as distinguished a Brahmsian – did not and lapsed into the obscurity of a premature old age, saved only by recorded extracts dating from the late 1920s of his Wagner performances, in particular his legendary performances of *Parsifal*.

This study focussed finally on the next generation of conductors, starting with Arturo Toscanini and including Willem Mengelberg, Bruno Walter, Hermann Abendroth and Wilhelm Furtwängler, Adrian Boult and Fritz Busch, each of them set against their particular backgrounds and musical influences.[10] In substance, therefore, it encompasses a century of Brahms symphony performances, commencing with the composer himself, Levi and Bülow, all from the 1870s, and closing with the performances of Adrian Boult from the 1950s to the 1970s.

---

[6]   See pp. 12 and 18.
[7]   See pp. 8, 29 and 48.
[8]   See respectively pp. 55 and 72.
[9]   See pp. 78 and 82.
[10] See pp. 96, 115, 122, 125, 134, 138 and 140.

But for the conflating tendency earlier referred to, it would be superfluous to remark that every one of the conductors mentioned had their own sharp individualities of style – in the earlier generations to a degree that has no modern parallel. The differences were most acute among, on the one hand, those who followed Wagner's more extreme personal practices in his own performances (of whom Mottl and Anton Seidl were the prime exponents) and, on the other, those who specialised in the Classical repertoire. By the early twentieth century both streams practised their art in their various ways across the entire repertoire; but adherents of one or the other tendency continued to exhibit those marked differences of approach that have lived on in subsequent generations of conductors whose recordings have caused so much heated debate among aficionados and musical historians today.

As the documentary evidence shows, the two recording conductors Abendroth and Furtwängler were in their distinct but related ways the descendants of ultra-Wagnerian practice through the persuasive and powerful example of their mentor, Felix Mottl. It is regrettable that Mottl, like Steinbach, left no reliable legacy in recorded sound, although Chapter 2 suggests that elements of what would probably appear to modern ears to be an extremely wayward style might be traced in certain Beethoven recordings made by the composer-conductor Hans Pfitzner, who was on close terms with Mottl.[11] What is clear beyond dispute is that Mottl failed utterly to understand Brahms's symphonies and was heavily criticised for his performances of them later in his career.[12] There can be little doubt that Abendroth and Furtwängler had to forge their interpretative way with Brahms against the vivid backdrop of Mottl's powerful example in the treatment of the Classical repertoire. Certainly, their individuality and distinction as musicians made them far more than mere carbon copies of their mentor[13] but, whether in Brahms or elsewhere, their sometimes extravagant response in terms of tempo variation surely had its validation in their eyes (and very probably its origin) in Mottl's typical freedom of approach. It cannot occasion surprise that the two friends, otherwise great beyond dispute, did not achieve their distinction in Brahms (in the ears of many) without criticism on the way centring variously on unacceptable or inauthentic freedom of tempo and liberties with the structure.

Remote though the recorded Brahms performances of these two conductors may be from Steinbach's approach, they have their undoubted attractions for those of a particular musical outlook: they often have an urgency, musical pliability and overwhelming conviction lacking in many more recent recordings of the canon. The Brahms performances of other fine conductors included in this study, such as Max Fiedler and Bruno Walter, also have their own considerable virtues. Although the evidence presented in Chapter 2 demonstrates that none of their performances points to

[11] See p. 135.
[12] See p. 52.
[13] But see the comments on Abendroth's rendering of Brahms's Third Symphony, p. 214.

the 'Meiningen way', with its particular characteristics which we know had Brahms's wholehearted approval, it does not follow that, in the absence of those characteristics, Brahms would have withheld his approval had he been able to hear them. Moreover, the composer's wholehearted welcome for Steinbach's interpretations seems to have been quite unaffected by the seeming clash between that conductor's views and his own markings in the Fourth Symphony pencilled in for the benefit of Joachim, intent on conducting the work in Berlin: the annotations in Walter Blume's book about the Meiningen way (the shortcomings of which have been examined in some detail[14]) suggest that Steinbach performed the passages in question in a rather different fashion.[15] As has been remarked elsewhere, this disparity is 'an index and valorisation of the tolerances of the readings endorsed and admired by Brahms',[16] an observation which leads inexorably to the conclusion adumbrated at the outset of this study: that in performances of his orchestral music Brahms was willing to look favourably upon a wide range of deeply felt and cogent solutions to problems of form, shape and nuance, save only for outcomes that smacked of an unartistic 'free performance style'. On that account he might have questioned, as he did explicitly in the case of Bülow, aspects of those recorded performances covered by this study where structure is disrupted too obviously and beyond repair.[17]

Turning from these relatively uncontroversial conclusions to the other conductors, the group in whom may be discerned some connection, direct or indirect, with styles having Brahms's unequivocal approbation, it should be remembered that those so identified were without doubt subject to many influences, including the example set by those sober members of the Wagner circle, Richter and Weingartner (the latter of whom, however, severed his connections with that circle at an early date, even before the events linking him with Brahms). Both these great conductors were recognised, certainly by Boult and Fritz Busch, as among the great interpreters of the Classics; Toscanini also recognised the greatness of Richter and admired the young Weingartner – although he disliked certain of the latter's performances he heard after the Great War.[18] In any event all three – Boult, Busch and Toscanini – singled out Steinbach as

---

[14] See pp. 150–5.

[15] See p. 216.

[16] Musgrave and Sherman, Ch. 8 (Pascall and Weller), p. 237.

[17] See e.g. comments on Fiedler (p. 77), Mengelberg (p. 119) and Abendroth (p. 133).

[18] In conversation with family members and friends on 9 May 1954, Toscanini said that at first he liked Weingartner, whom he met in Milan when he was young and good-looking, but after that war he found him aged and bald, conducting *The Magic Flute* in Vienna in a way he found boring. Likewise, in conversation with NBC musicians on 16 November 1953, Toscanini commented on a Paris performance in 1932 of Debussy's *L'Après-midi d'un faune* that 'put people to sleep, it never ended'. Information and translations courtesy Harvey Sachs. There is, however, no evidence of Toscanini's views on Weingartner's Brahms which, as shown in Table 1, p. 169, often

the Brahms interpreter of their younger days by whom they were explicitly influenced in their performances of the four symphonies.[19]

Save only to a significant extent in the performance of Brahms, it is clear beyond doubt from the documentation in Chapter 2 that Steinbach was, fundamentally, a Classicist in the company of others such as Richter and Weingartner.[20] Although he was, according to Busch, capable of turning in an excellent performance of Siegfried's *Trauermusik*, he abstained from the interpretative extravagances of musicians in Wagner's circle.[21] A more animated conductor than Richter, he nonetheless performed that supreme masterwork, Beethoven's Ninth Symphony, in a way that both Boult and Busch took as a model. Yet, even in Brahms, repeated critical observation about his stylistic approach demonstrates conclusively that, as distinct from the relative extremes perpetuated in the twentieth century by Mottl's followers, Steinbach's freedom operated for the most part with subtlety and within a moderately circumscribed range of flexibility and nuance.

Assessment in more detail of Steinbach's freedom of approach in Brahms and its possible perpetuation in twentieth-century performances has been one of the principal purposes of Chapter 3, dealing with recorded evidence. As foreshadowed by the preliminary conclusions there presented, the principal conclusion must be that, while no single recording conductor holds the key to Steinbach's practice and style, evidence of his approach is present to a varying degree in selected recordings of the already identified Steinbach witnesses, Boult, Busch and Toscanini. Not only do these recordings demonstrate the structural integrity and the particular type of freedom reflected in the descriptions of Steinbach's interpretative way delineated in Chapter 2, but they also accord significantly with some at least of the directions set out in Walter Blume's (it is true, sometimes questionable) book prescribing the Meiningen way for the performance of Brahms's four symphonies. Further, in the instances where other conductors examined in Chapter 3 cannot be proved to be among the Steinbach witnesses – that is, having no personal or musical connection with him – their performances coincide with Blume's prescriptions on relatively infrequent occasions. Thus, taken together, all the clues followed up throughout Chapters 2 and 3 lead to one solid conclusion: listen to certain selected performances of the Steinbach witnesses for at least some enlightenment about his stylistic approach to Brahms. That conclusion's evidential foundations, as well as the inferences to be drawn from it, are summarised in greater detail below.

---

outpaced Toscanini's. See also Dyment 2012, pp. 310–11 and Robert Charles Marsh, *Toscanini and the Art of Orchestral Performance*, London: Allen & Unwin, 1956, p. 53.

[19] See pp. 98, 138 and 141.
[20] See pp. 38–48.
[21] Fritz Busch, p. 57.

Further research may clarify uncertainties about the relationship between some of the major witnesses in this analysis, such as Abendroth and Mottl, Abendroth and his Cologne players, Blume and Steinbach in Munich, as well as other issues such as the frequency with which Boult attended Steinbach's concerts.[22] The results are, however, unlikely to change significantly the conclusions presented thus far and in the following pages.

The ultimate message for today and tomorrow – and a warning

This study of conductors having Brahms's explicit approbation has narrowed its 'assembly of witnesses' to three strands of authority – Weingartner, Nikisch and Steinbach. Of the first two, one, through his recordings, is very much with us; the other is frustratingly almost beyond capture.

Weingartner was forever proud of the praise bestowed by Brahms on his performance of the Second Symphony witnessed by the composer in 1895. However, as Chapter 2 demonstrates, the 'authenticity' of Weingartner's recordings of the Brahms symphonies cannot on that account be taken for granted.[23] Some forty-five years separated Brahms's expressions of approval for that Second Symphony and Weingartner's recording of it. The two readings may well have been similar – but how similar we cannot now determine. Moreover, as a determined Wagnerite in the 1890s, Weingartner did not conduct the other three symphonies until later in his career. Taken in the round, we can only conclude now that, on the evidence we have, Weingartner's rhythmically strong and subtly shaped but otherwise unadorned style in the performance of all four symphonies might well have pleased the composer had he been able to hear them – a conclusion entirely consonant with the summing up already given about other performances still more remote from the Meiningen tradition.

Nevertheless, whatever reservations may be needed about the strength and validity of the strand of authority linking Weingartner with the composer, for musicians today that strand, in the form of his recordings of all four symphonies, is at least readily accessible and, notwithstanding some limitations in the quality of sound, one which discloses its characteristics without ambiguity or obfuscation. Weingartner's legacy, as earlier noted, has already entered the musical bloodstream of eminent maestros of

---

[22] Material about the performance of Brahms still awaiting a detailed assessment includes correspondence between Steinbach and both the Busch brothers and Max Reger held by the Busch Brothers Foundation at the Max Reger Institute (Karlsruhe); however, the main thrust of this cache of correspondence is detailed at pp. 140 and 173. The Meiningen Museum's first edition Brahms symphony scores annotated by unknown hands may yield further relevant material: see Ch. 2, n. 360.

[23] See p. 86.

our day with some highly distinguished results that recognise how the example set by him, free of any hint of pose or wilfulness, may lead today's practitioner close to the heart of Brahms's creative process.[24] As far back as 1990 Roger Norrington with his 'authentic' instrument band, the London Classical Players, commenced his Brahms cycle with the First Symphony, which in terms of tempo alone strongly indicated a conscious reference to Weingartner as one at least of the precedents informing his approach, coupled with information about the duration of early performances such as Bülow's.[25] In terms of tempo variations, Weingartner was again one of the conductors whose practice was cited by Norrington in his accompanying notes for the adoption of minimal changes, as a conscious contrast with, by repute, the sharply differing approach of Nikisch.

Now, at the time of writing, the Weingartner influence has been absorbed into the bloodstream of the modern symphony orchestra, as witness the performances in 2012, live and recorded, of all Brahms's symphonic works by the Leipzig Gewandhaus Orchestra under their conductor, Riccardo Chailly.[26] As Chailly himself has put it, Weingartner's Brahms recordings are nothing less than 'the essence of these works: pure, devoid of extremes, firmly rooted in a tradition that seems buried today ... the freshness, the clarity of his interpretations still have the power to convince'. Once again the Weingartner influence is directed towards the flowing tempos, the extreme clarity of parts and the modest expansion and contraction of tempos for expressive purposes, although it is noteworthy that Chailly's interpretations are sometimes far from closely modelled on those to be heard in Weingartner's recordings: to take but one example, Weingartner's austere reserve and uniquely up-tempo *Andante moderato* second movement to be heard in his recording of the Fourth Symphony is not followed in Chailly's more expansive approach.

Whether this resuscitation of Weingartner's influence in the performance of Brahms will prove long-lasting and become more widespread is one of the interesting issues to emerge from the 'authentic' movement's search for the roots of a genuine Brahms performance style. Weingartner's connection with Brahms ensures that his recordings will, at any rate, continue to offer a reference point for all performers who feel compelled to search in the past for practical assistance in the task of moulding a convincing performance style for the third millennium. Properly handled, as it has been by the two conductors discussed here, his legacy provides an example from which all who aspire to conduct the canon may benefit.

By contrast with Weingartner, Nikisch's legacy is all too sparse, limited, as has

[24] See p. 95.
[25] See Norrington's notes for the first issue of this recording, EMI CDC 7548622.
[26] The recorded performances are on Decca 478 5344, also containing in the notes the quotations from Chailly cited here. Chailly's London performance of the cycle was given in October 2012.

been demonstrated in Chapter 2 and 3, to his possible ghostly influence in just one recording – that is, Leopold Stokowski's earliest recording of the First Symphony.[27] The evidence is too thin for any specifics to be constructed for the benefit of current or future generations: one is left with but a simple injunction – listen to this performance and do no more than dream that it may reflect, through the prism of Stokowski's supremely magnetic personality, something of the poetic abandon of his teacher; an example to ponder but not necessarily to follow.

Leaving aside Weingartner and Nikisch, the weight of conclusions hereafter must relate to the claims to authenticity – to a proven and documented connection with the Meiningen way – of those who witnessed Fritz Steinbach in action. In the frustrating absence of any recordings by Steinbach, recordings by those witnesses must form our strongest link with him; that historic link was subjected to thorough examination in Chapter 3.

Of the conductors examined, although documentary evidence is entirely lacking in the case of Hermann Abendroth, it is possible that he may on occasion have observed Steinbach's Cologne performances of Brahms while he was in post at Essen. But whatever he heard or noted was subsumed in the experiences of an already well-developed and dominant musical personality grounded in the earlier and antithetical influences already outlined. As the examination of the First Symphony suggests,[28] there may (just) be a few clues about some limited aspects of Steinbach's approach buried deep within Abendroth's recordings of the work, although the most distinctive of those clues suggesting this possibility, upheld elsewhere as of incontrovertible value, actually carry little or no weight.[29] Furthermore, Abendroth's recordings of the other symphonies contain negligible evidence of his having any familiarity with the Steinbach tradition and much that contradicts that contention. To rely on fragmentary and questionable evidence drawn from recordings of just one symphony as a key to our understanding of the Meiningen way would seem to demonstrate an unduly optimistic view of the strength of that evidence. It is true that, according to those who were well acquainted with the latter-day Abendroth, such as the distinguished Classical conductor Kurt Masur, it seems that he was so sure of his approach to the interpretation of Brahms that he felt able to take certain liberties in performance[30] – but that confidence of approach extended far back to the early years of his career, before his long Cologne tenure in succession to Steinbach.[31] As this study has demonstrated, his style owed very little to his predecessor: in lineage, in artistic connections, in virtually all his recorded performances, there is nothing to link the two conductors.

[27] See pp. 69 and 163.
[28] See pp. 184–202.
[29] See p. 198.
[30] See Walter Frisch's observations in the *New York Times*, Ch. 1, n. 4.
[31] See p. 127.

The influences shaping Sir Adrian Boult's approach to Brahms undoubtedly included Steinbach, whose performances were, he said, revelatory. But Boult witnessed him on only a relatively few occasions and it is by no means clear that he heard him conduct all the symphonies at a (musically) fully cognisant age. In any event, over a period of years before those occasions he also heard Richter conduct masterworks across the whole repertoire and there can be little no doubt that the latter's monumental, sometimes rhythmically unvaried approach remained a potent influence on a conductor whose musicianship was impeccable but whose temperament did not always match the intensity of his co-witnesses.[32] Boult's finest Brahms recordings, made when he was in his mid-sixties, appear to retain only intermittent reminders of the Steinbach influence, although individual movements are of substantial value in that connection, notably the outer movements of the First Symphony, the third movement of the Third and the finale of the Fourth.[33]

Fritz Busch's recorded Brahms legacy is relatively small but, given Steinbach's closeness to him as master and friend, immensely valuable. Virtually the whole of the First Symphony in his New York Philharmonic concert performance dating from February 1942 provides compelling evidence of his connection with the Meiningen way, particularly in the unique features of the extraordinarily exhilarating finale, the impact of which surely recreates something of the enormous excitement with which Steinbach's London performances of this movement were greeted before the Great War. Further, the performance's accordance in some key passages with the then unknown prescriptions of Walter Blume suggests a conductor who retained in his mind the supremely 'warm and convincing' way of his mentor in this work.[34]

In Busch's recording of the Second Symphony from 1931, the spontaneous exuberance and the pliable, individual shaping of phrase are highly suggestive of Steinbach's practice, although it is possible that in the outer movements Busch's tempos may outpace his master's.[35] However, the controlled expansiveness of the slow movements in both this recording and that of the First Symphony again strongly suggests Steinbach's unhurried approach. Busch's later recording of the Second Symphony, dating from 1947, has less fire and individuality although rather more polish; however, the constraints of the recording process in 1947 are strongly suggested in his tempo for the *Adagio*, far quicker than in 1931.[36] His recording of the Fourth Symphony from 1950 by no means lacks fire and, in addition to its considerable merits in terms of just tempos, fine phrasing (within the limits of a second-rate orchestra's capability)

[32] See p. 214.
[33] See pp. 214 and 221.
[34] See p. 200.
[35] See p. 209.
[36] See Table 1, p. 169.

and structural integrity, provides valuable corroborative evidence about his mentor's approach to structure, particularly in the passacaglia.[37]

Corroborative because of that finale's similarities to Arturo Toscanini's approach. The Italian maestro's lifelong admiration for Steinbach, whom he witnessed conducting all Brahms's symphonies and many another of his works at the Munich Brahms Festival in September 1909, is documented in Chapter 2;[38] the plethora of Toscanini's recorded performances of Brahms must therefore command the closest attention.

The focus in this study has for the greater part been on Toscanini's earliest Brahms recordings, many of them from live broadcasts. That choice was occasioned not merely because of his earlier tendency towards greater breadth of tempo, a tendency that in this composer in particular cannot be assumed, as Table 1 set out in Chapter 3 so clearly demonstrates.[39] Indeed, there are so many exceptions among Toscanini's recorded performances of the Brahms symphonies as almost to nullify the validity of that 'earlier tendency' as a generalisation: the late RCA versions of the Second (remarkably fine) and Third (a listless failure), for example, are his slowest complete recordings of the works. But what makes the early recordings most worthy of study is the degree to which they retain a constant flexibility and multiple nuancing that became less apparent and less frequent in Toscanini's later NBC years. He was already between sixty-seven and seventy-two years old at the time of those early recordings; he was just forty-two when he first heard Steinbach, probably little influenced until then by other interpretative approaches to Brahms. How he conducted Brahms in, say, the 1920s, when he invoked the shade of Steinbach in his exchange with Furtwängler,[40] can only be guessed at between the lines of reviews which, as Chapter 2 has shown, are of limited value.[41]

Nevertheless, as the analyses in Chapter 3 have demonstrated, some of Toscanini's early recordings are strongly suggestive of the Meiningen way. That conclusion should not be read as suggesting that the Maestro consciously sought to copy what he recollected of Steinbach's approach – although he admitted in old age that he had repeatedly failed in his attempts to embody certain elements in his performances of the Third Symphony, in which he regarded Steinbach as supremely successful.[42] For the most part, however, he had internalised deeply the lessons learned at that Munich Festival so many years before in the re-creative fire of his own stylistic approach, which was accompanied by his customarily prolonged, intensive and rigorous intellectual analysis of all the symphonies. Among the performances disclosing elements of those early

[37] See p. 220.
[38] See p. 98.
[39] See p. 170.
[40] See p. 100.
[41] See pp. 103–8.
[42] See p. 99.

lessons, Chapter 3 cites both the 1935 New York Philharmonic and the 1937 Christmas
night NBC SO debut performances of the First Symphony; in particular the former,
with the conductor at his peak as a symphonic conductor, contains much that may
well reflect Steinbach's practices.[43] Again, the NBC broadcast of the Second Symphony
from February 1938 and the 1935 New York Philharmonic Third Symphony show at
least some significant accordance with Walter Blume's prescriptions – the finale of the
Second Symphony is noteworthy in this regard – even if, as with his every recording
examined throughout this study, Toscanini's individual viewpoint wins out in other
aspects of the performances.[44]

Of all the available Toscanini recordings, however, his performance with the BBC
SO of the Fourth Symphony from the Queen's Hall in June 1935 retains the characteristics of his early approach at their most eloquent. An 'explosive and generating force'
recalling Nikisch, remarked Cardus of this performance of the passacaglia.[45] He was
right to locate Toscanini's achievement here as lying securely within Austro-German
traditions but, as detailed in Chapters 2 and 3, the direct and most obvious debt is
to the Steinbach heritage.[46] Offered the highly invidious choice, I would certainly
nominate it as the most remarkable recorded performance extant of any movement
of a Brahms symphony. But, whether or not one agrees with that summation, this
recording of the symphony as a whole, and especially its finale, undoubtedly locates
with some precision where, with the assistance of Blume and all other supporting
documentary and recorded evidence (Fritz Busch's recorded Brahms in particular),
the task of reconstructing the major elements of the Meiningen tradition may best be
taken forward.

Is that task worth the considerable effort? For all those with an interest in the performance of Brahms's symphonies, the question answers itself, for, as documented in
Chapters 1 and 2, Meiningen was the one venue where Brahms could both express
himself in fully rehearsed performances of his works and witness performances by
the conductor in whom, from the late 1880s onwards, he repeatedly showed his full
confidence.[47] No wonder he felt at home in Meiningen, where, pampered by the good
Herzog Georg and his wife, he heard his symphonies played during the 1890s with an
unerring understanding of the necessary balance between form and feeling always in
the mind of the orchestra's Kapellmeister conductor.

The task of reconstruction will, however, require a discriminating ear, since the
temptation to exaggerate what Brahms required in his own 'pushing forward and

---

[43] See pp. 184–201.
[44] See pp. 208 and 214. Details of all the performances, dates and issue numbers, are given in
the Table at p. 167.
[45] See p. 106.
[46] See pp. 107 and 221.
[47] See pp. 29–31.

holding back'[48] has already been evident in various quarters: attempts to follow the Meiningen way in contemporary performances have met with intermittent success at best. Thus far, contemporary practitioners intent on following in Steinbach's footsteps have sometimes espoused an extreme approach that appears to be based on insufficiently detailed scholarship: misconceptions concerning the nature of that conductor's general approach combined with a too literal attempt to implement the precepts of Walter Blume's work – too literal in the sense that some of his hints have been magnified into the obvious and the unjustifiably extravagant.

This is not the place for a detailed dissection of the work of contemporary conductors, for any survey must be a changing and, one trusts, endless parade. It may, however, be salutary to examine briefly the most obvious example: Sir Charles Mackerras's Brahms symphony cycle dating from 1997.[49] This cycle was the first to attempt to follow Blume's prescriptions; perhaps the attempt was premature. It was not reassuring to find Mackerras, in the interview accompanying the set, characterising Steinbach's interpretative approach to Brahms as approximating a combination of Toscanini's 'strict tempo' and Furtwängler's 'freely poetic' practices – substantially misleading as to both Toscanini's approach and Furtwängler's relevance, as the preceding chapters of the present study have demonstrated. And, sure enough, among convincing performances of individual movements in all four symphonies, as well as considerable textual illumination as a consequence of the Meiningen-strength orchestra employed, one also finds much that, interpretatively, is distant from a proper reckoning of Steinbach's practice.

The following examples are representative but far from exhaustive: the choice is ample but here highly selective. First off, drooping *pizzicati* at bar 9 of the First Symphony's opening movement, contra Blume and all the Steinbach witnesses, are succeeded by drastic successive reductions in tempo during bars 127–56 of that movement, an approach in accord with, say, Nikisch and Stokowski (although perhaps more extreme than either), and far from Steinbach's seemingly constrained approach to tempo changes in this much-pondered passage.[50] Again, the end of this symphony suffers from undue distension on the return of the chorale theme that probably exaggerates to a degree Steinbach's practice.[51] This tendency towards exaggeration is exceeded in the first movement of the Third Symphony, where the *crescendo* on the second chord

---

[48] See p. 16.
[49] Symphonies Nos. 1–4, *Academic Festival Overture*, the *Haydn* Variations and Symphony No. 1, alternate second movement, Scottish Chamber Orchestra, conducted by Sir Charles Mackerras, with notes and interview, Telarc CD 80450. See also *Charles Mackerras*, eds. Nigel Simeone and John Tyrrell, Woodbridge: Boydell & Brewer, 2015, pp. 82, 191.
[50] See further pp. 60, 69, 187 and 188; also p. 188 in regard to Fritz Busch's approach in the last-mentioned passage.
[51] See p. 197.

and headlong lunge through the first subject, the vast tempo reduction for the main second subject at bar 36 and the virtual stasis becalming the *poco sostenuto* transition to the recapitulation are all in close accord with Abendroth's wrongheaded treatment of this movement and almost certainly distant from Steinbach's.[52] Finally, the recapitulatory part of the Fourth's passacaglia from bar 129 onwards finds Mackerras adopting both a distinctly increased tempo, typical of those conductors foreign to the Steinbach way examined in Chapter 3, and in the *Più Allegro* coda a variety of tempos that does much to destroy the implacable grandeur of that peroration.[53]

Such efforts (in which Mackerras has not been not alone[54]) have doubtless been sincerely made; nor can the wholehearted enthusiasm of the conductors concerned be assailed. But, in the absence of a well-grounded scholarly approach, these performances have tended to undermine Brahms's real achievement in the symphonies, their combination at the deepest level of intellect and intense feeling, the Classical and the Romantic. They also bring to mind Blume's own warnings: his fear that his mere mention of Steinbach's very slight changes of tempo at various points would be misinterpreted in too crude a fashion.[55]

Blume's explicit, and in this instance seemingly well-grounded, warning in this context must be heeded in the future if progress is to be made in the search for Brahms's authentic voice; for a proper understanding of the composer's unique fusion of intellect and feeling – and the careful balance that has therefore to be made in performing practice – is essential in leading us to the heart of his creative process. Clearly drawing inspiration from memories of Steinbach in action, Toscanini exhibited that understanding conclusively in his early BBC SO recorded performance of the Fourth's passacaglia. That example may be multiplied from the many chosen from the recordings of the Steinbach witnesses – Boult, Fritz Busch and Toscanini – analysed in this study, subject always to the individual interpretative vision of these interpreters, but demonstrating nonetheless their achievement in maintaining that fundamental but precarious balance between the interests of form and expressive intensity so characteristic of the Meiningen way as analysed here.

It will be obvious that, in my view, the task of reconstructing the Meiningen way's approach to the performance of the four symphonies requires a more thoughtful and discriminating approach than has been adopted so far in contemporary attempts in performance practice. 'They all did that sort of thing' – meaning an unstructured licence in performance of Classical masterpieces seen as typical of conductorial

---

[52] See pp. 52 and 214.
[53] See further pp. 181 and 220.
[54] Sir John Eliot Gardiner's recording of Brahms's Third Symphony, Soli Deo Gloria SDG 704, particularly in its first and third movements, parallels Mackerras's recording in its similarity to Abendroth's approach and is therefore similarly remote from Steinbach's practice.
[55] See pp. 186 and 211.

practice in the late nineteenth century – for me received its quietus over four decades ago with Boult's tartly dismissive retort, 'a lot of *rot*';[56] and, as has been demonstrated in this study, such excesses played no part in the Meiningen way. As for what *did* characterise that way, it is to be hoped that the evidence offered here provides a well-documented foundation for a deeper understanding of it: an accurate perception both of what Brahms required by way of structural propriety combined with expressive nuance and fluctuations of pace, and of the intuitively appropriate response to those requirements so fully and consistently displayed by his 'dear conductor', Fritz Stein-bach. Other strands of authority linked with Brahms, few and sometimes tenuous, yield rather different perceptions; but it is only via a full appreciation of the Meiningen way that we draw nearest to the very spirit of the composer.

[56] See Preface, p. xii.

BIBLIOGRAPHY

Books

Aldrich, Richard. *Concert Life in New York 1902–1923*. New York: Putnam, 1941.

Arndt, Peri, and others (eds). *Das 'Reichs-Brahmsfest' 1933 in Hamburg*. Hamburg: Bockel Verlag, 1997.

Avins, Styra. *Johannes Brahms: Life and Letters*. Oxford and New York: Oxford University Press, 1997.

Barblan, Guglielmo. *Toscanini e La Scala*. Milan: Edizioni della Scala, 1972.

Bass, James K. 'Johannes Brahms the Conductor: Historical Context, Chronology and Critical Reception'. DMA dissertation, University of Miami, Florida, 2005.

Berrsche, Alexander. *Trösterin Musika*. Munich: Hermann Rinn, 1949 (2nd ed.).

Birkin, Kenneth. *Hans von Bülow: A Life for Music*. Cambridge: Cambridge University Press, 2011.

Blume, Walter. *Brahms in der Meininger Tradition. Seine Sinfonien und Haydn-Variationen in der Bezeichnung von Fritz Steinbach*. Stuttgart: Ernst Surkamp, 1933; repr. with intro. by Michael Schwalb, Hildesheim: Georg Olms Verlag, 2013.

Boult, Adrian. *Boult on Music*. London: Toccata Press, 1983.

Boult, Adrian. *My Own Trumpet*. London: Hamish Hamilton, 1973.

Boult, Adrian. *The Point of the Stick: A Handbook on the Technique of Conducting*. London: Paterson, 1968.

Boult, Adrian. *Thoughts on Conducting*. London: Phoenix House, 1963.

Brinkmann, Reinhold (transl. Pete Palmer). *Late Idyll: The Second Symphony of Johannes Brahms*. Cambridge, MA: Harvard University Press, 1995.

Brown, Jonathan. *Great Wagner Conductors: A Listener's Companion*. Canberra: Parrot Press, 2012.

Busch, Fritz. *Aus dem Leben eines Musikers*. Zürich: Rascher & Cie, 1949; transl. Marjorie Strachey as *Pages from a Musician's Life*. London: Hogarth, 1953.

Busch, Grete. *Fritz Busch, Dirigent*. Frankfurt: Fischer, 1970.

Busch-Serkin, Irene (compiled and transl. Russell Stockman). *Adolf Busch: Letters–Pictures–Memories*. 2 vols. Walpole, NH: Arts and Letters, 1991.

Chasins, Abram. *Leopold Stokowski: A Profile*. London: Dutton, 1979.

Chevalley, Heinrich (ed.). *Arthur Nikisch. Leben und Werken*. Berlin: Bote & Bock, 1922.

Clough, Francis J. and Cuming, G. J. *World Encyclopaedia of Recorded Music*. London: Sidgwick & Jackson, 1952.

Cooper, Barry. *Beethoven*. Oxford: Oxford University Press, 2000.

Cronheim, Paul (intro.). *Willem Mengelberg. Gedenkboek 1895–1920*. The Hague: Martinus Nijhoff, 1920.

Daniel, Oliver. *Stokowski: A Counterpoint of Views*. New York: Dodd Mead, 1982.

Dejmek, Gaston. *Max Fiedler*. Essen: Vulcan, 1940.

Dyment, Christopher. *Felix Weingartner: Recollections and Recordings*. Rickmansworth: Triad Press, 1976.

Dyment, Christopher. *Toscanini in Britain*. Woodbridge: The Boydell Press, 2012.

Erskine, John. *The Philharmonic-Symphony Society of New York: Its First Hundred Years*. New York: Macmillan, 1943; repr. Boston: Da Capo, 1979.

Fifield, Christopher. *True Artist and True Friend: A Biography of Hans Richter*. Oxford: Oxford University Press, 1993.

Finck, Henry T. *Anton Seidl: A Memorial by His Friends*. New York: Charles Scribner's Sons, 1899; repr. Boston: Da Capo 1983.

Fortner, Johannes (ed.). *Die Gewandhaus-Konzerte zu Leipzig, 1781–1981*. Leipzig: VEB Deutscher Verlag für Musik, 1981.

Foss, Hubert and Goodwin, Noel. *London Symphony: Portrait of an Orchestra*. London: Naldrett, 1954.

Frisch, Walter. *Brahms: The Four Symphonies*. New York: Schirmer, 1996.

Frisch, Walter and Karnes, Kevin (eds). *Brahms and His World*. Princeton: Princeton University Press, 2009 (2nd ed.).

Goltz, Maren. *Musiker-Lexikon des Herzogtums Sachsen-Meiningen (1680–1918)*. Meiningen, 2012.

Goltz, Maren and Müller, Herta. *Der Brahms Klarinettist Richard Mühlfeld*. Balve: Artivo 2007.

Gregor-Dellin, Martin and Mack, Dietrich (eds) (transl. Geoffrey Skelton). *Cosima Wagner's Diaries*. New York: Harcourt-Brace Jovanovich, 1978–80.

Grierson, Mary. *Donald Francis Tovey: A Biography Based on Letters*. Oxford: Oxford University Press, 1952; repr. Westport, CT: Greenwood Press, 1970.

Grümmer, Paul. *Begegnungen. Aus dem Leben eines Violoncellisten*. Munich: Bong, 1963.

Haas, Frithjof. *Der Magier am Dirigentenpult. Felix Mottl*. Karlsruhe: Hoepfner-Bibliothek, 2006.

Haas, Frithjof. *Zwischen Brahms und Wagner. Der Dirigent Hermann Levi*. Zürich: Atlantis Musikbuch-Verlag, 1995; transl. Cynthia Klohr as *Hermann Levi: From Brahms to Wagner*. Washington, DC: Scarecrow Press, 2012.

Haggin, B. H. *Music & Ballet 1973–1983*. New York: Horizon, 1984.

Henschel, George. *Personal Recollections of Johannes Brahms*. Boston: Gorham Press, 1907.

Herzfeld, Friedrich. *Magie des Taktstocks*. Berlin: Ullstein AG, 1953.

Hinrichsen, Joachim (ed.) (transl. Cynthia Klohr). *Hans von Bülow's Letters to Johannes Brahms*. Washington, DC: Scarecrow Press, 2012.

Hofmann, Renate and Hofmann, Kurt, *Johannes Brahms als Pianist und Dirigent. Chronologie seines Wirkens als Interpret*. Tutzing: Hans Schneider, 2006.

Holden, Raymond. *The Virtuoso Conductors*. New Haven: Yale University Press, 2005.

Huneker, J. G. *The Philharmonic Society of New York and its Seventy-fifth Anniversary: A Retrospect*. New York, 1917; repr. Boston: Da Capo, 1979.

Huschke, Konrad. *Johannes Brahms als Pianist, Dirigent und Lehrer*. Karlsruhe: Friedrich Gutsch, 1935.

Jacobs, Arthur. *Henry. J Wood: Maker of the Proms*. London: Methuen, 1994.

Jacobson, Robert. *Reverberations: Interviews with the World's Leading Musicians*. New York: William Morrow, 1974.

Johnson, H. Earle. *Symphony Hall, Boston*. Boston: Little, Brown, 1950.

Kalbeck, Max. *Johannes Brahms*. 4 vols, Berlin: Deutsche Brahms-Gesellschaft, 1904–14.

Kalbeck, Max. *Johannes Brahms Briefwechsel I: Johannes Brahms im Briefwechsel mit Heinrich und Elisabet von Herzogenberg*, vol. 1, Berlin: Deutsche Brahms-Gesellschaft, 1907; transl. Hannah Bryant as *Johannes Brahms: The Herzogenberg Correspondence*, London: John Murray, 1909; repr. with introduction by Walter Frisch, New York, 1987.

Kaut, Josef. *Festspiele in Salzburg*. Salzburg: Residenz, 1969.

Keller, Hans (ed. and transl., in collaboration with C. F. Flesch). *The Memoirs of Carl Flesch*. London: Rockliff, 1957; centenary ed. Harlow: Bois de Boulogne, 1973.

Kelsen, Hans (transl. from 2nd German ed. by Max Knight). *Pure Theory of Law*. Berkeley and Los Angeles: University of California Press, 1967.

Kennedy, Michael. *Adrian Boult*. London: Hamish Hamilton, 1987; repr. London: Papermac, 1989.

Lamond, Frederic. *The Memoirs of Frederic Lamond*, Glasgow: William McLennan, 1949.

Lehmann, Stephen and Faber, Marion. *Rudolf Serkin: A Life*. New York: Oxford University Press, 2003.

Litzmann, Berthold. *Letters of Clara Schumann and Johannes Brahms 1853–1896*. 2 vols. New York: Longmans, 1927.

Lucke-Kaminiarz, Irina. *Hermann Abendroth. Ein Musiker im Wechselspiel der Zeitgeschichte*. Weimar: WTV, 2007.

Marsh, Robert Charles. *Toscanini and the Art of Orchestral Performance*. London: Allen and Unwin, 1956; rev. as *Toscanini and the Art of Conducting*. New York: Collier, 1962.

Martin, George. *The Damrosch Dynasty: America's First Family of Music*. Boston: Houghton Miflin, 1983.

Millington, Barry and Spencer, Stewart (eds). *Wagner in Performance*. London: Yale University Press, 1992.

Miracco, Renato (ed.). *Maestro's Secret Music: The Artworks Collected by Arturo Toscanini*. Exhibition catalogue. New York and Livorno: Mazotta, 2007.

Mittag, Erwin. *The Vienna Philharmonic*. Vienna: Gerlach & Wiedling, 1950.

Moore, Jerrold Northrop (ed.). *Music and Friends: Letter to Adrian Boult*. London: Hamish Hamilton, 1979.

Morgan, Kenneth. *Fritz Reiner: Maestro and Martinet*. Urbana: Illinois University Press, 2005.

Moser, Andreas (ed.). *Johannes Brahms Briefwechsel V und VI. Johannes Brahms im Briefwechsel mit Joseph Joachim*. Berlin: Deutsche Brahms-Gesellschaft, 1912; repr. Tutzing: Hans Schneider, 1974.

Muck, Peter. *Karl Muck. Ein Dirigentenleben in Briefen und Documenten*. Tutzing: Hans Schneider, 2003.

Müller, Herta and Hoffman, Renate (eds). *Brahms Briefwechsel Vol. XVII. Johannes Brahms in Briefwechsel mit Herzog Georg II von Sachsen Meiningen und Helene Freifrau von Heldburg*. Rev. Otto Biba, Kurt Hoffman and Renate Hoffman, Tutzing: Hans Schneider, 1991.

Musgrave, Michael (ed.). *A Brahms Reader*. London and New Haven: Yale University Press, 2000.

Musgrave, Michael and Sherman, Bernard D. (eds). *Performing Brahms: Early Evidence of Performance Style*. Cambridge and New York: Cambridge University Press, 2003.

Neupert, Käte. *Die Besetzung der Bayreuther Festspiele 1876–1960*. Bayreuth: Edition Musica, 1961.

Ney, Elly. *Elly Ney. Briefwechsel mit Willem von Hoogstraten*. Vol. 1: 1910–26. Tutzing: Hans Schneider, 1970.

Pascall, Robert (ed.). *Symphonie Nr. 1 c-moll op. 68*. Series I/1 of *Johannes Brahms Gesamtausgabe*. Munich: G. Henle, 1996.

Pasternack, Jonathan R. 'Brahms in the Meiningen Tradition – His Symphonies and Haydn Variations According to the Markings of Fritz Steinbach, Edited by Walter Blume: A Complete Translation with Background and Commentary'. DMA dissertation, University of Washington, 2004.

Pearton, Maurice. *The LSO at Seventy*. London: Gollancz, 1974.

Philip, Robert. *Early Recordings and Musical Style*. Cambridge: Cambridge University Press, 1992.

Philip, Robert. *Performing Music in the Age of Recording*. London and New Haven: Yale University Press, 2004.

Pleasants, Henry (ed. and transl.). *Eduard Hanslick: Music Criticisms 1846–99*. Rev. ed. Harmondsworth: Penguin, 1963.

Potter, Tully. *Adolf Busch: The Life of an Honest Musician*. London: Toccata, 2010.

Reimann, Heinrich. *Johannes Brahms*. Berlin: Harmonie, 1903.

Riess, Curt (transl. Margaret Goldsmith). *Wilhelm Furtwängler*. London: Frederick Muller, 1955.

Russell, John. *Erich Kleiber: A Memoir*. London: Andre Deutsch, 1957.

Ryding, Erik and Pechefsky, Rebecca. *Bruno Walter: A World Elsewhere*. New Haven: Yale University Press, 2001.

Sachs, Harvey. *Reflections on Toscanini*. New York: Grove Weidenfeld, 1991.

Sachs, Harvey. *Toscanini*. London: Weidenfeld and Nicolson, 1978.

Sackville-West, Edward. (intro.) (transl. Hanns Hammelmann and Ewald Osers). *A Working Friendship: The Correspondence between Richard Strauss and Hugo von Hofmannsthal*. New York: Vienna House, 1961; repr. 1974.

Sanders, Alan. *Sir Adrian Boult: A Discography*. London: Gramophone, 1980.

Scharberth, Irmgard. *Gürzenich Orchester Köln 1888–1988*. Cologne: Wienand Verlag, 1988.

Scherbera, Jürgen. *Gustav Brecher und die Leipziger Oper 1923–1933*. Leipzig: Edition Peters, 1990.

Schindler, Anton Felix. *Biografie von Ludwig van Beethoven*. Münster: Aschendorf, 1860; 3rd. ed. transl. Donald MacArdle as *Beethoven as I Knew Him*. Chapel Hill, University of North Carolina Press, 1966; repr. New York: Norton, 1972.

Scholes, Percy A. *The Mirror of Music 1844–1944*. London: Novello/Oxford University Press, 1947.

Schuller, Gunther. *The Compleat Conductor*. Oxford: Oxford University Press, 1997.

Seltsam, William H. *Metropolitan Opera Annals: A Chronicle of Artists and Performances*. New York: H.W. Wilson, 1947.

Shaw, Bernard. *Music in London*. London: Constable, 1932.

Shirakawa, Sam S. *The Devil's Music Master: The Controversial Life and Career of Wilhelm Furtwängler*. New York: Oxford University Press, 1992.

Simeone, Nigel and Tyrrell, John (eds). *Charles Mackerras*. Woodbridge: Boydell & Brewer, 2015.

Specht, Richard (transl. Eric Blom). *Johannes Brahms*. London: J. M. Dent, 1930.

Speyer, Edward. *My Life and Friends*. London: Cobden-Sanderson, 1937.

Taubman, Howard, *Toscanini*, London: Odhams, 1951.

Turner, W. J. *Music and Life*. London: Methuen, 1921.

Walker, Alan. *Hans von Bülow: A Life and Times*. New York and Oxford: Oxford University Press, 2010.

Walter, Bruno (transl. Paul Hamburger). *Of Music and Music-Making*. London: Faber 1961; New York: Norton, 1961.

Walter, Bruno (transl. James A. Galston). *Theme and Variations*. London: Hamish Hamilton, 1947.

Weingartner, Felix. *Akkorde*. Leipzig: Breitkopf & Hartel, 1912; repr. Walluf-Nendein: Sandig, 1977.

Weingartner, Felix (transl. Marguerite Wolff). *Buffets and Rewards*. London: Hutchinson, 1937.

Weingartner, Felix. *Bayreuth (1876–1896)*. Berlin: Fischer Verlag 1897; transl. Lily Antrobus, London: Weekes, 1898 (repr. Christopher Dyment in *Felix Weingartner: Recollections and Recordings*); 2nd ed. Leipzig: Breitkopf & Hartel, 1904.

Weingartner, Felix. *Lebenserinnerungen*. 2 vols. Zürich: Orell Füssli, 1928–29.

Weingartner, Felix. *On Music & Conducting*. New York: Dover, 1969 (containing *On Conducting*, 3rd ed. 1905, transl. Ernest Newman with notes; *On the Performance of Beethoven's Symphonies*, 3rd ed. 1928, transl. Jessie Crosland; *The Symphony Since Beethoven*, 4th ed. 1928, transl. H. M. Schott).

Weingartner, Felix (transl. Arthur Bles). *The Symphony Writers Since Beethoven*. London: William Reeves, [1907] (translated from 2nd ed. *Die Symphonie nach Beethoven*, Berlin, c. 1901; 3rd (rev.) German ed. 1909, 4th (rev.) German ed. 1926).

Wilson, Elizabeth. *Shostakovich: A Life Remembered*. London: Faber and Faber, 2006 (2nd ed.).

Wood, Henry. *My Life of Music*. London: Gollancz, 1938.

Zwart, Frits. *Willem Mengelberg (1871–1951). Een Biografie 1871–1920*. Amsterdam: Prometheus, 1999.

Articles and pamphlets

Albrecht, Theodore. 'Anton Schindler as Destroyer and Forger of Beethoven's Conversation Books: A Case for Decriminalization'. http://www.rilm.org/historiography/talbrecht.pdf
Cardus, Neville. 'Toscanini: Some After-thoughts'. In Evan Senior (ed.), *The Concert-Goer's Annual No. 1*, London: John Calder, 1957, pp. 81–4
Caullier, Joëlle. 'Les chefs d'orchestre allemands à Paris entre 1894 et 1914', *Revue de Musicologie*, vol. 67, no. 2 (1981), pp. 191–210.
Dyment, Christopher. 'Adrian Boult: The Formative Years'. *Classic Record Collector*, Spring 2003, pp. 38–45.
Dyment, Christopher. 'Apostle of Brahms?' (Max Fiedler Part 1). *Classic Record Collector*, Summer 2002, pp. 26–32; 'Pauses for Thought' (Max Fiedler Part 2). *Classic Record Collector*, Autumn 2002, pp. 44–8.
Dyment, Christopher. 'Toscanini's European Inheritance'. *International Classic Record Collector*, Winter 1998, pp. 22–6.
Dyment, Christopher. 'Weingartner: Eastern Approaches'. *International Classic Record Collector*, Spring 2000, pp. 8–17.
Goltz, Maren. *Die Brahms-Programme auf den Konzertreisen der Meininger Hofkapelle (1882–1914)*. Meiningen, 2009, http://www.db-thueringen.de/servlets/DerivateServlet/Derivate-18050/goltz_brahmsprogramme.pdf.
Krienitz, Willy. 'Felix Mottls Tagebuchaufzeichnungen aus den Jahren 1873–1876'. In *Neue Wagner-Forschungen*. Karlsruhe: G. Braun, 1943.
Müller, Herta. 'Fritz Steinbachs Wirken in Meiningen und für Johannes Brahms von 1886–1903'. *Südthüringer Forschungen*, vol. 30 (1999), pp. 87–120.
Popp, Suzanne. 'Gratwanderung: Regers Brahms-Interpretation', in Suzanne Popp (ed.), *Auf Der Suche nach dem Werk. Max Reger – sein Schaffen – seine Sammlung*. Karlsruhe: Max Reger Institut, 1998, pp. 236–49.
Schmidt, Carsten. 'Richard Strauss and the Recording Media'. *Classical Recordings Quarterly*, Winter 2014, pp. 10–15.
Smith, T. Max. 'Toscanini at the Baton', *The Century*, vol. 85 (1913), pp. 691–701.
Zwart, Frits. 'Willem Mengelberg, Live: The Radio Recordings'. Essay with CD set. Amsterdam: Concertgebouw, 97016.

INDEX

www.ingramcontent.com/pod-product-compliance
Lightning Source LLC
Chambersburg PA
CBHW070410100426
42812CB00005B/1697